The houses of history

THE HOUSES
OF HISTORY

A critical reader
in twentieth-century history and theory

selected and introduced by
ANNA GREEN & KATHLEEN TROUP

NEW YORK UNIVERSITY PRESS
Washington Square, New York

First published in the U.S.A. in 1999 by
NEW YORK UNIVERSITY PRESS
Washinton Square
New York, N.Y. 10003

New York University Press edition published by special arrangement with
Manchester University Press, Oxford Road,
Manchester M13 9NR, UK
http://www.man.ac.uk/mup

Library of Congress Cataloging-in-Publication Data
The houses of history : a critical reader in twentieth-century history
   and theory / selected and introduced by Anna Green & Kathleen Troup.
      p.   cm.
   Includes bibliographical references and index.
   ISBN 0-8147-3126-0 (clothbound). — ISBN 0-8147-3127-9 (pbk.)
   1. Historiography—History—20th century.   2. History—Philosophy.
   3. Historians.   I. Green, Anna.   II. Troup, Kathleen.
   D13.2.H64   1999
   909.82′07′2—dc21   98-54087
                     CIP

Printed in Great Britain

Reprinted in paperback 2000

Contents

Preface

Every piece of historical writing has a theoretical basis on which evidence is selected, filtered and understood. This statement is as true of scientific empiricism as it is of poststructuralism, although the theory is more likely to be explicit in the latter case. As Loewenberg said: 'Each historian and each age redefines categories of evidence in the light of its needs, sensibilities, and perceptions. The value of any conceptual framework is what new combinations of data or inferences from the data it may contribute to the historian's ability to interpret documents and the other raw material of history.'[1] In our view, this is one of the enduring strengths of the historical profession, and one of the pleasures of working as an historian.

The idea for this book developed from an introductory History and Theory course which we have taught for several years now. We wanted to introduce students to the theories behind different kinds of historical writing in order that they might read more critically and reflect on their own historical practice. We hoped to provide our classes with stimulating examples from the various historical 'schools'. To our surprise, no textbook existed in English which fulfilled our dual purpose.

In our experience, history students often find theory more difficult than do students from other disciplines, mainly due to their thorough-going historical training in the empirical method. We have therefore tried to make this book as straightforward as possible, while pointing to more complex debates in the brief additional reading lists concluding each chapter. References will also assist further reading, although we have kept these to a minimum, partly due to constraints of space. We refer to articles as well as whole books since these shorter readings will be initially more accessible to students.

In considering the structure of this reader, we decided to limit ourselves to those schools of historical thought which have had the greatest influence on the historical profession during the twentieth century. This was in part due to the restrictions of length necessary in a book designed as a university text, and partly in accordance with our belief that these schools were of most relevance to contemporary students. For similar reasons, we have concentrated on works of history, although there are a few studies by political scientists, anthropologists and other theorists. The applied readings range from the classic, such as the extract from *The Making of the English Working Class*, to the recent, such as Henrietta Whiteman's work. Again we have aimed for accessibility, both in language and length, while trying to represent historical writing covering a range of chronological periods and geographical areas.

Clearly the twelve schools are not discrete: for example, Catherine Hall, who writes on gender, also addresses issues of class; Inga Clendinnen, our ethnohistorian, is concerned with gender roles as well as Mayan ritual in general. Almost all historians use empiricism in conjunction with any other theoretical perspective which they might adopt.

An enterprise of this nature inevitably incurs a number of debts. The History Department at the University of Waikato entrusted us with the development of its theory course: we're glad to have this opportunity to thank its members. We also thank the Vice-Chancellor of this university for his financial contribution. We had the good fortune to encounter Vanessa Graham from Manchester University Press at the beginning of this process: her enthusiasm assisted our first foray into the textbook market. We're also grateful to our students who have stimulated us with their questions, pushed us in our efforts for clarity and even designed a class T-shirt, aptly emblazoned with 'The Scream'. Many friends and colleagues have discussed our work with us and have thereby lightened the burden of writing. We also thank the anonymous reader for helpful comments and the staff at Manchester University Press for their efficient processing of the manuscript.

In particular, Peter Gibbons, Mark Houlahan, Radhika Mohanram and Tom Ryan have severally read drafts, provided obscure references and rushed to our assistance with apparently the only copy of *Representations* in New Zealand, and we're very grateful for their interest. Finally we thank our husbands, Jack Vowles and Kai Jensen, for their domestic support, theoretical and editorial comments and patience with constant historiographical conversations throughout the writing of this book: their presence has been invaluable.

Note

1 Peter Loewenberg, *Decoding the Past: The Psychohistorical Approach* (2nd ed., New Brunswick, 1996), p. 15.

Acknowledgements

The editors and publishers wish to thank the following for permission to use copyright material:

Little, Brown and the University of Chicago Press for material from Judith R. Walkowitz, *City of Dreadful Delight: Narratives of Sexual Danger in Late-Victorian London* (1992), pp. 171–83.

Cambridge University Press for Richard Wall, 'The Household: Demographic and Economic Change in England, 1650–1970', in R. Wall, J. Robin and P. Laslett (eds), *Family Forms in Historic Europe* (1983), pp. 493–512; and for Theda Skocpol, 'France, Russia, China: A Structural Analysis of Social Revolutions', in *Social Revolutions in the Modern World* (1994), pp. 133–46.

Columbia University Press for Hayden White, 'The Fictions of Factual Representation', in *The Literature of Fact*, ed. Angus Fletcher (1976), pp. 21–44. Copyright © 1976 by Columbia University Press.

Victor Gollancz Ltd and Pantheon Books, a division of Random House, Inc. for material from E. P. Thompson, *The Making of the English Working Class* (1963), pp. 189–204. Copyright © 1963 by E. P. Thompson.

HarperCollins Publishers, Inc. for material from Fernand Braudel, *The Mediterranean and the Mediterranean World in the Age of Philip II*, vol. 1 (2nd edn 1972), pp. 38–47. Copyright © Librairie Armand Colin 1966. English translation copyright © by Wm Collins Ltd and Harper & Row Publishers Inc.

Journal of Social History for Inga Clendinnen, 'Yucatec Maya Women and the Spanish Conquest: Role and Ritual in Historical Reconstruction', *Journal of Social History*, 15, 3 (Spring 1982), pp. 427–42.

W. W. Norton & Company, Inc. and Random House, UK for material from Erik H. Erikson, 'The Legend of Hitler's Childhood' in *Childhood and Society* (1950), pp. 294–310. Copyright 1950, © 1963 by W. W. Norton & Company, Inc., renewed © 1978, 1991 by Erik H. Erikson.

Oral History Society for Alistair Thomson, 'Anzac Memories: Putting Popular Memory Theory into Practice in Australia', *Oral History* (Spring 1990), pp. 25–8, 30–1.

Oxford University Press, Inc. for material from Henrietta Whiteman, 'White Buffalo Woman', in Calvin Martin, *The American Indian and the Problem of History* (1987), pp. 162–70. Copyright © 1987 by Calvin Martin.

Routledge for material from Geoffrey Elton, *England under the Tudors*, 3rd edn (1991), pp. ix–xi, 18–35; and Catherine Hall, 'Gender Divisions and Class Formation in the Birmingham Middle Class, 1780–1850', in *People's History and Socialist Theory*, ed. Raphael Samuel (1981), Routledge and Kegan Paul, pp. 164–75.

Every effort has been made to trace the copyright holders but if any have been inadvertently overlooked the publishers will be pleased to make the necessary arrangement at the first opportunity.

1

The empiricists

Empiricism is both a theory of knowledge, an epistemology, and a method of historical enquiry.[1] There are few historians who dissent from the use of empiricism as a research method, and most routinely employ the analytical tools and protocols developed over the past 150 years. But as a theory of knowledge empiricism has come under attack, most recently by postmodernism. Since the turn of the century philosophers have grappled with the epistemological difficulties of empiricism, and historians have been content to let them do so. Empiricist historians often prefer to describe their work as a 'craft', with all the connotations of hands-on knowledge and skill, and to emphasize the importance of methodology over theory. Yet all historical writing is constructed upon a theory of knowledge, and we cannot and should not leave these matters entirely to others. Let us begin with the origins of empiricism, which is, without doubt, the most influential school of historical thought over the course of this century.

The empirical approach to historical research has its origins in the 'scientific revolution' of the sixteenth and seventeenth centuries.[2] Central to the natural philosophy of the period, originating with Francis Bacon, was the belief that knowledge should be derived from observation of the material world. This, of course, challenged the control exercised by the Church and its clerics over the generation and dissemination of learning. The new ideas of scientific enquiry were carried forward by the philosophers of the eighteenth-century Enlightenment and applied to the study of human society. Many of the university disciplines with which we are now familiar, history, sociology and anthropology, emerged during the second and third quarters of the nineteenth century. Intrinsic to this new, university-led professionalism for historical study came an emphasis upon systematic archival research into material documents.

1

Leopold von Ranke was instrumental in establishing professional standards for historical training at the University of Berlin between 1824 and 1871. Rejecting many of the sources previously used by historians – particularly personal memoirs, or accounts written after the event – Ranke argued that historians should only use 'primary' or original sources, those which were generated at the time of the event under consideration. These should be subjected to the closest scrutiny, and only then 'by gathering, criticizing and verifying all the available sources, could [historians] put themselves in a position to reconstruct the past accurately'.[3] In its most extreme form, scientific history led to positivism. The nineteenth-century French philosopher Auguste Comte, with whom the term positivism originated in the 1830s, endeavoured to show that history could be understood like the natural world, in terms of general laws. Comte sought to move from the detailed examination of all phenomena to the formulation of broad laws which governed historical development. These ideas profoundly influenced many of the leading thinkers of the nineteenth century, including Karl Marx and Charles Darwin.

In a well-known phrase, Ranke also argued that historians should refrain from judging the past, and simply write what actually happened, *'wie es eigentlich gewesen'*.[4] Richard Evans, a British historian of Germany, has suggested that this phrase has been 'widely misunderstood', and that Ranke sought to 'understand the inner being of the past.'[5] He intended that each historical period should be understood on its own terms. In other words it should not be judged by the historian's own criteria. Nonetheless, Ranke perceived human history as the working out of God's will, and in consequence Georg Iggers concluded that '[t]he impartial approach to the past . . . for Ranke revealed the existing order as God had willed it . . . One cannot understand the new science of history as it was understood by Ranke without taking into account the political and religious context in which it emerged'.[6] That context was the nineteenth-century ferment arising from nationalism and the growth of European states. A prolific historian, Ranke wrote over sixty volumes of chronological narrative focusing upon the political and diplomatic history of Europe.

Ranke's influence was widespread; his pupils were appointed in the new universities being established throughout Europe and North America. The following exhortation by a French historian at the first International Congress of Historians in 1900 illustrates the preoccupation with factual evidence which had become the core of historical practice:

> We want nothing more to do with the approximations of hypotheses, useless systems, theories as brilliant as they are deceptive, superfluous moralities. Facts, facts, facts – which carry within themselves their lesson and their philosophy. The truth, all the truth, nothing but the truth.[7]

The core tenets of scientific, empirical history as it stood at the turn of the century might be codified as follows:

⦿ the rigorous examination and knowledge of historical evidence, verified by references;

⦿ impartial research, devoid of *a priori* beliefs and prejudices;

⦿ and an inductive method of reasoning, from the particular to the general.

Implicit within these research principles is a specific theory of knowledge. First of all, the past exists independently of the individual's mind, and is both observable and verifiable. Secondly, through adherence to the research principles above, the historian is able to represent the past objectively and accurately. In other words, the truth of an historical account rests upon its correspondence to the facts.[8] These principles represent the search for objective truth, 'the noble dream' of the historical profession, to use a phrase recurrent in American historiography.

These core tenets of empirical history remained deeply influential among the historical profession throughout the twentieth century. Reflections on the practice of history written many years apart by two regius professors of history at Cambridge University both focus upon these principles. The first, J. B. Bury, declared in his inaugural address in 1902 that 'history is a science, no less and no more'. For Bury, the writing of history was a science because of its 'minute method of analysing . . . sources' and 'scrupulously exact conformity to facts'. Believing that 'science cannot be safely controlled or guided by subjective interest', he stated that it was the role of universities to train students in objective analysis, setting aside the influence of their own time and place. 'There was indeed', Bury commented, 'no historian since the beginning of things who did not profess that his sole aim was to present to his readers untainted and unpainted truth'.[9]

Sixty-five years later G. R. Elton took up the same cudgels in defence of the scientific method in history, and his book, *The Practice of History*, remained continuously in print in Britain for thirty years. Bury and Elton believed that the correct historical method was the key to revealing the truth about the past. Both men compared the creation of historical knowledge to building with bricks and mortar. Each published piece of research represented a brick and the work of the historian was therefore analogous to that of a skilled craftsman. The analogy is revealing, for neither Bury nor Elton expected, or desired, the labourer to have knowledge of the larger edifice. Bury visualized historians as labourers painstakingly adding bricks to a grand building, the design of which was unknown to them.[10] Elton defended the work of the student 'journeyman' who might never raise his eyes beyond the detail of his own minute area of study.[11] The material foundations of this edifice, the labours of countless scholars, had to be sound and both men placed a great deal of importance upon the correct historical method for the evaluation and use of historical evidence.

With irrefutable, factual information located at the heart of historical enquiry, the method of establishing the veracity and adequacy of the evidence became paramount, and this leads us to the first principle of empirical history. The careful evaluation and authentication of primary source material is one of Ranke's most significant legacies. In a widely-read textbook on the study of history Arthur Marwick lists seven criteria which should be applied to historical documents. The first four steps involve the basic verification of authenticity.[12] One of the most famous forged documents in history, the Donation of Constantine, purported to show that the Emperor Constantine gave his crown and empire to Pope Sylvester I after the latter cured him of leprosy. The document was exposed as a forgery seven hundred years later by Renaissance writer Lorenzo Valla.[13] But forgeries are not confined to the medieval world; the comparatively recent revelation that the 'Hitler Diaries' were fraudulent suggests that authentication of sources remains an essential part of the historian's work.[14]

Marwick's three final criteria relate more to interpretation than verification. The aspiring historian is advised to ask, for example, 'what person, or group of persons, created the source [and] how exactly was the document understood by contemporaries?'[15] Taking this process a significant step further, one of the foremost historians in the field of intellectual history, Quentin Skinner, transformed the study of major political texts. First he insisted that the works of political thinkers be understood within the 'more general social and intellectual matrix out of which their works arose'.[16] While social context could help explain a text, however, this alone was not enough. The intellectual historian also needed to consider the intentions of the author, and how those intentions were to be achieved. In other words, Skinner argued that texts should be understood as acts of rhetorical communication.[17]

The limitations of the traditional criteria for documentary evaluation become apparent, however, when historians expand their focus beyond that of the literate elite. First of all, the records or artefacts that survive into the present are always incomplete and partial. Conclusions have to be based upon the extant records and these may reflect a very narrow range of experiences or perspectives. Most documentary material is created and/or preserved by the elite of a society, and to reconstruct the lives and perspectives of those further down the hierarchy the historian must find other sources and techniques beyond the limited range proposed by Marwick. Ethnohistorians, in particular those working in the area of culture contact, frequently work with evidence reflecting only the perspectives of the colonizer. They have learned from the discipline of anthropology how to read such evidence against the grain, and for its symbolic content, in order to reveal the subjugated peoples.

Secondly, even though much evidence is destroyed, it remains virtually impossible for any modern historian to read all existing archival source material bearing upon their research, for the time-scale (and endurance) is beyond any one individual. When the quantity of surviving documents exceeds human capacity Elton recommended the exhaustive study of one set of 'master' documents to guide the historian in his or her subsequent selective use of the remaining archives.[18] These strictures concerning selection may be applicable to source material consisting of a reasonably comprehensive documentary archive deriving from a known source, for example government records, preserved in only one or two depositories. They are, however, clearly inadequate when the research subject requires the historian to find the evidence in a wide range of sources, scattered all over the place, the quantity and relevance of which may not be known in advance.

Let us turn now to the second and third tenets of empirical history, which are closely linked: that of impartial research, devoid of *a priori* beliefs and prejudices, and the inductive method of reasoning. Elton argued that the historian should not impose his or her own questions upon the evidence; rather, the questions should arise spontaneously out of the material itself.[19] This is a useful warning, as Quentin Skinner has pointed out, to avoid 'the premature consignment of unfamiliar evidence to familiar categories'. But Skinner illustrates, through the hypothetical analysis of a material object (in this case a house), how 'we are already caught up in the process of interpretation as soon as we begin to describe any aspect of our evidence in words'.[20] This too is the basis for Abrams' opening comments on Elton's study of *Reformation Europe* where the title of the work, without further elaboration, prefigures the field of enquiry.[21] Abrams continues his critique by examining what he calls the 'Elton dilemma', the problem of narrative as an explanatory historical device. Rejecting the notion that facts speak for themselves, Abrams argues that every narrative contains implicit analysis because the historian must decide how to arrange the evidence. The device of telling a story allows the historian to evade critical scrutiny of the theorizing underpinning its structure.[22]

Furthermore, judgements concerning causation or motivation are often the product of the historian's inferences, and are impossible to prove.[23] Let us take the example of the decline in fertility in Britain, the United States and Australasia between 1870 and 1920. Based upon quantitative analysis of the census data, historians accept that there was a significant decline in the average number of live births per married woman during this period. In this case the overall trend appears to be clear. But the reasons for the fertility decline are less so; there are at least half a dozen explanations which range from the economic (fertility behaviour determined by inter-generational wealth flows) to the social (the increased authority of women within the home).[24] While the fertility decline was undoubtedly the consequence of a complex set of factors, historians continue to search for the principal causes.[25] In a world facing rapid population increase, understanding human motivation for fertility control in the past acquires particular contemporary salience.

But agreement among historians is remarkably difficult to achieve, and historical events are open to a multiplicity of interpretations. The same evidence can generate two quite different stories about the past, and problems arise when these are incompatible. For a striking example of this in practice, see the comparison by environmental historian William Cronon of two histories of the long drought which struck the Great Plains of North America in the 1930s.[26] The first study describes the drought as a natural disaster over which the people of the Dust Bowl triumphed; the second focuses upon the failure of human beings to understand the cyclical climate of this semi-arid environment leading to ecological collapse. Cronon ultimately concludes that 'to try to escape the value judgments that accompany storytelling is to miss the point of history itself, for the stories we tell, like the questions we ask, are all finally about value'.[27] Are we then to accept that all interpretations are relative? Relativism is the belief that absolute truth is unattainable, and that all statements about history are connected or relative to the position of those who make them. In the 1930s the American historical profession was convulsed by Charles A. Beard's critique of objectivity.[28] Beard, the brilliant revisionist historian and author of *An Economic Interpretation of the U.S. Constitution*, argued that historians could never be 'neutral mirror(s)' to the past:

> We do not acquire the colorless, neutral mind by declaring our intention to do so. Rather do we clarify the mind by admitting its cultural interests and patterns – interests and patterns that will control, or intrude upon, the selection and organization of historical materials. . . . What do we think we are doing when we are writing history? What kinds of philosophies or interpretations are open to us? Which interpretations are actually chosen and practiced? And why? By what methods or processes can we hope to bring the multitudinous and bewildering facts of history into any coherent and meaningful whole? Through the discussion of such questions the noble dream of the search for truth may be brought nearer to realization, not extinguished.[29]

In Britain a similar relativist critique came from the British historian E. H. Carr in *What is History?*, published in 1961. Carr shared Beard's perspective that historians wrote about the past in the context of contemporary concerns and perspectives. For Carr, the historian was a fisherman, choosing which pond in which to fish, and what tackle to use. All history writing, he insisted, was ultimately the product of the historian:

> In the first place, the facts of history never come to us 'pure', since they do not and cannot exist in a pure form: they are always refracted through the mind of the recorder. It follows that when we take up a work of history, our first concern should be not with the facts which it contains but with the historian who wrote it.[30]

The significance of individual subjectivity in the writing of history has gained reinforcement in recent years from the influence of postmodernism. From this perspective, the orthodox historical preoccupation with facts about the past becomes redundant, because there is no independent reality outside language. The historian is always constrained by the limitations of his or her own intellectual world, from which the concepts and categories of thought are invariably drawn. Postmodernists argue that while language shapes our reality, it does not necessarily reflect it. Further elaboration of this perspective will be found in chapter 12, but the major challenge to empiricism lies in the rejection of any correspondence between reality or experience, and the language employed to describe it.

One difficulty with subjectivism is that it leaves the door open to the unacceptable face of moral relativism. Is one interpretation of the past as good as any other? Should we not, for example, challenge those historians who attempt to refute the historical fact of the holocaust? An interpretation based upon such a travesty of the documentary and oral record indicates the moral deficiency of an unqualified subjectivist stance.[31] All this leaves empirical historians in a very unsatisfactory position, and as Dominick LaCapra has suggested, 'extreme documentary objectivism and relativistic subjectivism do not constitute genuine alternatives'.[32]

One way of addressing this unsatisfactory dichotomy between objectivism and subjectivism was developed by the philosopher of science Karl Popper, whose writings span a large part of the century. Persecuted by the Nazis in the 1930s, Popper retained his faith in science as a rational tool despite the destruction wrought by totalitarian regimes in Europe. Indeed, he agreed with Bertrand Russell's statement that epistemological relativism held a close relationship with authoritarian and totalitarian beliefs:

> the belief in the possibility of a rule of law, of equal justice, of fundamental rights, and a free society – can easily survive the recognition that judges are not omniscient and may make mistakes about facts and that, in practice, absolute justice is never fully realized in any particular legal case. But the belief in the possibility of a rule of law, of justice, and of freedom, can hardly survive the acceptance of an epistemology which teaches that there are no objective facts.[33]

In Popper's method, the historian begins with an hypothesis or 'conjecture', which he or she must then seek to disprove through examination of the evidence. The concept of refutation is central to Popper's goal of achieving objective knowledge. Such knowledge, he believed, could never be more than provisional, but 'those among our theories which turn out to be highly resistant to criticism, and which appear to us at a certain moment of time to be better approximations to truth than other known theories, may be described . . . as "the science" of that time'.[34] All theories should, in principle, be able to be refuted; for this reason Popper dismissed psychoanalysis, which he perceived as able to explain 'practically everything that happened'.[35]

In the 1960s Popper's method for the rigorous testing of theories was challenged by the revelations of a physicist, Thomas Kuhn. Kuhn argued that the actual research practice of the scientific community rarely correlated with Popper's ideals concerning the rigorous testing of theories for falsification. Scientific research, Kuhn suggested, was more likely to seek to validate existing paradigms. Eventually the contradictions between the paradigm and the research data become sufficiently intense to cause a paradigmatic revolution, a process which is as much determined by culture and language, as it is by scientific rationality.[36] Berkhofer might have this process in mind when he describes the principles of objective empirical history as the 'normal history paradigm' prior to the poststructural challenge of the last decade.[37] While philosophers of science continue to debate the merits of Popper's method of establishing objective knowledge, his approach does suggest a more explicit and fruitful relationship between theory and evidence from which empirical historians can learn. Should the historians' method of research commence with the conscious formulation of an hypothesis, grounded in theory? Should we employ a research method which is more objective because it actively seeks evidence to disprove, as well as prove, a hypothesis while accepting that the final interpretation will always be subject to revision?

Let us turn now to an example of empiricist history, taken from one of Geoffrey Elton's most influential works, *England under the Tudors*, first published in 1955. Born in Germany in 1921, Elton studied at the University of Prague before completing a doctoral thesis at Cambridge on Tudor government which 'made his reputation'.[38] His corpus of work focuses primarily upon administrative history, and he also became one of the leading defenders of empiricism as a theory of knowledge. The extract from his work which follows contains many of the distinguishing features of empiricist history. To begin with, examine the table of contents. What does it suggest about Elton's approach to this period of English history, both in terms of focus and organization? What historical factors appear to be missing from his account? The title suggests the study is about England, but in this case, is dynastic history equated with national history? It is interesting that Elton wrote his path-breaking study of the Tudor government in the 1950s, a time of unprecedented state expansion in Western Europe, the debate over which may well have influenced the focus of his work.

Elton was adamant that his own interpretation of the Tudor government 'came to my mind not (as some of my critics would have it) because mine was a naturally authoritarian mind looking for virtue in rulers, but because the evidence called them forth'.[39] This is an appeal to the orthodox inductive method. Throughout the chapter Elton identifies strongly with the interests of Henry VII, and nothing is more apparent than the dismissive treatment meted out to luckless pretenders. What other examples can you find in the reading which indicate Elton's implicit theory of the importance of strong leadership? One of the criticisms Abrams made of narrative history is the 'luring of the reader into accepting the author's preferred interpretation simply as a happening'.[40] Does Elton, as the omniscient narrator, allow the flow of the story to obscure the degree to which he is making judgements on the basis of undeclared criteria?

Notes

1 E. P. Thompson makes a clear distinction between empiricism as an 'ideological formation', and the empirical techniques of historical investigation in *The Poverty of Theory and Other Essays* (New York, 1978), p. 6.
2 Dorinda Outram makes the point that the terms science and scientist were not invented until the early nineteenth century, and the more common contemporary term would have been 'natural philosophy', see *The Enlightenment* (Cambridge, 1995), pp. 48–9.
3 See Richard Evans, *In Defence of History* (London, 1997), p. 18.
4 Cited in Ernst Breisach, *Historiography, Ancient, Medieval and Modern* (2nd edn, Chicago, 1994), p. 233.
5 Evans, *In Defence of History*, pp. 17–18.
6 Georg G. Iggers, *Historiography in the Twentieth Century* (Hanover, 1997), p. 26.
7 Cited in Peter Novick, *That Noble Dream: The 'Objectivity Question' and the American Historical Profession* (Cambridge, 1988), p. 26.
8 See Jonathan Dancy, *Introduction to Contemporary Epistemology* (Oxford, 1985), pp. 115–16 for further discussion of correspondence theory.
9 J. B. Bury, 'The Science of History', in *Selected Essays of J. B. Bury*, ed. Harold Temperley (Cambridge, 1930), pp. 4–6.
10 *Ibid.*, p. 17.
11 G. R. Elton, *The Practice of History* (Sydney, 1967), pp. 34–5.
12 Arthur Marwick, *The Nature of History* (3rd edn, London, 1989), pp. 220–4.
13 Norman F. Cantor (ed.), *The Medieval World, 300–1300* (London, 1968), pp. 131–2.
14 Robert Harris, *Selling Hitler: The Story of the Hitler Diaries* (London, 1986).
15 Marwick, *The Nature of History*, p. 223.
16 Quentin Skinner, *The Foundations of Modern Political Thought*, vol. 1 (Cambridge, 1978), p. x.
17 Quentin Skinner, 'Meaning and Understanding in the History of Ideas', *History and Theory*, 8, 1 (1969), pp. 48–9. I am grateful to Lyndan Warner for drawing my attention to this point.
18 Elton, *The Practice of History*, pp. 92–3.
19 *Ibid.*, p. 83.
20 Quentin Skinner, 'Sir Geoffrey Elton and the Practice of History', *Transactions of the Royal Historical Society*, 6th ser., 7 (1997), pp. 307–8.
21 Philip Abrams, *Historical Sociology* (Shepton Mallet, 1982), p. 307.

22 *Ibid.*, pp. 310, 307.
23 See John Tosh, *The Pursuit of History* (London, 1984), ch. 7, for an excellent discussion of these issues.
24 See Simon Szreter, *Fertility, Class and Gender in Britain 1860–1940* (Cambridge, 1996).
25 S. H. Rigby discusses the philosophical problems inherent in the search for principal causes in 'Historical Causation: Is One Thing more Important than Another', *History*, 80, 259 (June 1995), pp. 227–42.
26 See William Cronon, 'A Place for Stories: Nature, History and Narrative', *Journal of American History*, 78 (March 1992), pp. 1347–76.
27 *Ibid.*, p. 1376.
28 Novick, *That Noble Dream*, p. 259.
29 Charles A. Beard, 'That Noble Dream' (1935), in Fritz Stern (ed.), *The Varieties of History* (2nd edn, London, 1970), p. 328.
30 E. H. Carr, *What is History* (2nd edn, London, 1987), p. 22.
31 Deborah E. Lipstadt, *Denying the Holocaust: The Growing Assault on Truth and Memory* (New York, 1994).
32 Dominick LaCapra, *History and Criticism* (Ithaca, 1985), p. 137.
33 See Karl R. Popper, *Conjectures and Refutations: The Growth of Scientific Knowledge* (London, 1963), p. 5.
34 *Ibid.*, p. vii.
35 Peter Gay, *Freud for Historians* (Oxford, 1985), p. 63.
36 Thomas Kuhn, *The Structure of Scientific Revolutions* (Chicago, 1962).
37 Robert F. Berkhofer, Jr., *Beyond the Great Story: History as Text and Discourse* (Cambridge, Mass., 1995), pp. 28–31.
38 John Cannon, *et al.* (eds), *The Blackwell Dictionary of Historians* (Oxford, 1988), p. 122.
39 Elton, *The Practice of History*, p. 121.
40 Abrams, *Historical Sociology*, p. 307.

Additional reading

Acton, J. E. (ed.), *The Cambridge Modern History* (Cambridge, 1902–12).

Appleby, Joyce, Lynn Hunt and Margaret Jacob, *Telling The Truth About History* (New York, 1994).

Carr, E. H., *What is History?* (2nd edn, London, [1961] 1988).

Elton, G. R., *The Practice of History* (London, [1967] 1987).

Elton, G. R., *England under the Tudors* (3rd edn, London, 1991).

Evans, Richard J., *In Defence of History* (London, 1997).

Kenyon, J. P., *Stuart England* (2nd edn, Harmondsworth, 1985).

Marwick, Arthur, *The Nature of History* (London, [1970] 1989).

Novick, Peter, *That Noble Dream: The 'Objectivity Question' and the American Historical Profession* (Cambridge, 1988).

Powicke, Maurice, *The Thirteenth Century, 1216–1307* (Oxford, 1962).

Russell, Conrad, *Parliaments and English Politics 1621–1629* (Oxford, 1979).

Tosh, John, 'The Limits of Historical Knowledge', in *The Pursuit of History* (2nd edn, London, [1984] 1991).

ENGLAND UNDER THE TUDORS
G. R. Elton

Contents

Chapter II
HENRY VII: SECURING THE DYNASTY

1. Henry's claim to the crown

When victory was won at Bosworth, Lord Stanley, whose timely desertion of Richard III had made Henry's triumph possible, picked up the crown and put it on the victor's head; according to the chronicler, people rejoiced and clapped their hands and cried, 'King Henry, King Henry'. But while this acclamation must have been pleasant to his ears, it did not make the gold circlet sit any more securely on his head. Henry VII's first task was to convince the country and the world that he really was king. Though he could feel the task somewhat eased as his journey to London assumed the proportions of a triumph, there was probably no need to remind him of men's fickleness. The city of London, in particular, had distinguished itself by the readiness with which it had hailed each successive conqueror of the crown.

Henry's own claim to the crown was far from straightforward. Fifteenth-century England knew no proper law of succession. The judges had repeatedly declared that the common law did not extend to such exalted matters; they had, in fact, been too scared of the consequences to attempt a definition in the middle of the dynastic struggles. Henry IV, in 1399, had put forward a claim compounded of the (false) assertion that he represented the true line of succession, the proof of divine favour contained in his actual victory, and the duty of removing a lawless monarch like Richard II. There were points here which Henry VII might profitably remember. Richard, duke of York, in 1450, and his son Edward IV after him, opposed an out-and-out theory of legitimacy to the claims which the oath of allegiance gave to Henry VI, the king in possession. Legitimacy—the doctrine that the crown can descend only to one man at any given time and that this succession is determined by primogeniture—was the centre of the Yorkist position; being descended from John of Gaunt's elder brother, they found in it a useful weapon against Gaunt's issue. Richard III exploited it further when he took the crown by the simple step of declaring his nephews bastardised; this left him as the only legitimate heir of the only legitimate line. There was thus a general idea that the succession should pass to the eldest son, but the strict theory of legitimacy was still the property of a party, and the Lancastrians had never subscribed to it.

The theory was of no use at all to Henry VII. He claimed to represent the line of Lancaster; his mother Margaret was the last of the Beauforts, John of Gaunt's illegitimate descendants who had been legitimised by the pope and by Richard II. However, an insertion, itself of doubtful validity, in Henry IV's confirmation of his predecessor's grant had denied them the right to succeed to the crown. On the male side, Henry had no royal ancestry; if direct descent from Edward III was to be decisive, the young earl of Warwick, son of the late duke of Clarence, had undoubtedly the best claim. Legitimacy was thus valueless to the Tudor king. Nor did he intend to base his right on the much-mooted marriage to Elizabeth, daughter of Edward IV: it might be useful in appeasing the Yorkist faction, but Henry meant to be king in his own right. He therefore deliberately post-poned the marriage until he had established himself on the throne. In actual fact, he adopted the simplest solution of all: he said that he was king. In November 1485 he told his first parliament that he had come to the crown by inheritance (leaving the details studiously vague) and by the proof of God's will expressed in his victory: his right was, in his own view, divine to this extent that divine approval had clearly been given on the field of battle. This Tudor kind of divine right is the exact opposite to the Stuart brand. The Tudors appealed to fact—God spoke through the arbitrament of war. The Stuarts believed in an indefeasible right which no amount of adverse cir-cumstances could lessen or destroy.

Thus Henry certainly thought and acted as king of England as soon as Richard III was dead. Indeed, he arbitrarily fixed the begin-ning of his reign as the day before Bosworth, but this was only a typical piece of sharp practice designed to enable him to deal with Richard's supporters on that day as traitors to himself. There was no question of parliament conferring or even confirming his title. The very fact that the body which met in November 1485 counts as a real parliament is proof enough; only a true king can summon a true par-liament, and the writs of summons went out early in September. Henry VII merely followed a precedent set in 1406 by Henry IV who had the succession after him registered in parliament, and he did it for the same reason—to avoid all ambiguity and pave the way for a stable continuance of his dynasty. It was 'ordained, established, and enacted' by the parliament, not that Henry was king, but that the inheritance of the crown of England, with every right and possession belonging to it, should remain and abide with 'our now sovereign lord king Henry' and his heirs. The act thus recognised that Henry was king, and that therefore rightly the succession must pass to his line; its purpose, like that of many Tudor acts, was to put a matter beyond doubt by putting it on record. It served the ends of propa-ganda the importance of which all the Tudors understood very well.

These were matters of theory, but of legal theory and therefore important. The care with which Henry made sure that his title should not rest on parliament, nor, on the other hand, be too thoroughly investigated, shows that he knew the value of theory. But practical considerations mattered even more. Henry might allege his claim to be beyond cavil, but there were others who would dispute this hotly. It was therefore only sound policy to make sure of all who could pos-sibly raise a rival claim. Richard III had happily died without direct heirs and had—despite doubts, the point remains probable—eased Henry's way further by putting Edward IV's sons out of the way. There remained the daughters of Edward IV and the son of Clarence, the ten-year-old earl of Warwick. Henry dealt with the former by marrying Elizabeth, the eldest of them, in January 1486, and with the latter by securing his body in the Tower. The unfortunate boy was to live out his life there till the conspiracies of others of which he had neither knowledge nor part brought him to the block. There remained the claim of John de la Pole, earl of Lincoln, nephew of Edward IV and nominated as his successor by Richard III, but for the present he submitted to Henry. The marriage with Elizabeth of York also helped to keep quiet that section of Yorkists that had joined Henry against Richard III's usurpation and had made his victory possible; ultimately, in producing heirs to the claims of both Lancaster and York, it brought about that 'Union of the Two Noble and Illustrious Families' which the Tudor historian Edward Hall took for the subject of his discourse. For the moment, however, there remained many dissatisfied with the new king and many more to whom violent ups and downs in public life, with the chances they offered to the enterprising and unscrupulous, had become the normal state of things. Not until 1500 could the Spanish ambassador de Puebla report that no doubtful royal blood remained to unsettle the Tudor claim, and even a year or two later some royal officials at Calais, discussing politics and the king's illness, foresaw further dynastic difficulties. The reign was never quite free from the fact or threat of conspiracy, and for several years Henry VII had to defend his throne against the kind of enterprise which had secured it to him in the first place.

2. Conspiracies
One of the purposes for which the parliament of November 1485 assembled was to dispose of the king's late adversaries. The usual crop of attainders[1] ruined a number of leading Yorkist supporters; so far, Henry VII showed no special mercy or any intention to end the wars by composing the feuds. There was, in any case, another good reason behind these acts which deprived some of the richest men in the kingdom of their property. The great act of resumption of the same

---

[1] Attainders were acts of parliament registering somebody's conviction for treason and declaring all his property forfeit to the king and his blood 'corrupted'; only in 1539 did they come to be used in lieu of trials.

year declared void all crown grants made since the death of Henry VI and recovered for Henry VII a vast deal of land; clearly, the king was from the first determined to improve his finances. In the true spirit of the civil wars, each stage of which had been signalled by the attainder of the defeated and the reversal of attainders previously inflicted on the victors, the parliament marked a Tudor, or even a Lancastrian, triumph. For the time being the Yorkists—even those who, hating Richard as a usurper, had supported Henry's bid for the crown—were left rather in the cold; the long overdue marriage to Elizabeth of York, so often promised, came none too soon to prevent the complete alienation of moderate Yorkist sentiment.

Moreover, there were still the extremists. In March 1486, having married his queen and seeing the south at peace, Henry travelled north into the Yorkist stronghold of Yorkshire, to show his face and overcome opposition. At Lincoln he heard that Francis, Lord Lovell, Richard III's friend and chamberlain, had broken sanctuary at Colchester, together with Humphrey and Thomas Stafford, and had fled to unknown parts. As the king continued into Yorkshire, news came in of armed bands raised by the fugitives and of threatened risings in Henry's path. But nothing happened. York, which recently had recorded an official lament at Richard III's overthrow, received his conqueror with pageantry and pomp; a local conspiracy was promptly scotched, and Lovell's forces melted away before the promise of a pardon. Lovell fled abroad; the Staffords, who had failed to raise the west country against the king, were dragged from sanctuary and taken to the Tower. The question arose whether they ought to escape justice because the Church's right of sanctuary had been violated. In his natural desire to prevent an acquittal, Henry tried to get the judges' opinion before the case came to trial, but since they were reluctant to commit themselves in advance he had to be content with requesting a rapid decision. In the end the court of king's bench decided that sanctuary was a common-law matter in which the pope could not interfere—certainly a striking instance of the growing spirit of resistance to ecclesiastical pretensions—and that the privilege did not cover treasonable offences. Humphrey Stafford was executed, though Thomas benefited from Henry VII's awakening mercifulness. The rising itself was utterly insignificant, but the case deserves attention because it illustrates the Tudor principle of relying on the decisions of common-law judges, the Tudor readiness to respect the judges' independence, and the Tudor disregard for ancient franchises and immunities.

In September 1486, Henry's heart was gladdened by the birth of a son—Arthur (the revival of the ancient British name was meant to be significant)—who seemed to make the dynasty secure. The king himself was not yet thirty; there seemed no question that he would live long enough to see his heir of age. However, just at this juncture the first of the serious conspiracies of the reign came into the open. The country was much unsettled by rumours: many believed that the princes in the Tower were still alive and had perhaps managed to escape, or that the earl of Warwick, the true Yorkist claimant if Richard III had really disposed of Edward IV's sons, was again at large. There was plenty of credulity, plenty of Yorkist sentiment, and plenty of plain superstition for a skilful man to exploit. An Oxford priest of no birth but some brains, Richard Symonds, was the first to realise this. He planned to pass off a pupil of his, a harmless gentle boy called Lambert Simnel, as Richard of York, the younger of Edward's sons; soon after, when it was rumoured that Warwick had died in the Tower, Simnel's impersonation was changed to Warwick on the grounds that the government would not be able to disprove the fraud by exhibiting the real earl. The very fact that such a wildcat scheme could spring from an obscure priest's brain—and that it came within measurable distance of success—indicates the state of the country and the size of Henry's problem. Symonds found favour with the leaders of the Yorkist party—Margaret, the dowager duchess of Burgundy, sister of Edward IV and the centre of all the plots against the Tudors, and the exiled Lord Lovell who had taken refuge with her. John de la Pole, earl of Lincoln, Richard III's successor-designate whom Henry VII had treated with kindness, repaid the king by fleeing to join the rebels who had raised the White Rose in Ireland. That country had always nursed Yorkist sympathies, and its most powerful noble, the earl of Kildare, welcomed any opportunity to throw off English control.

Thus Henry was suddenly faced with a major threat, all the more dangerous in that it centred upon Ireland where he could not touch it. Subsidiary moves in Lancashire and Cornwall could be disregarded, but the menace from across the Irish channel demanded immediate action. In vain the real Warwick was paraded through London; in May 1487, the false Warwick was proclaimed Edward VI in Dublin, and all Ireland except the city of Waterford went over to him. His power rested on Kildare, the Yorkist leaders Lincoln and Lovell, and 2,000 German mercenaries contributed by Margaret of Burgundy. In June they landed in Lancashire and began their march on London. The familiar story of the Wars of the Roses seemed about to re-open. However, the country showed how tired it was of it all: even Yorkshire gave little support to the White Rose, and the rest of the country remained loyal to Henry. It is probable, also, that the inclusion in Lincoln's army of many wild Irishmen served to lose him much support. The decision came at Stoke, on 16 June 1487, where all the Yorkist leaders were killed, or disappeared never to be heard of again; Symonds and Simnel fell into the king's hands. Henry proved merciful in a politic manner; his treatment of Simnel, taken into the royal household where he made a career from scullion to falconer, bore an air of sardonic but not unkindly humour. Symonds was confined for life; there was no general proscription or holocaust of executions such as was to disgrace later Tudor victories, though a number of Simnel's followers paid for their treason in sizeable fines. One of the victims of the affair, for reasons which have remained obscure, was Henry's mother-in-law, the foolish and meddling Elizabeth Woodville; she ended her days in a convent. Throughout it is clear that Henry tried to play down the whole business, an endeavour in which he succeeded.

Before the next serious threat to Henry's throne arose, England became involved in a war with France. The full story is extremely complicated, and almost equally immaterial. But its main lines are important, for they indicate both Henry's VII's aims in foreign affairs and the European diplomatic situation which was to determine England's attitude to the continent until the fall of Wolsey in 1529. In the last twenty years of the fifteenth century Western Europe assumed a new aspect. France, consolidated by Louis XI (who died in 1483), and Spain, created by the personal union of Ferdinand of Aragon and Isabella of Castile (1469), took over the leadership of affairs, and their quarrels form the story of European diplomacy to which the machinations of Maximilian, king of the Romans, of Italian princes including the pope, and of the kings of England are subsidiary. Henry VII's immediate attitude in 1487 was decided by several considerations. The traditional hostility to France was far from dead; indeed, it was kept alive by the king's retention of a claim to the French throne which feeling in the country would not have allowed him to surrender even if he had felt so inclined. More materially, England's continued possession of Calais provided both a gateway into France and a permanent irritant to relations between the two countries. Furthermore, Henry earnestly wished to secure visible recognition for his dynasty from some European power, and common interests, mostly commercial, suggested the rising power of Spain. In 1488–9 he negotiated a treaty of marriage between his son Arthur and Catherine, the younger daughter of Ferdinand and Isabella. In return, Spain—who had ambitions for two French provinces in the Pyrenees—secured a promise of English help against France. The occasion of the quarrel was provided by the affairs of Brittany. That duchy alone had escaped the centralising activities of Louis XI, but his daughter (Anne of Beaujeu) and later his son (Charles VIII) were determined to remedy the omission. Though the French won a great victory in 1488 they lost its gains when the duke of Brittany died soon after, to be succeeded by his daughter Anne, aged twelve. Anne of Brittany was an important heiress whose hand was worth fighting for; Spain saw a chance of embarrassing France, and Anne of Beaujeu a chance of asserting French control of the duchy by claiming the wardship of the young duchess; the war revived.

England's part was decided for her by the danger of letting the Breton ports fall into French hands, by the fact that English volunteers had been killed in hundreds in the previous Breton defeat, and by Spanish pressure. In 1489 Henry prepared for war. With some difficulty he obtained a parliamentary grant of £100,000, only part of which was ever paid; its collection led to a major riot in the north in which the king's lieutenant, the earl of Northumberland, was killed. The garrison at Calais was reinforced. The treaty of Medina del Campo with Spain, in March 1489, bound England to the war. Henry gained big trading concessions, but Spain had much the best of the political bargain: either side could withdraw when it had achieved its ends, but since Spain wanted only the Pyrenean provinces while England spoke of recovering Henry V's conquests, it is plain where the advantage lay. However, Henry got what he wanted—trade on favoured terms and the betrothal of Arthur and Catherine; as events were to show, he had no intention of wasting blood or treasure over the affairs of Brittany or Spain. He fulfilled the terms of the treaty and assisted his other ally, Maximilian, in his struggle with Flemish rebels. Otherwise neither he nor anyone else made any move until in 1490 Maximilian suddenly married Anne of Brittany. Henry occupied 1491 in extracting money from his country by benevolences, that is, by forced gifts described as voluntary, a method declared illegal in 1484; but no one resisted Charles VIII when, stung to action by Anne's marriage, he proceeded gradually to conquer Brittany and in the end himself married Anne after she had secured the necessary dispensation from her non-consummated previous marriage.

The situation was now handsomely confused. Spain showed no intention of supporting her ally; not for the last time did kings of England regret an alliance with Ferdinand of Aragon. Brittany was irrevocably French, and the vast English ambitions for the recovery of Henry V's conquests were merely ridiculous. It need not be thought that the king shared them. But he could not afford to associate the Tudors with the surrender of claims so tenaciously held by Lancaster and York, nor did he wish to write off the considerable loans he had made to Brittany earlier in the war. He therefore spent 1492 in making demonstrations designed to impress France with the gravity of the English threat. He even crossed the channel in person and took an army to besiege Boulogne, an action which came to be considered the *sine qua non* of Tudor generalship in Northern France. Charles VIII had no reason for continuing the war, the more so as his restless ambition was turning to thoughts of Italy. Thus in December 1492 the two powers signed the treaty of Etaples by which Henry agreed to hold his claim to France in abeyance and received in return a sum which he could and did call a tribute, as well as repayment of the Breton debts. At relatively small expense he had obtained an honourable peace and a sizeable pension to compensate him for his outlay. He had thrown over Spain—but Ferdinand and Isabella had themselves been contemplating a separate peace, so that Henry had merely beaten them at their own game. His other ally, Maximilian, also felt himself deserted, but his own conduct had been extremely shifty, and no one ever at any time had any scruples in neglecting Maximilian. The war had demonstrated that England was once again a power to be reckoned with and entitled to play a part in European diplomacy. It had led to the official recognition of the Tudor dynasty by France and Spain, with both of whom Henry had concluded treaties. The king could feel that he had manoeuvred well in his first essay in this tricky game.

The treaty of Etaples came not a minute too soon, for Henry had to turn his attention to the most serious threat he was to face in his whole reign. In the year 1491, a young man of seventeen, servant to a Breton merchant, was walking up and down the streets of Cork, displaying on his person the silk clothes in which his master traded. His bearing and splendour made a great impression on the rather backward townsfolk, unsettled as they already were by tales of Plantagenet princes escaping hither and thither. They told the young man that he was the earl of Warwick, and when he denied this they obligingly changed him into a bastard of Richard III. He continued his denials, but they only turned him into Richard, duke of York, the younger son of Edward IV. Worn out by their importunity he agreed. This at least was the tale which the pretender later told in his confession which is now accepted as largely true, though it may still appear doubtful whether a man who for eight years pertinaciously maintained his identity as Richard of York really came by the imposture in so casual a manner. His real name was Perkin Warbeck—his parents were still alive in Tournai in 1497—and he had been travelling in the service of various merchants since he was eleven. The supposed miracle of his knowing the details which convinced others of his Plantagenet descent has been made too much of: it does not appear that he ever convinced anyone except people eager to use him against Henry VII. This also goes for his supposed aunt, Margaret of Burgundy, who was perfectly capable of taking up a pretender and swearing to his identity once she felt sure that no genuine Yorkist claimants survived at liberty. That she later coached him in his part is likely.

Warbeck's career as Richard of York was crowded and various; the story has been told often and at sufficient length, and only its salient points need concern us here. His appearance which had so impressed the Irish at Cork is known from a good drawing: his charm and intelligence cannot disguise a blatant weakness. Everything he undertook by himself ended in dismal failure; anyone less like the brutal and efficient Yorkist strain it is hard to imagine. It seems that of all the men who had to do with him only Henry VII, who treated him with weary contempt and almost offensive leniency, judged him fairly; others were too blinded by his usefulness to take his just measure. In consequence he served as the peg on which hung the events of eight disturbed years.

After the Irish lords had approved of him in their rough Irish fashion which counted not the truth when trouble could be stirred up against England, Warbeck's first protector was Charles VIII of France, then at war with Henry VII. The treaty of Etaples put a stop to this, and in 1493 Warbeck passed into Burgundy, there to find favour with the dowager duchess Margaret and gather round him the Yorkist exiles and their hopes. The support he received annoyed Henry VII to the point of breaking off all trade with the Low Countries, a boycott which hit the Flemish cloth industry very hard, dependent as it was on English wool and unfinished cloth. However, the embargo was naturally also unpopular with English merchants and could not be prolonged unduly; it was lifted after two years though it had not achieved the end for which it was imposed. Warbeck had sought and found a better protector than Margaret; late in 1493 he was at Vienna, winning over the unstable and foolish Maximilian who saw a chance of paying Henry VII out for his alleged treachery in the treaty of Etaples. Maximilian went so far as to recognise Warbeck as Richard IV, the rightful king of England, and to promise him full support in the recovery of the crown. In return, Warbeck signed a document in January 1495 which made Maximilian his heir, so that—should Warbeck die in the attempt to win the throne of England—the king of the Romans would succeed to the full Yorkist claim. Maximilian was himself good at making worthless promises, but one feels that on this occasion he had met his match. However, the mere fact that the pretender found all this support was significant. Maximilian and his son, the Archduke Philip, ruler of the Netherlands, made the Low Countries the centre of Warbeck's conspiracy to which many flocked even from England in hopes of a Yorkist revival. By this time Warbeck knew his part to perfection, and it is not surprising that he imposed on those eager partisans of the White Rose.

More dangerous still was the fact that the conspiracy had developed a branch in England—indeed, in the very court itself. One of those who had gone to Flanders to join Richard IV was Sir Robert Clifford who, however, had second thoughts on arrival—unless, as is possible, he was secretly in the service of Henry VII. At any rate, in December 1494 he officially made his peace with the king, received a pardon and reward, and returned to lay detailed information against the heads of disaffection in England. Probably Henry had had his eye on the men involved for some time, and Clifford's testimony only served to clinch matters. A number of lesser men, led by Lord Fitzwalter, died on block and gallows, their property being subsequently confiscated and their blood attainted in the parliament of 1495. One man fell with a crash: Clifford accused Sir William Stanley, lord chamberlain of the household and the man who had made the victory at Bosworth possible, of complicity in the plot. Nothing is known about the whole affair, but from the testimony of contemporaries we know that Henry VII was not easily persuaded of anyone's treasonable activity. It therefore seems likely that Stanley had aroused suspicion long before Clifford denounced him. After all, the Stanleys had changed sides in 1485 only after much hesitation; it is possible that Sir William did not think even a chamberlain's staff sufficient reward for his services.

The arrests and executions broke the conspiracy in England and made Warbeck's projected invasion hopeless. Nevertheless, it was attempted. In July 1495 he appeared off Deal and landed gradually the better part of his forces; he himself remained prudently on board ship. The royal officers were ready: the men who had landed were killed or taken, and the affair collapsed in ridicule as Warbeck sailed rapidly off to Ireland. Here he failed to take the loyal town of Waterford in an eleven days' siege and decided to try Scotland. King James IV had come to the throne as the head of the party bitterly hostile to England, after his mildly Anglophil father had been murdered. He was therefore more than ready to receive the pretender and offer him assistance. But this business too came to nothing. In January 1496 a Scottish force crossed the border and burnt and looted savagely—distressing Warbeck not a little, it must be added, much to the amazement of both Scots and English. They then withdrew again. Border raids were one thing; an expedition to put Richard IV on the throne of England was quite another. Henry VII was the less inclined to take serious countermeasures because his natural dislike of war was being encouraged by Spain who wanted his alliance against France (then too successful in Italy) and therefore tried to arrange peace between England and Scotland. Moreover, the heavy war taxation led to a really serious rising in Cornwall. The Cornishmen had no interest in Warbeck; what they wanted was relief from exactions demanded by affairs on the far northern border which they did not consider concerned them. They therefore rose in 1497, under the leadership of the blacksmith Joseph and the lawyer Flamank, to march to London and state their case. They were peaceable enough at first but killed a tax-collector at Taunton, probably thinking little of so obvious a deed. Then, led by Lord Audley, an impoverished peer, they marched right across England, for with the king's forces tied up on the border there was no one to oppose them. In June 1497 they sat down at Blackheath, but instead of being overawed—Henry never parleyed with rebels under arms—the king proceeded to surround and attack them. Two thousand died on the day; of the survivors only the leaders were hanged. All this, however, did not make the problem of Perkin Warbeck easier for Henry.

In actual fact Perkin left Scotland, where he was kept as a potential but unused asset, in July 1497, hoping to try his luck once more in Ireland. But things had changed there; Kildare was, for the moment, loyal; and Warbeck thought it better to follow an invitation from Cornwall where the king's clemency had by some been misinterpreted as weakness. Opposed by the new lord chamberlain, Giles Lord Daubeney, Perkin once again lost heart; at Taunton he stole away at midnight with some sixty leading followers, leaving his forces unofficered. Though he reached sanctuary at Beaulieu monastery, he was persuaded to throw himself on Henry's mercy, and so in August 1497 the king at last had the troublesome adventurer in his hands. It was now that the famous confession appeared, telling of Warbeck's true identity and early life; but there is sound proof that Henry knew all these details as early as 1493, and corroborative evidence exists to establish the truth of the confession. Warbeck was kept at court in honourable custody; once again Henry VII refused to make martyrs. In 1498, however, he tried to escape and on his recapture suffered a harsher confinement. Finally, he made another attempt in November 1499, as is supposed with the king's connivance, for now the government hoped to get at the real Yorkist, the earl of Warwick, through the pretended one. Warwick seems to have been quite innocent of any attempt against Henry VII, but for some reason of which we are ignorant the government had decided that his very existence constituted a danger. Indeed, the career of Perkin Warbeck, and that of Lambert Simnel before him, gave grounds for such a belief, and it may be that diplomatic difficulties—the insistence of Spain on a safe Tudor title before they would let Catherine of Aragon go to England—forced Henry's hand. At any rate, the government produced some sort of evidence of a conspiracy; Warbeck was hanged and Warwick beheaded; and the Tudor could sleep more easily. There is nothing to be said in extenuation of such judicial murders of which the reign of Henry VIII was to produce many more, except that those who saw a danger in so perfectly innocent a man as Edward of Warwick were far from wrong. It was not what he did or thought but what he stood for in other men's minds that brought him to his death. For Warbeck one may feel sorry, but he had certainly earned his fate several times over.

3. Ireland and Scotland

The stories of Lambert Simnel and Perkin Warbeck have served to underline an important truth: there was danger for the English crown within the British isles themselves. Ireland and Scotland were both trouble spots. The Norman conquest of Ireland in the twelfth century had imposed upon the native Celtic population a feudal ruling class, but though the kings of England might claim to be lords of Ireland they never, in fact, effectively ruled much of it. The so-called English Pale—a strip of coast stretching some 50 miles northwards from Dublin—was the real limit of English influence, though the few towns in the south, especially Waterford and Cork, also provided precarious centres of civilisation in a country not far removed from tribal barbarism. The Irish nobility, Anglo-Norman in origin, had long since suffered the common fate of English settlers in Ireland and become as Irish as the Irish, so that there was little to choose, from the king's point of view, between Anglo-Irish families like the Geraldines or Butlers and the purely Irish chieftains. Even within the Pale, Englishry was losing ground to Irish speech, dress, and habits. The wars of the Roses had further weakened the hold of the crown. The local feuds adopted the terminology of the English dynastic struggles: thus the Geraldines, led by the earls of Kildare and Desmond, championed the Yorkist cause, while their enemies, the Butlers under the earl of Ormond, espoused the side of Lancaster. The Geraldines won, with the result that Ireland became something of a Yorkist stronghold. But on the whole these were phrases rather than realities; what mattered to the Irish lords was independence from royal control and the fighting of their own internecine quarrels. The better part of the wild, wooded, boggy, and hilly country of the north and west had never so much as seen an English soldier or administrator.

The recovery and reduction of Ireland proved to be a general Tudor problem; to Henry VII its urgency was brought home by the fact that the country offered a safe and friendly springboard to any claimant, however absurd. In 1485 the power of Fitzgerald was paramount. The elder branch of the Butlers had moved to England, and though Henry VII restored them to their forfeited lands in Ireland, this did not affect the position of the great earl of Kildare whose many links with native families and wide personal possessions made him the virtual ruler of the country. He held the title of lord deputy and his brother was chancellor of Ireland; for the moment, Henry VII could not attempt to attack these strongholds of Geraldine power. Kildare was a curious character: arrogant and restless, he was yet gifted with some political skill, little rancour, and a roughish humour which, as it happened, appealed to the king. The support which the earl gave to Lambert Simnel was blatant and avowed, but Henry deliberately ignored it and permitted the two Fitzgeralds to continue in office when they admitted that they had been mistaken about the pretender. But forbearance was not the right treatment for a man who had earned the title of 'the great earl' by invariably getting his own way. In 1491, when Perkin Warbeck was acclaimed at Cork, Kildare showed himself cautiously ready to side with him, and in June 1492 Henry at last deprived him of the deputyship. Thomas Fitzgerald lost the great seal of Ireland, and the offices went instead to the archbishop of Dublin and Alexander Plunket, ancestor of a noble Irish line.

Kildare was sufficiently taken aback to seek the king's pardon, even asking his old enemy Ormond for help, but it was a full year before Henry would grant it (1493), and then only after the earl had come in person to seek it. The display of energy had at least produced signs of humility. Nothing, however, had been done to settle or even improve the state of Ireland. Government there was at the time managed at two removes: the king, as lord of Ireland, appointed a lord lieutenant (his uncle, the duke of Bedford) whose office was exercised for him by a lord deputy. More was required than the replacement of Kildare by a sequence of mediocrities, and in September 1494 Henry made his most determined attempt to solve the problem. He transferred the title of lord lieutenant to the infant prince Henry, his second son, so as to match in Ireland the nominal headship exercised by his elder son in Wales, and appointed as deputy Sir Edward Poynings, one of his most trusted and able ministers. The offices of chancellor and treasurer, too, were filled by Englishmen; the new policy announced itself from the first as hostile to all things Irish and determined to reduce the country to obedience to England.

Poynings was an experienced soldier and statesman, and the plan he had been sent to execute required the qualities of both. He was to conquer Ulster, the wildest part of the country where rebellion had always found safe refuge, and he was to impose on Ireland a constitution which would secure the full control of the English government. In the first he failed outright; in the second he succeeded after a fashion. His expedition against the tribesmen of the north got literally bogged down, and he had in the end to content himself with buying the clans off. The only positive result was the fall of Kildare, who had accompanied Poynings' forces, on a suspicion of treason to which his family's actions (Desmond assisted Warbeck in the siege of

Waterford) and Ormond's whispers gave colour. The parliament of Drogheda, summoned by Poynings in December 1494, attainted him, thus mightily impressing the Irish to whom the earl had seemed an almost more than human figure. The deputy promptly arrested him and shipped him to the Tower. Some other acts of this parliament, commonly known as Poynings' laws, were designed to achieve the second of Henry's aims. Their total effect was to decree that an Irish parliament could only be summoned, and could only legislate, with the king's previous approval; no future laws were to be discussed unless first agreed to by the king in council. Furthermore, all laws made in England were automatically to apply to Ireland. Poynings' laws thus destroyed the legislative independence of the Irish parliament and, in law at least, gave the king vastly greater powers in Ireland than he had in England. It may be noticed that when these and other acts against the lawlessness and wild violence of Irish conditions were passed, they had the approval of the English colonist element which in later years was to be foremost in the attack on Poynings' laws.

However, Henry VII's success proved illusory. The failure to subdue the wild Irish increased the Irish budget enormously by forcing Poynings to pay blackmail for peace, and though he had been so far successful as to deal easily with Warbeck's attack on Waterford, the king was not satisfied. Henry VII now showed one side of the Tudor character not often in evidence in his reign. When new difficulties rendered a pre-arranged policy doubtful or expensive, these inspired opportunists were always ready to give up, even though in consequence the work already done might be put in jeopardy. In effect Henry despaired of the success of the measures initiated in 1494 when in 1496 he recalled Poynings and restored Kildare to favour and the office of deputy. If—as is reported—he answered the bishop of Meath's complaint that all Ireland could not rule Kildare by saying that in that case Kildare had better rule all Ireland, he may have proved his wit but hardly his sagacity. The problem of Ireland had turned out to be too big for solution; the return of Kildare meant the end of effective English control, despite the operation of Poynings' laws; and Henry VIII, Elizabeth, and Oliver Cromwell had to face a problem grown even bigger in the interval. Henry VII had the best chance of all to win success, before the Reformation came to complicate matters; but parsimony (however necessary) and opportunism triumphed. There were no claimants about to disturb the peace from Ireland; why, then, waste good money on a probably futile policy of direct rule? Henry VII was lucky to die before the Irish problem revived, but revive it did—and largely because he gave up the fight.

Scotland constituted a very different problem—more serious and threatening on the face of it, though ultimately to prove much less insidious. The presence on one small island of two hostile powers had the most disastrous effects on both, but particularly on the politically more advanced kingdom of England. Since Edward I's ill-judged attempts to subdue Scotland, the northern kingdom had been persistently opposed to its larger neighbour, and by dint of its ancient alliance with France had managed to remain a very painful thorn in England's side. The border from Berwick to Carlisle was practically never at peace as raiding parties crossed from either side, to kill, rob, and burn on the other. Far too often these 'rodes' provided the ready pretext for more formal war. Truce followed truce with monotonous and pointless regularity. Compared with Scotland, harassed by perpetual feuds, gang warfare, murders, and dynastic upsets, even the England of the wars of the Roses was almost a law-abiding and peaceful state, and in Scotland such troubles were considered by the nobility as not only pleasurable but a necessity of life. One such conflagration resulted, in 1488, in the overthrow and murder of king James III, elevating to the throne a young king of romantically warlike ambitions, James IV. Little purpose would be served by reciting in detail his various attempts to instigate action on the border and the repeated treaties for a cessation of the trouble, now for three years and now for nine, none of which ever endured their appointed length. The revolution which had put James IV on the throne left, as was usual in Scotland, a powerful and dissatisfied opposition of nobles who intrigued with England and afforded Henry VII an opportunity to keep Scotland from getting dangerous. The French war of 1489–92 passed off without active interference from the north, but when Perkin Warbeck's wanderings took him to Scotland James IV seized upon this providential opportunity of embarrassing the enemy. The story of Scotland's share in Warbeck's Odyssey has already been told. At one time, in 1497, it looked as though Henry VII would accept the challenge and attempt serious war in the north, but the Cornish rebellion came just in time to save James IV from his ill-regulated combativeness. If one may judge from later events in Henry VIII's reign, the Scottish army would have stood but a poor chance against the forces which the earl of Surrey was marshalling on the border.

As it was, Henry VII preserved his peaceful reputation unsullied, to prove once more how well he could exploit difficult situations without precipitating war. Surrey did cross the border once to teach James a sharp lesson, incidentally refusing a typically chivalrous but unrealistic offer of single combat. The end of Warbeck left James rather at a loss, and his own position in a country some of whose chief lords were ready to throw in their lot with the enemy was none too comfortable. Henry even hinted that two could play at the game of supporting pretenders and showed signs of adopting the cause of a Stuart claimant, the duke of Albany, then living in France. All these things working together, and Henry still continuing to offer real peace, an agreement was finally arrived at in December 1497. It was to endure as long as both sovereigns lived. But this truce suffered the common fate of these border treaties; it was broken in the following year by a Scottish raid and English counter-raid. Something more permanent was required, and Henry VII, seriously intent on settling these tiresome difficulties, therefore proposed to marry his daughter Margaret to the king of Scots. Margaret, born in 1490, was of course too young for a real marriage, and the negotiations were dragged out not only by James's reluctance to make peace but also by a chance he thought he had of marrying a Spanish princess of rather riper years. However, in the end things fell out as Henry had designed. In July 1499, a treaty of peace and alliance was concluded between England and Scotland, and in September serious negotiations began for the marriage. After further delays James IV finally agreed to it in January 1502. The dynastic marriages of the time were commonly concluded when one party or both were yet children; one result of this was the frequent annulment of such unions and remarriage of these diplomatic pawns. However, the union of James of Scotland and Margaret Tudor was destined to be successful. It turned into a proper marriage agreeable to both parties before James crowned a warlike life by getting killed at Flodden, in 1513, fighting his wife's brother as he had once fought his wife's father. The real significance of the marriage lay in the distant future. If Henry VII had hoped to settle Anglo-Scottish difficulties at once he was disappointed; Scotland continued persistently hostile, and Henry VIII was twice at war with her. In the end, however, the marriage provided England with her Stuart kings;

though this was to prove anything but a blessing to her constitutional development, it did end the ancient feud on the border and opened the way to a union which was to be fruitful to both countries. Henry VII's Irish policy was right but not pursued long enough; his policy towards Scotland was wise and farseeing, and in the end completely successful.

2

Marxist historians

The single most influential theorist for twentieth-century historical writing is undoubtedly Karl Marx.[1] As Arthur Marwick has pointed out, 'most historians have in some way or another been affected by some aspect of Marxist thinking'.[2] This includes historians considered in other chapters of this book, for example, some historians of gender and the postcolonial historians of India. In this introduction, however, we will focus upon three historians of the British Marxist school, Eric Hobsbawm, Christopher Hill and E. P. Thompson. All were members of the Communist Party Historians Group, established in 1947, but the latter two severed their relationship with the Communist Party following the invasion of Hungary by the Soviet Union in 1956. Their combined body of historical writing, most influential during the three post-war decades, encompasses a wide range of subjects and centuries, including broad syntheses of history, biography, intellectual history and 'history from below' – studies of the 'common people'.

Raphael Samuel argues that the form that Marxist historiography took in Britain owed a great deal to its antecedents: 'Marxist historiography was chronologically preceded by, and has always had to co-exist with, a more broadly based and less theoretically demanding "people's history"'.[3] Taking this one step further, Arthur Marwick suggests that Thompson and Hill share in what might be called the 'main distinguishing characteristic of the contemporary British school of Marxist historians, an interest in ordinary people as such, rather than just in their political organisations or roles as revolutionary agents'.[4] The term 'history from below', coined by E. P. Thompson in 1966, is often used to reflect this interest.[5]

However, to conflate the broad body of social history with the work of Marxist historians may be to miss the very clear distinction between them. Harvey Kaye emphasizes the point that the British Marxist historians represent 'a theoretical tradition', the defining subject of which is 'the origins, development and expansion of capitalism as economic and social change'. Furthermore, their 'core proposition . . . is that class struggle has been central to the historical process'.[6] In contrast, social history has been fiercely criticized for its lack of explicit theorization, and a tendency to separate popular culture from the matrix of economic and political relationships in which it is embedded.[7] In order to understand the theoretical basis for Marxist historiography, we need to look at the ideas of Karl Marx.

Karl Marx was born in 1818 in Trier, Germany and spent his early adult life in Prussia and France. In the 1840s Paris was a ferment of revolutionary socialist ideas and movements, culminating in the 1848 revolution. Many of Marx's ideas about history emerged during this period, worked out in conjunction with his life-long collaborator, Friedrich Engels. Raphael Samuel rightly points out that Marx's published writings were primarily 'political interventions' arising out of the 'working class and revolutionary democratic movements in which Marx and Engels participated with such enthusiasm'.[8] Always under threat from the Prussian authorities, Marx lived an itinerant life in the late 1840s, moving between Prussia, Brussels and Paris. Finally, expelled from Paris, he left for England in 1849 where he spent the rest of his life.[9]

The theory of history for which Marx is known is not written down in one place, nor even developed coherently in a series of texts.[10] References are to be found scattered throughout his writings, and more than one generation of Marxist scholars have debated their meaning. Helmut Fleischer has identified three different historical approaches within Marx and Engels' writings, and these left an 'ambiguous and often contradictory legacy' to later Marxists.[11] Bear this qualification in mind as we consider the main strands of Marx's thought, and the concepts which have been most influential upon the writing of history.

Marx's interpretation of human history is known as the materialist conception of history, or 'historical materialism'. The basic principles were first developed in *The German Ideology*, written in 1846. Historical materialism locates the central dynamic of human history in the struggle to provide for physiological and material needs: 'life involves before everything else eating and drinking, a habitation, clothing and many other things. The first historical act is thus the production of the means to satisfy these needs, the production of material life itself'.[12] Secondly, Marx argues the fulfillment of these

needs is never completed, for 'the satisfaction of the first need . . .
leads to new needs'.[13] Marx identifies the way in which human
material needs are met as the most important influence in human
history: 'the multitude of productive forces accessible to men
determines the nature of society, hence, that the "history of humanity"
must always be studied and treated in relation to the history of
industry and exchange'.[14]

Consequently Marx believed that the economic structure of society
formed the base upon which all other aspects of society rested. Most
important are the forces of production – tools, technology, raw
materials – which when combined with human labour power are
transformed into goods to meet human needs. The interaction
between raw materials and human labour creates relations of
production between people, and these relations may rest upon
cooperation or subordination. For Marx, the rest of society – the
superstructure of political institutions and legal systems – was derived
from the forces and relations of production. In other words, he does
not ascribe an independent existence to the realm of human
consciousness and ideas, but perceives these as arising out of our
material existence. The premises and main ideas of historical
materialism are concisely described in the following, frequently cited,
statement from Contribution to the Critique of Political Economy (1859):

> In the social production of their life, men enter into definite relations that
> are indispensable and independent of their will, relations of production
> which correspond to a definite stage of development of their material
> productive forces. The sum total of these relations of production constitutes
> the economic structure of society, the real foundation, on which rises a legal
> and political superstructure and to which correspond definite forms of social
> consciousness. The mode of production of material life conditions the social,
> political and intellectual life process in general. It is not the consciousness of
> men that determines their being, but, on the contrary, their social being
> that determines their consciousness.[15]

How, then, does human society change over the centuries? Marx
separated human history into three historical epochs, each the product
of a progressively more advanced mode of production: ancient society
(Greece and Rome); feudal society; and capitalist (or modern
bourgeois) society.[16] Transition from one to another took place
through a process Marx described as a dialectic. Each mode of
production contained within it contradictions which would cause its
downfall; and each successive stage of human history contained both
a dominant class, and one which would overthrow it. In capitalist

society Marx anticipated that the proletariat, or working class, would eventually overthrow the bourgeoisie, and initiate another system of productive relations, a fourth epoch of socialism. His grand, overarching evolutionary theory of human history rested upon a dialectic of economic transformation. In placing economic relationships at the core of his philosophy of human history, Marx fundamentally differentiated himself from contemporaries, such as Leopold von Ranke.

The driving force in Marx's conception of history are classes, which arise from different economic roles in the productive process.[17] In order to overthrow the dominant class, subordinate people must become aware of their oppression, and consequently the concept of human agency is critical to Marx's conceptual framework. Marx's theory, therefore, contains a kind of paradox: the dialectic of productive transformation (a consequence of the inner contradictions within the production process itself) is, nonetheless, dependent upon the consciousness and actions of men and women. The following sentence, taken from *The Eighteenth Brumaire of Louis Bonaparte* (1859), lies at the heart of the matter:

> Men make their own history, but they do not make it just as they please; they do not make it under circumstances chosen by themselves, but under circumstances directly encountered, given, and transmitted from the past.[18]

This is an important phrase within Marx's work, for it challenges the economic determinism that can be seen as implicit within his formulation of historical change. Consequently, as Eric Hobsbawm has pointed out, 'the crucial argument about the materialist conception of history has concerned the fundamental relationship between social being and consciousness.'[19] This might be described as one of the strongest unifying themes in the work of Christopher Hill, Eric Hobsbawm and E.P. Thompson, to whose historical writings we will now turn.

Christopher Hill came to adulthood in the context of economic collapse and the rise of European fascism:

> The bottom fell out of our universe in 1931, the year I went up to Balliol. And there, the influence of undergraduate friends – a great deal of Marxist discussion went on in Oxford in the early thirties. Marxism seemed to me (and many others) to make better sense of the world situation than anything else, just as it seemed to make better sense of seventeenth-century English history.[20]

The seventeenth century has been the subject of Hill's historical writing, and his extensive body of published work includes biographies of Milton and Cromwell as well as the Marxist interpretation of the English Civil War of 1640 for which he is most widely known.[21] Hill argued that the Civil War was a revolutionary turning point in the development of capitalism, not merely a constitutional or religious dispute:

> The state power protecting an old order that was essentially feudal was violently overthrown, power passed into the hands of a new class, and so the freer development of capitalism was made possible. The Civil War was a class war . . . Parliament beat the King because it could appeal to the enthusiastic support of the trading and industrial classes in town and countryside, to the yeoman and progressive gentry, and to wider masses of the population.[22]

Hill drew upon economic evidence to support his thesis, for example, using maps of England to illustrate that support for Parliament came from the 'economically advanced south and east of England, the King's support from the economically backward areas of north and west'.[23] But here, as elsewhere in his writings, he also pays a great deal of attention to the world of ideas. A subsequent study focused upon the radical ideas which were able to emerge during the two decades between 1641 and 1660 when censorship was lifted and a flood of printed material emerged.[24] That his research and writing does not rest upon a very narrow economistic perspective of class struggle is borne out by his assertion in 1958 that 'we must widen our view so as to embrace the total activity of society. Any event so complex as a revolution must be seen as a whole. Large numbers of men and women were drawn into political activity by religious and political ideals as well as by economic necessities.'[25]

Over the next forty years Hill's Civil War thesis was the centre of a major historical debate. One critique focused upon the application of class and class consciousness to this period. Peter Laslett, for example, rejected the use of the concept of bourgeois class consciousness before the onset of the industrial revolution.[26] Hill later conceded that the revolution was not 'consciously willed' by the expanding rural and urban capitalist class, although he responded that 'I think of class as defined by the objective position of its members in relation to the productive process and to other classes. Men become conscious of shared interests in the process of struggling against common enemies, but this struggle can go a long way before one can call it "class consciousness"'.[27] Hill continued to argue that the '*outcome* [of the Civil War] was the establishment of conditions far more favourable to the development of capitalism than those which prevailed before 1640'.[28]

Certainly the conceptualization of society in terms of economic class became much more widely accepted by historians for the period of industrialization, and one of the most fertile areas of research for Marxist historians has been labour history. During the 1960s and 1970s labour historians were polarized around a debate over the degree to which people of the working class have been able to act as agents in the making of their own history. This arose, in part, from historians' recognition that increasing proletarianization during the nineteenth century had not been accompanied by an increasingly radical political consciousness. On the contrary, working-class organizations, such as trade unions, were primarily reformist in intent. Attempts to explain this reformism frequently circulated around the ideas expressed in an influential essay by Eric Hobsbawm, first published in 1954, and republished during the 1960s.[29]

Hobsbawm's argument rested upon the identification of an 'upper strata' of the working class whose level of security in terms of continuous employment and adequate wages separated them from the vast majority of labouring men. The perspective of this labour elite, he argues, was based upon 'the knowledge that they occupied a firm and accepted position just below the employers, but very far above the rest'.[30] The effect of this proximity to the employers explains, according to Hobsbawm, the political attitudes of the labour aristocracy, 'its persistent liberal-radicalism in the nineteenth century . . . [and] also its failure to form an independent working-class party'.[31] In Hobsbawm's analysis, the major determinant of political consciousness for this group was the economic factor of comparatively regular and high wages. Hobsbawm was widely criticized for drawing 'far too neat an equation between high wages and a quiescent labour force'.[32] Furthermore, later research indicated that skilled workers were far less secure, well paid, or politically likely to follow their employers than Hobsbawm suggested.[33] In his own defence, Hobsbawm stated that he had never sought to explain British 'reformism', only to establish the existence of a labour aristocracy. But on the matter of the relationship between wages and consciousness, he had not changed his mind, declaring that 'I remain sufficient of a traditionalist Marxist to stress its determination by the economic base . . . I may well have pushed the economism a bit farther in 1954 than I would do today, but the basic argument stands.'[34] Of the three historians considered here, Hobsbawm has remained closest to the economic determinism of the Marxist model of history.

Finally we turn to what was to become one of the most widely influential historical texts of the second half of the twentieth century. E. P. Thompson published *The Making of the English Working Class* in 1963, and William Sewell reminds us 'how much this book enriched and enlarged our conception of working class history', with its inclusion of not only trade unions and real wages, but popular culture, religion, festivals and beggars.[35] The central theme of Thompson's book is the emergence of a conscious working class between 1780 and 1832 in the context of proletarianization and political repression. Thompson draws our attention to the role of the cultural inheritance – popular traditions – and Methodism in shaping the critical response men made to the economic consequences of industrialization. It is this emphasis upon the role of ideas that has led Thompson to be characterized as a 'cultural' Marxist. While economic factors, such as wages and prices, are duly considered, Thompson is more interested in how the economic upheavals of industrialization are interpreted by those undergoing these experiences. By 1830, Thompson argues, a conscious working class identity formed the basis for collective political action. Thompson emphasized that the new consciousness and actions were due as much to human agency as to the economic structure within which people were born:

> [C]lass happens when some men, as a result of common experiences (inherited or shared), feel and articulate the identity of their interests as between themselves, and as against other men whose interests are different from (and usually opposed to) theirs. The class experience is largely determined by the productive relations in which men are born – or enter involuntarily. Class-consciousness is the way in which these experiences are handled in cultural terms: embodied in traditions, value-systems, ideas and institutional forms. If the experience appears as determined, class-consciousness does not.[36]

The Making of the English Working Class immediately drew a fierce critique from Tom Nairn and Perry Anderson, whose perspective was greatly influenced by the structuralism of French philosopher Louis Althusser. Writing within the Marxist paradigm, Althusser emphasized the hegemony of capitalist ideology in society, arguing that the dominant economic class also controlled the superstructure of ideology, law and politics.[37] Consequently, Anderson and Nairn perceived working class consciousness as structured by the economic, social and political environment, rather than as a product of human agency. From the structuralist perspective of Nairn and Anderson the ability of the working class to resist or form counter-ideology was perceived as minimal in the face of inescapable structural determination and capitalist ideological hegemony.[38] This debate, over the relative strengths of structure and agency, continued within labour history for two decades, albeit on slightly different terms.[39]

More recent criticism has centred around Thompson's characterization of the role played by radical working class women, that of 'giving moral support to the men'.[40] Joan Scott has described the book as 'a story about men, and class is, in its origin and its expression, constructed as a masculine identity, even when not all the actors are male'.[41] Thompson was unrepentant, explaining in personal correspondence that 'it *was* so gendered'.[42] His position is largely supported by the research of James Epstein, who found that women's intervention into public, male space was mediated in entirely traditional terms, and suggests 'nothing to alter the picture of radical women playing an active but fundamentally subordinate and supportive role to men'.[43] Nonetheless, Epstein concluded that Thompson's account failed to give sufficient recognition to the limited participation women did achieve in the face of widespread opprobrium.[44]

In later life E. P. Thompson refused to define himself simply as a Marxist, and argued that the best approach was a 'theoretically informed empiricism'.[45] Thompson strongly believed in the importance of evidence, tartly writing to *History Workshop Journal* in 1993 that '[w]riting history demands an engagement with hard evidence and is not as easy as some post-modernists suppose'.[46] This leads us to the last critique of Marxist historiography, that written from a poststructuralist perspective. A number of Marxist historians ultimately rejected the structuralism of Althusser, and turned to the study of ideology and language divorced from any relationship with the material world. Historians such as Gareth Stedman Jones and Patrick Joyce reject the idea that past experience can be retrieved through the medium of language, and consequently the vocabulary of class and radical politics has become de-materialized.[47] This is completely the opposite of Thompson's own views about the process of writing history, which he saw as a dialogue between theory and evidence:

Historical practice is above all engaged in this kind of dialogue; with an argument between received, inadequate, or ideologically-informed concepts or hypotheses on the one hand, and fresh or inconvenient evidence on the other; with the elaboration of new hypotheses; with the testing of these hypotheses against the evidence, which may involve interrogating existing evidence in new ways, or renewed research to confirm or disprove the new notions; with discarding those hypotheses which fail these tests, and refining or revising those which do, in the light of this engagement.[48]

The reading for this chapter is taken from E. P. Thompson's *The Making of the English Working Class*. Thompson's interest in both literature (reflected in the biographies of the socialist William Morris, and the poet William Blake) and history is evident in the emphasis he places upon human consciousness in making sense of, and responding to, the profound social and economic upheaval of industrial capitalism. In the extract from his work which follows, what do you think is Thompson's hypothesis? To what kinds of evidence does he give particular weight in supporting his hypothesis? Why does Thompson attach so much significance to the views contained within the address of the Journeyman Cotton Spinner? Does he see economic factors as paramount in the creation of working class consciousness? In this account do men make their own history, but in circumstances not of their own choosing?

Notes

1 Friedrich Engels correctly declared at Marx's funeral that 'his name will live on through the centuries and so will his work', cited in David McLellan, *Karl Marx: The Legacy* (London, 1983), p. 7.
2 Arthur Marwick, *The Nature of History* (3rd edn, London, 1989), p. 109.
3 Raphael Samuel, 'British Marxist Historians, 1880–1980: Part One', *New Left Review* 120 (1980), p. 37.
4 Marwick, *The Nature of History*, p. 113.
5 E. P. Thompson, 'History from Below', *The Times Literary Supplement*, 7 April 1966, pp. 279–80.
6 Harvey Kaye, *The British Marxist Historians* (Cambridge, 1984), pp. 5–6.
7 Tony Judt, 'A Clown in Regal Purple: Social History and the Historians', *History Workshop Journal*, 7 (1979), pp. 66–94. See also E. F. and E. D. Genovese, 'The Political Crisis of Social History', *Journal of Social History*, 10 (1976), pp. 205–21; Gareth Stedman Jones, 'From Historical Sociology to Theoretical History', *British Journal of Sociology*, 27 (1976), pp. 295–306.
8 Samuel, 'British Marxist Historians, 1800–1980', p. 22.
9 Peter Singer, *Marx* (Oxford, 1980), pp. 1–6.
10 See Erik Olin Wright *et al.*, *Reconstructing Marxism: Essays on Explanation and the Theory of History* (London, 1992), p. 13.
11 Helmut Fleischer, *Marxism and History* (New York, 1973), pp. 8–9; S. H. Rigby, 'Marxist Historiography', in Michael Bentley (ed.), *Companion to Historiography* (London, 1997), p. 889.

12 Karl Marx and Frederick Engels, *The German Ideology, Part One*, ed. C. J. Arthur (New York, 1970), p.48.
13 *Ibid.*, p. 49.
14 *Ibid.*, p. 50.
15 Karl Marx and Frederick Engels, *Selected Works* (New York, 1968), p.182.
16 Marx and Engels, 'Manifesto of the Communist Party', *Selected Works*, p. 36.
17 *Ibid.*, p. 35.
18 Marx and Engels, *Selected Works*, p. 97.
19 Eric Hobsbawm, 'Marx and History', in *On History* (London, 1997), p. 162.
20 Kaye, *The British Marxist Historians*, p. 102. E. P. Thompson fought in the Second World War, while Eric Hobsbawm's family came to live in England in 1933 following Hitler's ascent to power.
21 Christopher Hill, *The English Revolution 1640: An Essay* (3rd edn, London, [1940] 1955).
22 *Ibid.*, p. 6.
23 Christopher Hill, *The Century of Revolution, 1603–1714* (London, [1961] 1969), p. 112.
24 Christopher Hill, *The World Turned Upside Down* (London, [1972] 1991).
25 Christopher Hill, *Puritanism and Revolution* (London, 1958), p. 31.
26 Peter Laslett, *The World We Have Lost* (2nd edn, New York [1965] 1973), ch. 2.
27 Cited in Kaye, p. 126.
28 Christopher Hill, 'A Bourgeois Revolution?', in J. G. A. Pocock, *Three British Revolutions, 1641, 1688, 1776* (Princeton, 1980), p. 111.
29 E. J. Hobsbawm, 'The Labour Aristocracy in Nineteenth-century Britain', in *Labouring Men* (London, 1964), pp. 272–315; for other sources in this debate see Eric Hobsbawm, 'Debating the Labour Aristocracy', in *Worlds of Labour* (London, 1984), pp. 344–5.
30 Hobsbawm, 'The Labour Aristocracy in Nineteenth-century Britain', p. 296.
31 *Ibid.*, p. 274.
32 H. F. Moorhouse, 'The Marxist Theory of the Labour Aristocracy', *Social History*, 3, 1 (January 1978), p. 72.
33 Alastair Reid, 'Intelligent Artisans and Aristocrats of Labour: The Essays of Thomas Wright', in Jay Winter (ed.), *The Working Class in Modern British History* (Cambridge, 1983), p. 172.
34 Hobsbawm, 'Debating the Labour Aristocracy', pp. 216, 220.
35 In Harvey J. Kaye and Keith McClelland (eds), *E. P. Thompson: Critical Perspectives* (Cambridge, 1990), p. 50.
36 E. P. Thompson, *The Making of the English Working Class* (Harmondsworth, 1963), pp. 9–10.
37 For further elaboration of Althusser's theory, see S. H. Rigby, *Marxism and History* (Manchester, 1987), chapter 9.
38 Perry Anderson, 'Origins of the Present Crisis', *New Left Review*, 23 (January–February 1964), pp. 26–53; Tom Nairn, 'The English Working Class', *New Left Review*, 24 (March–April 1964), pp. 43–57.
39 See the debate in the journal *Social History*: Richard Price, 'The Labour Process and Labour History', 8 (1983), pp. 57–75; Patrick Joyce, 'Labour, Capital and Compromise: A Response to Richard Price', 9 (1984), pp. 67–76; Richard Price, 'Conflict and Co-operation: A Reply to Patrick Joyce', and Patrick Joyce, 'Languages of Reciprocity and Conflict: A Further Response to Richard Price', 9 (1984), pp. 217–24, 225–31.
40 Thompson, *The Making of the English Working Class*, p. 4.
41 Joan Scott, 'Women in *The Making of the English Working Class*', in *Gender and the Politics of History* (New York, 1988), p. 72.
42 Bryan D. Palmer, *E. P. Thompson: Directions and Oppositions* (London, 1994), p. 185.
43 James Epstein, 'Understanding the Cap of Liberty: Symbolic Practice and Social Conflict in Early Nineteenth-century England', *Past and Present*, 122 (February 1989), pp. 101–2.

44 *Ibid.*, p. 106.
45 Institute of Historical Research, *Interviews with Historians: Edward Thompson with Penelope Corfield* (1993), 28.40.
46 E. P. Thompson, 'Theory and Evidence', *History Workshop Journal*, 35 (Spring 1993), p. 274.
47 See Patrick Joyce (ed.), *Class* (Oxford, 1995); Marc W. Steinberg, 'Culturally Speaking: Finding a Commons between Post-structuralism and the Thompsonian Perspective', *Social History*, 21, 2 (May 1996), pp. 193–214.
48 E. P. Thompson, *The Poverty of Theory and Other Essays* (New York, 1978), p. 43.

Additional reading

Currie, R. and R. M. Hartwell, 'The Making of the English Working Class?', *Economic History Review*, 18 (December 1965), pp. 633–43.

Donnelly, F. K., 'Ideology and Early English Working-class History: Edward Thompson and his Critics', *Social History*, 2 (1976), pp. 219–38.

Genovese, Eugene D., *Roll, Jordan, Roll: The World the Slaves Made* (New York, 1974).

Hill, Christopher, *The Century of Revolution, 1603–1714* (London, [1961] 1969).

Hobsbawm, E. J., *Labouring Men* (London, [1964] 1979).

Johnson, Richard, 'Edward Thompson, Eugene Genovese, and Socialist-Humanist History', *History Workshop Journal*, 6 (1978), pp. 79–100.

Kaye, Harvey J., *The British Marxist Historians* (Cambridge, 1984).

Samuel, Raphael, 'British Marxist Historians, 1880–1980: Part One', *New Left Review*, 120 (1980), pp. 21–96.

Samuel, Raphael (ed.), *People's History and Socialist Theory* (London, 1981).

Scott, Joan Wallach, 'Women in *The Making of the English Working Class*', in *Gender and the Politics of History* (New York, 1988).

Steinberg, Marc W., 'Culturally Speaking: Finding a Commons between Post-structuralism and the Thompsonian Perspective', *Social History*, 21, 2 (May 1996), pp. 193–214.

Thompson, E. P., *The Making of the English Working Class* (Harmondsworth, 1963).

EXPLOITATION
E. P. Thompson

John Thelwall was not alone in seeing in every 'manufactory' a potential centre of political rebellion. An aristocratic traveller who visited the Yorkshire Dales in 1792 was alarmed to find a new cotton-mill in the 'pastoral vale' of Aysgarth—'why, here now is a great flaring mill, whose back stream has drawn off half the water of the falls above the bridge':

> With the bell ringing, and the clamour of the mill, all the vale is disturb'd; treason and levelling systems are the discourse; and rebellion may be near at hand.

The mill appeared as symbol of social energies which were destroying the very 'course of Nature'. It embodied a double threat to the settled order. First, from the owners of industrial wealth, those upstarts who enjoyed an unfair advantage over the landowners whose income was tied to their rent-roll:

> If men thus start into riches; or if riches from trade are too easily procured, woe to us men of middling income, and settled revenue; and woe it has been to all the Nappa Halls, and the Yeomanry of the land.

Second, from the industrial working population, which our traveller regarded with an alliterative hostility which betrays a response not far removed from that of the white racialist towards the coloured population today:

> The people, indeed, are employ'd; but they are all abandon'd to vice from the throng. . . . At the times when people work not in the mill, they issue out to poaching, profligacy and plunder. . . .[1]

The equation between the cotton-mill and the new industrial society, and the correspondence between new forms of productive and of social relationship, was a commonplace among observers in the years between 1790 and 1850. Karl Marx was only expressing this with unusual vigour when he declared: 'The hand-mill gives you society with the feudal lord: the steam-mill, society with the industrial capitalist.' And it was not only the mill-owner but also the working population brought into being within and around the mills

---

[1] *The Torrington Diaries*, ed. C. B. Andrews (1936), III, pp. 81–2.

which seemed to contemporaries to be 'new'. 'The instant we get near the borders of the manufacturing parts of Lancashire,' a rural magistrate wrote in 1808, 'we meet a fresh race of beings, both in point of manners, employments and subordination . . .'; while Robert Owen, in 1815, declared that 'the general diffusion of manufactures throughout a country generates a new character in its inhabitants . . . an essential change in the general character of the mass of the people.'

Observers in the 1830s and 1840s were still exclaiming at the novelty of the 'factory system'. Peter Gaskell, in 1833, spoke of the manufacturing population as 'but a Hercules in the cradle'; it was 'only since the introduction of steam as a power that they have acquired their paramount importance'. The steam-engine had 'drawn together the population into dense masses' and already Gaskell saw in working-class organisations an ' "imperium in imperio" of the most obnoxious description'.[2] Ten years later Cooke Taylor was writing in similar terms:

> The steam-engine had no precedent, the spinning-jenny is without ancestry, the mule and the power-loom entered on no prepared heritage: they sprang into sudden existence like Minerva from the brain of Jupiter.

But it was the human consequence of these 'novelties' which caused this observer most disquiet:

> As a stranger passes through the masses of human beings which have accumulated round the mills and print works . . . he cannot contemplate these 'crowded hives' without feelings of anxiety and apprehension almost amounting to dismay. The population, like the system to which it belongs, is NEW; but it is hourly increasing in breadth and strength. It is an aggregate of masses, our conceptions of which clothe themselves in terms that express something portentous and fearful . . . as of the slow rising and gradual swelling of an ocean which must, at some future and no distant time, bear all the elements of society aloft upon its bosom, and float them Heaven knows whither. There are mighty energies slumbering in these masses. . . . The manufacturing population is not new in its formation alone: it is new in its habits of thought and action, which have been formed by the circumstances of its condition, with little instruction, and less guidance, from external sources. . . .[3]

---

[2] P. Gaskell, *The Manufacturing Population of England* (1833), p. 6; Asa Briggs, 'The Language of "Class" in Early Nineteenth-century England', in *Essays in Labour History*, ed. Briggs and Saville (1960), p. 63.

[3] W. Cooke Taylor, *Notes of a Tour in the Manufacturing Districts of Lancashire* (1842), pp. 4–6.

For Engels, describing the *Condition of the Working Class in England in 1844* it seemed that 'the first proletarians were connected with manufacture, were engendered by it . . . the factory hands, eldest children of the industrial revolution, have from the beginning to the present day formed the nucleus of the Labour Movement.'

However different their judgements of value, conservative, radical, and socialist observers suggested the same equation: steam power and the cotton-mill = new working class. The physical instruments of production were seen as giving rise in a direct and more-or-less compulsive way to new social relationships, institutions, and cultural modes. At the same time the history of popular agitation during the period 1811–50 appears to confirm this picture. It is as if the English nation entered a crucible in the 1790s and emerged after the Wars in a different form. Between 1811 and 1813, the Luddite crisis; in 1817 the Pentridge Rising; in 1819, Peterloo; throughout the next decade the proliferation of trade union activity, Owenite propaganda, Radical journalism, the Ten Hours Movement, the revolutionary crisis of 1831–2; and, beyond that, the multitude of movements which made up Chartism. It is, perhaps, the scale and intensity of this multiform popular agitation which has, more than anything else, given rise (among contemporary observers and historians alike) to the sense of some *catastrophic* change.

Almost every radical phenomenon of the 1790s can be found reproduced tenfold after 1815. The handful of Jacobin sheets gave rise to a score of ultra-Radical and Owenite periodicals. Where Daniel Eaton served imprisonment for publishing Paine, Richard Carlile and his shopmen served a total of more than 200 years imprisonment for similar crimes. Where Corresponding Societies maintained a precarious existence in a score of towns, the post-war Hampden Clubs or political unions struck root in small industrial villages. And when this popular agitation is recalled alongside the dramatic pace of change in the cotton industry, it is natural to assume a direct causal relationship. The cotton-mill is seen as the agent not only of industrial but also of social revolution, producing not only more goods but also the 'Labour Movement' itself. The Industrial Revolution, which commenced as a description, is now invoked as an explanation.

From the time of Arkwright through to the Plug Riots and beyond, it is the image of the 'dark, Satanic mill' which dominates our visual reconstruction of the Industrial Revolution. In part, perhaps, because it is a dramatic visual image—the barrack-like buildings, the great mill chimneys, the factory children, the clogs and shawls, the dwellings clustering around the mills as if spawned by them. (It is an image which forces one to think first of the industry, and only secondly of the people connected to it or serving it.) In part, because the cotton-mill and the new mill-town—from the swiftness of its growth, ingenuity of its techniques, and the novelty or harshness of its discipline—seemed to contemporaries to be dramatic and portentous: a more satisfactory symbol for debate on the 'condition-of-England' question than those anonymous or sprawling manufacturing *districts* which figure even more often in the Home Office 'disturbance books'. And from this both a literary and an historical tradition is derived. Nearly all the classic accounts by contemporaries of conditions in the Industrial Revolution are based on the cotton industry—and, in the main, on Lancashire: Owen, Gaskell, Ure, Fielden, Cooke Taylor, Engels, to mention a few. Novels such as *Michael Armstrong* or *Mary Barton* or *Hard Times* perpetuate the tradition. And the emphasis is markedly found in the subsequent writing of economic and social history.

But many difficulties remain. Cotton was certainly the pace-making industry of the Industrial Revolution,[4] and the cotton-mill was the pre-eminent model for the factory-system. Yet we should not assume any automatic, or over-direct, correspondence between the dyamic of economic growth and the dynamic of social or cultural life. For half a century after the 'breakthrough' of the cotton-mill (around 1780) the mill workers remained as a minority of the adult labour force in the cotton industry itself. In the early 1830s the cotton hand-loom weavers alone still outnumbered all the men and women in spinning and weaving mills of cotton, wool, and silk combined.[5] Still, in 1830, the adult male cotton-spinner was no more typical of that elusive figure, the 'average working man', than is the Coventry motor-worker of the 1960s.

The point is of importance, because too much emphasis upon the newness of the cotton-mills can lead to an underestimation of the continuity of political and cultural traditions in the making of working-class communities. The factory hands, so far from being the 'eldest children of the industrial revolution', were late arrivals. Many of their ideas and forms of organisation were anticipated by domes-

---

[4] For an admirable restatement of the reasons for the primacy of the cotton industry in the Industrial Revolution, see E. J. Hobsbawm, *The Age of Revolution* (1962), Ch. 2.

[5] Estimates for U.K., 1833. Total adult labour force in all textile mills, 191,671. Number of cotton hand-loom weavers, 213,000. See below, p. 311.

tic workers, such as the woollen workers of Norwich and the West Country, or the small-ware weavers of Manchester. And it is questionable whether factory hands—except in the cotton districts—'formed the nucleus of the Labour Movement' at any time before the late 1840s (and, in some northern and Midland towns, the years 1832–4, leading up to the great lock-outs). Jacobinism, as we have seen, struck root most deeply among artisans. Luddism was the work of skilled men in small workshops. From 1817 onwards to Chartism, the outworkers in the north and the Midlands were as prominent in every radical agitation as the factory hands. And in many towns the actual nucleus from which the labour movement derived ideas, organisation, and leadership, was made up of such men as shoemakers, weavers, saddlers and harnessmakers, booksellers, printers, building workers, small tradesmen, and the like. The vast area of Radical London between 1815 and 1850 drew its strength from no major heavy industries (shipbuilding was tending to decline, and the engineers only made their impact later in the century) but from the host of smaller trades and occupations.[6]

Such diversity of experiences has led some writers to question both the notions of an 'industrial revolution' and of a 'working class'. The first discussion need not detain us here.[7] The term is serviceable enough in its usual connotations. For the second, many writers prefer the term working *classes*, which emphasises the great disparity in status, acquisitions, skills, conditions, within the portmanteau phrase. And in this they echo the complaints of Francis Place:

> If the character and conduct of the working-people are to be taken from reviews, magazines, pamphlets, newspapers, reports of the two Houses of Parliament and the Factory Commissioners, we shall find them all jumbled together as the 'lower orders', the most skilled and the most prudent workman, with the most ignorant and imprudent labourers and paupers, though the difference is great indeed, and indeed in many cases will scarce admit of comparison.[8]

Place is, of course, right: the Sunderland sailor, the Irish navvy, the Jewish costermonger, the inmate of an East Anglian village workhouse, the compositor on *The Times*—all might be seen by their 'betters' as belonging to the 'lower classes' while they themselves might scarcely understand each others' dialect.

[6] Cf. Hobsbawm, op. cit., Ch. 11.

[7] There is a summary of this controversy in E. E. Lampard, *Industrial Revolution*, (American Historical Association, 1957). See also Hobsbawm, op. cit., Ch. 2.

[8] Cit. M. D. George, *London Life in the 18th Century* (1930). p. 210.

Nevertheless, when every caution has been made, the outstanding fact of the period between 1790 and 1830 is the formation of 'the working class'. This is revealed, first, in the growth of class-consciousness: the consciousness of an identity of interests as between all these diverse groups of working people and as against the interests of other classes. And, second, in the growth of corresponding forms of political and industrial organisation. By 1832 there were strongly-based and self-conscious working-class institutions—trade unions, friendly societies, educational and religious movements, political organisations, periodicals—working-class intellectual traditions, working-class community-patterns, and a working-class structure of feeling.

The making of the working class is a fact of political and cultural, as much as of economic, history. It was not the spontaneous generation of the factory-system. Nor should we think of an external force—the 'industrial revolution'—working upon some nondescript undifferentiated raw material of humanity, and turning it out at the other end as a 'fresh race of beings'. The changing productive relations and working conditions of the Industrial Revolution were imposed, not upon raw material, but upon the free-born Englishman—and the free-born Englishman as Paine had left him or as the Methodists had moulded him. The factory hand or stockinger was also the inheritor of Bunyan, of remembered village rights, of notions of equality before the law, of craft traditions. He was the object of massive religious indoctrination and the creator of new political traditions. The working class made itself as much as it was made.

To see the working class in this way is to defend a 'classical' view of the period against the prevalent mood of contemporary schools of economic history and sociology. For the territory of the Industrial Revolution, which was first staked out and surveyed by Marx, Arnold Toynbee, the Webbs and the Hammonds, now resembles an academic battlefield. At point after point, the familiar 'catastrophic' view of the period has been disputed. Where it was customary to see the period as one of economic disequilibrium, intense misery and exploitation, political repression and heroic popular agitation, attention is now directed to the rate of economic growth (and the difficulties of 'take-off' into self-sustaining technological reproduction). The enclosure movement is now noted, less for its harshness in displacing the village poor, than for its success in feeding a rapidly growing population. The hardships of the period are seen as being due to the dislocations consequent upon the Wars, faulty communications, immature banking and exchange, uncertain markets, and the trade-cycle, rather than to exploitation or cut-throat competition. Popular unrest is seen as consequent upon the unavoidable coincidence of high wheat prices and trade depressions, and explicable in terms of an elementary 'social tension' chart derived from these data.[9] In general, it is suggested that the position of the industrial worker in 1840 was better in most ways than that of the domestic worker of 1790. The Industrial Revolution was an age, not of catastrophe or acute class-conflict and class oppression, but of improvement.[10]

The classical catastrophic orthodoxy has been replaced by a new anti-catastrophic orthodoxy, which is most clearly distinguished by its empirical caution and, among its most notable exponents (Sir John Clapham, Dr. Dorothy George, Professor Ashton) by an astringent criticism of the looseness of certain writers of the older school. The studies of the new orthodoxy have enriched historical scholarship, and have qualified and revised in important respects the work of the classical school. But as the new orthodoxy is now, in its turn, growing old and entrenched in most of the academic centres, so it becomes open to challenge in its turn. And the successors of the great empiricists too often exhibit a moral complacency, a narrowness of reference, and an insufficient familiarity with the actual movements of the working people of the time. They are more aware of the orthodox empiricist postures than of the changes in social relationship and in cultural modes which the Industrial Revolution entailed. What has been lost is a sense of the whole process — the whole political and social context of the period. What arose as valuable qualifications have passed by imperceptible stages to new generalisations (which the evidence can rarely sustain) and from generalisations to a ruling attitude.

The empiricist orthodoxy is often defined in terms of a running critique of the work of J. L. and Barbara Hammond. It is true that the Hammonds showed themselves too willing to moralise history, and to arrange their materials too much in terms of 'outraged emotion'.[11]

---

[9] See W. W. Rostow, *British Economy in the Nineteenth Century* (1948), esp. pp. 122–5.

[10] Some of the views outlined here are to be found, implicitly or explicitly, in T. S. Ashton, *Industrial Revolution* (1948) and A. Radford, *The Economic History of England* (2nd edn. 1960). A sociological variant is developed by N. J. Smelser, *Social Change in the Industrial Revolution* (1959), and a knockabout popularisation is in John Vaizey, *Success Story* (W.E.A., n.d.).

[11] See E. E. Lampard, op. cit., p. 7.

There are many points at which their work has been faulted or qualified in the light of subsequent research, and we intend to propose others. But a defence of the Hammonds need not only be rested upon the fact that their volumes on the labourers, with their copious quotation and wide reference, will long remain among the most important source-books for this period. We can also say that they displayed throughout their narrative an understanding of the political context within which the Industrial Revolution took place. To the student examining the ledgers of one cotton-mill, the Napoleonic Wars appear only as an abnormal influence affecting foreign markets and fluctuating demand. The Hammonds could never have forgotten for one moment that it was also a war against Jacobinism. 'The history of England at the time discussed in these pages reads like a history of civil war.' This is the opening of the introductory chapter of *The Skilled Labourer*. And in the conclusion to *The Town Labourer*, among other comments of indifferent value, there is an insight which throws the whole period into sudden relief:

> At the time when half Europe was intoxicated and the other half terrified by the new magic of the word citizen, the English nation was in the hands of men who regarded the idea of citizenship as a challenge to their religion and their civilisation; who deliberately sought to make the inequalities of life the basis of the state, and to emphasise and perpetuate the position of the workpeople as a subject class. Hence it happened that the French Revolution has divided the people of France less than the Industrial Revolution has divided the people of England. . . .

'Hence it happened . . .'. The judgement may be questioned. And yet it is in this insight—that the revolution which did *not* happen in England was fully as devastating, and in some features more divisive, than that which did happen in France—that we find a clue to the truly catastrophic nature of the period. Throughout this time there are three, and not two, great influences simultaneously at work. There is the tremendous increase in population (in Great Britain, from 10.5 millions in 1801 to 18.1 millions in 1841, with the greatest rate of increase between 1811–21). There is the Industrial Revolution, in its technological aspects. And there is the political *counter*-revolution, from 1792–1832.

In the end, it is the political context as much as the steam-engine, which had most influence upon the shaping consciousness and institutions of the working class. The forces making for political reform in the late 18th century—Wilkes, the city merchants, the Middlesex

small gentry, the 'mob'—or Wyvill, and the small gentry and
yeomen, clothiers, cutlers, and tradesmen—were on the eve of
gaining at least some piecemeal victories in the 1790s: Pitt had been
cast for the rôle of reforming Prime Minister. Had events taken their
'natural' course we might expect there to have been some show-down
long before 1832, between the oligarchy of land and commerce and
the manufacturers and petty gentry, with working people in the tail
of the middle-class agitation. And even in 1792, when manufacturers and professional men were prominent in the reform movement,
this was still the balance of forces. But, after the success of *Rights of
Man*, the radicalisation and terror of the French Revolution, and the
onset of Pitt's repression, it was the plebeian Corresponding Society
which alone stood up against the counter-revolutionary wars. And
these plebeian groups, small as they were in 1796, did nevertheless
make up an 'underground' tradition which ran through to the end
of the Wars. Alarmed at the French example, and in the patriotic
fervour of war, the aristocracy and the manufacturers made common
cause. The English *ancien régime* received a new lease of life, not only
in national affairs, but also in the perpetuation of the antique
corporations which misgoverned the swelling industrial towns.
In return, the manufacturers received important concessions: and
notably the abrogation or repeal of 'paternalist' legislation covering
apprenticeship, wage-regulation, or conditions in industry. The aristocracy were interested in repressing the Jacobin 'conspiracies' of
the people, the manufacturers were interested in defeating their
'conspiracies' to increase wages: the Combination Acts served both
purposes.

Thus working people were forced into political and social *apartheid*
during the Wars (which, incidentally, they also had to fight). It is true
that this was not altogether new. What was new was that it was coin-
cident with a French Revolution: with growing self-consciousness
and wider aspirations (for the 'liberty tree' had been planted from
the Thames to the Tyne): with a rise in population, in which the
sheer sense of numbers, in London and in the industrial districts,
became more impressive from year to year (and as numbers grew, so
deference to master, magistrate, or parson was likely to lessen): and
with more intensive or more transparent forms of economic exploitation. More intensive in agriculture and in the old domestic industries: more transparent in the new factories and perhaps in mining.
In agriculture the years between 1760 and 1820 are the years of
wholesale enclosure, in which, in village after village, common rights

are lost, and the landless and—in the south—pauperised labourer is left to support the tenant-farmer, the landowner, and the tithes of the Church. In the domestic industries, from 1800 onwards, the tendency is widespread for small masters to give way to larger employers (whether manufacturers or middlemen) and for the majority of weavers, stockingers, or nail-makers to become wage-earning outworkers with more or less precarious employment. In the mills and in many mining areas these are the years of the employment of children (and of women underground); and the large-scale enterprise, the factory-system with its new discipline, the mill communities— where the manufacturer not only made riches out of the labour of the 'hands' but could be *seen* to make riches in one generation—all contributed to the transparency of the process of exploitation and to the social and cultural cohesion of the exploited.

We can now see something of the truly catastrophic nature of the Industrial Revolution; as well as some of the reasons why the English working class took form in these years. The people were subjected simultaneously to an intensification of two intolerable forms of relationship: those of economic exploitation and of political oppression. Relations between employer and labourer were becoming both harsher and less personal; and while it is true that this increased the potential freedom of the worker, since the hired farm servant or the journeyman in domestic industry was (in Toynbee's words) 'halted half-way between the position of the serf and the position of the citizen', this 'freedom' meant that he felt his *unfreedom* more. But at each point where he sought to resist exploitation, he was met by the forces of employer or State, and commonly of both.

For most working people the crucial experience of the Industrial Revolution was felt in terms of changes in the nature and intensity of exploitation. Nor is this some anachronistic notion, imposed upon the evidence. We may describe some parts of the exploitive process as they appeared to one remarkable cotton operative in 1818—the year in which Marx was born. The account—an Address to the public of strike-bound Manchester by 'A Journeyman Cotton Spinner'— commences by describing the employers and the workers as 'two distinct classes of persons':

'First, then, as to the employers: with very few exceptions, they are a set of men who have sprung from the cotton-shop without education or address, except so much as they have acquired by their intercourse with the little world of merchants on the exchange at Manchester; but to counterbalance that deficiency, they give you enough of appearances by an ostentatious display of elegant mansions, equipages, liveries, parks, hunters, hounds, &c. which they take care to shew off to the merchant stranger in the most pompous manner. Indeed their houses are gorgeous palaces, far surpassing in bulk and extent the neat charming retreats you see round London . . . but the chaste observer of the beauties of nature and art combined will observe a woeful deficiency of taste. They bring up their families at the most costly schools, determined to give their offspring a double portion of what they were so deficient in themselves. Thus with scarcely a second idea in their heads, they are literally petty monarchs, absolute and despotic, in their own particular districts; and to support all this, their whole time is occupied in contriving how to get the greatest quantity of work turned off with the least expence. . . . In short, I will venture to say, without fear of contradiction, that there is a greater distance observed between the master there and the spinner, than there is between the first merchant in London and his lowest servant or the lowest artisan. Indeed there is no comparison. I know it to be a fact, that the greater part of the master spinners are anxious to keep wages low for the purpose of keeping the spinners indigent and spiritless . . . as for the purpose of taking the surplus to their own pockets.

'The master spinners are a class of men unlike all other master tradesmen in the kingdom. They are ignorant, proud, and tyrannical. What then must be the men or rather beings who are the instruments of such masters? Why, they have been for a series of years, with their wives and their families, patience itself—bondmen and bondwomen to their cruel taskmasters. It is in vain to insult our common understandings with the observation that such men are free; that the law protects the rich and poor alike, and that a spinner can leave his master if he does not like the wages. True; so he can: but where must he go? why to another, to be sure. Well: he goes; he is asked where did you work last: "did he discharge you?" No; we could not agree about wages. Well I shall not employ you nor anyone who leaves his master in that manner. Why is this? Because there is an abominable *combination existing amongst the masters*, first established at Stockport in 1802, and it has since become so general, as to embrace all the great masters for a circuit of many miles round Manchester, though not the little masters: they are excluded. They are the most obnoxious beings to the great ones that can be imagined. . . . When the combination first took place, one of their first articles was, that no master should take on a man until he had first ascertained whether his last master had discharged him. What then is the man to do? If he goes to the parish, that grave of all independence, he is there told—We shall not relieve you; if you dispute with your master, and don't support your family, we will send you to prison; so that the man is bound, by a combination of circumstances, to submit to his master. He cannot travel and get work in any town like a shoe-maker, joiner, or taylor; he is confined to the district.

'The workmen in general are an inoffensive, unassuming, set of well-informed men, though how they acquire their information is almost a mystery to me. They are docile and tractable, if not goaded too much; but this is not to be wondered at, when we consider that they are trained to work from six years old, from five in a morning to eight and nine at night. Let one of the advocates for obedience to his master take his stand in an avenue leading to a factory a little before five o'clock in the morning, and observe the squalid appearance of the little infants and their parents taken from their beds at so early an hour in all kinds of weather; let him examine the miserable pittance of food, chiefly composed of water gruel and oatcake broken into it, a little salt, and sometimes coloured with a little milk, together with a few potatoes, and a bit of bacon or fat for dinner; would a London mechanic eat this? There they are, (and if late a few minutes, a quarter of a day is stopped in wages) locked up until night in rooms heated above the hottest days we have had this summer, and allowed no time, except three-quarters of an hour at dinner in the whole day: whatever they eat at any other time must be as they are at work. The negro slave in the West Indies, if he works under a scorching sun, has probably a little breeze of air sometimes to fan him: he has a space of ground, and time allowed to cultivate it. The English spinner slave has no enjoyment of the open atmosphere and breezes of heaven. Locked up in factories eight stories high, he has no relaxation till the ponderous engine stops, and then he goes home to get refreshed for the next day; no time for sweet association with his family; they are all alike fatigued and exhausted. This is no overdrawn picture: it is literally true. I ask again, would the mechanics in the South of England submit to this?

'When the spinning of cotton was in its infancy, and before those terrible machines for superseding the necessity of human labour, called steam engines, came into use, there were a great number of what were then called *little masters*; men who with a small capital, could procure a few machines, and employ a few hands, men and boys (say to twenty or thirty), the produce of whose labour was all taken to Manchester central mart, and put into the hands of brokers. . . . The brokers sold it to the merchants, by which means the master spinner was enabled to stay at home and work and attend to his workmen. The cotton was then always given out in its raw state from the bale to the wives of the spinners at home, when they heat and cleansed it ready for the spinners in the factory. By this they could earn eight, ten, or twelve shillings a week, and cook and attend to their families. But more are thus employed now; for all the cotton is broke up by a machine, turned by the steam engine, called a devil: so that the spinners wives have no employment, except they go to work in the factory all day at what can be done by children for a few shillings, four or five per week. If a man then could not agree with his master, he left him, and could get employed elsewhere. A few years, however, changed the face of things. Steam engines came into use, to purchase which, and to erect buildings sufficient to contain them and six or seven hundred hands, required a great capital. The engine power produced a more marketable (though not a better) article than the little master could at the same price. The consequence was their ruin in a short time; and the overgrown capitalists triumphed in their fall; for they were the only obstacle that stood between them and the complete controul of the workmen.

'Various disputes then originated between the workmen and masters as to the fineness of the work, the workmen being paid according to the number of hanks or yards of thread he produced from a given quantity of cotton, which was always to be proved by the overlooker, whose interest made it imperative on him to lean to his master, and call the material coarser than it was. If the workman would not submit *he must summon his employer before a magistrate*; the whole of the acting magistrates in that district, with the exception of two worthy clergymen, being gentlemen who have sprung from the *same* source with the master cotton spinners. The employer generally contented himself with sending his overlooker to answer any such summons, thinking it beneath him to meet his servant. The magistrate's decision was generally in favour of the master, though on the statement of the overlooker only. The workman dared not appeal to the sessions on account of the expense. . . .

'These evils to the men have arisen from that dreadful monopoly which exists in those districts where wealth and power are got into the hands of the few, who, in the pride of their hearts, think them-selves the lords of the universe.'[12]

This reading of the facts, in its remarkable cogency, is as much an *ex parte* statement as is the 'political economy' of Lord Brougham. But the 'Journeyman Cotton Spinner' was describing facts of a different order. We need not concern ourselves with the soundness of all his judgements. What his address does is to itemise one after another the grievances felt by working people as to changes in the character of capitalist exploitation: the rise of a master-class without traditional authority or obligations: the growing distance between master and man: the transparency of the exploitation at the source of their new wealth and power: the loss of status and above all of independence for the worker, his reduction to total dependence on the master's instruments of production: the partiality of the law: the disruption of the traditional family economy: the discipline, monotony, hours and conditions of work: loss of leisure and amenities: the reduction of the man to the status of an 'instrument'.

That working people felt these grievances at all—and felt them passionately—is itself a sufficient fact to merit our attention. And it reminds us forcibly that some of the most bitter conflicts of these years turned on issues which are not encompassed by cost-of-living series. The issues which provoked the most intensity of feeling were very often ones in which such values as traditional customs, 'justice', 'independence', security, or family-economy were at stake, rather than straightforward 'bread-and-butter' issues. The early years of the 1830s are aflame with agitations which turned on issues in which wages were of secondary importance; by the potters, against the Truck System; by the textile workers, for the 10-Hour Bill; by the building workers, for co-operative direct action; by all groups of workers, for the right to join trade unions. The great strike in the north-east coalfield in 1831 turned on security of employment, 'tommy shops', child labour.

The exploitive relationship is more than the sum of grievances and mutual antagonisms. It is a relationship which can be seen to take distinct forms in different historical contexts, forms which are related to corresponding forms of ownership and State power. The classic exploitive relationship of the Industrial Revolution is depersonalised, in the sense that no lingering obligations of mutuality—of paternalism or deference, or of the interests of 'the Trade'—are

[12] *Black Dwarf*, 30 September 1818.

admitted. There is no whisper of the 'just' price, or of a wage justified in relation to social or moral sanctions, as opposed to the operation of free market forces. Antagonism is accepted as intrinsic to the relations of production. Managerial or supervisory functions demand the repression of all attributes except those which further the expropriation of the maximum surplus value from labour. This is the political economy which Marx anatomised in *Das Kapital*. The worker has become an 'instrument', or an entry among other items of cost.

In fact, no complex industrial enterprise could be conducted according to such a philosophy. The need for industrial peace, for a stable labour-force, and for a body of skilled and experienced workers, necessitated the modification of managerial techniques—and, indeed, the growth of new forms of paternalism—in the cotton-mills by the 1830s. But in the overstocked outwork industries, where there was always a sufficiency of unorganised 'hands' competing for employment, these considerations did not operate. Here, as old customs were eroded, and old paternalism was set aside, the exploitive relationship emerged supreme.

3
Freud and psychohistory

One of the most controversial areas of twentieth-century historiography is psychohistory, the use of psychoanalysis to aid our understanding of historical personalities, groups or trends. Reactions to psychohistory have been diverse, from Loewenberg's belief that it is 'the most powerful of interpretive approaches to history', to Barzun's assertion that, 'events and agents lose their individuality and become illustrations of certain automatisms'.[1] Even sympathetic accounts differ radically. For example, Ashplant comments that '[t]he central concerns of psychoanalysis are at first sight considerably removed from those of most historical writing' whereas Meyerhoff suggests that '[p]sychoanalysis and history . . . have a great deal in common'.[2]

Many historians apply some psychological understanding to history. We talk about the application of 'common sense', our knowledge of 'human nature', the possession of 'fellow feeling': in short, a belief that we have something in common, our humanity perhaps, with people in the past which allows us to understand them.[3] This idea is currently under challenge on a number of fronts and has clear flaws.[4] Nevertheless, it would be useful if we could use psychology in a more systematic way, applying universal laws which govern individual and group behaviour. The experience of historians, psychoanalysts and psychohistorians to date, however, suggests that no such simple solution exists.

Psychohistory does not refer to psychological interpretations in general but specifically to the use of psychoanalysis. Psychoanalytic theory was developed by Freud during the early part of the twentieth century, but was little employed by historians until about 1960. Its take-off was spurred by two events, the publication of Erik Erikson's *Young Man Luther* and the presidential address to the American Historical Association by William Langer, both of which appeared in print in 1958. Langer, often quoted, requested 'the urgently needed deepening of our historical understanding through exploitation of the concepts and findings of modern psychology'.[5] In what did the psychoanalysis which Langer went on to specify consist?

While Freud's development of his psychoanalytic theory runs to many volumes, Penelope Hetherington elegantly summarized this into four basic propositions, upon which, she suggested, 'the whole body of theory ultimately rests'. These are:

Freud's theory:

1. That the experience of infancy and childhood have primacy in determining the shape of adult behaviour.
2. That there are stages of development through which all individuals pass in their very long period of maturation.
3. That adult behaviour is largely determined by the unconscious.
4. That there is a dialectical process in operation in adult behaviour, implying the existence of psychic conflict.[6]

Freud's ideas about childhood sexuality are inherent in the first two of these propositions. He believed that all humans were born biologically equipped with a powerful sexual drive. During infancy and childhood up to about five years of age, this (at this early stage) generalized desire for pleasure was expressed through various developmental stages, the oral, anal and genital. These stages occur both in 'normal' development and in those individuals who later exhibit psychopathological symptoms; adult personality and behaviour are influenced primarily through the child's experience of this development and the experience is different for boys and girls. Because childhood gratification of these desires for pleasure is frequently frowned upon by society, embodied usually in the parents, awareness of the desires is repressed into a part of the brain known as the unconscious. The unconscious is inaccessible, except during the process of psychoanalysis, but reveals itself in daily life through dreams, word association and slips of the tongue, neurotic symptoms and 'irrational' or conflicting behaviours. Since the unconscious is not a 'thing' nor situated in a particular part of the brain, its existence cannot be proven but only inferred from otherwise hard to explain but ubiquitous data.[7]

Freud's theory has sometimes been seen as deterministic, in that he saw an adult as a product of a small group of people, the family, who interpreted the nature of society for her or him. Concomitantly, the range of adult choices is ultimately determined by childhood experiences and, for Freud, these childhood developmental stages are universal. While Freud did consider that the environment played a part in the construction of the adult personality, his followers and critics have modified his theories, sometimes in ways which give a greater role to culture in relation to biology. Some feminist psychoanalysts, for example, have explained the clinical findings about women, such as the notorious penis envy, in terms of women's oppression by society and their subsequent discontent with their position, rather than positing that the cultural devaluation of women is a result of their lack of male genitalia, and consequent rejection of their femininity leading to low self-esteem.[8] As well, post-Freudian theorists have placed more emphasis on data gathered from 'normal' people, as compared to Freud's evidence, mainly derived from himself and his clinical practice. Thus, some would argue that later modifications to Freud's theory are of more use to the historian, although Freud's theory remains basic to these modifications.

In particular, Erikson's theory of ego psychology has suggested fruitful amalgamations of history and psychoanalysis. Rather than continuing to study the development of neuroses, Erikson posited a model of normal development in terms of the 'eight ages of man', and contended that human development was a matter of 'integrat[ing] the timetable of the organism with the structure of social institutions'. He outlined these ideas in *Childhood and Society*. In Loewenberg's words: 'A psychosocial identity is the sense of continuity between one's personal, family, ethnic, and national past and one's current role and interaction with the present.' Thus Erikson could argue that '[c]ultures . . . elaborate upon the biologically given', and that the 'psychoanalytic method is essentially a historical method'.[9]

As part of his theory, Erikson suggested that psychological development continued beyond childhood. He used these ideas in biographical studies of Luther and Gandhi, where material from early childhood was scanty.[10] Erikson's theories suggested new possibilities for historians. According to Loewenberg, '[e]go psychology and character analysis are particularly important and welcome to historians because they are based on the evidence of adult behaviour. They do not require reconstruction of infantile experience or reductions to origins – the behaviour and patterns of accommodating to the world exist in adulthood and the evidence is historical.'[11] Erikson's work has therefore been pivotal in the field of psychobiography.

Object-relations theory has also been useful in combining a psychoanalytic account of human development with an analysis of environment. Rather than focusing on the relatively autonomous development of one individual, object-relations theorists argue that development happens in the context of a social and psychic relationship. The nature of the mother–infant relationship is most important, although contacts with other developmental figures are significant. Since the mother–child link is a social relationship, as well as an instinctual one, it is historically constructed and therefore changes with time and place.[12] Clearly individual childhood experiences vary, but historians often know in general terms when and how significant events occur. The age of weaning, the approximate age of birth of the next sibling, and ideas about nurturing and disciplining children are all factors which historians can take into account in psychohistorical explanations.

Psychohistorians have wanted to study the behaviour and motivations not only of individuals but of groups in the past. Langer, for example, discussed mass emotional reactions to the Black Death. Freud concentrated initially upon the relationship between a group and its leader, seeing the group as regressing to a state of dependency. But this approach does not deal with the dynamics of the group itself. What is it about groups, then, that allows their members to act collectively in ways which conflict with members' usual individual behaviour and values?[13]

Wilhelm Reich attempted to blend history, in the form of historical materialism, with group psychoanalysis.[14] In *The Mass Psychology of Fascism*, written in the early 1930s, Reich synthesized the theories of Freud and Marx. He argued that Nazism, like all political movements, was grounded in the psychological structure of the German masses, in particular of the lower middle class. This group was anxious due to their increasing poverty in the face of depression and German war debts. Lower-middle-class fathers were authoritarian, and able to sexually repress their children on account of the correspondence of familial and economic structures: that is, the family lived and worked together. These psychically damaged children therefore became submissive, and were relieved to rely on an authoritarian *Führer* in later life. At the same time they craved authority, and so acted in an authoritarian manner towards those below them. This is, of course, a simplified account but it serves to show how Reich enriched his analysis of a concrete historical situation with psychoanalytic insights.[15]

How have these psychohistorical approaches been applied and received by the historical community? In general we have been and are suspicious: psychohistory, for example, does not rate a chapter in

Routledge's massive *Companion to Historiography*.[16] Much current criticism revolves around either classic studies such as Freud's *Leonardo* and Erikson's *Luther*, or investigations of near-contemporary or at least twentieth-century individuals or group phenomena.[17] In the latter case, subjects can often be asked to make sense of their own lives, perhaps using oral interviews: that is, a relationship of sorts exists between the subject and the researcher, comparable to that between the analysand and the analyst in classic psychoanalysis. Moreover, the subject creates at least some of the evidence and may be available for the deeper exploration of areas thought to be crucial to psychohistorical explanation.[18] A fairer test of psychohistory, however, might be to examine research from an earlier age, where the researcher has only the extant primary sources with which to work and thus is on equal terms with other historians. The following two examples therefore derive from the medieval period. They may illustrate some of the advantages and pitfalls discussed by critics of psychohistory.

In 1976 Kantor examined the memoirs of Abbot Guibert of Nogent, written in 1116, with the aim of 'better understand[ing] the relation between the man and the society of twelfth-century northern France in which he lived'.[19] Unusually, Guibert wrote at length about his childhood and upbringing, in a 'dreamy confessional narrative', where the rather fragmentary historical story contains sermons and anecdotes, usually of a judgemental and violent nature. Kantor argues that Guibert has unconsciously distorted the historical picture, but that this means that the memoirs are an ideal psychohistorical source.

In Kantor's view, Guibert's interior life was dominated by his mother, who was responsible for his upbringing, his father having died during Guibert's infancy. She was 'beautiful yet chaste', both saint and whore, and apparently had similarly contradictory impulses regarding the choice of a monastic career for Guibert. Kantor traces Guibert's sexual repression to that of his mother, as he does Guibert's own opposing 'ambition to glory' (which he seems to equate with lust) and 'submission to God'. Kantor explains that Guibert exhibits an imperfectly desexualized Oedipal attachment to his mother, and by transference to that 'seductive' cultural icon, the Virgin Mary. Rather than Guibert's superego forming in relation to his father, it developed along matriarchal lines due to his feminine upbringing, with the result that an internalized Virgin acts as superego. These opposing characteristics set up a conflict between erotic and non-erotic impulses with regard to the Virgin – in any case a paradox in her own right.

Thus women are threatening accusers and castrators as well as temptresses. In addition, the oedipal drama ascends to heaven: Guibert identifies with Christ, whose unconscious desires for the Virgin are chastened by God the Father (also a castrator in Guibert's fantasy life). Guibert's resultant guilt and self-hate leads him to aggressive and violent denunciations of those around him, especially the women.

Kantor also draws analogies between Guibert's interior and exterior worlds, contrasting the external masculine world of twelfth-century France with its adventure and loose morals, with Guibert's interior feminine one, attuned to the need for protection. His drama is thus linked to the courtly love scene as well as to the twelfth- and thirteenth-century cult of the Virgin. Parallels with the Madonna/whore paradox of twentieth-century southern Italy are also drawn.

Kantor's account is a plausible one, and he goes some way to situating an individual in the context of his time, although his classic Freudianism is now rather out-dated. His analysis does, however, exhibit some of the features for which psychohistorians have been criticized, rightly or wrongly. For instance, the study is a psychopathology and thus tells us little about normal life, despite Kantor's reminder that 'neurosis is but an extreme form of "normality"'. Nevertheless, the general importance of the Virgin in Guibert's internal life does seem likely to have been common among monks, given the emphasis on her cult in France at this time. Perhaps rather than the usual criticism that psychopathology serves to discredit leaders of society, in this version it appears to cast doubt on the possibility of psychic health within monasticism, at least in its medieval form. Kantor infers infantile psychological development from adult fantasy and inner experience, an approach sometimes labelled reductionist. In this sense, he treats the structure of the unconscious as constant over time, an analysis borne out by Kantor's comparison of Guibert's psyche with those of twentieth-century Italian men. He is therefore assuming that psychoanalysis is, even in its classic statement, applicable to the past. Historians have been uncomfortable with this view.

Kantor situates Guibert's ambivalence towards women in the context of medieval misogyny, but again does not separate 'normal' misogyny from Guibert's extreme form. Feminists might also argue that Kantor's statement, '[w]e know that [Guibert's mother] was the probable cause of her husband's impotence for many years', displays a rather unreflective contemporary misogyny, or at least echoes that dating from Freud's own era.

One of the greatest problems for psychohistorians is obtaining the appropriate evidence on which to base a psychoanalytic interpretation, both for an individual and to determine the psychological norms of society. Kantor has paid careful attention to the language and the structure of his source, an autobiographical document unique for its time. In this way he makes full use of a source previously deemed problematic for its lack of historical veracity and continuity, and its unusual content.[20]

A more sustained analysis of aspects of the medieval psyche is Rudolph Bell's *Holy Anorexia*. Bell compares holy women who starved themselves with modern sufferers of anorexia nervosa, both in terms of symptoms and causes. His study is historically specific, based on urban Italian saints as portrayed in their hagiographies, letters, confessors' accounts and canonization records. He contextualized their lives within a broader statistical picture of the characteristics of saints and then examined the lives of several women in detail. As his publisher states, Bell found that '[f]or both the anorexic and the fasting saint, self-starvation is part of a larger struggle for liberation from a patriarchal family and society. Both contemporary anorexics and "holy anorexics" seek autonomy in culturally defined ideal states: energetic slenderness today, spiritual purity in the Middle Ages.'[21]

While rooted in psychology, Bell's account seems more historically convincing than Kantor's, perhaps because it uses a range of sources, examines a number of different women and develops its context. Bell engages in speculation, but fleshes out his analysis with considerable primary evidence. Examining in detail the experience of several women allows Bell to investigate the workings and outcomes of a desire for feminine autonomy in different settings – illustrating both a cure and its opposite, death by starvation. This approach seems more based in social history than does Kantor's. In contrast to Bynum's more culturally oriented study of the same phenomenon, Bell does emphasize the negative aspects of women's relationship to food, and food itself as material rather than symbolic.[22] While he still compares past with present, his psychological interpretation is historically nuanced. The sources are undoubtedly problematic, as Bell points out, but he argues that at least they allow us access to the feelings of non-elite medieval women. His approach can help us to ascertain the 'mood' of a time in accordance with Langer's agenda.

A recent and highly praised example of group psychology comes in John Demos's *Entertaining Satan*.[23] Like many historians, Demos aims to explicate the seventeenth-century outbreak of witchcraft at Salem. He points out that the witch documents focus on symbols of maternal function, aggression and issues of boundaries (the witch often intruded upon a household or the body of a person), and sees these features as 'a distinctive mode of "object relations"'. Defence mechanisms of projection are also important and relate to a definable phase of very early childhood. Demos argues that particular child-rearing practices coupled with age-specific sibling rivalry help account for the virulent 'antagonism to women' seen during the witchcraze.[24] Gay suggests that Demos's psychohistorical work is enhanced by its eclectic nature – controversially, he uses a variety of psychoanalytic schools in his explanation. More importantly, it is his solid grounding as an historian that allows him to contextualize the psychohistory in a persuasive and non-reductionist manner.[25]

Psychohistory can, however, explain more than the irrational in history. Many historians are committed to explanations based on individual or group self-interest, although we admit that individuals do not always appear to recognize their best interests nor do they always act for their own short-term or even ultimate good. This is particularly clear in economic history: as Cochran says, '[e]ach culture has its own forms of economic irrationality or inconsistency.' Surely psychohistory can be of use here.[26]

Lacan's recent rereading of Freud, with its insistence that a person's subjectivity is not a given, but is created, may point to new possibilities for psychohistory. Previous theorists argued that the unconscious and sexuality, essential to the subject, always existed. Lacan, in contrast, says that an infant acquires subjectivity, including the unconscious and sexuality, through its interaction with society, mediated mainly by language. The infant learns about human culture through the speech of others, and forms his image of himself in accordance with the picture that others reflect to him. Lacan's emphasis on language and society in the formation of the psyche leave a greater role for historians in describing that formation than does a psychology which asserts a subjectivity biological in origin.[27]

One final issue worth examining in the context of psychohistory is that of subjectivity and objectivity. Psychoanalytic interpretations are by their nature individual and subjective, whether or not we label them scientific. Loewenberg makes the point that the empathy and reaction of the researcher to her subject, known as counter-transference, is an essential part of the psychohistorical process. In this sense, presumably no two researchers will interpret the data in an identical way. This issue has been debated in the broader historical context for many years, however, since it is generally true that no two historians produce an identical interpretation of a collection of data. Therefore, this argument should not be used as justification for abandonment of the psychohistorical enterprise.

Overall, and despite the above reservations, psychohistory has much to offer. At the least, it can help reveal the rational roots of apparently irrational behaviour, and assist in explanation of the extreme situations of history, such as the persecution of witchcraft.[28] It can certainly be enriching, and adds a further perspective from which to examine both the past and our own interpretations of it.

Gay takes this rather minimalist picture of psychohistory further:

> Psychoanalytic history, then, is at its most ambitious an orientation rather than a specialty. I cannot reiterate often enough that psychoanalysis offers the historian not a handbook of recipes but a style of seeing the past. That is why Freudian history is compatible with all the traditional genres – military, economic, intellectual – as well as with most of their methods.[29]

Like the *Annales* historians, whom we examine in the next chapter, he calls for a total history, including the unconscious as well as our conscious world.

Erik Erikson, in his development of ego psychology, modified some of Freud's ideas. Like Freud, he saw the psychoanalytic method as an historical method, arguing that 'the history of humanity is a gigantic metabolism of individual life cycles'.[30] The following extract uses as its source Hitler's supposed autobiographical account of his childhood. Rather than carrying out a straightforward analysis of Hitler's pathology, Erikson examines the mythical Hitler and how his psyche fitted into the collective psyche of the German people.

Erikson discussed the unconscious as well as the conscious nature of myth. What does he mean by myth and how might a myth help to create or to explain historical events? Erikson also critiques those theorists interpreting the beginning of *Mein Kampf* in terms of Hitler's Oedipus complex. This is the way some psychohistorians have used apparently autobiographical material. What are Erikson's objections to this practice? Why, in particular, does he believe it is 'inexpedient to apply ordinary diagnostic methods to [Hitler's] words'?

Erikson claims that Hitler uses his father and mother as symbols which appeal to a particular part of Germany's population. How then does Erikson explain Hitler's wider appeal? Overall, how well do you think this account serves to elucidate the psychological background to the rise of National Socialism? How does it compare with any other explanations of which you are aware?

Notes

1 Peter Loewenberg, *Decoding the Past: The Psychohistorical Approach* (2nd edn, New Brunswick, 1996), p. 3; Jacques Barzun, *Clio and the Doctors: Psycho-History Quanto-History & History* (Chicago, 1974), p. 23.
2 T. G. Ashplant, 'Fantasy, Narrative, Event: Psychoanalysis and History', *History Workshop Journal*, 23 (1987), p. 167; Hans Meyerhoff, 'On Psychoanalysis as History', in Geoffrey Cocks and Travis L. Crosby (eds), *Psycho/History: Readings in the Method of Psychology, Psychoanalysis, and History* (New Haven, 1987), p. 17.
3 As George M. Kren and Leon H. Rappoport point out, this idea goes back as early as Herodotus and Thucydides. See 'Clio and Psyche', printed in Kren and Rappoport (eds), *Varieties of Psychohistory* (New York, 1976), p. 64.
4 In the past, and still in some historical writing, it has led, for example, to the misrepresentation or the omission of the experience of groups such as women, people of colour, or members of the working class.
5 W. Langer, 'The Next Assignment', *American Historical Review*, 63 (1958), p. 284.
6 Penelope Hetherington, 'Freud, Psychoanalysis and History', unpublished paper presented to the History Department Research Seminar, University of Western Australia, 1980, p. 4.
7 J. A. C. Brown, *Freud and the Post-Freudians* (London, 1963), ch. 2.
8 Nancy Chodorow, *The Reproduction of Mothering: Psychoanalysis and the Sociology of Gender* (Berkeley, 1978), p. 47. Simone de Beauvoir critiqued the idea of penis envy much earlier: see *The Second Sex*, trans. and ed. H. M. Parshley (Harmondsworth, [1949] 1972), pp. 72–5.
9 Erik H. Erikson, *Childhood and Society* (London, [1950] 1995), pp. 221, 95, 14, and ch. 7; Loewenberg, *Decoding the Past*, p. 20.
10 Erikson, *Young Man Luther: A Study in Psychoanalysis and History* (New York, 1958); *Gandhi's Truth: On the Origins of Militant Nonviolence* (New York, 1969).
11 Loewenberg, *Decoding the Past*, p. 24.
12 Chodorow, *Reproduction of Mothering*, p. 47.
13 Langer, 'The Next Assignment'; Ashplant, 'Psychoanalysis in Historical Writing', *History Workshop Journal*, 26 (1988), p. 111; Bruce Mazlish, 'What Is Psycho-history?', in Kren and Rappoport, *Varieties of Psychohistory*, p. 33.
14 Reich (1897–1957) is a controversial figure within the psychoanalytic community. Once regarded as Freud's most promising follower, he was expelled from the International Psychoanalytic Association in 1934, and labelled 'psychotic'. See Myron Sharaf, *Fury on Earth: A Biography of Wilhelm Reich* (London, 1983).
15 Wilhelm Reich, *The Mass Psychology of Fascism*, trans. Vincent R. Carfagno (3rd edn, Harmondsworth, 1970), p. 111; Paul A. Robinson, *The Freudian Left* (New York, 1969), ch. 1, esp. pp. 40–8. Erich Fromm also discussed the psychological underpinnings of the Nazi movement: see *The Fear of Freedom* (London, 1942), ch. 6.
16 Michael Bentley (ed.), *Companion to Historiography* (London, 1997).
17 Sigmund Freud, *Leonardo da Vinci and a Memory of His Childhood*, trans. Alan Tyson, *Standard Edition of the Complete Psychological Works of Sigmund Freud*, ed. James

Strachey with the collaboration of Anna Freud (London, [1910] 1957), vol. 11, pp. 63–137; Erikson, *Young Man Luther*.

18 See, for example, John Byng-Hall, 'The Power of Family Myths', in Raphael Samuel and Paul Thompson (eds), *The Myths We Live By* (London, 1990), pp. 216–24.

19 Jonathan Kantor, 'A Psycho-historical Source: The *Memoirs* of Abbot Guibert of Nogent', *Journal of Medieval History*, 2 (1976), pp. 281–304. The following account draws heavily on Kantor's ideas and words.

20 These general critiques are derived from Loewenberg, *Decoding the Past*; Ashplant, 'Psychoanalysis in Historical Writing'; Frank E. Manuel, 'The Use and Abuse of Psychology in History', in Kren and Rappoport, *Varieties of Psychohistory*, pp. 38–62; Peter Burke, *History and Social Theory* (Cambridge, 1992), pp. 114–18; and John Tosh, *The Pursuit of History: Aims, Methods and New Directions in the Study of Modern History* (2nd edn, London, 1991), pp. 79–80.

21 Rudolph M. Bell, *Holy Anorexia* (Chicago, 1985).

22 Carolyn Walker Bynum, *Holy Feast and Holy Fast: The Religious Significance of Food to Medieval Women* (Berkeley, 1987), esp. p. 14.

23 John Demos, *Entertaining Satan: Witchcraft and the Culture of Early New England* (Oxford, 1982); see the discussion in Peter Gay, *Freud for Historians* (New York, 1985), pp. 203–5.

24 See his chapter 'Accusers, Victims, Bystanders: The Innerlife Dimension', reprinted in Cocks and Crosby (eds), *Psycho/History*, pp. 254–66.

25 Gay, *Freud for Historians*, p. 203.

26 Thomas Cochran, 'Economic History, Old and New', *American Historical Review*, 74 (1969), p. 1567, cited in Gay, *Freud for Historians*, p. 101. See also Gay's discussion of self-interest, pp. 99–115.

27 For a succinct description of Lacan's theory, see Juliet Mitchell, 'Introduction – I', in Juliet Mitchell and Jacqueline Rose (eds), *Feminine Sexuality: Jacques Lacan and the École Freudienne* (New York, 1982), pp. 1–26. For an example of historical practice, see Sally Alexander, 'Women, Class and Sexual Difference', *History Workshop Journal*, 17 (1984), pp. 125–49.

28 Burke, *History and Social Theory* , p. 115; Ashplant, 'Psychoanalysis in Historical Writing', p. 104.

29 Gay, *Freud for Historians*, p. 210.

30 Erikson, *Childhood and Society*, p. 14.

Additional reading

Ashplant, T. G., 'Psychoanalysis in Historical Writing', *History Workshop Journal*, 26 (1988), pp. 102–19.

Barzun, Jacques, *Clio and the Doctors: Psycho-History Quanto-History & History* (Chicago, 1974).

Certeau, Michel de, *The Writing of History*, trans. Tom Conley (New York, [1975] 1988).

Cocks, Geoffrey and Travis L. Crosby (eds), *Psycho/History: Readings in the Method of Psychology, Psychoanalysis, and History* (New Haven, 1987).

Erikson, Erik H., *Childhood and Society* (London, [1950] 1995).

Erikson, Erik H., *Young Man Luther: A Study in Psychoanalysis and History* (New York, 1958).

Gay, Peter, *Freud for Historians* (New York, 1985).

George, Alexander L. and Juliette L. George, *Woodrow Wilson and Colonel House: A Personality Study* (New York, 1956).

Kren, George M. and Leon H. Rappoport (eds), *Varieties of Psychohistory* (New York, 1976).

Lifton, Robert Jay (ed.), *Explorations in Psychohistory: The Wellfleet Papers* (New York, 1975).

Loewenberg, Peter, *Decoding the Past: The Psychohistorical Approach* (2nd edn, New Brunswick, 1996).

Mazlish, Bruce (ed.), *Psychoanalysis and History* (Englewood Cliffs, N.J., 1963).

Reich, Wilhelm, *The Mass Psychology of Fascism*, trans. Vincent R. Carfagno (3rd edn, Harmondsworth, 1970).

THE LEGEND OF
HITLER'S CHILDHOOD
Erik H. Erikson

The most ruthless exploiters of any nation's fight for a safe identity have been Adolf Hitler and his associates, who for a decade were the undisputed political and military masters of a great, industrious, and studious people. To stop these experts of the cheap word from becoming a threat to the whole of Western civilization the combined resources of the industrial nations of the world were mobilized.

The West would now prefer to ignore the question mark which thus challenges the idea of unilinear progress. It hopes that, after some feeding and policing by occupation troops, these same Germans will once more emerge as good customers, easily domesticated; that they will return to the pursuit of *Kultur*, and forever forget the martial foolishness they were once more trapped into.

Men of good will must believe in psychological as well as in economic miracles. Yet I do not think that we are improving the chances of human progress in Germany or anywhere else by forgetting too soon what happened. Rather, it is our task to recognize that the black miracle of Nazism was only the German version—superbly planned and superbly bungled—of a universal contemporary potential. The trend persists; Hitler's ghost is counting on it.

For nations, as well as individuals, are not only defined by their highest point of civilized achievement, but also by the weakest one in their collective identity: they are, in fact, defined by the distance, and the quality of the distance, between these points. National Socialist Germany has provided a clear-cut illustration of the fact that advancing civilization is potentially endangered by its own advance, in that it splits ancient conscience, endangers incomplete identities, and releases destructive forces which now can count on the cold efficiency of the super-managers. I shall therefore go back this one step in our history and restate here a few formulations written for a U.S. government agency at the beginning of World War II, in preparation for the arrival of the—oh, so arrogant—first Nazi prisoners. Some of these formulations may already sound dated. Yet the psychological problems presented here do not vanish overnight either from Germany proper, or from the continent of which she is the

71

center. At any rate, history only teaches those who are not overeager to forget.

I shall take as my text the Brown Piper's sweetest, most alluring tune: the account of his childhood, in *Mein Kampf*.

> In this little town on the river Inn, Bavarian by blood and Austrian by nationality, gilded by the light of German martyrdom, there lived, at the end of the eighties of last century, my parents: the father a faithful civil servant, the mother devoting herself to the cares of the household and looking after her children with eternally the same loving care.[1]

The sentence structure, the tone quality, indicate that we are to hear a fairy tale; and indeed we shall analyze it as part of a modern attempt to create a myth. But a myth, old or modern, is not a lie. It is useless to try to show that it has no basis in fact; nor to claim that its fiction is fake and nonsense. A myth blends historical fact and significant fiction in such a way that it 'rings true' to an area or an era, causing pious wonderment and burning ambition. The people affected will not question truth or logic; the few who cannot help doubting will find their reason paralyzed. To study a myth critically, therefore, means to analyze its images and themes in their relation to the culture area affected.

1. Germany

> This little town. . . . Bavarian by blood and Austrian by nationality, gilded by the light of German martyrdom. . . .

Hitler was born in the Austrian town of Braunau, near the German border. He thus belonged to the Austrian Empire's German minority.

It had been in Braunau, he records, that a man named Palm was shot by Napoleon's soldiers for printing a pamphlet: *In the Hour of Germany's Deepest Humiliation*. Palm's memorial stands in the center of the town.

There was, of course, no German Reich in Palm's time. In fact, some of the German states were Napoleon's military allies. But having used the all-inclusive, the magic term 'Germany,' Palm, when delivered to Napoleon by the Austrian police, became the idol of the nationalist movement calling for a greater Germany.

---

[1] Adolf Hitler, *Mein Kampf*, Reynal & Hitchcock edition, New York, 1941, by arrangement with Houghton-Mifflin Company.

Having pointed to Palm's resistance to and martyrdom under the sinister *Bonaparte*, the story proceeds to describe young Adolf's heroic opposition to his *father*, and tells of the German minority's hatred of the Austrian *emperor*. Little Adolf belonged, so he says, to 'those who in painful emotion long for the hour that will allow them to return to the arms of the beloved mother'—Germany.

It is here that his imagery begins to involve terms of family relations which openly identify his 'oedipus' situation with his country's national problems. He complains that this 'beloved mother, . . . the *young* Reich,' by her 'tragic alliance with the *old Austrian sham state* . . . herself sanctioned the slow extermination of the German nationality.'

Hitler's mother was twenty-three years younger than his father; and, as we shall see, the mother, as a good woman of her day, valiantly stood up for the man who beat her. The father was a drunkard and a tyrant. The equation suggests itself that in Hitler's national as well as domestic imagery, the young mother betrays the longing son for a senile tyrant. Little Adolf's personal experience thus blends with that of the German minority which refuses to sing 'God Save Emperor Francis,' when the Austrian anthem is sung and substitutes for it 'Germany over All.' Hitler continues: 'The direct result of this period was: first, I became a nationalist; second, I learned to grasp and to understand the meaning of history . . . so that at fifteen, I already understood the difference between dynastic patriotism and popular nationalism.'

Such seemingly naïve coincidence of themes lends itself easily—much too easily—to a psychoanalytic interpretation of the first chapter of *Mein Kampf* as an involuntary confession of Hitler's oedipus complex. This interpretation would suggest that in Hitler's case the love for his young mother and the hate for his old father assumed morbid proportions, and that it was this conflict which drove him to love and to hate and compelled him to save or destroy people and peoples who really 'stand for' his mother and his father. There have been articles in psychoanalytic literature which claim such simple causality. But it obviously takes much more than an individual complex to make a successful revolutionary. The complex creates the initial fervor; but if it were too strong it would paralyze the revolutionary, not inspire him. The striking use of parental and familial images in Hitler's public utterances has that strange mixture of naïve confession and shrewd propaganda which characterizes the histrionic genius. Goebbels knew this and he guided his barking master well—until very close to the end.

I shall not now review the psychiatric literature which has described Hitler as a 'psychopathic paranoid,' an 'amoral sadistic infant,' an 'overcompensatory sissy,' or 'a neurotic laboring under the compulsion to murder.' At times, he undoubtedly was all of that. But, unfortunately, he was something over and above it all. His capacity for acting and for creating action was so rare that it seems inexpedient to apply ordinary diagnostic methods to his words. He was first of all an adventurer, on a grandiose scale. The personality of the adventurer is akin to that of an actor, because he must always be ready to personify, as if he had chosen them, the changing roles suggested by the whims of fate. Hitler shares with many an actor the fact that he is said to have been queer and unbearable behind the scenes, to say nothing of in his bedroom. He undoubtedly had hazardous borderline traits. But he knew how to approach the borderline, to appear as if he were going too far, and then to turn back on his breathless audience. Hitler knew how to exploit his own hysteria. Medicine men, too, often have this gift. On the stage of German history, Hitler sensed to what extent it was safe to let his own personality represent with hysterical abandon what was alive in every German listener and reader. Thus the role he chose reveals as much about his audience as about himself; and precisely that which to the non-German looked queerest and most morbid became the Brown Piper's most persuasive tune for German ears.

2. Father

> ... the father a faithful civil servant ...

Despite this sentimental characterization of the father, Hitler spends a heated portion of his first chapter in reiterating the assertion that neither his father nor 'any power on earth could make an official' out of him. He knew already in earliest adolescence that the life of an official had no appeal for him. How different he was from his father! For though his father, too, had rebelled in early adolescence and at the age of thirteen had run away from home to become 'something "better,"' he had, after twenty-three years, returned home— and become a minor official. And 'nobody remembered the little boy of long ago.' This futile rebellion, Hitler says, made his father old early. Then, point for point, Hitler demonstrates a rebellious technique superior to that of his father.

Is this the naïve revelation of a pathological father-hate? Or if it is shrewd propaganda, what gave this Austrian German the right to expect that the tale of his boyhood would have a decisive appeal for masses of Reichs-Germans?

Obviously, not all Germans had fathers of the kind Hitler had, although many undoubtedly did. Yet we know that a literary theme, to be convincing, need not be true; it must sound true, as if it reminded one of something deep and past. The question, then, is whether the German father's position in his family made him act— either all of the time, or enough of the time, or at memorable times— in such a way that he created in his son an *inner* image which had some correspondence to that of the older Hitler's publicized image.

Superficially, the position in his family of the German middle-class father of the late nineteenth and the early twentieth century may have been quite similar to other Victorian versions of 'life with Father.' But patterns of education are elusive. They vary in families and persons; they may remain latent only to appear during memorable crises; they may be counteracted by determined attempts to be different.

I shall present here an impressionistic version of what I consider one pattern of German fatherhood. It is representative in the sense in which Galton's blurred composites of photography are representative of what they are supposed to show.

When the father comes home from work, even the walls seem to pull themselves together (*'nehmen sich zusammen'*). The mother— although often the unofficial master of the house—behaves differently enough to make a baby aware of it. She hurries to fulfill the father's whims and to avoid angering him. The children hold their breath, for the father does not approve of 'nonsense'—that is, neither of the mother's feminine moods nor of the children's playfulness. The mother is required to be at his disposal as long as he is at home; his behavior suggests that he looks with disfavor on that unity of mother and children in which they had indulged in his absence. He often speaks to the mother as he speaks to the children, expecting compliance and cutting off any answer. The little boy comes to feel that all the gratifying ties with his mother are a thorn in the father's side, and that her love and admiration—the model for so many later fulfillments and achievements—can be reached only without the father's knowledge, or against his explicit wishes.

The mother increases this feeling by keeping some of the child's 'nonsense' or badness from the father—if and when she pleases;

while she expresses her disfavor by telling on the child when the father comes home, often making the father execute periodical corporal punishment for misdeeds, the details of which do not interest him. Sons are bad, and punishment is always justified. Later, when the boy comes to observe the father in company, when he notices his father's subservience to superiors, and when he observes his excessive sentimentality when he drinks and sings with his equals, the boy acquires that first ingredient of *Weltschmerz*: a deep doubt of the dignity of man—or at any rate of the 'old man.' All this, of course, exists concurrently with respect and love. During the storms of adolescence, however, when the boy's identity must settle things with his father image, it leads to that severe German *Pubertät* which is such a strange mixture of open rebellion and 'secret sin,' cynical delinquency and submissive obedience, romanticism and despondency, and which is apt to break the boy's spirit, once and for all.

In Germany, this pattern had traditional antecedents. It always just happened to happen, although it was, of course, not 'planned.' Indeed, some fathers who had resented the pattern deeply during their own boyhood wished desperately not to inflict it on their boys. But this wish again and again traumatically failed them in periods of crisis. Others tried to repress the pattern, only to augment both their and their children's neuroticisms. Often the boy sensed that the father himself was unhappy about his inability to break the vicious circle; for this emotional impotence the boy felt pity and disgust.

What, then, made this conflict so universally fateful? What differentiates—in an unconscious but decisive way—the German father's aloofness and harshness from similar traits in other Western fathers? I think the difference lies in the German father's essential lack of true inner authority—that authority which results from an integration of cultural ideal and educational method. The emphasis here definitely lies on *German* in the sense of *Reichs-German*. So often when discussing things German, we think and speak of well-preserved German *regions*, and of 'typical' yet isolated instances where the German father's inner authority seemed deeply justified, founded as it was on old rural and small urban *Gemütlichkeit*; on urban *Kultur*; on Christian *Demut*; on professional *Bildung*; or on the spirit of social *Reform*. The important point is that all of this did not assume an integrated meaning on a national scale as the imagery of the Reich became dominant and industrialization undermined the previous social stratification.

Harshness is productive only where there is a sense of obligation in command, a sense of dignity in voluntary obedience. This, however, only an integrating cause can provide: a cause that unites past and present in accord with changes in the economic, political, and spiritual institutions.

The other Western nations had their democratic revolutions. They, as Max Weber demonstrated, by gradually taking over the privileges of their aristocratic classes, had thereby identified with aristocratic ideals. There came to be something of the French chevalier in every Frenchman, of the Anglo-Saxon gentleman in every Englishman, and of the rebellious aristocrat in every American. This something was fused with revolutionary ideals and created the concept of 'free man'—a concept which assumes inalienable rights, indispensable self-denial, and unceasing revolutionary watchfulness. For reasons which we shall discuss presently, in connection with the problem of *Lebensraum*, the German identity never quite incorporated such imagery to the extent necessary to influence the unconscious modes of education. The average German father's dominance and harshness was not blended with the tenderness and dignity which comes from participation in an integrating cause. Rather, the average father, either habitually or in decisive moments, came to represent the habits and the ethics of the German top sergeant and petty official who—'dress'd in a little brief authority'—would never be more but was in constant danger of becoming less; and who had sold the birthright of a free man for an official title or a life pension.

In addition, there was the breakdown of the cultural institution which had taken care of the adolescent conflict in its traditional—and regional—forms. In the old days, for example, the custom of *Wanderschaft* existed. The boy left home in order to be an apprentice in foreign lands at about the age—or a little later—at which Hitler announced his opposition, and at which Hitler's father had run away from home. In the immediate pre-Nazi era, some kind of break either still took place, with paternal thunder and maternal tears; or it was reflected in more moderate conflicts which were less effective because more individualized and often neurotic; or it was repressed, in which case not the father-boy relation, but the boy's relation to himself, was broken. Often the—exclusively male—teachers had to bear the brunt of it; while the boy extended his idealistic or cynical hostility over the whole sphere of *Bürgerlichkeit*—the German boy's contemptible world of 'mere citizens.' The connotation of this word *Bürger* is hard to transmit. It is not identical with the solid burgher;

nor with the glutted bourgeois of the class-conscious revolutionary youth; and least of all with the proud citoyen or the responsible citizen, who, accepting his equal obligations, asserts his right to be an individual. Rather it means a kind of adult who has betrayed youth and idealism, and has sought refuge in a petty and servile kind of conservatism. This image was often used to indicate that all that was 'normal' was corrupt, and that all that was 'decent' was weak. As 'Wanderbirds,' adolescent boys would indulge in a romantic unity with Nature, shared with many co-rebels and led by special types of youth leaders, professional and confessional adolescents. Another type of adolescent, the 'lone genius,' would write diaries, poems, and treatises; at fifteen he would lament with Don Carlos' most German of all adolescent complaints: 'Twenty years old, and as yet nothing done for immortality!' Other adolescents would form small bands of intellectual cynics, of delinquents, of homosexuals, and of race-conscious chauvinists. The common feature of all these activities, however, was the exclusion of the individual fathers as an influence and the adherence to some mystic-romantic entity: Nature, Fatherland, Art, Existence, etc., which were superimages of a pure mother, one who would not betray the rebellious boy to that ogre, the father. While it was sometimes assumed that the mother would openly or secretly favor, if not envy, such freedom, the father was considered its mortal foe. If he failed to manifest sufficient enmity, he would be deliberately provoked: for his opposition was the life of the experience.

At this stage, the German boy would rather have died than be aware of the fact that this misguided, this excessive initiative in the direction of utter utopianism would arouse deep-seated guilt and at the end lead to stunned exhaustion. The identification with the father which in spite of everything had been well established in early childhood would come to the fore. In intricate ways treacherous Fate (= reality) would finally make a *Bürger* out of the boy—a 'mere citizen' with an eternal sense of sin for having sacrified genius for Mammon and for a mere wife and mere children such as anyone can have.

Naturally, this account is made typical to the point of caricature. Yet I believe that both the overt type and the covert pattern existed, and that, in fact, this regular split between precocious individualistic rebellion and disillusioned, obedient citizenship was a strong factor in the political immaturity of the German: this adolescent rebellion was an abortion of individualism and of revolutionary spirit. It is my belief that the German fathers not only did not oppose this rebellion, but, indeed, unconsciously fostered it, as one sure way of maintaining their patriarchal hold over youth. For once a patriarchal superego is firmly established in early childhood, you can give youth rope: they cannot let themselves go far.

In the Reichs-German character, this peculiar combination of idealistic rebellion and obedient submission led to a paradox. The German conscience is self-denying and cruel; but its ideals are shifting and, as it were, homeless. The German is harsh with himself and with others; but extreme harshness without inner authority breeds bitterness, fear, and vindictiveness. Lacking co-ordinated ideals, the German is apt to approach with blind conviction, cruel self-denial, and supreme perfectionism many contradictory and outright destructive aims.

After the defeat and the revolution of 1918 this psychological conflict was increased to the point of catastrophe in the German middle classes; and the middle classes anywhere significantly include the worker class in so far as it aspires to become middle-class. Their servility toward the upper class, which had lost the war, was now suddenly robbed of any resemblance to a meaningful subordination. The inflation endangered pensions. On the other hand, the groping masses were not prepared to anticipate or usurp either the role of free citizens or that of class-conscious workers. It is clear that only under such conditions could Hitler's images immediately convince so many—and paralyze so many more.

I shall not claim, then, that Hitler's father, as described in derogatory accounts, was, in his manifestly rude form, a typical German father. It frequently happens in history that an extreme and even atypical personal experience fits a universal latent conflict so well that a crisis lifts it to a representative position. In fact, it will be remembered here that great nations are apt to choose somebody from just beyond the borders to become their leader: as Napoleon came from Corsica, Stalin came from Georgia. It is a universal childhood pattern, then, which is the basis for the deep wonderment which befell the German man who read about Hitler as a youth. 'No matter how firm and determined my father might be . . . his son was just as stubborn and obstinate in rejecting an idea which had little or no appeal for him. I did not want to become an official.' This combination of personal revelation and shrewd propaganda (together with loud and determined action) at last carried with it that universal conviction for which the smoldering rebellion in German youth had been waiting: that no old man, be he father, emperor, or god, need stand in the way of his love for his mother Germany. At the same time it proved to the grown-up men that by betraying their rebellious adolescence they had become unworthy of leading Germany's youth, which henceforth would 'shape its own destiny.' Both fathers and sons now could identify with the Führer, an adolescent who never gave in.

Psychologists overdo the father attributes in Hitler's historical image; Hitler the adolescent who refused to become a father by any connotation, or, for that matter, a kaiser or a president. He did not repeat Napoleon's error. He was the Führer: a glorified older brother, who took over prerogatives of the fathers without overidentifying with them: calling his father 'old while still a child,' he reserved for himself the new position of the one who remains young in possession of supreme power. He was the unbroken adolescent who had chosen a career apart from civilian happiness, mercantile tranquillity, and spiritual peace: a gang leader who kept the boys together by demanding their admiration, by creating terror, and by shrewdly involving them in crimes from which there was no way back. And he was a ruthless exploiter of parental failures.

'The question of my career was to be settled more quickly than I had anticipated. . . . When I was thirteen my father died quite suddenly. My mother felt the obligation to continue my education for the career of an official.' Thus thwarted, Hitler developed a severe pulmonary illness, and 'all that I had fought for, all that I had longed for in secret, suddenly became reality. . . .' His mother had to grant the sick boy what she had denied the healthy and stubborn one: he could now go and prepare to be an artist. He did—and failed the entrance examination to the national art school. Then his mother died, too. He was now free—and lonely.

Professional failure followed that early school failure which in retrospect is rationalized as character strength and boyish toughness. It is well known how in picking his sub-leaders Hitler later redeemed similar civilian failures. He got away with this only because of the German habit of gilding school failure with the suspicion of hidden genius: 'humanistic' education in Germany suffered all along from the severe split of fostering duty and discipline while glorifying the nostalgic outbreaks of poets.

In his dealings with the 'old' generation inside or outside Germany, Hitler consequently played a role as stubborn, as devious, and as cynical as he reports his to have been in relation to his father. In fact, whenever he felt that his acts required public justification and apology, he was likely to set the stage as he did in the first chapter of *Mein Kampf*. His tirades were focused on one foreign leader— Churchill or Roosevelt—and described him as a feudal tyrant and a senile fool. He then created a second image, that of the slick, rich son and decadent cynic: Duff-Cooper and Eden, of all men, are the ones he selected. And, indeed, Germans acquiesced to his broken pledges, as long as Hitler, the tough adolescent, seemed merely to be taking advantage of other men's senility.

3. Mother

> ... the mother devoting herself to the cares of the household and looking after her children with eternally the same loving care.

Beyond this continuation of his fairy tale, Hitler says little of his mother. He mentions that she was sometimes lovingly worried about the fights he, the boy hero, got into; that after the father's death, she felt 'obliged'—out of duty rather than inclination—to have him continue his education; and that soon she, too, died. He had respected his father, he says, but loved his mother.

Of 'her children' there is no further word. Hitler never was the brother of anyone.

That Hitler, the histrionic and hysterical adventurer, had a pathological attachment to his mother, there can be little doubt. But this is not the point here. For, pathological or not, he deftly divides his mother image into the two categories which are of the highest propagandistic value: the loving, childlike, and slightly martyred cook who belongs in the warm and cozy background—and the gigantic marble or iron virgin, the monument to the ideal. In contrast to the sparsity of reference to his personal mother, then, there is an abundance of superhuman mother figures in his imagery. His Reichs-German fairy tale does not simply say that Hitler was born in Braunau because his parents lived there; no, it was 'Fate which designated my birthplace.' This happened when it happened not because of the natural way of things; no, it was an 'unmerited mean trick of Fate' that he was 'born in a period between two wars, at a time of quiet and order.' When he was poor, 'Poverty clasped me in her arms'; when sad, 'Dame Sorrow was my foster mother.' But all this 'cruelty of Fate' he later learned to praise as the 'wisdom of Providence,' for it hardened him for the service of Nature, 'the cruel Queen of all wisdom.'

When the World War broke out, 'Fate graciously permitted' him to become a German foot soldier, the same 'inexorable Goddess of Fate, who uses wars to weigh nations and men.' When after the defeat he stood before a court defending his first revolutionary acts, he felt certain 'that the Goddess of History's eternal judgment will smilingly tear up' the jury's verdict.

Fate, now treacherously frustrating the hero, now graciously catering to his heroism and tearing up the judgment of the bad old men: this is the infantile imagery which pervades much of German idealism; it finds its most representative expression in the theme of the young hero who becomes great in a foreign country and returns to free and elevate the 'captive' mother: the romantic counterpart to the saga of King Oedipus.

Behind the imagery of superhuman mothers there thus lurks a two-faced image of maternity: the mother at one time appears playful, childlike, and generous; and at another, treacherous, and in league with sinister forces. This, I believe, is a common set of images in patriarchal societies where woman, in many ways kept irresponsible and childlike, becomes a go-between and an in-between. It thus happens that the father hates in her the elusive children, and the children hate in her the aloof father. Since 'the mother' regularly becomes and remains the unconscious model for 'the world,' under Hitler the ambivalence toward the maternal woman became one of the strongest features of German official thinking.

The Führer's relationship to motherhood and family remained ambiguous. In elaboration of a national fantasy he saw in himself a lonely man fighting and pleasing superhuman mother figures which now try to destroy him, now are forced to bless him. But he did not acknowledge women as companions up to the bitter end, when he insisted on making an honest woman out of Eva Braun, whom he presently shot with his own hands—or so the legend ends. But the wives of other men gave birth to their children in the shelter of the chancellery, while he himself, according to his official biographer, 'is the embodiment of the national will. He does not know any family life; neither does he know any vice.'

Hitler carried this official ambivalence toward women over into his relationship to Germany as an image. Openly despising the masses of his countrymen, who, after all, constitute Germany, he stood frenziedly before them, and implored them with his fanatical cries of 'Germany, Germany, Germany' to believe in a mystical national entity.

But then, the Germans have always been inclined to manifest a comparable attitude of ambivalence toward mankind and the world at large. That the world is essentially perceived as an 'outer world' is true for most tribes or nations. But for Germany the world is constantly changing its quality—and always to an extreme. The world is experienced either as vastly superior in age and wisdom, the goal of eternal longing and *Wanderlust*; or as a mean, treacherous, encircling encampment of enemies living for one aim—namely, the betrayal of Germany; or as a mysterious *Lebensraum* to be won by Teutonic courage and to be used for a thousand years of adolescent aggrandizement.

4. Adolescent

In this country, the word 'adolescence,' to all but those who have to deal with it professionally, has come to mean, at worst, a no man's land between childhood and maturity, and at best, a 'normal' time of sports and horseplay, of gangs and cliques and parties. The adolescent in this country offers less of a problem and feels less isolated because he has, in fact, become the cultural arbiter; few men in this country can afford to abandon the gestures of the adolescent, along with those of the freeman forever dedicated to the defeat of autocrats.

From here, then, it is hard to see what adolescence may mean in other cultures. In the primitive past, dramatic and bizarre adolescence rites were performed in an endeavor to modify and sublimate the adolescent's budding manhood. In primitive rituals the adolescent was forced to sacrifice some of his blood, some of his teeth, or a part of his genitals; in religious ceremonies he is taught to admit his sinfulness and bow his knee. Ancient rites confirmed the boy's intention of becoming a man in his father's world but at the same time of remaining eternally the modest son of a 'Great Father.' Leaders of the ritual dance, redeemers, and tragic actors were the representatives of guilt and expiation. Germany's adolescent rebellion was a climactic step in a universal psychological development which parallels the decline of feudalism: the inner emancipation of the sons. For while there are close parallels between primitive adolescence rites and those of National Socialism, there is one most significant difference. In Hitler's world, the adolescent marched with his emancipated equals. Their leader had never sacrificed his will to any father. In fact, he had said that conscience is a blemish like circumcision, and that both are Jewish blemishes.

Hitler's horror of Jewry—an 'emasculating germ' represented by less than 1 per cent of his nation of 70 million—is clothed in the imagery of phobia; he describes the danger emanating from it as a weakening infection and a dirtying contamination. Syphilophobia is the least psychiatry can properly diagnose in his case. But here again, it is hard to say where personal symptom ends and shrewd propaganda begins. For the idealistic adolescent's imagery is typically one of purest white and blackest black. His constant preoccupation is with the attainment of what is white, and the phobic avoidance and extirpation of everything black, in others and in himself. Fears of sexuality, especially, make the adolescent suggestible to words like these: 'Alone the loss of purity of the blood destroys the inner happiness forever; it eternally lowers man, and never again can its consequences be removed from body and mind.'[2]

The pre-Nazi German adolescent was passionately cruel with himself; it was not in order to indulge himself that he opposed his father. When he 'fell,' his guilt was great. Hitler, so this adolescent was made to feel, was the man who had the right to be cruel against black everywhere because he was not lenient with himself. What aroused suspicions in sensible non-Germans—namely, Hitler's proclaimed abstinence from meat, coffee, alcohol, and sex—here counted as a heavy propaganda factor. For Hitler thus proved his moral right to free the Germans from their postwar masochism and to convince them that they, in turn, had a right to hate, to torture, to kill.

In the children, Hitler tried to replace the complicated conflict of adolescence as it pursued every German, with simple patterns of hypnotic action and freedom from thought. To do so he established an organization, a training, and a motto which would divert all adolescent energy into National Socialism. The organization was the Hitler Youth; the motto, 'Youth shapes its own destiny.'

God no longer mattered: 'At this hour when the earth is consecrating itself to the sun, we have only one thought. Our sun is Adolph Hitler.'[3] Parents did not matter: 'All those who from the perspective of their "experience," and from that alone combat our

---

[2] *Ibid.*
[3] Quoted in G. Ziemer, *Education for Death*, Oxford University Press, New York, 1941.

method of letting youth lead youth, must be silenced. . . .'[4] Ethics did not matter: 'An entirely fresh, newborn generation has arisen, free from the preconceived ideas, free from compromises, ready to be loyal to the orders which are its birthright.'[5] Brotherhood, friendship did not matter: 'I heard not a single song expressing any tender emotion of friendship, love of parents, love for fellow-man, joy of living, hope for future life.'[6] Learning did not matter: 'National Socialist ideology is to be a sacred foundation. It is not to be degraded by detailed explanation.'[7]

What mattered was: to be on the move without looking backward. 'Let everything go to pieces, we shall march on. For today Germany is ours; tomorrow, the whole world.'

On such a foundation Hitler offered a simple racial dichotomy of cosmic dimensions: the German (soldier) versus the Jew. The Jew is described as small, black, and hairy all over; his back is bent, his feet are flat; his eyes squint, and his lips smack; he has an evil smell, is promiscuous, and loves to deflower, impregnate, and infect blond girls. The Aryan is tall, erect, light, without hair on chest and limbs; his glance, walk, and talk are *stramm*, his greeting the outstretched arm. He is passionately clean in his habits. He would not knowingly touch a Jewish girl—except in a brothel.

This antithesis is clearly one of ape man and superman. But while in this country such imagery may have made the comics, in Germany it became official food for adult minds. And let us not forget (for the Germans will not forget) that for long years German youth and the German army seemed to indicate a success for Hitler's imagery. Healthy, hard, calm, obedient, fanatic, they 'challenge everything that is weak in body, in intensity, and in loyalty.'[8] They were arrogant in the extreme; and it was only in their sneering arrogance that the old German fear of succumbing to foreign 'cultured' influence could be recognized.

In women, too, National Socialist race consciousness established a new pride. Girls were taught to accept joyfully the functions of their bodies if mated with selected Aryans. They received sexual enlightenment and encouragement. Childbirth, legitimate or illegitimate,

[4] Quoted in Hans Siemsen, *Hitler Youth*, Lindsay Drummond, London, 1941.
[5] Quoted in Ziemer, *op. cit.*
[6] Ziemer, *op. cit.*
[7] Quoted in Ziemer, *op. cit.*
[8] Ziemer, *op. cit.*

was promoted by propaganda, by subsidies, by the institution of 'State children,' who were born 'for the Führer.' Breast feeding was advocated; what American psychiatrists at that time dared suggest only in professional journals, the German state decreed: 'Stillfähigkeit ist Stillwille'—ability to nurse is the will to nurse. Thus German babyhood was enriched for the sake of the race and of the Führer.

In his imagery no actor and no effective innovator is really independent, nor can he dare to be entirely original: his originality must consist in the courage and singular concentration with which he expresses an existing imagery—at the proper time. If he does so, however, he is convincing to himself and to others—and paralyzes his adversaries, in so far as they unconsciously partake of his imagery, so that they will wait, become insecure, and finally surrender.

In Germany, then, we saw a highly organized and highly educated nation surrender to the imagery of ideological adolescence. We have indicated that we cannot lay the blame for this on the power of the leaders' individual neuroses. Can we blame the childhood patterns of the led?

4

The *Annales*

The group of historians now known as the *Annales* 'school' has produced some of the most exciting innovations in twentieth-century history writing. One of their admirers wrote: 'it was the *Annales* itself that over the years undermined the positivist definition of historical fact, destroyed the taboo on unwritten evidence, imposed a dialogue with the sister disciplines, discredited the history of events, rejected the primacy of political history by insisting on its interaction with economic and cultural history, repudiated traditional biography which isolated the individual, and succeeded, finally, in making "sensibility" or modes of feeling the object of serious historical research.'[1] This programme was not carried out by a single historian, nor does it employ a clear-cut paradigm, so the term 'school' is problematic in describing the *Annales* historians. Their work is united, however, in terms of theoretical and methodological principles embodied in the journal *Annales: Économies, Sociétés, Civilisations* whence their name derives.

The conceptual foundations of the *Annales* were laid in 1929 when the journal (then entitled *Annales d'histoire économique et sociale*) was first published by the Strasbourg professors Lucien Febvre and Marc Bloch. Febvre and Bloch rejected the near-monopoly of French history by political and diplomatic topics, an approach they saw as sterile. They wanted to break down the boundaries between the human sciences, with historians incorporating as many of these disciplines as possible in their work. Two decades later, a second milestone was reached: the publication of *La Méditerranée et le monde Méditerranéen à l'époque de Philippe II* by Fernand Braudel. Braudel introduced a multi-layered historical chronology, and initiated a strong focus on quantitative history among the historians influenced by him. From the early 1970s, those researchers labelled the 'third generation' of the *Annales* added an emphasis on the mental structures or *mentalités* of past societies to the already formidable range of new topics.[2]

Bloch and Febvre's approaches to history were complementary. In Febvre's doctoral thesis, *Philippe II and the Franche-Comté*, he examined the geographical background of this region and the effect of its material situation on its social, cultural and political development. Febvre later turned to religious history. His best known book, *The Problem of Unbelief in the Sixteenth Century*, asked not whether Rabelais was an atheist but whether such a stance was possible in his era. Thus what might have been a history of the Reformation became a broader examination of culture. By this means, Febvre anticipated the *Annales'* later interest in mentality.[3]

Bloch, however, concentrated overall on analysing the material structures of society. In *Feudal Society* he analysed not only the medieval aristocracy and the details of their land holdings and political dealings, but also their relationships with peasants, the customs by which each group held land, and the rituals by which property transfer was effected and formalized. He also emphasized the influence of the environment as part of the historical material world.[4] In contrast, *The Royal Touch* examined the importance of popular belief in legitimizing the power of medieval monarchy, and the ways in which kings utilized that belief for their own purposes. Bloch discussed touching in order to heal scrofula as a deliberately developed part of royal mystique.[5]

In this way Febvre and Bloch between them promulgated an ideal of *histoire totale* (total history), arguing that all aspects of a society were part of historical reality. Some of these ideas had been proposed previously, for example, in the historical geography of Vidal de la Blache and the issues of Henri Berr's *Revue de Synthèse Historique*, founded in 1900. It was left to Febvre and Bloch, however, to argue for this broad synthesis from an historical point of view, and thus to assert the place of history in the forefront of the human sciences.[6]

In 1947 the Sixième Section of the École Pratique des Haute Études was founded. This was a research centre in economics and the social sciences, outside the French university programme, and under Febvre's presidency it promoted a variety of *Annales* research. The event that rocketed the *Annales* version of history to the fore in France, however, was the production of a thesis by a student of Febvre's. In *The Mediterranean*, Braudel proposed a new model of historical time, and broke from the objective empirical methods of his historical contemporaries.[7]

Braudel expressed his schema of time in a metaphor of the ocean. He envisaged three layers of historical time, each moving at a different speed, and each aligned with different historical topics. The slowest moving, 'man in his relationship to the environment', was geographical time, the 'almost imperceptible' shifting of geology and climate, entailing examination of communications and limits of production. This *longue durée* moved in slow cycles of hundreds of years or more. The medium *durée*, or *conjonctures*, was equivalent to the 'swelling currents' with 'slow but perceptible rhythms', and revolved in ten to fifty year cycles. This middle layer comprised economic cycles, trade, population fluctuations, and prices. His third aspect of time Braudel called *histoire événementielle*, 'the ephemera of history', 'crests of foam that the tides of history carry on their strong backs'. This is the concern of a more traditional political and diplomatic history.[8]

The similarities between Braudel's work and Lévi-Strauss's structural anthropology are marked, although a direct influence is hard to trace.[9] One can certainly say that as contemporary French scholars they were subject to the same collection of intellectual influences.[10] Structuralists believe that we, as humans, make our world comprehensible by imposing mental structures upon it, consciously or unconsciously. Conversely, an analyst of society will seek to elucidate these structures. Kurzweil thus defines structuralism as 'the systematic attempt to uncover deep universal mental structures as these manifest themselves in kinship and larger social structures, . . . and in the unconscious psychological patterns that motivate human behaviour'.[11]

Some of these structures are synchronic, that is, unchanging with time. In the case of Braudel, the elements of the *longue durée* change so slowly that alteration is imperceptible to humans: these structures are effectively synchronic. Structures may also change over time and this diachronic change may manifest itself in an oscillatory form (for example, the cyclical *conjonctures*). Change over time can also be irreversible, as in the dramatic historical event. In all cases, it is the relationship between the structures which illuminates society and its history.

As well as using the three *durées* to organize his narrative, Braudel conceived time in a new way. For example, his famous phrase 'the Mediterranean was 99 days long' vividly evoked the effect of sea and horseback travel upon early modern communications. His spatial approach to the sea was equally novel; for Braudel, the Mediterranean extended as far north as the Baltic and eastward to India. Land and sea were inextricably connected: the history of the Mediterranean 'can no more be separated from that of the lands surrounding it than the clay can be separated from the hands of the potter who shapes it'.[12]

Braudel in fact argued that there were many durées, not only three, and thus he converged with Febvre's and Bloch's aim of writing a total history. In Braudel's case the totality was to be expressed in a range of durées rather than by topic, although chronology and subject were linked. This was an avowedly structuralist approach, and the deepest layer was ultimately the most influential: 'the long run always wins in the end'. Thus he largely overturned the traditional emphasis on the importance of events and people as the agents of history. Braudel's agents are the mountains and the sea itself. Eschewing direct statement, he conveys his sense of agency through an expansive and emotional approach to writing. His style is evocative and by its wealth of detail transports the reader into the region which Braudel loved 'with passion'.[13]

Braudel's work, while widely applauded, also had its critics.[14] Their main arguments fell into two groups. Firstly, reviewers found problems with the structure of The Mediterranean, especially in terms of fulfilling its author's aim of histoire totale. To some, 'total history' seemed an impossibility, and others agreed that The Mediterranean certainly could not be so described, as Braudel had omitted key topics, such as culture, agriculture, law and religion.[15] Bailyn argued that the three sections of The Mediterranean lacked connection, and Le Goff (himself an Annaliste) in particular condemned the section dealing with events for its lack of relation to the early parts of the book.[16] Historians who accepted the idea of the durées suggested even so that Braudel had located some of his discussions under the wrong chronological heading; there were suggestions that his linkages of topic and chronology were arbitrary.[17]

Secondly, in the same way that Marxist historians have been accused of economic determinism, Braudel was labelled a 'geographical determinist'. As we noted above, Braudel seemed to attribute any historical agency which did exist to large and unchanging landforms, and his book was curiously devoid of people. Apparently lacking a theory of historical change, his structuralism tends to the synchronic, rather than the diachronic normally deemed appropriate to history.[18]

Despite these possible flaws The Mediterranean is one of the great works of twentieth-century history, combining earlier ideas into a novel paradigm of historical writing. Braudel set new trends in historical thinking and methodology, made history one of the most important

subjects in French academia, and, as institutional and pedagogical
leader of the *Annales* group of historians from 1956 to the early 1970s,
provided intellectual and financial support for a burgeoning French
historical profession.[19]

Braudel's immediate followers focused mainly on the statistical aspect
of his work. Ernest Labrousse, a pioneering researcher on prices and
wage series since the 1930s, influenced and encouraged this trend.[20]
While Braudel himself continued to explore great vistas, historians like
Goubert and Duby seized upon the computer as a tool, and French
notarial, financial and population registrations records as sources, to
generate series and tables which elucidated a wide variety of
problems.[21] Pierre and Huguette Chaunu, for example, produced
twelve number-laden volumes in an effort to do for the Atlantic Ocean
what Braudel had achieved for the Mediterranean Sea. Historical
geography was certainly important in this work, but the main focus
was on economic structures and trends.[22]

Rather than *histoire totale*, these quantitative historians were pursuing
histoire problème, that is, a problem-solving approach to history. As we
see in a later chapter, quantification assisted the identification of
important causal factors, and led to a more narrowly focused *Annales*
group. Computerization of data also meant that large projects could
be tackled by groups of historians, and a number of collaborative
programmes originated in the laboratories of the Sixième Section.[23]

The move to quantification has had its detractors, one recent reviewer
reporting that the 1960s *Annales* group were seen as 'naive positivists'
who 'claim[ed] that only those things which can be counted are worth
studying'.[24] Another remarked that the 'fascination with hard data . . .
has relieved *Annales* historians of the task of critically confronting past
and present'.[25] He alludes here both to the descriptive rather than
analytic nature of some research, and to the unveiling of structures
rather than the explanation of historical change. It is true that at times
numbers seem to rob history of its humanity, in the sense that we
study groups rather than individuals, and thus inevitably omit detail.
This is, however, by no means invariably the case. Goubert, for
example, studied demographic data for the Beauvais region in the
seventeenth and eighteenth centuries. His analysis extended beyond
the statistical, and showed that female fertility not only followed
biological cycles, but differed according to region, reflecting the
varying impact of religious sexual ethics.[26] Iggers argues that here
Goubert was linking mental structures with biological processes, whose

effects on populations in turn brought about economic change.[27] The human is thus to the forefront in Goubert's account.

Nevertheless, from the 1970s the *Annales* changed direction again. Le Goff summed up the mood of the turn away from the quantitative in his allusion to the 'imperialistic designs of economic history'.[28] Replacing the claims to objective scientific history was a new and more subjective interpretation of the collective thought structures or mind-sets of the past. We can see links here both to the structuralism of Lévi-Strauss and to the twentieth century's interest in psychology.

The study of *mentalités*, as it was called, foregrounded ordinary people's own experience of their lives and sought to display the inner workings of society. One famous example of the history of *mentalité* was Emmanuel Le Roy Ladurie's *Montaillou*. Using a cache of inquisitorial records, Le Roy Ladurie reconstructed the households of the medieval village of Montaillou, and discussed the villagers' views on love, sex, religion, death, work and magic. The first section, on the 'ecology' of Montaillou, provided the material setting for individuals who speak to the reader seemingly in their own words, straight from the trial documents. In one sense, this is a return to Braudel's *longue durée* but with the added dimension of mental structures. In another, it overturns any ecological determinism, demonstrating the historical agency of people, both of fourteenth-century peasants and of the bishop who ordered their arrest.[29]

Georges Duby, using an entirely different source, examined *mentalité* through an analysis of medieval art and architecture. Arguing that the period 980 to 1420 encompassed a move from the primacy of monasteries to cathedrals and finally to palaces as community nexuses, Duby shows the effects of urbanization and cultural expansion on people's attitudes to power, money, education, gender and, above all, personal salvation.[30]

The study of *mentalités* has been viewed as the *Annales* means of addressing the objectivity-subjectivity dilemma which historians continually confront. Burguière remarked that '[t]he study of *mentalités* is the surest way of avoiding anachronism, that is, the absence of distance, the loss of the meaning of change and of what is relative that affects our reasoning when we project our own categories onto another epoch'.[31] However, if a knowledge of *mentalités* is to help us explain past human behaviour, rational and irrational, especially collective but also individual, the *Annales* historians may have to explore further, 'to trace these states back to their roots in the unconscious mind'. When these words were published in 1985, Gay accused the *Annales* school of 'stop[ping] short'. He did, however, consider some of the work of Le Roy Ladurie, Alain Besançon and Le Goff to be exceptional in this regard.[32]

The changes from the 1970s did not herald a complete break with the *Annales* past. There are clear links between the study of *mentalités* and the interests pursued by Febvre and Bloch, for example, while others returned to earlier themes. Le Roy Ladurie's study of climate supplemented Braudel's geology, and Duby used an event, the battle of Bouvines, as a window onto both medieval warfare and early thirteenth-century French politics.[33]

There may now be a fourth generation of *Annales* scholars, more historiographically diverse than previously. Iggers links this new group with the 1994 change in the journal title to *Annales: Histoire, Sciences Sociales*.[34] The parameters of this trend are not yet clear, however.

As well as specific criticisms of the *Annales* works, more general comments have been made. The lack of a meta-narrative for historical change, mentioned above in reference to Braudel, has been levelled at the *Annales* as a whole and is the criticism most difficult to refute. It follows that, while the *Annales* methods have been applied very successfully to pre-industrial societies, they generally have not been and perhaps cannot be used to interrogate faster-paced modern societies where change is quick and sometimes of paramount historical importance. Recently some *Annales* historians have studied the modern period and times of sudden change: Marc Ferro, for example, worked on revolutionary Russia.[35] Nonetheless, the tension between structures and events, quantification and *mentalités*, remains.

Another blind spot in the *Annales* programme is gender. While both men and women are discussed in some *Annales* work, women are frequently ignored and gender as an analytical category is not used, despite the possibility of including patriarchal values as part of the *longue durée*. This gap has at least been addressed, however, with the recent publication of the multi-volume *A History of Women*, jointly edited by Duby and Michèle Perrot, although Huppert sees this series as 'mediocre' compared to other more serious and ground-breaking work.[36]

This discussion has been confined to the work of French historians, but the influence of the *Annales* has been widespread, at least since the rapid translation of their work into English in the 1970s. Hobsbawm argued that Cambridge historians were reading the *Annales* in the 1930s, the impact of the French mainly deriving from economic and social history. Huppert recalls discussion of the journal in the United States in the late 1950s, while Iggers refers to their widespread European influence. In 1978, Immanuel Wallerstein founded the Fernand Braudel center at SUNY, which produces its own *Annales*-oriented journal. Consequently, the *Annales* has been described as 'ferociously, aggressively global in scope, both in its recruitment of contributors and in its choice of topics to pursue'.[37]

Overall, the *Annales* historians' search for underlying structures, their attempt at total history and their use of the methods and subjects of the social sciences has led to a great expansion of the subjects of history. Likewise, with their examination of *mentalité*, they have furnished the historical profession with a new mode of reconstructing the past. Difficulties remain with the *Annales* historians' attempt to combine scientific history and historicism (the determination to see the past in its own terms). Nevertheless, twentieth-century historiography has been tremendously stimulated by Bloch and Febvre's expansive vision coupled with Braudel's passionate and courageous leadership.

Throughout his life, Braudel remained committed to exposing the big picture. So, for example, *Civilization and Capitalism* is a synthesis of primary and secondary material, especially quantitative data, tackling that large question, how and why did the modern world develop In the following extract from the *longue durée* section of *The Mediterranean*, we meet the mountains and hear their story. Here Braudel is at his best while still posing problems for many historians. What is the range of historical topics included in this extract? Braudel connects the environment with what we now label *mentalités*: the physical barrier of the mountains is 'an obstacle, and therefore also a refuge'. Find examples of the way in which Braudel links geography with society and culture. Consider his picturesque language. Here he imbues the mountain people with particular character traits through a vivid visual image. What might be the consequences of this practice for his readers?

Braudel's copious notes refer to archival evidence from the 1500s, references to literature from the succeeding centuries and even a 1963 film. Why do many historians find this disquieting? Braudel has also been accused of substituting description for explanation, for example, when he says 'it was above all for the simple reason that mountains are mountains'. Find some other examples of these kinds of statements, and consider them in the light of other types of historical explanation with which you are familiar.

Notes

1 Jean Glénisson, 'France', trans. John Day, in Georg G. Iggers and Harold T. Parker (eds), *International Handbook of Historical Studies: Contemporary Research and Theory* (Westport, Conn., 1979), p. 176.
2 See Peter Burke, *The French Historical Revolution: The Annales School, 1929–89* (Cambridge, 1990), ch. 1, for a discussion of the various resistances to political history. Burke also mentions the idea of three 'generations' of *Annales* historians.
3 Burke, *French Historical Revolution*, pp. 13–14; Lucien Febvre, *The Problem of Unbelief in the Sixteenth Century: The Religion of Rabelais*, trans. Beatrice Gottlieb (Cambridge, Mass., [1942] 1982).
4 Marc Bloch, *Feudal Society*, trans. L. A. Manyon, 2 vols (London, [1940] 1961).
5 Bloch, *The Royal Touch: Sacred Monarchy and Scrofula in England and France*, trans. J. E. Anderson (London, [1924] 1973).
6 See François Dosse, *New History in France: The Triumph of the Annales*, trans. Peter V. Conroy Jr. (Urbana, Ill., [1987] 1994), chs 1 and 2.
7 Fernand Braudel, *The Mediterranean and the Mediterranean World in the Age of Philip II*, trans. Siân Reynolds, 2 vols (London, [1949] 1975).
8 *Ibid.*, pp. 20–1.
9 They both taught in Brazil in the 1930s, for example, and may have influenced each other. However, Lévi-Strauss's important book on myth where he laid out his theory of structural anthropology was not published until 1955, well after Braudel's thesis.
10 See Howard Gardner, *The Quest for Mind: Piaget, Lévi-Strauss and the Structuralist Movement* (New York, 1972), ch. 2.
11 Edith Kurzweil, *The Age of Structuralism: Lévi-Strauss to Foucault* (New York, 1980), p. 1.
12 Braudel, *The Mediterranean*, pp. 17, 168–70, 360.
13 *Ibid.*, pp. 17, 1238, 1244.
14 For praise, see, for example, Febvre, 'On livre qui grandit: La Méditerranée . . .', *Revue Historique*, 203 (1950), pp. 216–24; J. H. Elliott, 'Mediterranean Mysteries', *New York Review of Books*, May 3 1973, pp. 25–8.
15 J. H. Hexter, 'Fernand Braudel and the *Monde Braudellien*', *Journal of Modern History*, 44 (1972), pp. 519–20, 530; Peter Burke, 'Fernand Braudel', in John Cannon (ed.), *The Historian at Work* (London, 1980), pp. 196–7; Traian Stoianovich, *French Historical Method: The Annales Paradigm* (Ithaca, 1976), ch. 4.
16 Bernard Bailyn, 'Braudel's Geohistory – A Reconsideration', *Journal of Economic History*, 11 (1951), p. 279; Jacques Le Goff, 'Is Politics Still the Backbone of History?', trans. B. Bray, *Daedalus* 100 (1971), p. 4.
17 Hexter, 'Fernand Braudel', p. 533.
18 See, however, Kinser's balanced discussion of these issues in '*Annaliste* Paradigm? The Geohistorical Structuralism of Fernand Braudel', *American Historical Review*, 86 (1981), pp. 63–105.
19 See Hexter, 'Fernand Braudel' for an appraisal of Braudel's role in the development of French scholarship.
20 Georg G. Iggers, *New Directions in European Historiography* (Middletown, Conn., 1975), p. 61.
21 For example, Braudel, *Capitalism and Material Life 1400–1800*, trans. Miriam Kochan (London, [1967] 1973); Pierre Goubert, *Beauvais et le Beauvaisis de 1600 à 1730, contribution à histoire sociale de la France du XVIIe siècle* (Paris, 1960); Georges Duby, *La Société aux XIe et XIIe siècles dans la région mâconnaise* (Paris, 1953).

22 P. and H. Chaunu, *Séville et l'Atlantique* (Paris, 1955–60), 12 vols. See also discussion in Burke, *French Historical Revolution*, p. 56.
23 See Hexter, 'Fernand Braudel', pp. 491–2, and Emmanuel Le Roy Ladurie, *The Territory of the Historian*, trans. Ben and Siân Reynolds (Hassocks, Sussex, [1973] 1979), pp. 27–31.
24 George Huppert, 'The *Annales* Experiment', in Michael Bentley (ed.), *Companion to Historiography* (London, 1997), p. 880.
25 Iggers, *New Directions*, p. 75.
26 Discussed in Iggers, *New Directions*, pp. 63–4.
27 *Ibid.*, p. 63.
28 Quoted in Glénisson, 'France', p. 181.
29 Emmanuel Le Roy Ladurie, *Montaillou: Cathars and Catholics in a French Village 1294–1324*, trans. Barbara Bray (Harmondsworth, [1978] 1981). Note that Braudel later included mental frameworks in the *longue durée*: 'History and the Social Sciences: The *Longue Durée*', in *On History*, trans. Sarah Matthews (Chicago, [1969] 1980), p. 31.
30 Georges Duby, *The Age of the Cathedrals: Art and Society 980–1420*, trans. Eleanor Levieux and Barbara Thompson (rev. edn, Chicago, [1976] 1981).
31 André Burguière, 'The Fate of the History of *Mentalités* in the *Annales*', *Comparative Studies in Society and History*, 24, 3 (1982), p. 430.
32 Peter Gay, *Freud for Historians* (New York, 1985), pp. 119, 209.
33 Le Roy Ladurie, *Times of Feast, Times of Famine: A History of Climate since the Year 1000*, trans. Barbara Bray (New York, [1967] 1971); Georges Duby, *The Legend of Bouvines: War, Religion and Culture in the Middle Ages*, trans. Catherine Tihanyi (Cambridge, [1973] 1990).
34 Georg G. Iggers, *Historiography in the Twentieth Century: From Scientific Objectivity to the Postmodern Challenge* (Hanover, N. H., 1997), pp. 61–2.
35 Marc Ferro, *The Russian Revolution of February 1917*, trans. J. L. Richards (London, 1972). Note Iggers' discussion of other work concerning the modern period in *Historiography in the Twentieth Century*, p. 62.
36 Natalie Zemon Davis, 'Women and the World of the *Annales*', *History Workshop Journal*, 33 (1992), pp. 212–37. See brief discussion in Burke, *French Historical Revolution*, pp. 65–6, and Huppert, '*Annales* Experiment', p. 874, n. 5.
37 Eric Hobsbawm, 'British History and the *Annales*: A Note' [1978], rep. in *On History* (London, 1997), pp. 178–9; Huppert, '*Annales* Experiment', p. 875; Iggers, *Historiography in the Twentieth Century*, pp. 62–3. See *Review: A Journal of the Fernand Braudel Center for the Study of Economies, Historical Systems, and Civilizations*, and also Burke, *French Historical Revolution*, ch. 5, and Miri Rubin (ed.), *The Work of Jacques Le Goff and the Challenges of Medieval History* (Woodbridge, 1997) for an extensive discussion of the *Annales*' influence.

Additional reading

Braudel, Fernand, *On History*, trans. Sarah Matthews (Chicago, [1969] 1980).

Braudel, Fernand, *The Mediterranean and the Mediterranean World in the Age of Philip II*, trans. Siân Reynolds, 2 vols (London, [1949] 1975).

Burke, Peter, *The French Historical Revolution: The Annales School, 1929–89* (Cambridge, 1990).

Dosse, François, *New History in France: The Triumph of the Annales*, trans. Peter V. Conroy Jr. (Urbana, Ill., [1987] 1994).

Duby, Georges, *The Three Orders: Feudal Society Imagined*, trans. Arthur Goldhammer (Chicago, [1978] 1980).

Forster, Robert and Orest Ranum (eds), *Deviants and the Abandoned in French Society: Selections from the Annales: économies, sociétés, civilisations 4*, trans. Elborg Forster and Patricia M. Ranum (Baltimore, 1978).

Hexter, J. H., 'Fernand Braudel and the *Monde Braudellien'*, *Journal of Modern History*, 44 (1972), pp. 480–539.

Hunt, Lynn, 'French History in the Last Twenty Years: The Rise and Fall of the *Annales* Paradigm', *Journal of Contemporary History*, 21 (1986), pp. 209–24.

Le Goff, Jacques, *The Birth of Purgatory*, trans. Arthur Goldhammer (Chicago, [1981] 1984).

Le Roy Ladurie, Emmanuel, *Carnival in Romans: A People's Uprising at Romans 1579–1580*, trans. Mary Feeney (New York, 1979).

Le Roy Ladurie, Emmanuel, *The Mind and Method of the Historian*, trans. Siân Reynolds and Ben Reynolds (Chicago, [1978] 1981).

Review: A Journal of the Fernand Braudel Center for the Study of Economies, Historical Systems, and Civilizations, vol. 1 (1978).

Stoianovich, Traian, *French Historical Method: The Annales Paradigm* (Ithaca, 1976).

THE MEDITERRANEAN AND THE
MEDITERRANEAN WORLD IN THE
AGE OF PHILIP II
Fernand Braudel

Mountain freedom[1]

There can be no doubt that the lowland, urban civilization penetrated to the highland world very imperfectly and at a very slow rate.
This was as true of other things as it was of Christianity. The feudal
system as a political, economic, and social system, and as an instrument of justice failed to catch in its toils most of the mountain
regions and those it did reach it only partially influenced. The resistance of the Corsican and Sardinian mountains to lowland influence
has often been noted and further evidence could be found in Lunigiana, regarded by Italian historians as a kind of mainland Corsica,
between Tuscany and Liguria.[2] The observation could be confirmed
anywhere where the population is so inadequate, thinly distributed,
and widely dispersed as to prevent the establishment of the state,
dominant languages, and important civilizations.

A study of the vendetta would lead one towards a similar conclusion. The countries where the vendetta was in force—and they were
all mountainous countries—were those that had not been moulded
and penetrated by mediæval concepts of feudal justice,[3] the Berber

---

[1] As observed by contemporaries; Loys Le Roy, *De l'excellence du gouvernement royal*,
Paris, 1575, p. 37, writes 'A country covered with mountains, rocks, and forests, fit only
for pasture, where there are many poor men, as is most of Switzerland, is best suited for
democracy . . . The lands of the plain, where there are greater numbers of rich and noble
men, are better suited to an aristocratic form of government'. Jean Bodin, in *Les six livres
de la République* (English translation, *The Six Books of the Commonwealth*, by Knolles, 1606,
facs. edition Harvard, 1962, p. 694) reports that Leo Africanus was astonished by the
robust physique of the mountain folk of Mount Megeza, while the plain-dwellers were
smaller men. 'This force and vigour doth cause the mountaineers to love popular liberty
. . . as we have said of the Swissers and Grisons'. The Midlle Ages in Corsica, says Lorenzi
de Bradi, *La Corse inconnue*, 1927, p. 35, were a great period for liberty. 'The Corsican
would not suffer any man to rob him of the product of his labour. The milk from his
goat and the harvest from his field were his alone.' And H. Taine in his *Voyage aux
Pyrénées*, 1858, p. 138, says 'freedom took root here deep in the past, a gruff and wild
sort of freedom'.

[2] Arrigo Solmi, 'La Corsica' in *Arch. st. di Corsica*, 1925, p. 32.

[3] For a general picture, see the penetrating but legalistic work by Jacques Lambert, *La
vengeance privée et les fondements du droit international*, Paris, 1936. In the same order of

countries, Corsica, and Albania, for example. Marc Bloch,[4] writing about studies of Sardinia, points out that during the Middle Ages the island was an 'extensively manorialized, but not feudalized society' as a result of having been 'long isolated from the great currents which swept the continent'. This is putting the accent on the insularity of Sardinia, and it is quite true that it has been a decisive factor in Sardinian history. But the mountains are an equally important factor, just as responsible for the isolation of the people of Sardinia as the sea, if not more so; even in our own time they have produced those cruel and romantic outlaws, at Orgosolo and elsewhere, in revolt against the establishment of the modern state and its *carabinieri*. This moving phenomenon has been portrayed by anthropologists and film directors. 'He who does not steal', says a character in a Sardinian novel, 'is not a man'.[5] 'Law?' says another, 'I make my own laws and I take what I need.'[6]

In Sardinia, as in Lunigiana and Calabria, and everywhere where observation (when it is possible) reveals a hiatus between the society and the broad movements of history—if social archaisms (the vendetta among others) persisted, it was above all for the simple reason that mountains are mountains: that is, primarily an obstacle, and therefore also a refuge, a land of the free. For there men can live out of reach of the pressures and tyrannies of civilization: its social and political order, its monetary economy. Here there was no landed nobility with strong and powerful roots (the 'lords of the Atlas' created by the Maghzen were of recent origin); in the sixteenth century in Haute-Provence, the country nobleman, the *'cavaier salvatje'*, lived alongside his peasants, cleared the land as they did, did not scorn to plough and till the ground, or to carry wood and dung on the back of his donkey. He was a constant irritation 'in the eyes of the Provençal nobility, who are essentially city-dwellers like the

ideas, cf. Michelet's remark on the Dauphiné, where 'feudalism (never) exerted the same influence as it did upon the rest of France.' And Taine again: *op. cit.*, p. 138, 'These are the *fors* of Béarn, in which it is said that in Béarn in the old days there was no *seigneur'*. On blood feuds in Montenegro and upper Albania, see Ami Boué, *La Turquie d'Europe*, Paris, 1840, II, p. 395 and 523.

[4] Marc Bloch, *Feudal Society*, (trans. L. Manyon), London, 1961, p. 247. See also his useful remarks on Sardinia, 'La Sardaigne' in *Mélanges d'histoire sociale*, III, p. 94.

[5] Maurice Le Lannou, 'Le bandit d'Orgosolo', *Le Monde*, 16/17 June, 1963. The film was directed by Vittorio de Seta, the anthropological study carried out by Franco Caguetta, French transl.: *Les Bandits d'Orgosolo*, 1963; the novels mentioned are by Grazia Deledda, *La via del male*, Rome, 1896; *Il Dio dei viventi*, Rome, 1922.

[6] *Ibid.*

Italians'.[7] Here there were no rich, well-fed clergy to be envied and mocked; the priest was as poor as his flock.[8] There was no tight urban network so no administration, no towns in the proper sense of the word, and no gendarmes either we might add. It is only in the low-lands that one finds a close-knit, stifling society, a prebendal clergy, a haughty aristocracy, and an efficient system of justice. The hills were the refuge of liberty, democracy, and peasant 'republics'.

'The steepest places have been at all times the asylum of liberty', writes the learned Baron de Tott in his *Memoirs*.[9] 'In travelling along the coast of Syria, we see despotism extending itself over all the flat country and its progress stopt towards the mountains, at the first rock, at the first defile, that is easy of defence; whilst the Curdi, the Drusi, and the Mutuali, masters of the Lebanon and Anti-Lebanon, constantly preserve their independence'[10]. A poor thing was Turkish despotism—ruler indeed of the roads, passes, towns, and plains, but what can it have meant in the Balkan highlands, or in Greece and Epirus, in the mountains of Crete where the Skafiotes defied, from their hilltops, all authority from the seventeenth century onward, or in the Albanian hills, where, much later, lived 'Alī Pasha Tepedelenlī? Did the Wali Bey, installed at Monastir by the Turkish conquest of the fifteenth century, ever really govern? In theory his authority extended to the Greek and Albanian hill-villages, but each one was a fortress, an independent enclave and on occasion could become a hornets' nest.[11] It is hardly surprising, then, that the Abruzzi, the highest, widest, and wildest part of the Apennines, should have escaped Byzantine rule, the rule of the Exarchs of Ravenna, and finally the domination of Papal Rome, although the Abruzzi lie directly behind the city and the Papal State ran north through Umbria as far as the Po valley.[12] Nor is it astonishing that in Morocco the *bled es siba*, lands unsubdued by the sultan, should be essentially mountain regions.[13]

[7] Fernand Benoit, *La Provence et le Comtat Venaissin*, 1949, p. 27.

[8] For the high Milanese, see S. Pugliese, 'Condizioni economiche e finanziarie della Lombardia nella prima meta del secolo XVIII' in *Misc. di Storia italiana*, 3rd series, vol. xxi, 1924.

[9] *Mémoires sur les Turcs et les Tartares* (Eng. trans. *Memoirs of the Baron de Tott on the Turks and Tartars* . . . London 1785, I, p. 398): 'asylum of liberty, or,' he adds, 'the haunt of tyrants.' This was in connection with the Genoese installations in the Crimea.

[10] *Ibid.*, Preliminary Discourse, I, 11.

[11] Cf. Franz Spunda in Werner Benndorf, *Das Mittelmeerbuch*. 1940, pp. 209–210.

[12] A. Philippson, 'Umbrien und Etrurien', in *Geogr. Zeitung*, 1933, p. 452.

[13] Further examples: Napoleon was unable to control the mountains round Genoa, a refuge for deserters, in spite of the searches organized (Jean Borel, *Gênes sous Napoléon*

Sometimes this freedom of the hills has survived into our own time and can be seen today in spite of the immense weight of modern administration. In the Moroccan High Atlas, notes Robert Montagne,[14] 'the villages which are ranged along the sunny banks of the mountain torrents, near immense walnut trees watered by the turbulent Atlas streams, have no *chikhs'* or *Khalifats'* houses. It is impossible to distinguish between a poor man's house and a rich man's. Each of these little mountain cantons forms a separate state, administered by a council. The village elders, all clad alike in brown wool garments, meet on a terrace and discuss for hours on end the interests of the village. No one raises his voice and it is impossible from watching them to discover which is their president.' All this is preserved, if the mountain canton is sufficiently high and sufficiently inaccessible, away from the main roads, which is a rare case today but was less so in former times before the expansion of road systems. This is why the Nurra, although connected to the rest of the island of Sardinia by an easily accessible plain, remained for a long time out of the reach of roads and traffic. The following legend was inscribed on an eighteenth century map by the Piedmontese engineers: 'Nurra, unconquered peoples, who pay no taxes'![15]

The mountains' resources: an assessment

As we have seen, the mountains resist the march of history, with its blessings and its burdens, or they accept it only with reluctance. And yet life sees to it that there is constant contact between the hill population and the lowlands. None of the Mediterranean ranges resembles the impenetrable mountains to be found in the Far East, in China, Japan, Indochina, India, and as far as the Malaya peninsula.[16] Since they have no communication with sea-level civilization, the communities found there are autonomous. The Mediterranean

---

Ier, 2nd ed. 1929, p. 103). In about 1828, the Turkish police were powerless to prevent outbreaks of brigandage by the peoples of Mt. Ararat (Comte de Sercey, *op. cit.*, p. 95); they seem to be equally unsuccessful today in protecting the mountain's forest wealth from the ravages of the flocks (Hermann Wenzel, 'Agrargeographische Wandlungen in der Türkei', in *Geogr. Zeitschr.* 1937, p. 407). Similarly in Morocco: 'In reality, in southern Morocco, the sultan's authority did not reach beyond the plain', writes R. Montagne, *op. cit.*, p. 134.

[14] *Ibid.*, p. 131.

[15] M. Le. Lannou, *Pâtres et paysans de la Sardaigne*, 1941, p. 14, n. 1.

[16] J. Blache, *op. cit.*, p. 12. On this contrast see Pierre Gourou, *L'homme et la terre en Extrême-Orient*, 1940, and the review of the same book by Lucien Febvre in: *Annales d'hist. sociale*, XIII, 1941, p. 73. P. Vidal de la Blache, *op. cit.*, Eng. trans. pp. 371–2.

mountains, on the other hand, are accessible by roads. The roads may be steep, winding, and full of potholes, but they are passable on foot. They are a 'kind of extension of the plain' and its power through the hill country.[17] Along these roads the sultan of Morocco sent his *harkas*, Rome sent its legionaries, the king of Spain his *tercios*, and the Church its missionaries and travelling preachers.[18]

Indeed, Mediterranean life is such a powerful force that when compelled by necessity it can break through the obstacles imposed by hostile terrain. Out of the twenty-three passes in the Alps proper, seventeen were already in use at the time of the Romans.[19] Moreover, the mountains are frequently overpopulated—or at any rate over-populated in relation to their resources. The optimum level of population is quickly reached and exceeded; periodically the overflow has to be sent down to the plains.

Not that their resources are negligible: every mountain has some arable land, in the valleys or on the terraces cut out of the hillside. Here and there among the infertile limestone are strips of flysch (a mixture of slate, marls, and sandstone) and marls on which wheat, rye, and barley can be grown. Sometimes the soil is fertile: Spoleto lies in the middle of a fairly wide and comparatively rich plain, and Aquila in the Abruzzi grows saffron. The further south one goes, the higher is the upper limit for the cultivation of crops and usable trees. In the northern Apennines today, chestnut trees grow as far up as 900 metres; at Aquila, wheat and barley are found up to 1,680 metres; at Cozenza, maize, a new arrival in the sixteenth century, grows at 1,400 metres, and oats at 1,500 metres; on the slopes of Mount Etna, vines are grown up to a level of 1,100 metres and chestnut trees at 1,500 metres.[20] In Greece wheat is grown up to a level of 1,500 metres and vines up to 1,250 metres.[21] In North Africa the limits are even higher.

[17] R. Montagne, *op. cit.*, p. 17.

[18] I am thinking in particular of the travels of Sixtus V, in his youth and middle age, as described by Ludwig von Pastor, *Geschichte der Papste*, Freiburg-im-Breisgau, 1901–31, X, 1913, p. 23 and 59. They would make a good map.

[19] W. Woodburn Hyde, 'Roman Alpine routes', in *Memoirs of the American philosophical society*, Philadelphia, X, II, 1935. Similarly the Pyrenees have not always been the barrier one might imagine (M. Sorre, *Géog. univ.*, vol. VII, 1st part, p. 70; R. Konetzke, *op. cit.*, p. 9).

[20] Richard Pfalz, 'Neue wirtschaftsgeographische Fragen Italiens', in *Geogr. Zeitschr.*, 1931, p. 133.

[21] A. Philippson, *Das Mittelmeergebiet, op. cit.*, p. 167.

One of the advantages of the mountain region is that it offers a variety of resources, from the olive trees, orange trees, and mulberry trees of the lower slopes to the forests and pasturelands higher up. To the yield from crops can be added the produce of stockraising. Sheep and goats are raised, as well as cattle. In comparatively greater numbers than today, they used to be plentiful in the Balkans, and even in Italy and North Africa. As a result, the mountains are a source of milk, cheeses[22] (Sardinian cheese was exported in boatloads all over the western Mediterranean in the sixteenth century), butter, fresh or rancid, and boiled or roasted meat. The typical mountain house was a shepherd's or herdsman's dwelling, built for animals rather than for human beings.[23] In 1574, Pierre Lescalopier, when crossing the Bulgarian mountains, preferred to sleep 'under some tree' than in the peasants' huts of beaten clay where beasts and humans lived 'under one roof, and in such filth that we could not bear the stench'.[24]

The forests in those days, it should be pointed out, were thicker than they are today.[25] They can be imagined as something like the National Park of the Val di Corte, in the Abruzzi, with its thick beechwoods climbing up to 1,400 metres. The population of the forests included foxes, wolves, bears, and wildcats. The Monte Gargano's oak forests supported a whole population of woodcutters and timber merchants, for the most part in the service of the shipyards of Ragusa. Like the summer pastures, the forests were the subject of much dispute among mountain villages and against noble landowners. Even the scrubland, half forest, can be used for grazing, and sometimes for gardens and orchards; it also supports game and bees.[26] Other advantages of the mountains are the profusion of springs, plentiful water, that is so precious in these southern

---

[22] Victor Bérard, *La Turquie et l'hellénisme contemporain, op. cit.*, p. 103, writes on leaving Albania: 'After three days of goat cheese . . .'.

[23] P. Arqué, *op. cit.*, p. 68.

[24] *Op. cit.*, f° 44 and 44 v°.

[25] There used to be forests on the slopes of Mount Vesuvius. On the forests in general, the observations of Theobald Fischer are still useful (in *B. zur physischen Geogr. der Mittelmeerländer besonders Siciliens*, 1877, pp. 155 ff.) On the forests of Naples, Calabria and the Basilicata, in 1558, cf. Eugenio Albèri, *Relazioni degli ambasciatori veneti durante il secolo XVI*, Florence, 1839–63, II, III, p. 271. Even today there are many remains of the great forests of the past, forest ruins. They are listed for Corsica in Philippe Leca (preface by A. Albitreccia) *Guide blue de la Corse*, Paris, 1935, p. 15; See also the latter's *La Corse, son évolution au XIXe siècle et au début du XXe siècle*, 1942, pp. 95 ff.

[26] Comte Joseph de Bradi, *Mémoire sur la Corse*, 1819, pp. 187, 195 ff.

countries, and, finally, mines and quarries. Almost all the mineral resources of the Mediterranean, in fact, are found in its mountain regions.

But these advantages are not all found in every region. There are chestnut tree mountains (the Cévennes, Corsica) with their precious 'tree bread',[27] made from chestnuts, which can replace wheat bread if necessary. There are mulberry tree mountains like those Montaigne saw near Lucca in 1581,[28] or the highlands of Granada. 'These people, the people of Granada, are not dangerous', explained the Spanish agent, Francisco Gasparo Corso, to Euldj 'Alī, 'King' of Algiers in 1569.[29] 'What could they do to injure the Catholic King? They are unused to arms. All their lives they have done nothing but dig the ground, watch their flocks, and raise silkworms. . . .' There are also the walnut tree mountains: it is under the century-old walnut trees that even today, in the centre of the village, on moonlit nights, the Berbers of Morocco still celebrate their grand festivals of reconciliation.[30]

All told, the resources of the mountains are not as meagre as one might suppose. Life there is possible, but not easy. On the slopes where farm animals can hardly be used at all, the work is difficult. The stony fields must be cleared by hand, the earth has to be prevented from slipping down hill, and, if necessary, must be carried up to the hilltop and banked up with dry stone walls. It is painful work and never-ending; as soon as it stops, the mountain reverts to a wilderness and man must start from the beginning again. In the eighteenth century when the Catalan people took possession of the high rocky regions of the coastal massif, the first settlers were astonished to find dry stone walls and enormous olive trees still growing in the middle of the undergrowth, proof that this was not the first time that the land had been claimed.[31]

---

[27] P. Vidal de la Blache, *op. cit.* (Eng. trans.) pp. 141, 147, 221, 222. There are some excellent observations in D. Faucher, *Principes de géogr. agraire*, p. 23. 'The people eat bread from the trees', near Lucca, Montaigne, *Journal de voyage en Italie*, (ed. E. Pilon, 1932), p. 237.

[28] Montaigne, *ibid.*, p. 243.

[29] *Relacion de lo que yo Fco Gasparo Corso he hecho en prosecucion del negocio de Argel*, Simancas E° 333 (1569).

[30] R. Montagne, *op. cit.*, pp. 234–5.

[31] Franchesci Carreras y Candi, *Geografía general de Catalunya*, Barcelona, 1913, p. 505; Jaime Carrera Pujal, *H. política y económica de Cataluña*, vol. 1, p. 40. Similarly Belon, *op. cit.*, p. 140, v° notes that there had formerly been terraced fields, abandoned when he saw them, in the mountains round Jerusalem.

Mountain dwellers in the towns

It is this harsh life,[32] as well as poverty, the hope of an easier existence, the attraction of good wages, that encourages the mountain
people to go down to the plain: 'baixar sempre, mountar no', 'always
go down, never go up', says a Catalan proverb.[33] Although the mountain's resources are varied, they are always in short supply. When
the hive becomes too full,[34] there is not enough to go around and
the bees must swarm, whether peacefully or not. For survival, any
sacrifice is permitted. As in the Auvergne, and more especially as in
the Cantal in the recent past, all the extra mouths, men, children,
artisans, apprentices, and beggars are expelled.[35]

The history of the mountains is chequered and difficult to trace.
Not because of lack of documents; if anything there are too many.
Coming down from the mountain regions, where history is lost in
the mist, man enters in the plains and towns the domain of classified
archives. Whether a new arrival or a seasoned visitor, the mountain
dweller inevitably meets someone down below who will leave a
description of him, a more or less mocking sketch. Stendhal saw the
peasants from the Sabine hills at Rome on Ascension Day. 'They come
down from their mountains to celebrate the feast day at St. Peter's,
and to attend *la funzione*.[36] They wear ragged cloth cloaks, their legs
are wrapped in strips of material held in place with string cross-
gartered; their wild eyes peer from behind disordered black hair; they
hold to their chests hats made of felt, which the sun and rain have
left a reddish black colour; these peasants are accompanied by their
families, of equally wild aspect.[37] . . . The inhabitants of the mountains between Rome, Lake Turano, Aquila, and Ascoli, represent fairly
well, to my way of thinking,' Stendhal adds, 'the moral condition of

---

[32] Life in Haute-Provence for example: 'The farm of Haute-Provence' writes Marie
Mauron ('Le Mas provençal', in *Maisons et villages de France*, 1943, preface by R.
Cristoflour, p. 222) 'which endures long winters, fear of avalanches, and indoor life for
months on end, behind the snowy window panes with prospects confined to winter
rations, the cowshed, and fireside work'.

[33] Maximilien Sorre, *Les Pyrénées méditerranéennes*, 1913, p. 410.

[34] This surplus population which makes the move to the plains necessary is indicated
in the geographical survey by H. Wilhelmy, *Hochbulgarien*, 1936, p. 183. But there are
other motives: whether life is agreeable or not, for example, cf. A. Albitreccia in Philippe
Leca, *La Corse, op. cit.*, p. 129 who also notes of Corsica: 'in other places the presence of
roads encourages emigration; here their absence does so.'

[35] J. Blache, *op. cit.*, p. 88, according to Philippe Arbos, *L'Auvergne*, 1932, p. 86.

[36] The mass.

[37] *Promenades dans Rome*, ed. Le Divan, 1931, I, pp. 182–183.

Italy in about the year 1400'.[38] In Macedonia, in 1890, Victor Bérard met the eternal Albanian, in his picturesque cavalry soldier's costume.[39] In Madrid, Théophile Gautier came across water-sellers, 'young Galician *muchachos*, in tobacco-coloured jackets, short breeches, black gaiters and pointed hats'.[40] Were they already wearing this dress when they were to be found, both men and women, scattered all over sixteenth-century Spain in the *ventas* mentioned by Cervantes, along with their Asturian neighbours?[41] One of the latter, Diego Suárez, who was to become a soldier and chronicler of the events of Oran at the end of the sixteenth century, describes his own adventures, his escape, while still a child, from his father's house, his arrival at the builders' yards of the Escorial where he works for a while, finding the fare to his taste, *el plato bueno*. But some of his relatives, from the mountains of Oviedo, arrive in their turn, no doubt to find summer work on the farms of Old Castile, like so many others. And he has to move on so as not to be recognized.[42] The whole region of Old Castile was continually being crossed by immigrants from the mountains of the North who sometimes returned there. The Montaña, the continuation of the Pyrenees from Biscay to Galicia, provided little sustenance for its inhabitants. Many of them were *arrieros*, muleteers, like the Maragatos[43] whom we shall meet again, or the peasant-carriers from the *partido* of Reinosa, travelling south, their wagons laden with hoops and staves for casks, and returning to their northern towns and villages with wheat and wine.[44]

---

[38] *Ibid.*, p. 126. A similar picture, this time of the Caucasus, is to be found in *Souvenirs* of the Comte de Rochechouart, 1889, pp. 76–77, on the occasion of the capture of Anapa by the Duc de Richelieu: the Caucasian warriors, some clad in iron, armed with arrows, are reminiscent of the thirteenth or fourteenth century.

[39] Victor Bérard, *La Turquie et l'hellénisme contemporain, op. cit., passim.*

[40] *Voyage en Espagne*, 1845, pp. 65, 106. On the *gallegos*, both harvesters and emigrants, see *Los Españoles pintados por si mismos*, Madrid, 1843. This collection contains: *El Indiáno*, by Antonio Ferrer Del Rio, *El segador, El pastor trashumante* and *El maragato* by Gil y Curraso, *El aguador* by Aberramar.

[41] At Toledo, at the house of the Sevilian, there are two *mocetonas gallegas* (Galician girls) (*La ilustre fregona*). Galicians and Asturians do heavy work in Spain, especially in the mines: J. Chastenet, *Godoï*, 1943, p. 40. On *gallegos* as harvest workers in Castile in the eighteenth century, see Eugenio Larruga, *Memorias políticas y económicas sobre los frutos, comercio, fabricas y minas de España*, Madrid, 1745, I, p. 43.

[42] Diego Suárez, MS in the former *Gouvernement-Général* of Algeria, a copy of which was kindly passed on to me by Jean Casenave, f° 6.

[43] See below, p. 484.

[44] Jesús García Fernández, *Aspectos del paisaje agrario de Castilla la Vieja*, Valladolid, 1963, p. 12.

In fact, no Mediterranean region is without large numbers of mountain dwellers who are indispensable to the life of town and plains, striking people whose costume is often unusual and whose ways are always strange. Spoleto, whose high plain Montaigne passed through in 1581 on the way to Loreto, was the centre for a special kind of immigrant: pedlars and small traders who specialized in all the reselling and intermediary activities that call for middlemen, flair, and not too many scruples. Bandello describes them in one of his novellas as talkative, lively and self-assured, never short of arguments and persuasive whenever they want to be. There is nobody to beat the Spoletans, he says, for cheating a poor devil while calling the blessing of St. Paul upon him, making money out of grass-snakes and adders with drawn fangs, begging and singing in marketplaces, and selling bean meal as a remedy for mange. They travel all over Italy, baskets slung around their necks, shouting their wares.[45]

The people of the Bergamo Alps[46]—in Milan commonly known as the people of the *Contado*—are equally familiar in sixteenth-century Italy. They were everywhere. They worked as dockers in the ports, at Genoa and elsewhere. After Marignano, they came back to work the small-holdings of the Milanese, left abandoned during the war.[47] A few years later Cosimo de' Medici tried to attract them to Leghorn, the fever town where no one wanted to live. Rough men, clumsy, stocky, close-fisted, and willing for heavy labour, 'they go all over the world', says Bandello[48] (there was even an architect to be found working at the Escorial, Giovan Battista Castello, known as *el Bergamasco*[49]), 'but they will never spend more than four *quattrini* a day, and will not sleep on a bed but on straw'. When they made money they bought rich clothes and fed well, but were no more generous for it, nor any less vulgar and ridiculous. Real-life comedy characters,

---

[45] Matteo Bandello, *Novelle*, VII, pp. 200–201. Spoletans often served as soldiers, particularly in foreign armies, L. von Pastor, *op. cit.*, XVI, p. 267. On their cunning, see M. Bandello, *ibid.*, I. p. 418.

[46] M. Bandello, *op. cit.*, II, pp. 385–386. It was poverty which obliged the people of Bergamo to emigrate. Sober at home, they were said to be great eaters elsewhere. At least one native of Bergamo could be found in every place in the world. Most of the Venetian subjects in Naples were *Bergamaschi*, E. Albèri, *op. cit.*, Appendix, p. 351 (1597).

[47] Jacques Heers, *Gênes au XVe siècle. Activité économique et problèmes sociaux*, 1961, p. 19. M. Bandello, *op. cit.*, IV, p. 241. Similarly, after the restoration of Francesco Sforza, many peasants arrived in Milan from Brescia.

[48] *Op. cit.*, IX, pp. 337–338.

[49] L. Pfandl, *Philippe II*, French trans. 1942, pp. 353–354. Both the famous Colleoni and the Jesuit Jean-Pierre Maffei, the author of *L'histoire des Indes*, Lyons, 1603, came from Bergamo.

they were traditionally grotesque husbands whom their wives sent to *Corneto*: like the bumpkin in one of Bandello's novellas who has the excuse, if it is one, that he found his wife in Venice, among the women who sell love for a few coppers behind St. Mark's.[50]

The picture, as we see, quickly turns to caricature. The mountain dweller is apt to be the laughing stock of the superior inhabitants of the towns and plains. He is suspected, feared, and mocked. In the Ardèche, as late as 1850, the people from the *montagne* would come down to the plain for special occasions. They would arrive riding on harnessed mules, wearing grand ceremonial costumes, the women bedecked with jangling gold chains. The costumes themselves differed from those of the plain, although both were regional, and their archaic stiffness provoked the mirth of the village coquettes. The lowland peasant had nothing but sarcasm for the rude fellow from the highlands, and marriages between their families were rare.[51]

In this way a social and cultural barrier is raised to replace the imperfect geographical barrier which is always being broken in a variety of ways. It may be that the mountain dweller comes down with his flocks, one of the two annual movements of stock in search of pasture, or he may be hired in the lowlands at harvest time, and this is a seasonal emigration which is fairly frequent and much more widespread than is usually supposed: Savoyards[52] on their way to the lower Rhône valley, Pyrenean labourers hired for the harvest near Barcelona, or even Corsican peasants who regularly in summer, in the fifteenth century, crossed over to the Tuscan Maremma.[53] Or he may have settled permanently in the town, or as a peasant on the land of the plain: 'How many villages in Provence or even in the County of Avignon recall, with their steep, winding streets and tall houses, the little villages of the southern Alps'[54] from which their inhabitants originally came? Not so long ago, at harvest time the people from the mountains, young men and girls alike, would flock down as far as the plain and even the coast of lower Provence, where

[50] *Op. cit.*, IV, p. 335. He came from Brescia and had settled at Verona.

[51] Result of personal research. In fact, this opposition between highland and lowland is even more marked further north. Gaston Roupnel reports it in *Le vieux Garain*, 1939, on the Burgundy Côte, around Gevrey and Nuits-Saint-Georges. In 1870 the 'mountain folk' still wear smocks when they come to the lowland fairs.

[52] P. George, *La région du Bas-Rhône*, 1935, p. 300: mentions bands of Savoyards going to work at harvest time in the Arles region, in the first years of the seventeenth century.

[53] Grotanelli, *La Maremma toscana, Studi storici ed economici*, II, p. 19.

[54] P. George, *op. cit.*, p. 651.

the *gavot*, the man from Gap, which is really a generic name, is still known 'as typically a hard worker, careless of sartorial elegance, and used to coarse food'.[55]

A host of similar and even more striking observations could be made if one included the plains of Languedoc and the uninterrupted flow of immigrants coming to them from the North, from Dauphiné, and even more from the Massif Central, Rouergue, Limousin, Auvergne, Vivarais, Velay, and the Cévennes. This stream submerged lower Languedoc, but regularly went on beyond it towards wealthy Spain. The procession reformed every year, almost every day, and was made up of landless peasants, unemployed artisans, casual agricultural workers down for the harvest, the grape harvest, or threshing, outcasts of society, beggars and beggar-women, travelling preachers, *gyrovagues*—vagabonds—street musicians, and shepherds with their flocks. Mountain poverty was the great spur of this journey downwards. 'Behind this exodus', says one historian, 'there lies an obvious disparity of living standards, to the advantage of the Mediterranean plains.'[56] These beggars would arrive, set off again and die on the road or in the hospices, but in the long run they contributed to the human stock of the lowlands, so that for centuries there persisted the aberrant type, the man of the North, taller than average, with fair hair and blue eyes.

[55] Fernand Benoit, *op. cit.*, p. 23.
[56] Emmanuel Le Roy Ladurie, *op. cit.*, pp. 97 ff.

5

Historical sociology

In the late twentieth century, many theorists seem to agree that a sociology which explains as well as describes must be an historical sociology. Abrams went so far as to call historical sociology 'the essence of the discipline', arguing that it is 'almost natural to the modern western mind' to explain the contemporary world at least partly in historical terms.[1] What is historical sociology? Skocpol lists four characteristics of historical sociological studies:

1 'they ask questions about social structures or processes understood to be concretely situated in time and space';
2 'they address processes over time, and take temporal sequences seriously in accounting for outcomes';
3 they mostly 'attend to the interplay of meaningful actions and structural contexts, in order to make sense of the unfolding of unintended as well as intended outcomes in individual lives and social transformations';
4 they 'highlight the *particular* and *varying* features of specific kinds of social structures and patterns of change'.[2]

As well as the focus on active process, rather than a static model, historical sociology addresses directly the distinction between explanations based on structure and those based on agency. This is an issue at the core of controversy among most historical theorists as well as central to the ordering of most historical writing. Thus one might assume that the historical profession would welcome the insights of historical sociology. In fact this does not seem to be the case; a glance at lists of contributors to collections on historical sociology, at least those focusing upon theoretical and methodological considerations, shows that they tend to be employed by departments of sociology.

The term 'sociology' was coined in the mid-nineteenth century by Auguste Comte. Due perhaps to his training in the natural sciences, when Comte turned to the philosophy of history, he employed an evolutionary model of human development. Comte followed the inductive method, developing his general theories from empirical data, and was followed in this by the three social theorists whose work has been most influential in twentieth-century historical sociology. They are Marx, Weber and Durkheim.[3]

Like many sociologists and historians since, Marx, Weber and Durkheim were interested in the growth of capitalism and the transition to a modern industrialized society in Europe. Marx, with his associate Engels, looked at the process of class formation and the concomitant struggle between classes based on economic inequity. Weber examined the bureaucratization which went along with the transition to modernity, and the world view which fostered the growth of capitalism. And Durkheim investigated the social and moral disorder (anomie) which, he argued, accompanied the increasing specialization of labour during industrialization. While each of these writers developed large-scale explanatory theories, it is important to remember that they did not regard the kind of historical changes that they postulated as inevitable: although the circumstances which removed constraints to and even encouraged change might be present, this did not necessarily mean that the movement which they predicted would occur.

While this early theorizing took place in Europe and frequently in a university context, the main growth of sociology over the next fifty years occurred in the United States. In 1892, for example, the University of Chicago formed the first department of sociology. The new discipline tended to move away from the production of overarching historical theories, and focus on the socialization of individuals within the 'exceptional' climate of American democracy. Studies of the interaction of individuals led to an interest in social systems and how they work. This process of development in sociological thinking through the first half of the twentieth century culminated in the structural-functionalism of Talcott Parsons.

Parsons incorporated elements of the theories of each of Marx, Weber and Durkheim in his work, but in particular saw himself as carrying on the investigation into social action begun by Weber. He examined the function of various elements that structured a social system, and charted their interaction. His work also had its historical aspect: Parsons postulated an evolutionary system where the modern United States was the end product toward which all other economic, social and political systems progressed. Historical change occurred when solutions to functional problems within a given system were discovered, and so the system moved to a higher level of social organization. In practice, however, Parson's teleology broke down. Empirical evidence adduced by his critics did not support his claims: for example, developing countries did not all aspire to or work for evolution towards American-style capitalism. Thus the way was clear for a new empirically-based historical sociology.

In the United Kingdom, sociology tended to be linked with anthropology and was often functionalist; in addition radical theorists in various disciplines used Marx's work on class conflict as a base. In Europe, the Nazi movement was not sympathetic to sociology and so the earlier European developments in sociology were not continued. During the 1950s, however, throughout the Western world, a blending of the disciplines of history and sociology took place and historical sociology was established as a discipline. In 1958, for example, Sylvia Thrupp founded the journal *Comparative Studies in Society and History*, while the Past and Present society entitled their 1963 conference 'History, Sociology and Social Anthropology'.[4]

Historical sociology, both in its inception and during the last forty years, has tended to focus on several major topics. Probably the most developed of these areas has been the growth of modernity in all its guises. As mentioned above, Marx, Weber and Durkheim investigated various facets of capitalism and industrialization, and thus more recent scholars have often been writing in response to their work. We have already examined the influence of Marx in detail: here we will concentrate on Weber and his theories.[5]

Where Marx and Durkheim had seen the actions of an individual as largely determined by social structures, and therefore of little interest in themselves, Weber was interested in the meanings of action for an individual, and on a larger scale, in how the subjective world affected or even helped to implement societal change. He saw sociology and history as connected but separate enterprises: sociology formulated models or types and general rules or patterns of social events, whereas history 'aims at the causal analysis and causal attribution of individual actions, structures and personalities that have cultural significance'.[6] In both these fields he moved away from previous evolutionary models which tended to see historical change as a linear process, driven by one main causal engine. Weber's view of causation has thus been labelled 'multivocal' and 'polymorphous'. For example, he rejected the primacy of economics in historical processes, as postulated by Marx.[7]

As Abrams elaborates, '[f]or Weber the mere availability of capital and labour power, necessary as both were as preconditions for capitalism, could not in itself explain the actual growth of capitalism into a dominant economic and cultural order'. Weber argued this through a method of comparative history in what is probably his best known book, *The Protestant Ethic and the Spirit of Capitalism*. In this work, he juxtaposed Western Europe with other regions, for example, India and China, which also had the requirements for capitalism but where capitalism did not develop, and wondered what was different about the European situation.[8]

Weber saw the difference as the development of Occidental rationalism. Simply put, this rationalism was an offshoot of the ethos of Protestantism, where works were an important route to salvation, in contrast to the earlier more mystical Catholicism. Once rationalism, however, ceases to become the means to an end, but an end in itself, it is in fact a source of irrationality and lack of freedom, as values other than rational action disappear.[9]

The 'spirit' in the title of his book is 'a type of social action involving the rational calculative pursuit of profit-maximisation'. Weber has been accused of tautologous reasoning in this argument, with critics suggesting that the 'spirit of modern capitalism' is in fact no different from 'modern capitalism' itself. The spirit then is both the essence of capitalism and its cause. Holton, however, by reminding us of Weber's refusal of monocausality, argues that Weber did make the distinction, with the 'spirit' only one of many preconditions for the growth of capitalism.[10]

One of Weber's strengths from the modern historian's point of view was a belief in the scientific nature of history and the importance of evidence. However, his definition of the nature of historical evidence went further than, say, Ranke's: evidence can be 'either of a rational (logical, mathematical) or of an empathetic, emotional, artistic-receptive character'.[11] The multiplicity of possible evidence available to the historian assisted Weber to theorize the existence of four types of rationality (practical, theoretical, formal and substantive) and four types of social action (affectual, traditional, value-rational and means-end rational). Some but not all of these were linked. For example, Kalberg describes practical rationality as 'every way of life that views and judges worldly activity in relation to the individual's purely pragmatic and egoistic interests', which is therefore 'a manifestation of man's capacity for means-end rational action'.[12] It is clear that this breaking down of the category 'rationality' leads Weber away from any simplistic historical explanation to an extremely complex model.

Weber's similarly complex view of the workings of society led Collins to characterize him as a conflict sociologist along with Marx. While conflict is easily identified in Marx's discussion of class struggles, it is less obvious in Weber's work. Collins, however, argues that conflict is implicit in Weber's multidimensional view of society. If the world is made up of many spheres, there will probably be some consensus and solidarity, but conflict will definitely exist, both within and between spheres.[13] Overall Weber analysed the stratification of society in terms of three realms, class, status and party: each of these spheres struggles for dominance.[14]

Weber's model of social action has been influential in the twentieth century.[15] Recently, for example, Mann argued that societies and their histories were best described in terms of the interrelations of four sources of social power, ideological, economic, military and political relationships. These relationships are both individual and institutional. Very simply, in Mann's view, historical change occurs as humans in pursuit of their goals form social networks, which coalesce into the four spheres mentioned above. One of these spheres becomes institutionalized as the dominant power structure in a given area, and, in this context, further rival power networks form. Surrounding the process of change in the four major spheres are numerous other causal sequences which Mann sees as too complex to theorize. Using this model in the first two of three projected volumes, he discusses world history up to AD 1914 in great detail. Mann explicitly described his view of history as 'adhering to [Weber's] general vision of the relationship between society, history, and social action'.[16]

The nineteenth-century trend towards explaining the development of the modern world has been continued in the second half of the twentieth century. Some major historical sociologists in this area are S. N. Eisenstadt, Barrington Moore, Jr., W. W. Rostow, Immanuel Wallerstein, Perry Anderson, Reinhard Bendix and R. J. Holton.[17] Here we will discuss Wallerstein, an historical sociologist whose work, derived in part from Marxist theory, is influential in both the fields of global and postcolonial history.

Wallerstein began working as an Africanist, which led him to speculate more broadly on the reasons for the 'underdevelopment', continued poverty and rebellion in the non-Western world. Modernization theory,

which argued that all countries would gradually become rich and
technologically developed under liberal capitalism, seemed to be an
explanatory and predictive failure. In 1974, Wallerstein published *The
Modern World-System*, where he explained his observations in terms of
the economic system of development of the modern world. His
argument hinged around his assertion that, in about 1450, north-
western Europe was a little more technologically and organizationally
advanced than elsewhere, but, over the course of several centuries and
certainly by the present day, had become more highly developed due
to its exploitation of the non-Western peripheral countries by means of
an economic system organized on a world scale. Wallerstein divided
his world-system into three geographical areas, the capitalist core, the
semi-periphery and the peripheral areas. The peripheral zone supplied
primary resources to the core very cheaply due to coerced cheap
labour, and as the core became richer it could increase its economic
control over non-core regions. A particular economic and labour
structure characterized each zone, and within each, different versions
of a dominant class arose: the dominance of the capitalist core,
however, was paramount and it was able to manipulate the overall
economy with the assistance of extra-economic activities. In the face
of this deliberate and calculated exploitation, it was close to impossible
for the peripheral regions to develop dynamic economies and political
structures of their own.[18]

Wallerstein's thesis, predictably, has generated much controversy, not
least due to its explicitly political, even polemical, argument. There
seems to be general agreement that his work is groundbreaking, but
that, in Skocpol's words, '[l]ike many other important pioneering
works, . . . overreaches itself and falls short of its aims'.[19] The critiques
are variously historical, theoretical and methodological.

J. L. Anderson outlined three valuable aspects of Wallerstein's model.
Firstly, 'it directs attention to economically integrated and politically
connected systems as wholes, rather than simply to the separate
polities that are their parts'. Secondly, Wallerstein points to the
economic manipulation inherent in supposedly free trade, and, thirdly,
he shows how historical possibilities at any given time are dependent
on what has gone before.[20]

O'Brien criticized Wallerstein mainly on historical grounds, pointing to
important historical and statistical inaccuracies. He argues that in fact
the level of commerce between the core and the peripheral zones
during the period 1450 to 1750 was quite small and not a statistically

significant part of the explanation for the quickened rate of economic growth in the core after 1750. He also suggests that the idea of a 'world economy' in the sixteenth century is ahistorical.[21] Wesseling concurs, adding that the pre-industrial economy was not able to produce a surplus large enough to support Wallerstein's claims, and that anyway transportation systems were not sufficiently developed to service such an economy.[22] Skocpol also endorses this view when she suggests that Wallerstein often argues in an *a posteriori* way and tends to omit or dismiss as accidental historical data which does not support his theory.[23] In contrast, having seen Wallerstein's theories in action on a small scale in her own research, Thirsk finds his delineation of detail 'both accurate and sensitive'.[24]

Critics have also been unhappy with the way Wallerstein has modified Marxist theory. For example, Tilly suggests that Wallerstein's focus on relations of exchange rather than relations of production, and the consequent removal of the class confrontation which transforms the means of production, removes the historical dynamism from Marx's original thesis. Thus, Wallerstein does not explain how the capitalist system arose from feudalism and similarly cannot persuasively suggest how it might be superseded.[25] Similarly, Brenner critiqued 'Wallerstein's systematic refusal to integrate innovation and technical change as a regular feature of capitalist development'. Again this means a failure to examine the development of class structures and the productivity of labour as part of historical change.[26]

Despite, and perhaps because of, these and other criticisms, *The Modern World-System* has generated a new wave of historical sociology. Tilly commented on its similar usefulness for history: 'Wallerstein's special contribution is to propose a synthesis . . . between a well-known line of thought about the capitalist world-economy and Fernand Braudel's broad treatment of the entire Mediterranean world during the formative years of European capitalism as a single, interdependent system'.[27] And, as we saw in the *Annales* chapter, Wallerstein has opened a centre for the study of large-scale processes of historical sociology.

In addition to examining the development of the modern world, historical sociologists have been especially interested in revolutions and collective action. One of the most important theorists in this area is Charles Tilly. Hunt describes Tilly's basic agenda thus: 'How did collective action in Europe evolve under the influence of long-term structural transformations?' Tilly examines topics as varied as urbanization and the growth of capitalism, mainly through detailed historical investigations of particular rebellions, strikes and other collective activity. These projects have often used quantitative methods involving long periods, and Tilly 'bombard[s] the data bases with alternative causal hypotheses'. His work is particularly noteworthy for its dual approach – he is insistently both historian and sociologist – and as well as writing within each paradigm, he has tried to merge the two methodologies.[28]

Like Tilly, Theda Skocpol explicitly merges the disciplines of history and sociology in her book, *States and Social Revolutions: A Comparative Analysis of France, Russia and China*.[29] She studied three examples of a single type of revolution, each of which can be explained in a similar manner through a structuralist approach. As we see in the excerpt from her article which follows, Skocpol argues that 'social revolution [in France, China and Russia] was a conjuncture of three developments: (1) the collapse or incapacitation of central administrative and military machineries; (2) widespread peasant rebellions; and (3) marginal elite political movements'.[30]

We shall see some of the details of Skocpol's argument below; here we shall examine the responses to her book. For William Sewell, one of the strengths of Skocpol's work was her approach to the problem of multiple causation. He suggests that most analysts choose a prime cause, or try to convey the complexity of causation through a chronological narrative. These are not sufficiently analytical approaches, however, and he applauds Skocpol's explanation that these successful revolutions occurred at the conjuncture of three separate causal processes.[31] Bailey Stone, commenting that her account of the French revolution was the 'most persuasive' at its time of publication, commends Skocpol's distinction between voluntarist and structural explanations, that is, between explanations which attribute the revolution to a deliberate attempt by a mass movement to overthrow a government, and those where the pre-revolutionary state is the 'key actor', respectively.[32] Nevertheless, both Sewell and Stone criticize Skocpol's lack of attention to ideological factors, Stone arguing that her 'non-voluntarist, structural' account needs to 'accommodate some of the concerns of voluntarist history within a framework of structuralism – in other words, to evaluate sociocultural change within a matrix of power relationships in (and between) governments and societies'.[33]

Of great interest to historians intending sociological explanations is the preface to Skocpol's book. She relates how she read extensive and detailed histories of Russia, France and China before she read the theoretical analyses of revolution written by social scientists. She suggests that this was the reverse of the practice of most sociologists, and it may explain why her interpretation of revolution has been so palatable to historians. For Skocpol, the social science literature was 'frustrating', because its explanations did not accord with the historical evidence. She interpreted this as an ideological problem: that is, the theories derived from hypothetical models of change in liberal-democratic or capitalist societies. Marxist theories were as problematic as those proposed by non-Marxists. She suggests therefore that comparative historical sociology should only be attempted in areas where a large historical literature already exists, since most sociologists have neither the time nor all the historical skills to do the necessary primary research.[34]

Let us examine the following excerpt from Skocpol's work with these precepts in mind. How is a comparative historical method illustrated in this article, and what are its strengths and weaknesses? In what ways is Skocpol's work historical and in what ways sociological? In this excerpt, we can see the author's indebtedness to earlier historical sociologists, in particular, Wallerstein. How does Skocpol's explanation of modernization resemble his and in what ways does it differ? Finally, consider Skocpol's differentiation between short-term precipitants and fundamental underlying causes. Is this distinction useful to the historian and how might it affect our analyses of topics other than comparative revolution?

Notes

1 Philip Abrams, *Historical Sociology* (Shepton Mallet, 1982), pp. 1–2; Theda Skocpol (ed.), *Vision and Method in Historical Sociology* (Cambridge, 1984), p. 1.
2 Skocpol, *Vision and Method*, p. 1.
3 Randall Collins, *Four Sociological Traditions* (New York, 1994), pp. 38–46.
4 For the preceding paragraphs and for more detail, see Abrams, *Historical Sociology*, pp. 4, 112–28; Collins, *Four Sociological Traditions*, pp. 38–46; Dorothy Ross, 'The New and Newer Histories: Social Theory and Historiography in an American Key', *Rethinking History*, 1 (1997), pp. 126–33; Victoria E. Bonnell, 'The Uses of Theory, Concepts and Comparison in Historical Sociology', *Comparative Studies in Society and History*, 22 (1980), p. 156, n. 3; 'History, Sociology and Social Anthropology', *Past and Present*, 27 (1964), p. 102.
5 Durkheim, while originating the 'core tradition of sociology', tended to investigate systems, rather than processes of change, and so has been less influential for *historical* sociology: Collins, *Four Sociological Traditions*, p. 119.

6 Guenther Ross, 'History and Sociology in the Work of Max Weber', *British Journal of Sociology*, 27 (1976), pp. 310, 307; Max Weber, *Economy and Society*, ed. G. Roth and C. Wittich (New York, 1968), p. 19.

7 Stephen Kalberg, 'Max Weber's Types of Rationality: Cornerstones for the Analysis of Rationalization Processes in History', *American Journal of Sociology*, 85 (1980), p. 1151.

8 Abrams, *Historical Sociology*, pp. 74–5, 83; Weber, *The Protestant Ethic and the Spirit of Capitalism*, trans. Talcott Parsons (London, [1904] 1930).

9 Abrams, *Historical Sociology*, pp. 82–107.

10 R. J. Holton, *The Transition from Feudalism to Capitalism* (London, 1985), pp. 104, 109. See pp. 109–24 for further discussion of Weber.

11 Weber, *The Theory of Social and Economic Organization*, trans. A. M. Henderson and Talcott Parsons (New York, 1947), p. 90, cited in Werner J. Cahnman, 'Max Weber and the Methodological Controversy in the Social Sciences', in Werner J. Cahnman and Alvin Boskoff (eds), *Sociology and History: Theory and Research* (New York, 1964), p. 108.

12 Kalberg, 'Max Weber's Types of Rationality', pp. 1151–2. See the rest of this article for more detail on rationality and social action.

13 Collins, *Four Sociological Traditions*, pp. 84–5.

14 *Ibid.*, pp. 86–92; these terms come from Gerth and Mills' translation: Hans Gerth and C. Wright Mills (eds), *From Max Weber: Essays in Sociology* (New York, 1958), Section VII, 'Class, Status, Party'.

15 For example, see the work of W. G. Runciman, and the ideas contained within *A Critique of Max Weber's Philosophy of Social Science* (Cambridge, 1972).

16 Michael Mann, *The Sources of Social Power*, 2 vols (Cambridge 1986–93), vol. 1, ch. 1, esp. pp. 1–4, 29, 32, fig. 1.2.

17 See, for example, S. N. Eisenstadt, *The Political Systems of Empires* (New York, 1963); Barrington Moore, Jr., *Social Origins of Dictatorship and Democracy: Lord and Peasant in the Making of the Modern World* (Boston, 1966); W. W. Rostow, *Politics and the Stages of Growth* (Cambridge, 1971); Immanuel Wallerstein, *The Modern World-System: Capitalist Agriculture and the Origins of the European World-Economy in the Sixteenth Century* (New York, 1974); Perry Anderson, *Passages from Antiquity to Feudalism* (London, 1974); Reinhard Bendix, *Kings or People: Power and the Mandate to Rule* (Berkeley, 1978); Holton, *The Transition from Feudalism to Capitalism*.

18 This summary is derived from Charles Ragin and Daniel Chirot, 'The World System of Immanuel Wallerstein: Sociology and Politics as History', in Skocpol, *Vision and Method in Historical Sociology*, pp. 276–7 and Theda Skocpol, 'Wallerstein's World Capitalist System: A Theoretical and Historical Critique', *American Journal of Sociology*, 82 (1977), p. 1077.

19 Skocpol, 'Wallerstein's World Capitalist System', p. 1076.

20 J. L. Anderson, *Explaining Long-term Economic Change* (London, 1991), p. 66.

21 Patrick O'Brien, 'European Economic Development: The Contribution of the Periphery', *Economic History Review*, 2nd series, 35 (1982), pp. 1–18.

22 Hank Wesseling, 'Overseas History', in Peter Burke (ed.), *New Perspectives on Historical Writing* (Oxford, 1991), p. 81.

23 Skocpol, 'Wallerstein's World Capitalist System', p. 1088.

24 Joan Thirsk, 'Economic and Social Development on a European-World Scale', *American Journal of Sociology*, 82 (1977), p. 1098.

25 Charles Tilly, *As Sociology Meets History* (New York, 1981), pp. 41–2; Skocpol, 'Wallerstein's World Capitalist System', p. 1088. There are other criticisms from a Marxist viewpoint, for example, considering Wallerstein's use of 'class'. See Anthony Brewer, *Marxist Theories of Imperialism: A Critical Survey* (London, 1980), pp. 159–81.

26 Robert Brenner, 'The Origins of Capitalist Development: A Critique of Neo-Smithian Marxism', *New Left Review*, 104 (1977), pp. 25–92, esp. p. 56.

27 Tilly, *As Sociology Meets History*, p. 42.

28 For example, see Tilly, *The Vendée* (Cambridge, Mass., 1964); Lynn Hunt, 'Charles Tilly's Collective Action', in Skocpol, *Vision and Method*, pp. 244–5; Skocpol, 'Sociology's Historical Imagination', in *ibid.*, p. 16. For an excellent analysis of Tilly's work, see Hunt's full chapter.

29 Skocpol, *States and Social Revolutions: A Comparative Analysis of France, Russia and China* (Cambridge, 1979).

30 Skocpol, 'France, Russia, China: A Structural Analysis of Social Revolutions', reprinted in *Social Revolutions in the Modern World* (Cambridge, 1994), p. 135.

31 William H. Sewell, Jr., 'Ideologies and Social Revolutions: Reflections on the French Case', *Journal of Modern History*, 57 (1985), pp. 57–8.

32 Bailey Stone, *The Genesis of the French Revolution: A Global-Historical Interpretation* (Cambridge, 1994), pp. 13, 1–2. I am grateful to Simon Burrows for this reference.

33 Sewell, 'Ideologies and Social Revolutions', p. 57; Skocpol, *States and Social Revolutions*, p. 33; Stone, *The Genesis of the French Revolution*, p. 14.

34 Skocpol, *States and Social Revolutions*, pp. xiii–xiv. For further analyses of comparative historical sociological method, see Bonnell, 'The Uses of Theory, Concepts and Comparison in Historical Sociology'; Skocpol and Margaret Somers, 'The Uses of Comparative History in Macrosocial Inquiry', *Comparative Studies in Society and History*, 22 (1980), pp. 174–97; Bendix, 'Concepts and Generalizations in Comparative Sociological Studies', *American Sociological Review*, 28 (1963), pp. 532–9.

Additional reading

Abrams, Philip, *Historical Sociology* (Shepton Mallet, 1982).

Bonnell, Victoria E., 'The Uses of Theory, Concepts and Comparison in Historical Sociology', *Comparative Studies in Society and History*, 22 (1980), pp. 156–73.

Cahnman, Werner J. and Alvin Boskoff (eds), *Sociology and History: Theory and Research* (New York, 1964).

Collins, Randall, *Four Sociological Traditions* (Oxford, 1994).

Eisenstadt, S. N., *The Political Systems of Empires* (New York, 1963).

Lipset, Seymour Martin and Richard Hofstadter, *Sociology and History: Methods* (New York, 1968).

Mann, Michael, *The Sources of Social Power*, 2 vols (Cambridge 1986–93).

Moore, Barrington, Jr., *Social Origins of Dictatorship and Democracy: Lord and Peasant in the Making of the Modern World* (Boston, 1966).

Skocpol, Theda (ed.), *Vision and Method in Historical Sociology* (Cambridge, 1984).

Skocpol, Theda, *States and Social Revolutions: A Comparative Analysis of France, Russia, and China* (Cambridge, 1979).

Tilly, Charles, *As Sociology Meets History* (New York, 1981).

Wallerstein, Immanuel, *The Modern World-System: Capitalist Agriculture and the Origins of the European World-Economy in the Sixteenth Century* (New York, 1974).

Weber, Max, *The Protestant Ethic and the Spirit of Capitalism*, trans. Talcott Parsons (London, [1904] 1930).

FRANCE, RUSSIA, CHINA: A STRUCTURAL ANALYSIS OF SOCIAL REVOLUTIONS
Theda Skocpol

'A revolution', writes Samuel P. Huntington in *Political Order in Changing Societies*, 'is a rapid, fundamental, and violent domestic change in the dominant values and myths of a society, in its political institutions, social structure, leadership, and government activities and policies'.[1] In *The Two Tactics of Social Democracy in the Democratic Revolution*, Lenin provides a different, but complementary perspective: 'Revolutions', he says, 'are the festivals of the oppressed and the exploited. At no other time are the masses of the people in a position to come forward so actively as creators of a new social order'.[2]

Together these two quotes delineate the distinctive features of *social revolutions*. As Huntington points out, social revolutions are rapid, basic transformations of socio-economic and political institutions, and—as Lenin so vividly reminds us—social revolutions are accompanied and in part effectuated through class upheavals from below. It is this combination of thoroughgoing structural transformation and massive class upheavals that sets social revolutions apart from coups, rebellions, and even political revolutions and national independence movements.

If one adopts such a specific definition, then clearly only a handful of successful social revolutions have ever occurred. France, 1789, Russia, 1917, and China, 1911–49, are the most dramatic and clear-cut instances. Yet these momentous upheavals have helped shape the fate of the majority of mankind, and their causes, consequences, and

This article represents a shortened and revised version of a paper presented at the Session on Revolutions of the 1973 Meetings of the American Sociological Association. For criticism, advice (not all of it heeded), intellectual stimulation and encouragement offered to the author in the long course of preparing this paper, thanks go to: Daniel Bell, Mounira Charrad, Linda Frankel, George Homans, S. M. Lipset, Gary Marx, John Mollenkopf, Barrington Moore, Jr., Bill Skocpol, Sylvia Thrupp and Kay Trimberger.

[1] Samuel P. Huntington, *Political Order in Changing Societies* (New Haven: Yale University Press, 1968), p. 264.

[2] Stephan T. Possony, ed., *The Lenin Reader* (Chicago: Henry Regnery Company, 1966), p. 349.

potentials have preoccupied many thoughtful people since the late eighteenth century.

Nevertheless, recently, social scientists have evidenced little interest in the study of social revolutions as such. They have submerged revolutions within more general categories—such as 'political violence', 'collective behavior', 'internal war', or 'deviance'—shorn of historical specificity and concern with large-scale social change.[3] The focus has been mostly on styles of behavior common to wide ranges of collective incidents (ranging from riots to coups to revolutions, from panics to hostile outbursts to 'value-oriented movements', and from ideological sects to revolutionary parties), any of which might occur in any type of society at any time or place. Revolutions tend increasingly to be viewed not as 'locomotives of history', but as extreme forms of one or another sort of behavior that social scientists, along with established authorities everywhere, find problematic and perturbing.

Why this avoidance by social science of the specific problem of social revolution? Ideological bias might be invoked as an explanation, but even if it were involved, it would not suffice. An earlier generation of American social scientists, certainly no more politically radical than the present generation, employed the 'natural history' approach to analyze handfuls of cases of great revolutions.[4] In large part, present preoccupation with broader categories can be understood as a reaction against this natural history approach, deemed by its critics too 'historical' and 'a-theoretical'.

In the 'Introduction' to a 1964 book entitled *Internal War*, Harry Eckstein defines 'a theoretical subject' as a 'set of phenomena about which one can develop informative, testable generalizations that hold for all instances of the subject, and some of which apply to those instances alone'.[5] He goes on to assert that while 'a statement about two or three cases is certainly a generalization in the dictionary sense, a generalization in the methodological sense must usually

---

[3] For important examples see: Ted Robert Gurr, *Why Men Rebel* (Princeton, N.J.: Princeton University Press, 1970); Neil J. Smelser, *Theory of Collective Behavior* (New York: The Free Press of Glencoe, 1963), and Harry Eckstein, 'On the Etiology of Internal Wars', *History and Theory* 4(2) (1965).

[4] Crane Brinton, *The Anatomy of Revolution* (New York: Vintage Books, 1965; original edition, 1938); Lyford P. Edwards, *The Natural History of Revolution* (Chicago: University of Chicago Press, 1971; originally published in 1927); George Sawyer Petee, *The Process of Revolution* (New York: Harper and Brothers, 1938); and Rex D. Hopper, 'The Revolutionary Process', *Social Forces* 28 (March, 1950): 270–9.

[5] Harry Eckstein, ed., *Internal War* (New York: The Free Press, 1964), p. 8.

be based on more; it ought to cover a number of cases large enough for certain rigorous testing procedures like statistical analysis to be used'.[6] Even many social scientists who are not statistically oriented would agree with the spirit of this statement: theory in social science should concern itself only with general phenomena; the 'unique' should be relegated to 'narrative historians'.

Apparently it directly follows that no theory specific to social revolution is possible, that the *explanandum* of any theory which sheds light on social revolutions must be something more general than social revolution itself. Hence the efforts to conceptualize revolution as an extreme instance of patterns of belief or behavior which are also present in other situations or events.

This approach, however, allows considerations of technique to define away substantive problems. Revolutions are not just extreme forms of individual or collective behavior. They are distinctive conjunctures of socio-historical structures and processes. One must comprehend them as complex wholes—however few the cases—or not at all.

Fortunately social science is not devoid of a way of confronting this kind of problem. Social revolutions *can* be treated as a 'theoretical subject'. To test hypotheses about them, one may employ the comparative method, with national historical trajectories as the units of comparison. As many students of society have noted, the comparative method is nothing but that mode of multivariate analysis to which sociologists necessarily resort when experimental manipulations are not possible and when there are 'too many variables and not enough cases'—that is, not enough cases for statistical testing of hypotheses.[7] According to this method, one looks for concomitant variations, contrasting cases where the phenomena in which one is interested are present with cases where they are absent, controlling in the process for as many sources of variation as one can, by contrasting positive and negative instances which otherwise are as similar as possible.

---

[6] *Ibid.*, p. 10.

[7] See: Ernest Nagel, ed., *John Stuart Mill's Philosophy of Scientific Method* (New York: Hafner Publishing Co., 1950); Marc Bloch, 'Toward a Comparative History of European Societies', pp. 494–521 in Frederic C. Lane and Jelle C. Riemersma, eds., *Enterprise and Secular Change* (Homewood, Ill.: The Dorsey Press, 1953); William H. Sewell, Jr., 'Marc Bloch and the Logic of Comparative History', *History and Theory* 6(2) (1967): 208–18; Neil J. Smelser, 'The Methodology of Comparative Analysis', (unpublished draft); and S. M. Lipset, *Revolution and Counterrevolution* (New York: Anchor Books, 1970), part I.

Thus, in my inquiry into the conditions for the occurrence and short-term outcomes of the great historical social revolutions in France, Russia and China, I have employed the comparative historical method, specifically contrasting the positive cases with (a) instances of non-social revolutionary modernization, such as occurred in Japan, Germany and Russia (up to 1904), and with (b) instances of abortive social revolutions, in particular Russia in 1905 and Prussia/Germany in 1848. These comparisons have helped me to understand those aspects of events and of structures and processes which distinctively rendered the French, Chinese and Russian Revolutions successful social revolutions. In turn, the absence of conditions identified as positively crucial in France, Russia and China constitutes equally well an explanation of why social revolutions have not occurred, or have failed, in other societies. In this way, hypotheses developed, refined, and tested in the comparative historical analysis of a handful of cases achieve a potentially general significance.

Explaining the historical cases: revolution in modernizing agrarian bureaucracies

Social revolutions in France, Russia and China occurred, during the earlier world-historical phases of modernization, in agrarian bureaucratic societies situated within, or newly incorporated into, international fields dominated by more economically modern nations abroad. In each case, social revolution was a conjuncture of three developments: (1) the collapse or incapacitation of central administrative and military machineries; (2) widespread peasant rebellions; and (3) marginal elite political movements. What each social revolution minimally 'accomplished' was the extreme rationalization and centralization of state institutions, the removal of a traditional landed upper class from intermediate (regional and local) quasi-political supervision of the peasantry, and the elimination or diminution of the economic power of a landed upper class.

In the pages that follow, I shall attempt to explain the three great historical social revolutions, first, by discussing the institutional characteristics of agrarian states, and their special vulnerabilities and potentialities during the earlier world-historical phases of modernization, and second, by pointing to the peculiar characteristics of old regimes in France, Russia and China, which made them uniquely vulnerable among the earlier modernizing agrarian states to social-revolutionary transformations. Finally, I shall suggest reasons for similarities and differences in the outcomes of the great historical social revolutions.

An agrarian bureaucracy is an agricultural society in which social control rests on a division of labor and a coordination of effort between a semi-bureaucratic state and a landed upper class.[8] The landed upper class typically retains, as an adjunct to its landed property, considerable (though varying in different cases) undifferentiated local and regional authority over the peasant majority of the population. The partially bureaucratic central state extracts taxes and labor from peasants either indirectly through landlord intermediaries or else directly, but with (at least minimal) reliance upon cooperation from individuals of the landed upper class. In turn, the landed upper class relies upon the backing of a coercive state to extract rents and/or dues from the peasantry. At the political center, autocrat, bureaucracy, and army monopolize decisions, yet (in varying degrees and modes) accommodate the regional and local power of the landed upper class and (again, to varying degrees) recruit individual members of this class into leading positions in the state system.

Agrarian bureaucracies are inherently vulnerable to peasant rebellions. Subject to claims on their surpluses, and perhaps their labor, by landlords and state agents, peasants chronically resent both. To the extent that the agrarian economy is commercialized, merchants are also targets of peasant hostility. In all agrarian bureaucracies at all times, and in France, Russia and China in non-revolutionary times, peasants have had grievances enough to warrant, and recurrently spur, rebellions. Economic crises (which are endemic in semi-commercial agrarian economies anyway) and/or increased demands from above for rents or taxes might substantially enhance the likelihood of rebellions at particular times. But such events ought to be treated as short-term precipitants of peasant unrest, not fundamental underlying causes.

Modernization is best conceived not only as an *intra*-societal process of economic development accompanied by lagging or leading

---

[8] In formulating the 'agrarian bureaucracy' societal type concept, I have drawn especially upon the work and ideas of S. N. Eisenstadt in *The Political Systems of Empires* (New York: The Free Press, 1963); Barrington Moore, Jr., in *Social Origins of Dictatorship and Democracy* (Boston: Beacon Press, 1967); and Morton H. Fried, 'On the Evolution of Social Stratification and the State', pp. 713–31 in Stanley Diamond, ed., *Culture in History* (New York: Columbia University Press, 1960). The label 'agrarian bureaucracy' is pilfered from Moore. Clear-cut instances of agrarian bureaucratic societies were: China, Russia, France, Prussia, Austria, Spain, Japan, Turkey.

changes in noneconomic institutional spheres, but also as a world-historic *inter*-societal phenomenon. Thus,

> a necessary condition of a society's modernization is its incorporation into the historically unique network of societies that arose first in Western Europe in early modern times and today encompasses enough of the globe's population for the world to be viewed for some purposes as if it consisted of a single network of societies.[9]

Of course, societies have always interacted. What was special about the modernizing inter-societal network that arose in early modern Europe was, first, that it was based upon trade in commodities and manufactures, as well as upon strategic politico-military competition between independent states,[10] and, second, that it incubated the 'first (self-propelling) industrialization' of England after she had gained commercial hegemony within the Western European-centered world market.[11]

In the wake of that first commercial-industrial breakthrough, modernizing pressures have reverberated throughout the world. In the first phase of world modernization, England's thoroughgoing commercialization, capture of world market hegemony, and expansion of manufactures (both before and after the technological Industrial Revolution which began in the 1780s), transformed means and stakes in the traditional rivalries of European states and put immediate pressure for reforms, if only to facilitate the financing of competitive armies and navies, upon the other European states and especially upon the ones with less efficient fiscal machineries.[12] In the second phase, as Europe modernized and further expanded its influence around the globe, similar militarily compelling pressures were brought to bear on those non-European societies which escaped immediate colonization, usually the ones with pre-existing differentiated and centralized state institutions.

During these phases of global modernization, independent responses to the dilemmas posed by incorporation into a modernizing world were possible and (in some sense) necessary for governmental

---

[9] Terence K. Hopkins and Immanuel Wallerstein, 'The Comparative Study of National Societies', *Social Science Information* 6 (1967): 39.

[10] See Immanuel Wallerstein, *The Modern World System: Capitalist Agriculture and the Origins of the European World-Economy in the Sixteenth Century* (New York and London: Academic Press, 1974).

[11] E. J. Hobsbawm, *Industry and Empire* (Baltimore, Md.: Penguin Books, 1969).

[12] See Walter L. Dorn, *Competition for Empire, 1740–1763* (New York: Harper and Row, 1963; originally, 1940).

elites in agrarian bureaucracies. Demands for more and more efficiently collected taxes; for better and more generously and continuously financed militaries; and for 'guided' national economic development, imitating the available foreign models, were voiced within these societies especially by bureaucrats and the educated middle strata. The demands were made compelling by international military competition and threats. At the same time, governmental leaders did have administrative machineries, however rudimentary, at their disposal for the implementation of whatever modernizing reforms seemed necessary and feasible (at given moments in world history). And their countries had not been incorporated into dependent economic and political positions in a world stratification system dominated by a few fully industrialized giants.

But agrarian bureaucracies faced enormous difficulties in meeting the crises of modernization. Governmental leaders' realm of autonomous action tended to be severely limited, because few fiscal or economic reforms could be undertaken which did not encroach upon the advantages of the traditional landed upper classes which constituted the major social base of support for the authority and functions of the state in agrarian bureaucracies. Only so much revenue could be squeezed out of the peasantry, and yet landed upper classes could often raise formidable obstacles to rationalization of tax systems. Economic development might mean more tax revenues and enhanced military prowess, yet it channelled wealth and manpower away from the agrarian sector. Finally, the mobilization of mass popular support for war tended to undermine the traditional, local authority of landlords or landed bureaucrats upon which agrarian bureaucratic societies partly relied for the social control of the peasantry.

Agrarian bureaucracies could not indefinitely 'ignore' the very specific crises, in particular fiscal and martial, that grew out of involvement with a modernizing world, yet they could not adapt without undergoing fundamental structural changes. Social revolution helped accomplish 'necessary' changes in some but was averted by reform or 'revolution from above' in others. Relative stagnation, accompanied by sub-incorporation into international power spheres, was still another possibility (e.g., Portugal, Spain?). Social revolution was never deliberately 'chosen'. Societies only 'backed into' social revolutions.

All modernizing agrarian bureaucracies have peasants with grievances and face the unavoidable challenges posed by modernization abroad. So, in some sense, potential for social revolution has been built into all modernizing agrarian bureaucracies. Yet, only a handful have succumbed. Why? A major part of the answer, I believe, lies in the insight that 'not oppression, but weakness, breeds revolution'.[13] It is the breakdown of a societal mode of social control which allows and prompts social revolution to unfold. In the historical cases of France, Russia and China, the unfolding of social revolution depended upon the emergence of revolutionary crises occasioned by the incapacitation of administrative and military organizations. That incapacitation, in turn, is best explained not as a function of mass discontent and mobilization, but as a function of a combination of pressures on state institutions from more modernized countries abroad, and (in two cases out of three) built-in structural incapacities to mobilize increased resources in response to those pressures. France, Russia and China were also special among all agrarian bureaucracies in that their agrarian institutions afforded peasants not only the usual grievances against landlords and state agents but also 'structural space' for autonomous collective insurrection. Finally, once administrative/military breakdown occurred in agrarian bureaucracies with such especially insurrection-prone peasantries, then, and only then, could organized revolutionary leaderships have great impact upon their societies' development—though not necessarily in the ways they originally envisaged.

Breakdown of societal controls: foreign pressures and administrative/military collapse

If a fundamental cause and the crucial trigger for the historical social revolutions was the incapacitation of administrative and military machineries in modernizing agrarian bureaucracies, then how and why did this occur in France, Russia and China? What differentiated these agrarian bureaucracies which succumbed to social revolution from others which managed to respond to modernizing pressures with reforms from above? Many writers attribute differences in response to qualities of will or ability in governmental leaders. From a sociological point of view, a more satisfying approach might focus on the interaction between (a) the magnitude of foreign pressures brought to bear on a modernizing agrarian bureaucracy, and (b) the

[13] Christopher Lasch, *The New Radicalism in America* (New York: Vintage Books, 1967), p. 141.

particular structural characteristics of such societies that underlay contrasting performances by leaders responding to foreign pressures and internal unrest.

Overwhelming foreign pressures on an agrarian bureaucracy could cut short even a generally successful government program of reforms and industrialization 'from above'. Russia is the obvious case in point. From at least the 1890s onward, the Czarist regime was committed to rapid industrialization, initially government-financed out of resources squeezed from the peasantry, as the only means of rendering Russia militarily competitive with Western nations. Alexander Gerschenkron argues that initial government programs to promote heavy industry had succeeded in the 1890s to such an extent that, when the government was forced to reduce its direct financial and administrative role after 1904, Russia's industrial sector was nevertheless capable of autonomously generating further growth (with the aid of foreign capital investments).[14] Decisive steps to modernize agriculture and free peasant labor for permanent urban migration were taken after the unsuccessful Revolution of 1905.[15] Had she been able to sit out World War I, Russia might have recapitulated the German experience of industrialization facilitated by bureaucratic guidance.

But participation in World War I forced Russia to fully mobilize her population including her restive peasantry. Army officers and men were subjected to years of costly fighting, and civilians to mounting economic privations—all for nought. For, given Russia's 'industrial backwardness . . . enhanced by the fact that Russia was very largely blockaded . . .', plus the 'inferiority of the Russian military machine to the German in everything but sheer numbers . . . , military defeat, with all of its inevitable consequences for the internal condition of the country, was very nearly a foregone conclusion'.[16] The result was administrative demoralization and paralysis, and the disintegration of the army. Urban insurrections which brought first middle-strata moderates and then the Bolsheviks to power could not be suppressed, owing to the newly-recruited

[14] Alexander Gerschenkron, 'Problems and Patterns of Russian Economic Development', pp. 42–72 in Cyril E. Black, ed., *The Transformation of Russian Society* (Cambridge, Mass.: Harvard University Press, 1960).

[15] Geroid Tanquary Robinson, *Rural Russia Under the Old Regime* (Berkeley and Los Angeles: University of California Press, 1969; originally published in 1932), Chap. 11.

[16] William Henry Chamberlin, *The Russian Revolution*, Volume I (New York: Grosset and Dunlap, 1963; originally published in 1935), pp. 64–5.

character and war weariness of the urban garrisons.[17] Peasant grievances were enhanced, young peasant men were politicized through military experiences, and, in consequence, spreading peasant insurrections from the spring of 1917 on could not be controlled.

It is instructive to compare 1917 to the Revolution of 1905. Trotsky called 1905 a 'dress rehearsal' for 1917, and, indeed, many of the same social forces with the same grievances and similar political programs took part in each revolutionary drama. *What accounts for the failure of the Revolution of 1905 was the Czarist regime's ultimate ability to rely upon the army to repress popular disturbances.* Skillful tactics were involved: the regime bought time to organize repression and assure military loyalty with well-timed liberal concessions embodied in the October Manifesto of 1905 (and later largely retracted). Yet, it was of crucial importance that the futile 1904–05 war with Japan was, in comparison with the World War I morass, circumscribed, geographically peripheral, less demanding of resources and manpower, and quickly concluded once defeat was apparent.[18] The peace treaty was signed by late 1905, leaving the Czarist government free to bring military reinforcements back from the Far East into European Russia.

The Russian Revolution occurred in 1917 because Russia was too inextricably entangled with foreign powers, friend and foe, economically and militarily more powerful than she. Foreign entanglement must be considered not only to explain the administrative and military incapacitation of 1917, but also entry into World War I. That involvement cannot be considered 'accidental'. Nor was it 'voluntary' in the same sense as Russia's entry into the 1904 war with Japan.[19] Whatever leadership 'blunders' were involved, the fact remains that in 1914 both the Russian state and the Russian economy depended heavily on Western loans and capital. Moreover, Russia was an established part of the European state system and could not remain neutral in a conflict that engulfed the whole of that system.[20]

---

[17] Katharine Chorley, *Armies and the Art of Revolution* (London: Faber and Faber, 1943), Chap. 6.

[18] *Ibid.*, pp. 118–19.

[19] In 1904, '[t]he Minister of Interior, von Plehve, saw a desirable outlet from the [turbulent domestic] situation in a "little victorious war"' (Chamberlin, *op. cit.*, p. 47).

[20] See: Leon Trotsky, *The Russian Revolution* (selected and edited by F. W. Dupee) (New York: Anchor Books, 1959; originally published in 1932), Volume I, Chap. 2; and Roderick E. McGrew, 'Some Imperatives of Russian Foreign Policy', pp. 202–29 in Theofanis George Stavrou, ed., *Russia Under the Last Tsar* (Minneapolis: University of Minnesota Press, 1969).

Foreign pressures and involvements so inescapable and over-whelming as those that faced Russia in 1917 constitute an extreme case for the earlier modernizing agrarian bureaucracies we are considering here. For France and China the pressures were surely no more compelling than those faced by agrarian bureaucracies such as Japan, Germany and Russia (1858–1914) which successfully adapted through reforms from above that facilitated the extraordinary mobilization of resources for economic and military development. Why were the Bourbon and Manchu regimes unable to adapt? Were there structural blocks to effective response? First, let me discuss some general characteristics of all agrarian states, and then point to a peculiar structural characteristic shared by Bourbon France and Manchu China which I believe explains these regimes' inability to meet snow-balling crises of modernization until at last their feeble attempts triggered administrative and military disintegration, hence revolutionary crises.

Weber's ideal type of bureaucracy may be taken as an imaginary model of what might logically be the most effective means of purposively organizing social power. According to the ideal type, fully developed bureaucracy involves the existence of an hierarchically arrayed officialdom, where officials are oriented to superior authority in a disciplined manner because they are dependent for jobs, livelihood, status and career-advancement on resources and decisions channelled through that superior authority. But in preindustrial states, monarchs found it difficult to channel sufficient resources through the 'center' to pay simultaneously for wars, culture and court life on the one hand, and a fully bureaucratic officialdom on the other. Consequently, they often had to make do with 'officials' recruited from wealthy backgrounds, frequently, in practice, landlords. In addition, central state jurisdiction rarely touched local peasants or communities directly; governmental functions were often delegated to landlords in their 'private' capacities, or else to non-bureaucratic authoritative organizations run by local landlords.

Inherent in all agrarian bureaucratic regimes were tensions between, on the one hand, state elites interested in preserving, using, and extending the powers of armies and administrative organizations and, on the other hand, landed upper classes interested in defending locally and regionally based social networks, influence over peasants, and powers and privileges associated with the control of land and agrarian surpluses. Such tensions were likely to be exacerbated once the agrarian bureaucracy was forced to adapt to modernization abroad because foreign military pressures gave cause, while foreign economic development offered incentives and models, for state elites to attempt reforms which went counter to the class interests of traditional, landed upper strata. Yet there were important variations in the ability of semi-bureaucratic agrarian states to respond to modernizing pressures with reforms which sharply and quickly increased resources at the disposal of central authorities. What can account for the differences in response?

Not the values or individual qualities of traditional bureaucrats: Japan's Meiji reformers acted in the name of traditional values and authority to enact sweeping structural reforms which cleared the way for rapid industrialization and military modernization. Russia's Czarist officialdom was renowned for its inefficiency and corruption, and yet it implemented basic agrarian reforms in 1861 and 1905 and administered the first stages of heavy industrialization.

Leaving aside value-orientations and individual characteristics, we must look at the class interests and connections of state officials. *The adaptiveness of the earlier modernizing agrarian bureaucracies was significantly determined by the degree to which the upper and middle ranks of the state administrative bureaucracies were staffed by large landholders*. Only state machineries significantly differentiated from traditional landed upper classes could undertake modernizing reforms which almost invariably had to encroach upon the property or privileges of the landed upper class.

Thus, in an analysis of what she calls 'elite revolutions' in Japan (1863) and Turkey (1919), Ellen Kay Trimberger argues that segments of the traditional leaderships of those agrarian bureaucracies were able to respond so effectively to intrusions by more modern powers only because 'the Japanese and Turkish ruling elites were political bureaucrats without vested economic interests. . . .'[21] Similarly Walter M. Pintner concludes from his careful research into 'The Social Characteristics of the Early Nineteenth-Century Russian Bureaucracy' that:

> By the end of the eighteenth century the civil bureaucracy in the central agencies, and by the 1850s in the provinces also, was an essentially self-perpetuating group. Recruits came from a nobility that was in large measure divorced from the land, and from among the sons of nonnoble government workers (military, civil, and ecclesiastical). . . . What is impor-

[21] Ellen Kay Trimberger, 'A Theory of Elite Revolutions', *Studies in Comparative International Development* 7(3) (Fall, 1972): 192.

tant is that the state's civil administration, even at the upper levels, was staffed with men who were committed to that career and no other and who seldom had any other significant source of income. The competence, efficiency, and honesty of the civil service were undoubtedly very low, ... however, it should have been a politically loyal instrument, and indeed it proved to be when the tsar determined to emancipate the serfs and assign to them land that was legally the property of the nobility.[22]

But where—as in Bourbon France and late Manchu China— regionally-based cliques of landed magnates were ensconced within nominally centralized administrative systems, the ability of the state elites to control the flow of tax resources and implement reform policies was decisively undermined. By their *resistance* to the mobilization of increased resources for military or economic purposes in modernization crises, such landed cliques of officials could engender situations of acute administrative/military disorganization—potentially revolutionary crises of governmental authority.

The French monarchy struggled on three fronts throughout the eighteenth century.[23] Within the European state system, France's 'amphibious geography' forced her to compete simultaneously with the great continental land powers, Austria and (after mid-century) Prussia, and with the maritime powers, above all, Britain. Britain's accelerating commercial and industrial development put France at ever increasing disadvantage in trade and naval strength and the extraordinary efficiency of Prussia's bureaucratic regime, its special ability to extract resources from relatively poor people and territories and to convert them with minimal wastage to military purposes, tended to compensate for France's advantages of national wealth and territorial size. And the French monarchy had to fight on a 'third front' at home—against the resistance of its own privileged strata to rationalization of the tax system.

Perceptive as he was in pointing to rationalization and centralization of state power as the most fateful outcomes of the French Revolution, Alexis de Tocqueville[24] surely exaggerated the extent to

---

[22] Walter M. Pintner 'The Social Characteristics of the Early Nineteenth-Century Russian Bureaucracy', *Slavic Review* 29(3) (September, 1970): 442–3. See also, Don Karl Rowney, 'Higher Civil Servants in the Russian Ministry of Internal Affairs: Some Demographic and Career Characteristics, 1905–1916', *Slavic Review* 31(1) (March, 1972): 101–10.

[23] Dorn, *op. cit.*: and C. B. A. Behrens, *The Ancien Regime* (London: Harcourt, Brace, and World, 1967).

[24] Alexis de Tocqueville, *The Old Regime and the French Revolution* (New York: Anchor Books, 1955; originally published in French in 1856).

which monarchical authority already exhibited those qualities before the Revolution. To be sure:

> At first view France, the historic center of continental statecraft, presents the picture of a clear, homogeneous and consistent governmental structure. The king was the sole legislator, the supreme chief of the administrative hierarchy and the source of all justice. . . . All authority was delegated by the crown, and its agents, whether ministers, provincial intendants or subdelegates, were its mandatories. . . . In the matter of justice the council of state, acting as the king's private court, could override judgements of all ordinary courts. The sovereign's *parlements*, the intermediary and lower courts pronounced justice in the king's name, and even the seigneurial, municipal, and ecclesiastical courts were subject to his control . . . The Estates General were no more and the few remaining provincial estates were reduced to pure administrative bodies.[25]

Such was the system in theory, an absolute monarch's dream. But in practice? Quite aside from general qualities which set the French administrative system in the eighteenth century in sharp contrast to the Prussian—as 'more disjointed, less uniform, less effectively geared by control devices, above all less firmly co-ordinated by a single driving purpose penetrating the entire administrative hierarchy'[26]— the system afforded landlords (and wealth-holders generally) strategic points of institutional leverage for obstructing royal policies.

> A substantial number of the First and Second Estates was obviously still trying to live in terms of the old feudal structure that had lost its functional justification at least two centuries before . . . [T]he residue is not hard to identify or describe. Characteristically it was composed of the larger landowners, but not the princes of the realm nor even the constant residents at Versailles. The latter had obviously, if not necessarily willingly, cast their lot with the King. Similarly, many of the lesser nobles had, whether from ambition or necessity, taken service in the army or, occasionally, in the administration. The remaining survivors of the old feudal classes, however, tended to live on their properties in the provinces, serve and subvert the local bureaucracy, seek preferment in the Church, and find expression and defense of their interests through the provincial estates and *parlements*.[27]

The *parlements*, or sovereign courts, nominally a part of the administrative system, were the most avid and strategically located of the institutional defenders of property and privilege. 'The French monar-

[25] Dorn, *op. cit.*, p. 23.
[26] *Ibid.*, p. 30.
[27] Edward Whiting Fox, *History in Geographic Perspective: The Other France* (New York: W. W. Norton, 1971), p. 69.

chy never remedied its fatal error of having sold judicial offices just at the moment when it became master of the political machine. The monarch was almost completely powerless in the face of his judges, whom he could not dismiss, transfer, or promote'.[28]

Magistrates of the *parlements* varied markedly in the length of their noble pedigrees, but virtually all were men of considerable wealth, ' . . . for their fortunes included not only their offices, in themselves representing large investments, but also a formidable accumulation of securities, urban property, and rural seigneuries'.[29] As courts of appeal for disputes about seigneurial rights, the *parlements* played a crucial role in defending this 'bizarre form of property' held by noble and bourgeois alike.[30] Indeed, without the juridical backing of the parlements the whole system of seigneurial rights might have collapsed, for the royal officials had no interest in the maintenance of a system which removed income from those who were taxable into the hands of those who could not be taxed'.[31]

Not surprisingly, given their property interests and extensive connections with non-magisterial propertied families, the *parlementaires* were avid defenders of the rights and privileges of the upper classes in general. 'By their remonstrances and by their active participation in the surviving provincial estates the magistrates proceeded to uphold . . . opposition to undifferentiated taxation, encroachments on seigneurial autonomy, and ministerial assaults on the fortress of regional particularism.'[32] By their dogged defense of tax and property systems increasingly inadequate to the needs of the French state in a modernizing world, the *parlements* throughout the eighteenth century repeatedly blocked attempts at reform. Finally, in 1787–88,

---

[28] Dorn, *op. cit.*, p. 26.

[29] Franklin L. Ford, *Robe and Sword* (New York: Harper and Row, 1965; originally published in 1953), p. 248.

[30] Alfred Cobban, *The Social Interpretation of the French Revolution* (Cambridge: Cambridge University Press, 1968), Chaps. 4 and 5. There is growing agreement among historians that, at the end of the *Ancien Régime*, there was, 'between most of the nobility and the proprietary sector of the middle classes, a continuity of investment forms and socio-economic values that made them, economically, a single group. In the relations of production they played a common role. The differentiation between them was not in any sense economic; it was juridical'. From George Taylor, 'Noncapitalist Wealth and the Origins of the French Revolution', *American Historical Review* 72(2) (January, 1967): 487–8. Similar views are expressed by J. McManners, 'France', pp. 22–42 in Albert Goodwin, ed., *The European Nobility in the Eighteenth Century* (New York: Harper and Row, 1967; originally published in 1953); and Behrens, *op. cit.*, pp. 46–84.

[31] Alfred Cobban, *A History of Modern France, Volume I: 1715–1799* (Baltimore, Md.: Penguin Books, 1963; originally published in 1957), p. 155.

[32] Ford, *op. cit.*, p. 248.

they '. . . opened the door to revolution'[33] by rallying support against now indispensable administrative fiscal reforms, and by issuing the call for the convening of the Estates General.

France fought at sea and on land in each of the general European wars of the eighteenth century: the War of the Austrian Succession; the Seven Years War; and the war over American Independence. In each conflict, her resources were strained to the utmost and her vital colonial trade disrupted, yet no gains, indeed losses in America and India, resulted.[34] The War for American Independence proved to be the last straw. '[T]he price to be paid for American Independence was a French Revolution':[35] royal treasurers finally exhausted their capacity to raise loans from financiers, and were forced (again) to propose reforms of the tax system. The usual resistance from the *parlements* ensued, and an expedient adopted by Calonne in an attempt to circumvent it—the summoning of an Assembly of Notables in 1787— only provided privileged interests yet another platform for voicing resistance. A last-ditch effort to override the *parlements* (by Brienne in 1787–88) crumbled in the face of concerted upper-class defiance, popular demonstrations, and the unwillingness of army officers to direct forcible suppression of the popular resistance.[36]

The army's hesitance was especially crucial in translating fiscal crises and political unrest into general administrative and military breakdown. Recruited from various privileged social backgrounds— rich noble, rich non-noble, and poor country noble—the officers had a variety of long-standing grievances, against other officers and, significantly, against the Crown, which could never satisfy them all.[37] But it is likely that the decisive explanation for their behavior lies in the fact that they were virtually all privileged, socially and/or economically, and hence identified during 1787–88 with the *parlements*. In her *Armies and the Art of Revolution*, Katharine Chorley concludes from comparative historical studies that, in pre-industrial societies, army officers generally identify with and act to protect the interests of the privileged strata from which they are recruited. During its opening phases, until after the King had capitulated and agreed to convene the Estates General, the French Revolution pitted all strata,

[33] Cobban, *A History* . . . , p. 68.
[34] Dorn, *op. cit.*
[35] Cobban, *A History* . . . , p. 122.
[36] Jean Egret, *La Pré-Revolution Française, 1787–1788* (Paris: Presses Universitaires de France, 1962).
[37] Chorley, *op. cit.*, pp. 138–9.

led by the privileged, against the Crown. The army officers' under-standable reluctance to repress popular unrest during that period created a general crisis of governmental authority and effectiveness which in turn unleashed social divisions, between noble and non-noble, rich and poor, that made a subsequent resort to simple repres-sion by the Old Regime impossible.

The officers' insubordination early in the Revolution was all the more easily translated into rank-and-file insubordination in 1789 and after, because of the fact that French soldiers were not normally insu-lated from the civilian population. Soldiers were billeted with civil-ians, and those from rural areas were released during the summers to help with the harvest at home. Thus, during 1789, the *Gardes Françaises* (many of whom were married to Parisian working-class women) were won over to the Paris revolution in July, and peasant soldiers spread urban news in the countryside during the summer and returned to their units in the autumn with vivid tales of peasant revolt.[38]

Like the Bourbon Monarchy, the Manchu Dynasty proved unable to mobilize resources sufficient to meet credibly the challenges posed by involvement in the modernizing world. '[T]he problem was not merely the very real one of the inadequate resources of the Chinese economy as a whole. In large measure the financial straits in which the Peking government found itself were due to . . . [inability to] command such financial capacity as there was in its empire'.[39] Part of the explanation for this inability lay in a characteristic which the Chinese state shared with other agrarian states: lower and middle level officials were recruited from the landed gentry, paid insufficient salaries, and allowed to engage in a certain amount of 'normal' cor-ruption, withholding revenues collected as taxes from higher author-ities.[40] Yet, if the Manchu Dynasty had encountered the forces of modernization at the height of its powers (say in the early eighteenth century) rather than during its declining phase, it might have con-trolled or been able to mobilize sufficient resources to finance modern industries and equip a centrally controlled modern army. In

---

[38] *Ibid.*, p. 141.

[39] Albert Feuerwerker, *China's Early Industrialization* (New York: Atheneum, 1970; origi-nally published in 1958), p. 41.

[40] Chung-li Chang, *The Chinese Gentry* (Seattle: University of Washington Press, 1955); Ping-ti Ho, *The Ladder of Success in Imperial China* (New York: Columbia University Press, 1962); and Franz Michael, 'State and Society in Nineteenth Century China', *World Politics* 7 (April, 1955): 419–33.

that case, officials would never have been allowed to serve in their home provinces, and thus local and regional groups of gentry would have lacked institutional support for concerted opposition against central initiatives. But, as it happened, the Manchu Dynasty was forced to try to cope with wave after wave of imperialist intrusions, engineered by foreign industrial or industrializing nations anxious to tap Chinese markets and finances, immediately after a series of massive mid-nineteenth-century peasant rebellions. The Dynasty had been unable to put down the Taiping Rebellion on its own, and the task had fallen instead to local, gentry-led, self-defense associations and to regional armies led by complexly interrelated gentry who had access to village resources and recruits. In consequence of the gentry's role in putting down rebellion, governmental powers formerly accruing to central authorities or their bureaucratic agents, including, crucially, rights to collect and allocate various taxes, devolved upon local, gentry-dominated, sub-district governing associations and upon provincial armies and officials increasingly aligned with the provincial gentry against the center.[41]

Unable to force resources from local and regional authorities, it was all Peking could do simply to meet foreign indebtedness, and after 1895 even that proved impossible.

> Throughout the period from 1874 to 1894, the ministry [of Revenue in Peking] was engaged in a series of largely unsuccessful efforts to raise funds in order to meet a continuing series of crises—the dispute over Ili with Russia, the Sino-French War [1885], floods and famines, the Sino-Japanese War [1895]. . . . After 1895 the triple pressure of indemnity payments, servicing foreign loans, and military expenditures totally wrecked the rough balance between income and outlay which Peking had maintained [with the aid of foreign loans] until that time.[42]

The Boxer Rebellion of 1900, and subsequent foreign military intervention, only further exacerbated an already desperate situation.

Attempts by dynastic authorities to remedy matters through a series of 'reforms' implemented after 1900—abolishing the Confucian educational system and encouraging modern schools,[43] organizing the so-called 'New Armies' (which actually formed around the

[41] Philip Kuhn, *Rebellion and Its Enemies in Late Imperial China* (Cambridge, Mass.: Harvard University Press, 1970).

[42] Feuerwerker, *op. cit.*, pp. 40–1.

[43] Mary C. Wright, ed., *China in Revolution: The First Phase, 1900–1913* (New Haven: Yale University Press, 1968), pp. 24–6.

nuclei of the old provincial armies),[44] transferring local governmental functions to provincial bureaus,[45] and creating a series of local and provincial gentry-dominated representative assemblies[46]—only exacerbated the sorry situation, right up to the 1911 breaking point. 'Reform destroyed the reforming government'.[47] With each reform, dynastic elites thought to create powers to counterbalance entrenched obstructive forces, but new officials and functions were repeatedly absorbed into pre-existing local and (especially) regional cliques of gentry.[48] The last series of reforms, those that created representative assemblies, ironically provided cliques of gentry with legitimate representative organs from which to launch the liberal, decentralizing 'Constitutionalist movement' against the Manchus.

What ultimately precipitated the 'revolution of 1911' was a final attempt at reform by the central government, one that directly threatened the financial interests of the gentry power groups for the purpose of strengthening central government finances and control over national economic development:

> The specific incident that precipitated the Revolution of 1911 was the central government's decision to buy up a [railroad] line in Szechwan in which the local gentry had invested heavily. . . . The Szechwan uprising, led by the moderate constitutionalists of the Railway Protection League, sparked widespread disturbances that often had no connection with the railway issue. . . .[49]

Conspiratorial groups affiliated with Sun Yat Sen's T'eng Meng Hui, and mainly composed of Western-educated students and middle-rank New Army officers, joined the fray to produce a series of military uprisings. Finally,

> . . . the lead in declaring the independence of one province after another was taken by two principal elements: the military governors who commanded the New Army forces and the gentry-official-merchant leaders of

[44] Yoshiro Hatano, 'The New Armies', pp. 365–82 in Wright, ed., *op. cit.*; and John Gittings, 'The Chinese Army', pp. 187–224 in Jack Gray, ed., *Modern China's Search for a Political Form* (London: Oxford University Press, 1969).

[45] John Fincher, 'Political Provincialism and the National Revolution', in Wright, ed., *op. cit.*, p. 202.

[46] Fincher, *op. cit.*; and P'eng-yuan Chang, 'The Constitutionalists', in Wright, ed., *op. cit.*

[47] Wright, ed., *op. cit.*, p. 50.

[48] Fincher, *op. cit.*

[49] Wright, ed., *loc. cit.*

the provincial assemblies. These elements had more power and were more conservative than the youthful revolutionarists of the T'eng Meng Hui.[50]

The Chinese 'Revolution of 1911' irremediably destroyed the integument of civilian elite ties—traditionally maintained by the operation of Confucian educational institutions and the central bureaucracy's policies for recruiting and deploying educated officials so as to strengthen 'cosmopolitan' orientations at the expense of local loyalties—which had until that time provided at least the semblance of unified governance for China. 'Warlord' rivalries ensued as gentry interests attached themselves to regional military machines, and this condition of intra-elite disunity and rivalry (only imperfectly and temporarily overcome by Chiang Kai-Shek's regime between 1927 and 1937)[51] condemned China to incessant turmoils and provided openings (as well as cause) for lower-class, especially peasant, rebellions and for Communist attempts to organize and channel popular unrest.

---

[50] John King Fairbank, *The United States and China* (third edition) (Cambridge, Mass.: Harvard University Press, 1971), p. 132.

[51] Martin C. Wilbur, 'Military Separatism and the Process of Reunification Under the Nationalist Regime, 1922–1937', pp. 203–63 in Ping-ti Ho and Tang Tsou, eds., *China in Crisis*, Volume I, Book I (Chicago: University of Chicago Press, 1968).

6

Quantitative history

The term 'quantitative history' covers a range of methodologies and theoretical bases, linked by their reliance on numerical data. Almost all historical writing involves quantification, however, whether implicit or explicit. We may produce statistics concerning literacy among merchants' daughters in sixteenth-century Italy, or we may model the Canadian economy, referring to gross national product. We may compare individuals in the past according to the age at which they entered parliament or the size of their families. Or we may say, using Floud's example, 'the middle class supported the government', an apparently qualitative statement the veracity of which can only be proven by quantitative means.[1]

Some strands of quantitative history are not new phenomena. Malthus, for example, produced his essay on population history in 1798, and economic history gained in importance from the mid-nineteenth century, partly due to the influence of Marx. During the twentieth century, historians have increasingly wanted to study the mass of people in the past rather than a few well-documented individuals. Frequently we need to use quantitative methods to do so, thereby reducing a large amount of data to manageable proportions. In addition, examining the experience of many can compensate for the paucity of information concerning individuals. Historians also apply such possibilities to the study of minority or oppressed groups in the past, for whom specific historical data is similarly scarce. This broadening of historical focus, coupled with the advances in computer technology since the 1960s, has facilitated the development of increasingly sophisticated modes of quantitative analysis. The new methods, in turn, have enabled us to examine a host of novel historical questions.

While quantitative methods are frequently used for microstudies, narrowly delineated by time, place or problem, Lockridge described how apparently dull records of births, deaths and marriages in a small town led him to ponder the 'big questions', implicitly, the theoretical ones. He analysed the demographic behaviour of families in a town in colonial America, and realized how similar they were to the seventeenth- and eighteenth-century French of the Beauvais region. This led him to ask '[w]hat did it mean that the American environment did not transform these Europeans immediately into "new men", either demographically or socially, not for 150 years anyway?'[2] The comparative sweep which quantitative history can afford gives historians enormous scope for raising, theorizing and answering questions that more traditional narrative history might not.

What has become known as the 'new' economic history (or econometrics or cliometrics) flourished from the late 1950s. According to Davis, four practices characterize this 'new' history. It attempts 'to state precisely the questions subject to examination and to define operationally the relevant variables'; 'to build explicit models that are relevant to the questions at hand'; 'to produce evidence . . . of the world as it actually existed'; and 'to test the model . . . against the evidence . . . and the counterfactual deduction'.[3] While historians generally aim to formulate their questions precisely and unambiguously, building models prior to the collection of data is unacceptable to those many historians accustomed to the inductive method. There is controversy, too, about the kinds of data for which model building is most appropriate. At first glance, a complex statistical model might seem inappropriate to use in conjunction with poor economic data. Fogel argues, however, that the opposite is often true. The historian can compensate for scarce material by using efficient and powerful statistical methods, while similarly complex procedures are unnecessary if data is plentiful.[4] Economic models which utilize different variables can produce identical results thus compensating for inconsistencies in data. Modelling procedures therefore allow a wider scope of investigation than does traditional economic history.

More controversial than modelling historical economies is the use of counterfactual constructions. Here the new economic historian compares a real situation with that predicted in the absence of a particular circumstance (the counterfactual situation). The most famous example is Fogel's model of a late nineteenth-century America in which the railroads did not exist. Fogel aimed to test the traditional premise that the introduction of rail transport was crucial to the boom in the American economy during the second half of the century. By modelling the economics of agricultural transport, he calculated the gross national product (GNP) for 1890 in the counterfactual situation where only boat and wagon transport was available. He then compared this figure to the real GNP in 1890 and estimated that the agricultural social saving of the railroads in 1890 was 3.1 per cent or less of GNP (the figure varied according to several assumptions, for example, concerning the extension of the canal network).[5] Thus he concluded that rail transportation could hardly be called crucial to American economic growth.

In more general terms, Fogel argued that much 'old' economic history uses counterfactual explanation. Any statement such as 'slavery retarded the development of the South' implicitly compares the real world with an imagined one: it is the work of new economic historians to make these comparisons explicit and to test them.[6] While Fogel's overall logic has been applauded, his work has been criticized on two fronts. Firstly, Hunt suggests that Fogel has not taken account of important variables in his analysis, for example, 'the force of railway experience and example in developing new forms of company organization and encouraging innovation in financial enterprise'. More important for the method itself, however, is the charge that it is impossible to remove one variable from the economy without affecting others, and that such a multitude of changes is too complex to allow quantification.[7]

The whole idea of producing models of the economy with both explanatory and predictive power (in the counterfactual case) rests on two assumptions: that humans behave in an economically rational way, and that there are no exogenous variables, such as a climatic disaster of the proportions of the European famine of 1315 to 1317. Cipolla suggested that while economists may be able to ignore economic irrationality and exogeneity, economic historians cannot. In fact they must take account of many more historical variables than does the economist, to the extent that each historical situation is unique. In consequence, history is not well-served by economic models.[8] Conversely, Floud had argued that any explanatory model can only take into account a finite number of variables; certainly no historian can take account of all possible explanatory factors. Indeed, all historians pick out what seems the evidence most relevant to their problem. While the evidence chosen by an economic historian tends to be determined in advance by the model, a process unpalatable to many critics, the validity of the model can then be tested statistically, and the strength of its predictive power measured.[9] Still implicit, however, seems to be the assumption that cultural factors are less important than economics in historical explanation. Temin, himself a new economic historian, suggested that 'the methodological rigour of the new economic history needs to be allied with the willingness to contemplate diverse modes of behaviour characteristic of the old economic history'.[10]

Less methodologically controversial than the new economic history is the use of data to produce historical series, that is, serial history.[11] The historian finds or constructs homogeneous units of data which can be compared over long periods of time. Long-term changes, such as the gradual increase in literacy in Western Europe over the past four centuries, thus become visible and quantifiable. Similarly, series analysis shows up short-term fluctuations, such as alterations in the price of wheat, perhaps due to famine or climatic disaster. Some of the earliest series constructed related to wages and prices,[12] but, from the 1960s, the French *Annales* historians in particular have used serial history to throw light on cultural as well as economic and demographic phenomena. Vovelle, for example, investigated changing attitudes to death, both through a study of the contents of wills from eighteenth-century Provence, and by examining representations of Purgatory in Provençal churches of the fifteenth to twentieth centuries.[13] Serial history can therefore be used to tackle an extraordinary range of historical problems, and has engendered an ingenious approach to sources. In addition, Furet believes that one of the side benefits of this approach is the necessity for historians to become historiographically self-aware, focusing on the way in which we construct our data and our objects of research.[14]

One of the difficulties in producing a series lies in ensuring that the units of comparison are consistent. In using census data, for example, we may find that the work associated with a particular occupational group varied over time, despite an identical label. In a related instance, we may use series which show the yearly changes in the types of cases appearing in a medieval manorial court. Constructing the series is straightforward, but interpreting its meaning is more problematic. An increase in the proportion of thefts of firewood, for example, may reflect increasing levels of poverty, a decrease in the area of available woodland, more efficient policing of woodland regulations under a particular bailiff, a new attitude to crime, or merely a change in the types of business brought to that court. Here again we see that quantification can increase the amount of data at an historian's disposal, but cannot replace thoughtful interpretive practice.

One simple but frequently reiterated warning regards the risk of oversimplification. The following quote from Twain illustrates the point:

> the Mississippi between Cairo and New Orleans was twelve hundred and fifteen miles long one hundred and seventy-six years ago. It was eleven hundred and eighty after the cut-off of 1722. . . . its length is only nine hundred and seventy-three miles at present. In the space of one hundred and seventy-six years the Lower Mississippi has shortened itself two hundred and forty-two miles. That is an average of a trifle over one mile and a third per year. Therefore, any calm person, who is not blind or idiotic, can see that in the Old Oölitic Silurian Period, just a million years ago next November, the Lower Mississippi River was upwards of one million three hundred thousand miles long, and stuck out over the Gulf of Mexico like a fishing-rod.[15]

While this passage is obviously a joke, Twain nevertheless indicates the care which must be taken while using models and extrapolating from data. There is considerable value in standing back from one's results and using some common sense.

Historical demography, in part based on serial analysis, is the study of population in the past. Historians reconstruct rates of birth, marriage and death, and from there can examine topics such as family and household structure, migration, social structure and gender roles. These patterns can then be considered alongside economic data, like price and wage series, immeasurably broadening our historical perspective. These techniques give us access to a much greater proportion of historical societies than does the analysis of most historical documents: this is particularly true of pre-industrial communities. Tosh suggests that, since members of pre-industrial societies lived so much closer to the margins of subsistence than we do, demographic patterns themselves were crucial and, in fact, that 'demography was *the* determinant of social and economic life'.[16]

Historical demography is based broadly on two types of source and two analytic techniques. The first category of source consists of lists of people in existence at a particular time and may include other information about their lives such as age, sex, occupation, marital status and income. Census returns and taxation lists fall into this class. The second group, most importantly parish registers, gives dates and usually places of baptism, marriage and burial for individuals.[17]

In theory, if such documents were accurate and consistent in terms of their contents, frequent and regular over long time periods in the case of census material, and geographically encompassing, both nationally and internationally, demographic historians could calculate totals of births, marriages and deaths at any given time and place in the past. From here, rates of fertility, nuptiality and mortality per 1,000 of population could be produced and changes in these rates interpreted, a process known as aggregative analysis. While the modern census was first used in Scandinavia in the mid-eighteenth century, census material is not usually extant before the nineteenth century, and European parish registers, while they may extend back in time to the sixteenth century, do not translate into complete records of 'vital events', due to vagaries of recording and chronological gaps in the series.[18] Furthermore, these bald totals give us little information concerning, for example, household structure.

One means of overcoming this problem has been nominative analysis, where individuals are identified (by name) in the registers, the dates of their vital events and, ideally, kin relationships determined. Other source material relating to them, found in censuses, wills, land transactions, etc., is attached to their name. Once the researcher has painstakingly drawn up these sketchy biographies, often with computer assistance, he can reconstruct successive generations of a family, a technique known as family reconstitution.[19] This method produces a plethora of information about the age, kinship, inheritance and mobility patterns in society and the means through which these change. The drawback here, apart from the inherent difficulties in tracing individuals and the irregularities of the sources, is the enormous amount of time such an enterprise consumes, even for a small number of families.

A method of compensating for gaps in the census records, known as back projection, and later refined as inverse projection, was therefore developed. This produced quantitative measures of the size and structure of the population, working backwards from known statistics into the less certain past.[20] These techniques used together can show us demographic detail about the past and help us to interpret that information.

While to outline the conclusions reached by historical demographers would take more space than is available here, there are limitations to this approach which bear discussion. One of the most pressing of these, the difficulty of producing meaning from statistics, akin to that of producing soft data from hard data as Burke puts it, applies to most quantitative history.[21] In demographic terms, Anderson reminds us of the lack of evidence among our statistics concerning attitudes. Does a narrow age gap between spouses, for example, suggest a companionate marriage? Should a co-resident grandmother be seen as a 'revered and powerful matriarch', a nuisance whose death was eagerly awaited or 'an old friend'?[22]

Despite these and other problems with the demographic method, Wrigley suggests that, if we can develop 'organising concepts to link population characteristics to their socioeconomic context and to do justice to the mutual interaction between the two', we can extend the 'list of topics which promise well' 'almost indefinitely'.[23] An early example of such work is Laslett's *The World We Have Lost*, a perhaps flawed but enormously influential use of demographic and economic data to examine social structure as well as social and political change. Another very different but similarly groundbreaking book was Goubert's study of the Beauvais.[24]

A further powerful tool has been the development of content analysis. Here one takes an apparently qualitative document, such as a newspaper or an election speech, and codes the information it contains in order to facilitate a quantitative analysis. This technique can produce surprising conclusions: a quantitative analysis may point to the importance of items glossed over or taken for granted in a more subjectively structured reading.

Richard Merritt, for example, examined the development of American self-awareness by content analysis of eighteenth-century newspapers. He argued that '[t]he point at which the colonists stopped considering themselves Englishmen and began more often to think of themselves as Americans was of signal importance in the rise of American nationalism'. To pinpoint this moment, Merritt analysed variables such as words or symbols, regularities of speech usage and images. He points out, however, that the content analyst has to choose her or his variables carefully since the assumption is made that the words used by a writer or speaker reflect that person's attitudes.[25] Again this is a quantitative technique the use of which requires sensitivity but which can add enormously to knowledge derived from more conventional historical techniques.

The increasing use of computers as a tool is extremely important for historians. Computers are clearly well-suited to the complex models used by economic historians. Social and demographic historians are increasingly turning to the use of historical databases. Harvey and Press, for example, pointed out that, by 1992, one guide listed 376 projects carried out in the United Kingdom which used databases of some sort. And this was 'far from being an exhaustive or definitive inventory'.[26] As well, database programs, for example, NUD*IST, oriented to the quantitative and qualitative analysis of textual data, are being developed. In 1968, Le Roy Ladurie controversially wrote, 'tomorrow's historian will have to be able to programme a computer in order to survive'. Harvey and Press issued a similar challenge of their own: 'The use of databases in historical research is set to increase to the point where a basic knowledge of database systems will be regarded as an essential skill for all professionally trained historians.'[27]

Overall, quantitative methods in history have encouraged us to extend our range of historical sources and topics, made possible more exact comparisons between societies over time, and focused our minds on specific historical problems and on the ways in which we as historians construct our material. We have seen that the techniques can be controversial, the sources not as accurate as we once hoped, and the interpretation of our data less straightforward than it seemed in the early days of quantification. Nevertheless, rather than leaving out the people in history as some critics have alleged, the use of techniques such as economic modelling and demographic reconstruction has greatly increased our access to the mass of participants in our past.

Richard Wall, as a member of the Cambridge Group for the Study of Population and Social Structure, was part of a group of historical demographers who challenged the idea that the typical medieval family was an extended one, and that Western family structure has become more nuclear over time. As a result, much of Wall's work has dealt with issues of household structure in the modern world. The following chapter illustrates demographic history at its best. Not only does Wall produce useful statistics concerning the English household and changes in its composition, but he is critical of his own interpretive practice. Thus he highlights both the possibilities and limitations of historical demography.

Table 16.2 in this article shows the variation over time of the structure of the English household. What important trends does Wall identify from this table? What does he mean when he suggests that studies of the role of the kin group in working-class families may have 'unduly influenced expectations about the size and nature of the kin group in "traditional" English households'? Wall suggested an explanation for the decline in the number of servants included in English households from the late eighteenth century. What was this explanation and why did he think that his explanation might be inadequate? Overall, what does this article suggest to you about the processes involved in demographic history and the interpretation of data?

Notes

1 Roderick Floud, *An Introduction to Quantitative Methods for Historians* (2nd edn, London, 1979), pp. 1–2.
2 Kenneth Lockridge, 'Historical Demography', in Charles F. Delzell (ed.), *The Future of History* (Nashville, 1977), p. 55.
3 Lance Davis, 'The New Economic History: II. Professor Fogel and the New Economic History', *Economic History Review*, 19 (1966), p. 657.
4 R. W. Fogel, 'The New Economic History: I. Its Findings and Methods', *Economic History Review*, 19 (1966), pp. 652–3.
5 *Ibid.*, pp. 650–5.
6 *Ibid.*, p. 655.
7 E. H. Hunt, 'The New Economic History: Professor Fogel's Study of American Railways', *History*, 53 (1968), pp. 6, 10–15. See Hawke's commentary on Hunt's critique in the same volume. For a more detailed discussion of counterfactual history, see George G. S. Murphy, 'On Counterfactual Propositions', *History and Theory Beiheft 9: Studies in Quantitative History and the Logic of the Social Sciences* (1969), pp. 14–38.
8 Carlo M. Cipolla, *Between History and Economics: An Introduction to Economic History*, trans. Christopher Woodall (Oxford, 1991), pp. 9–10.
9 Roderick Floud, 'Introduction', in Floud (ed.), *Essays in Quantitative Economic History* (Oxford, 1974), pp. 2–4.
10 Peter Temin, 'The Future of the New Economic History', in Theodore K. Rabb and Robert I. Rotberg (eds), *The New History: The 1980s and Beyond* (Princeton, 1982), p. 179.
11 See François Furet, 'Quantitative History', *Daedalus*, 100 (1971), pp. 151–67, for a detailed discussion of this topic.
12 For example, William Beveridge, *Prices and Wages in England, from the Twelfth to the Nineteenth Century* (London, 1939), vol. 1.
13 Michel Vovelle, 'On Death', in *Ideologies and Mentalities*, trans. Eamon O'Flaherty (Cambridge, 1990), p. 73.
14 Furet, 'Quantitative History', p. 155.
15 Mark Twain, *Life on the Mississippi* (New York, 1883), pp. 128–9.
16 John Tosh, *The Pursuit of History: Aims, Methods and New Directions in the Study Of Modern History* (2nd edn, London, 1991), p. 188.
17 *Ibid.*
18 *Ibid.*
19 E. A. Wrigley, 'The Prospects for Population History', in Rabb and Rotberg, *The New History*, pp. 211–13.
20 *Ibid.*, pp. 213–16. For a detailed discussion of the method, see E. A. Wrigley and R. S. Schofield, *The Population History of England 1541–1871: A Reconstruction* (Cambridge, Mass., 1981), App. 15.
21 Peter Burke, *History and Social Theory* (Cambridge, 1992), pp. 36–8.
22 Michael Anderson, *Approaches to the History of the Western Family 1500–1914* (London, 1980), pp. 33–8.

23 Wrigley, 'The Prospects for Population History', pp. 207, 224. See his list of suggested research areas on p. 224.
24 Peter Laslett, *The World We Have Lost* (London, 1965). Laslett's work may have been influenced by modernization theory: see W. W. Rostow, *Politics and the Stages of Growth* (London, 1971), and S. N. Eisenstadt, *Modernization: Protest and Change* (London, 1966). For a discussion of Goubert, see Robert Harding, 'Pierre Goubert's *Beauvais et le Beauvaisis*: An Historian "*parmi les hommes*"', *History and Theory*, 22 (1983), pp. 178–98.
25 Richard L. Merritt, *Symbols of American Community, 1735–75* (New Haven, 1966); Merritt, 'The Emergence of American Nationalism: A Quantitative Approach', in Seymour Martin Lipset and Richard Hofstadter (eds), *Sociology and History: Methods* (New York, 1968), pp. 138–58.
26 K. Schürer and S. J. Anderson (eds), *A Guide to Historical Datafiles Held in Machine-Readable Form* (London, 1992), cited in Charles Harvey and Jon Press, *Databases in Historical Research: Theory, Methods and Applications* (London, 1996), p. xi.
27 Emmanuel Le Roy Ladurie, *The Territory of the Historian*, trans. Ben and Siân Reynolds (Hassocks, Sussex, [1973] 1979), p. 6; Harvey and Press, *Databases in Historical Research*, p. xi.

Additional reading

Anderson, Michael, *Approaches to the History of the Western Family 1500–1914* (London, 1980).

Barzun, Jacques, *Clio and the Doctors: Psycho-History Quanto-History & History* (Chicago, 1974).

Cipolla, Carlo M., *Between History and Economics: An Introduction to Economic History*, trans. Christopher Woodall (Oxford, 1991).

Floud, Roderick, *An Introduction to Quantitative Methods for Historians* (2nd edn, London, 1979).

Floud, Roderick (ed.), *Essays in Quantitative Economic History* (Oxford, 1974).

Fogel, Robert William, *Railroads and American Economic Growth: Essays In Econometric History* (Baltimore, 1964).

Furet, François and Jacques Ozouf, *Reading and Writing: Literacy in France from Calvin to Jules Ferry,* Cambridge Studies in Oral and Literate Culture 5 (Cambridge, [1977] 1982).

Laslett, Peter, *The World We Have Lost: Further Explored* (3rd edn, Cambridge, [1965] 1983).

Rabb, Theodore K. and Robert I. Rotberg (eds), *The New History: The 1980s and Beyond* (Princeton, 1982).

Rotberg, Robert I. and Theodore K. Rabb (eds), *Population and Economy: Population and History from the Traditional to the Modern World* (Cambridge, 1986).

Tosh, John, 'History by Numbers', in *The Pursuit of History: Aims, Methods and New Directions in the Study of Modern History* (2nd edn, London, 1991).

Wrigley, E. A. and R. S. Schofield, *The Population History of England 1541–1871: A Reconstruction* (Cambridge, Mass., 1981).

THE HOUSEHOLD: DEMOGRAPHIC AND ECONOMIC CHANGE IN ENGLAND, 1650–1970
Richard Wall

The basic structure of English households in the pre-industrial era is now well known. Households were small. The majority contained fewer than five persons, and membership was customarily confined to parents and their unmarried children. If the family was sufficiently wealthy, or involved in farming or trade, then the household might well contain servants, but there were remarkably few complex households containing grandparents, parents, and grandchildren.[1] Untimely death in the older generation and average age at marriage in the mid- to late 20s for both sexes naturally curtailed the number of three-generational households that it was possible to form. But the number that were formed never came anywhere near the potential number.[2] It was not because children married late while their parents died early that few households spanned three generations, but because the vast majority of children who had not already left the parental home to become servants in the households of others would establish separate households on marrying.

The implication of the link between marriage and the formation of a household is that English households must have varied in structure over time. Nationally, the crude marriage rate fell steadily to reach a low point in the late seventeenth century, from which it rose to a high plateau between 1771 and 1796 before falling again.[3] On each occasion the turning point followed a reversal in the trend of real wages some 30 years earlier, a sustained fall in real wages ushering in a fall in the marriage rate, a sustained rise in real wages prompting a comparable rise in the marriage rate. In terms of house-

I would like to thank my colleagues Dr R. S. Schofield, Dr R. M. Smith, and Dr E. A. Wrigley for their comments on an earlier draft of this chapter.

[1] P. Laslett and Wall (eds.), *Household and family* (1972): 146–54.

[2] Wachter with Hammel and Laslett, *Statistical studies of historical social structure* (1978): 80.

[3] R. M. Smith, 'Fertility, economy and household formation in England' (1981b): 601, fig. 3. Marriages per 1,000 persons aged 15–34 derived from Wrigley and Schofield, *The population history of England* (1981), which contains the base data and an explanation of the procedures underpinning the calculations.

Table 16.1. *Headship rates and proportions ever married: males aged 20–9*

| Parish | Date | Males aged 20–9 | | | Proportions | |
		No. ever married	No. heading households	All	Ever married (%)	Heading households (%)
Ealing	1599	4	7	31	12.9	22.6
Grasmere	1683	2	2	21	9.5	9.5
Chilvers Coton	1684	17	19	43	39.5	44.2
Lichfield	1695	29	37	116	25.0	31.9
Ringmore	1698	3	2	13	23.1	15.4
Stoke	1701	38	39	116	32.8	33.6
Wembworthy	1779	4	5	18	22.2	27.8
Corfe Castle	1790	24	24	80	30.0	30.0
Ardleigh	1796	35	30	94	37.2	31.9
Elmdon	1861	20	20	37	54.1	54.1

hold composition this relationship would be reflected most obviously in the headship rate, that is the proportion of persons by age who headed their own households. The expectation would be that more men in their 20s and 30s would marry and form their own households in the late sixteenth and late eighteenth centuries than during the seventeenth century, this behaviour being occasioned, as with the marriage rate, by an earlier rise in real income.

The information that is available on headship rates in pre-industrial England is unfortunately limited.[4] It is derived from those nine listings[5] which give the ages of the inhabitants and is presented for men in their 20s in table 16.1. Contrary to expectation, there is no sign of higher headship rates in the late eighteenth century, or indeed in the one solitary example from the late sixteenth. However, it could be argued that this is caused not by any lack of correlation between headship rates and proportions married, since at the level of the community such an association is visible (see the final two columns of table 16.1), but because the extremely wide variation in

[4] One nineteenth-century community, Elmdon in Essex, has been included for comparative purposes and had a very high headship rate.

[5] Listings are population counts including surviving enumeration schedules of the first four national censuses of England (1801–31) in which the population is divided into households. A brief description of the information provided by each list can be found in the journal *Local Population Studies* beginning with issue 24 (Spring 1980). For a discussion of some of the issues underlying the identification of the blocks of names as households, see ch. 1 above.

headship rates between communities completely masks any shift in headship rates between the seventeenth and eighteenth centuries. For example, the two large towns of Stoke and Lichfield yielded high rates, with more than 3 of every 10 men aged between 20 and 29 heading households. In the nascent industrial centre of Chilvers Coton, the headship rate was even higher. At the other extreme were Grasmere, nestling among the Westmorland fells, where only 9.5% of men aged 20–9 were household heads, and Ringmore, a coastal parish in Devon, where 15% of men in their 20s headed households.

These inter-community differences in headship rates, however, pose a further set of problems. Movement over time in headship rates may be explained by trends in the real wage, but it is less clear that such trends account for the range of headship rates among communities. Other and probably more relevant factors governing the process of household formation are the period of training considered necessary before an individual became free to pursue a particular occupation; the labour requirements of other households, which might involve at certain times a greater or lesser preference for labour within the household (i.e. unmarried servants)[6] over out-labour (labourers, mainly married persons); even, as might be the case in Grasmere, ease of access to land. Mortality too could vary markedly in level from place to place, altering the speed at which land or employment opportunities could be taken up by younger adults.[7]

The importance that should be given to each of these factors must await the detailed examination of the local economies of these communities, and even so there will be a limit to what can be based on no more than nine self-selected settlements. In practice, therefore, for charting both temporal and spatial variation in the English household before 1821 it will continue to be necessary to rely on the much larger body of listings which do not give ages.[8] This material has now

[6] Kussmaul, *Servants in husbandry in early-modern England* (1981): 97, 101.

[7] For example, unpublished estimates by the SSRC Cambridge Group, derived from 12 reconstitutions and relating to the period 1750–99, indicate that if the average chances of a man surviving from age 25 to age 50 is expressed as 100, in Gainsborough, Lincs. his survival chances were only 85.2, while in Gedling, Notts. they rated 112.7. The strength of regional variations in mortality in the nineteenth century is assessed by Benson, 'Mortality variation in the north of England' (1980).

[8] 1821 was the first of the national English censuses to include a question on age, and a number of enumeration schedules have survived giving the ages of the inhabitants. The first national census for which a full set of enumeration schedules has survived is 1841, but only in 1851 did it become standard to give the relationship to the head of the household and the exact age of every individual.

been thoroughly resurveyed,[9] and with the information now beginning to emerge from Michael Anderson's mammoth random sample of the 1851 enumerators' schedules, together with some near-contemporary sample surveys of households, it is possible to modify and add much greater detail to the overview of the household presented by Peter Laslett in 1969.[10] However, one major problem remains. There are simply too few listings to enable a random selection of communities to be drawn up for the pre-industrial period. General statements about the household based, as is inevitably the case, on the few lists of acceptable quality (cf. notes to table 16.2) need careful consideration. This is a difficulty to which further reference will be made below.

The main outlines of English households since the seventeenth century are set out in table 16.2. Two factors account for the fact that English households are now much smaller in size: the reduction in the number of children and the virtual elimination from the household of resident labour, represented by servants. On the other hand, the number of kin in the household seems to have declined only after 1947. Indeed, kin (relatives of the household head other than spouse or offspring) were at their maximum in 1947 rather than in some remote period in the past. It may be significant that the decade following 1947 saw a number of pioneering studies of the role of the kin group in working-class communities, studies that can be seen, in retrospect, to have unduly influenced expectations about the size and nature of the kin group in 'traditional' English households.

[9] The principles on which this fresh selection of listings was made were as follows: that divisions between households should be clearly identified, that the relationships of all or nearly all persons to the head of the household should be specified, and that the terms used should be unambiguous (for example some listmakers used 'child' as an age category rather than as a relationship indicating the offspring of the household head, and listings of this type were excluded). The differences between this selection and the one made in P. Laslett, 'Size and structure of the household in England over three centuries' (1969) is that Laslett made use of a variable number of listings depending on the subject under investigation (for example, 100 listings yielded information on mean household size but only 46 on kin), whereas the present selection uses fewer listings but has the same 'population' in all calculations. According to the new selection there were more households headed by married couples and more kin, but rather fewer offspring, servants, and attached lodgers than was previously suggested, but the revisions to the figures are generally slight; cf. table 16.2 below and P. Laslett and Wall (eds.) (1972): 83, table 1.13. Corrections of a similar order apply to the results in Wall, 'Regional and temporal variations in English household structure' (1977), in which Laslett's original selection of listings was rearranged according to time period (enumerated before or after 1750); cf. nn. 12, 26, 49 below.

[10] P. Laslett (1969). A revised and extended version formed ch. 4 of P. Laslett and Wall (eds.) (1972).

Table 16.2. *Mean number of persons per 100 households: England, seventeenth to twentieth centuries*

Relationship to household head	1650–1749	1750–1821	1851 Rural	1851 Urban[a]	1947	1970
Head + spouse	163	175	171	164	180	170
Offspring	177	209	210	191	134	109
Relatives	16	22	33	27	42	11
Servants	61	51	33	14	2	0[b]
SUBTOTAL	418[c]	457	447	396	358	290
Attached lodgers	26	24	24	50	9	3[b]
TOTAL	444	481	471	446	367	293
N (households)	866	1,900	2,467	1,961	5,997	796

[a] Excludes London.
[b] Servants and lodgers are not separately distinguished in the 1970 survey, and the division suggested here is entirely arbitrary.
[c] Proportions have been rounded to the nearest whole number. This accounts for any slight discrepancy between totals or subtotals and the sum of the figures in columns or rows.

Sources:
1650–1749 Cambridge Group listings: Puddletown, Dorset (1724); Southampton, Holy Rhood and St Lawrence (1696); Southampton, St John (1695); Goodnestone, Kent (1676); London, St Mary Woolchurch (1695); Harefield, Middx. (1699); Clayworth, Notts. (1676).
1750–1821 Cambridge Group listings: Binfield, Berks. (1801); West Wycombe, Bucks. (1760); Littleover, Derby. (1811); Mickleover, Derby. (1811); Morley, Derby. (1787); Corfe Castle, Dorset (1790); Ardleigh, Essex (1796); Forthampton, Gloucs. (1752); Barkway and Reed, Herts. (1801); Heyford and Caldecote, Oxon. (1771); Bampton, Barton, Hackthorpe, Kings Meaburn, Lowther, Morland, Newby, and Great Strickland, Westmor. (1787).
1851 Calculated from data supplied by Michael Anderson in a personal communication, derived from a one-sixteenth subsample of enumerators' schedules.
1947 Gray, 'The British household' (1947).
1970 R. Barnes and Durant, 'Pilot work on the General Household Survey' (1970).

It is not possible to produce a fine measure of change in household composition when the evidence is contained in a series of snapshot pictures of the household, but there are some very clear trends visible in table 16.2. The first phase (seventeenth to eighteenth centuries)[11] involved the decline in the number of servants in the household, but this was more than offset by a rise in the number of kin

[11] The time periods adopted for the analysis were 1650–1749 and 1750–1821, but most of the listings within the former period date from the late seventeenth century and within the latter period from the late eighteenth century; cf. notes to table 16.2.

and, more particularly, in the number of offspring, with the result that households were, on average, some 8% larger in the latter period.[12] During the second phase (up to 1851) there was a much sharper fall in the number of servants and a further rise in the number of kin, but it was only in the third phase that there occurred a fundamental transformation with marked falls in the numbers of offspring, servants, and attached lodgers. Owing to the failure of successive generations of census officials to conduct inquiries into the structure of the household, and the 100-year closure period that operates before the enumerators' schedules can be examined, this third phase is unsatisfactorily long. It is unclear when exactly the household changed and difficult therefore to frame hypotheses as to why it changed. It may also provide a false perspective from which to view the fourth phase, the changes that occurred to the household after 1947.[13] On the figures as they stand, the decline in kin and the further falls in the number of offspring and attached lodgers during the quarter century after the Second World War seem the most dramatic in the English experience, as they have occurred in such a short period. Hidden perhaps in the nineteenth century or the early twentieth, however, there might be other periods of equally dramatic change, although it has to be said that the evidence of the headship rate is that the rules governing the formation of households varied little between 1861 and 1951.[14]

At the same time it is important to remember, when referring to aspects of the household that have changed over time, that some surprising parallels can be drawn between the households of 1970 and those of the seventeenth century. This becomes clear if the focus is placed on the proportion of persons of various types present in the

[12] Cf. Wall (1977): 94, which indicated a more modest rise in mean household size of 2.3% based on a different set of listings (and in particular more London parishes in the earlier period), a subdivision of the material used by Laslett for his 1969 study (cf. n. 9 above).

[13] The economic uncertainties of the 1970s and the decline in real incomes and the contraction of the housing market in the early 1980s suggest the possibility of a fifth phase: a reversal of the fall in household size and more households containing kin. However, the latest available figures covering 1979, on household size and gross type (two-, one-, or no-family households with some subdivisions showing some of the households with dependent children or retired people or headed by married couples), provide no evidence of a halt to the process of fragmentation. See the journal *Social Trends*, 11 (1981): 28.

[14] My interpretation of the findings of Hole and Pountney, *Trends in population, housing and occupancy rates 1861–1961* (1971); see Wall, 'Regional and temporal variation in the structure of the British household since 1851' (1982a).

Table 16.3. *Household members by relationship to household head: England, seventeenth to twentieth centuries*

Relationship to household head	Proportion of total membership of household plus attached lodgers					
	1650–1749 (%)	1750–1821 (%)	1851		1947 (%)	1970 (%)
			Rural (%)	Urban (%)		
Head	22.5	20.8	21.2	22.4	27.3	34.1
Spouse	14.3	15.6	15.2	14.3	21.9	24.0
Offspring	39.9	43.4	44.4	42.8	36.5	37.2
Relatives	3.6	4.6	7.1	6.1	11.5	3.8
Servants	13.8	10.7	7.1	3.1	0.5 ⎱	1.1
Attached lodgers	5.8	4.9	5.0	11.2	2.3 ⎰	
TOTAL	99.9	100.0	100.0	99.9	100.0	100.2
N (population)	3,850	9,133	11,630	8,734	21,985	2,337

Sources: As for table 16.2.

household, as in table 16.3. Admittedly, the fact that households were so much smaller in 1970, with many persons living entirely on their own, means that more than half of the total membership of the household fell into two categories of household head and spouse of head.[15] On the other hand, the share of certain other persons in the household of the total membership was unchanged. This is true both for children and for kin despite the fact that the number of children and kin present was at an all-time low in 1970 (cf. table 16.2).

A more detailed examination of the structure of the household, however, is sufficient to bring out a further set of differences between the households of the seventeenth century and those of the present day. For example, an analysis of the range of kin accepted into the household (table 16.4) reveals that in both 1947 and 1970 a larger proportion of relatives could be defined as 'close kin' (parents and spouses of offpring) than had been the case in previous centuries.[16]

[15] Households containing just one person made up 23% of all households in 1979 compared with 5.7% in pre-industrial England; cf. *Social Trends*, 11 (1981) and P. Laslett and Wall (eds.) (1972): 142. Some data on the proportions of persons living alone in past and present populations are included in Wall 'Woman alone in English society' (1981).

[16] Information on kin (resident relatives) in 1851 is derived from an analysis of the enumerators' schedules for the same settlements for which listings had been drawn up between 1750 and 1821 and avoids the problem of a comparison between a random

Table 16.4. *Resident relatives by relationship to household head: England, seventeenth to twentieth centuries*

Relationship to household head	Mean relatives per 100 households					Proportion of all relatives				
	1650–1749	1750–1821	1851	1947[a]	1970[a]	1650–1749 (%)	1750–1821 (%)	1851 (%)	1947[a] (%)	1970[a] (%)
Parents[b]	2	3	4	10	3	16	17	12	24	30
Siblings[b]	2	3	7	–	2	22	18	21	–	23
Sons- or daughters-in-law	1	1	2	8	2	8	7	8	19	14
Nephews or nieces	1	2	5	–	–	9	11	16	–	–
Grandchildren	3	7	12	–	2	27	38	39	–	19
Other relatives	2	1	1	24	2	17	8	4	57	15
TOTAL	11	18[c]	32[c]	42	11	99	99	100	100	101
N (households)	2,765	2,231	2,804	5,997	796 (Kin)	293	409	943	2,531	88

[a] Dashes in these columns indicate that persons with this relationship have not been separately distinguished and are subsumed into the category 'Other relatives'.

[b] Includes in-laws.

[c] Values have been rounded to the nearest whole number. This accounts for any slight discrepancy between totals or subtotals and the sum of the figures in columns or rows.

Sources: As for table 16.2 with the following exceptions:

1650–1749: additional listings of Stoke Edith, Herefs. (1647); Monckton, Kent (1705); London, All Hallows Staining and St Mary le Bow (1695).

1750–1821: additional listings of Braintree, Essex (1821); Leverton, Lincs. (1762); Hartsop and Sockbridge, Westmor. (1787); but excluding Ardleigh, Essex (1796); Barkway and Reed, Herts. (1801); and Heyford and Caldecote, Oxon. (1771).

1851: enumerators' schedules for same settlements as 1750–1821.

In fact, looking at the kin group in detail, it is clear that this has been the most decisive shift in its composition. The earlier expansion of the kin group, even that between the late eighteenth century and the mid-nineteenth involving an increase in the number of grand-children, nephews, nieces, and siblings present in the household, produced no marked change in the proportion of kin of various types, other than a modest fall in the proportion of kin who were the parents or parents-in-law of the household head.[17] Put another way, the situation is one in which prior to 1851 the kin group expanded without materially altering the balance among the various types of relative present, whereas by 1947, despite the fact that the kin group grew even larger than it was in 1851, the range of kin in the household had already narrowed to what it was to be in 1970.

There has, therefore, been a considerable amount of change over the past three centuries in the structure of English households, and various suggestions can be put forward to explain the key elements of the process. For example, one explanation of the decline in farm service between the late eighteenth and mid-nineteenth centuries would be to see it as a consequence of the rise in population and fall in real wages which made labour relatively abundant and cheap at the same time as it made feeding that labour in one's home relatively expensive. It was, it could be argued, a natural response on the part of the farmers to switch from using living-in farm servants to day labourers who had to fend for themselves and could be employed on a more casual basis.[18] Similarly, reference is made to living standards in the twentieth century (only this time to rising standards) as a cause of the fragmentation of households.[19] It has to be recognized,

---

sample of schedules, the source of the data for 1851 in tables 16.2 and 16.3, and a much smaller and non-random selection of listings. See also n. 40 below for an illustration of the differences in the composition of the households in the random sample and in the schedules selected to provide a 'match' with 1750–1821.

[17] Table 16.4 also records an expansion between the seventeenth and eighteenth centuries in the number and proportion of all relatives who were the grandchildren of the household head. The difficulty is to decide whether this change is genuine, because the category of 'other relatives' (kin whose relationship to the household head was not specified) was sufficiently large in the period 1650–1749 (and much lower thereafter) to account for much of the registered increase in grandchildren. It is an unfortunate feature that the specification of relationships is not more exact even in the most detailed English listings of the seventeenth century (cf. n. 9).

[18] Cf. R. M. Smith (1981b): 604, who also stresses the relevance of the agrarian economy (grain as opposed to pasture), though his argument is formulated a little differently from that of the present chapter.

[19] For example Michael, Fuchs, and Scott, 'Changes in the propensity to live alone' (1980), interpreting trends in the United States between 1950 and 1976.

though, that such explanations do not provide a complete solution.

The first issue is the question of timing. The decline in farm service cannot be charted precisely, because the surviving listings are too scattered both geographically and over time. Nevertheless, farm service lingered on, particularly in pastoral areas, as is evident from the census returns of 1851.[20] It is clear, therefore, that population growth in the eighteenth century by itself cannot provide an entirely satisfactory explanation for the decline in farm service. The management of livestock required, or at least benefited from, a resident labour force (i.e. the farm servant) in a way arable farming did not.[21] However, one of the indirect consequences of population growth was that it induced farmers to meet the increased demand for basic (grain-based) food and a reduced demand for high-quality dairy products by abandoning pasture for arable wherever the geographical situation did not preclude such a change. In other words the economic pressures produced by population growth that led farmers to shed resident labour were largely confined to the arable sector, though population growth also tended to increase the relative importance of that sector in agriculture as a whole.

The question of timing also arises, but in a different sense, in connection with the association between changes in household structure in the twentieth century and rising living standards. No one doubts that living standards have risen. The problem is that such a rise has occurred in other periods without promoting change in the household. It is necessary, therefore, to conceive of living standards as subject to a certain (but as yet undefined) threshold which has to be crossed before the structure of the household is to be transformed. The principal difficulty in the concept of 'threshold' is that there is evidence to suggest that the household is 'fragmenting' in much the same way over much of Europe, and indeed in the United States,[22]

---

[20] Kussmaul (1981): 20, fig. 2.3.
[21] Kussmaul (1981): 23 argues that farm servants were common in pastoral areas not only because dairy farms required continuous labour but because labour was often scarce in such areas as a result of the combination of dispersed settlements and alternative employment opportunities in rural crafts. A further possibility, however, is that the real cost to the farmer of providing board and lodging for his employees was lower in mixed farming than in wholly agrarian regions, and it is a pity that information on this point and on the level of real wages in pastoral as opposed to agrarian regions is still unavailable.
[22] Some of this evidence is discussed in ch. 1, and see also Wall (1982a) and references, but it has to be admitted that determining the exact point of change from decadal

despite the fact that living standards could scarcely be described as uniform. It is necessary, therefore, to elaborate the hypothesis further to take account of the possibility that the point of change might differ from one country to another. Such differences might arise if a cultural pattern specific to a particular population discouraged members of families from breaking away to establish their own households, even though they had acquired sufficient resources for this purpose. A more plausible explanation, in my opinion, given the present ease with which ideas and tastes are communicated, is that once a particular pattern has established itself in a culturally dominant population, such as the United States, the pattern will spread rapidly to other populations in quite different economic circumstances. A less economically developed population will adopt, or at least tries to adopt, a household formation pattern that has emerged in the economic context of a more affluent neighbour. Obviously such a process would impose considerable strain on the familial system in the poorer population.

Issues of timing apart, further problems of interpretation arise because changes in attitudes about the type of household that is considered desirable are often associated with modifications in the composition of households. It is often claimed today, for example, that family ties are looser; that people value their independence more than they did; that individuals may still want to see their relatives, but not too often, and that they certainly do not want to live with them if it can be avoided. What is not so clear, however, is whether these attitudes existed, perhaps in a latent form, prior to the onset of the fragmentation process, or whether such attitudes are really new, as is sometimes claimed.[23]

A comparable situation occurs in connection with the decline in farm service after the late eighteenth century. Farmers, it is said, came to value their privacy and were therefore glad to distance themselves, both socially and geographically, from their employees.[24] This, too, could have been a previously held attitude, merely awaiting the right economic climate to be put into effect, or, alternatively, it could be

or even quinquennial censuses and the occasional survey must be subject to a considerable margin of error.

[23] A point raised in connection with the elderly in Britain by Hole and Pountney (1971): 26, and with one-person households in Austria by Findl and Helczmanovszki, *The population of Austria* (1977): 120.

[24] See the responses to Question 38 of the Poor Law Report of 1834 summarized by Kussmaul (1981): 128–9.

an attempt to rationalize a behaviour pattern that economic forces had made advantageous.

It is difficult to see how the conceptual difficulty is to be satisfactorily resolved, because of the problem of placing any attitudinal evidence in a sufficiently specific context. Nonetheless, changes in opinions about families and households are likely to be in evidence at a time when the shape of a household is undergoing modification, for whatever reason, and may well assist that process. On another front, however, further progress is possible in that there is much more information on the structure of English households that could be assembled, particularly for the nineteenth century.[25] A survey of the strength of regional variation in the frequency with which households contained relatives of the head (kin) has already been included in chapter 1 above, and in the present chapter I intend to look in more detail at the degree of change in household forms between the seventeenth and nineteenth centuries. Apart from the fall in the number of servants, there is also the rise in the number of offspring and kin to be explained (see table 16.2). In addition, two results of a previous analysis of changes in the English household need consideration: namely the fall from the seventeenth to the eighteenth century in the proportion of households headed by women, and a rise in the proportion of households headed by non-married men (whether by bachelors or by widowers could not be determined).[26]

How many of these developments can be ascribed to demographic factors? First, variations in the age at contracting a first marriage, it has already been argued, exerted a powerful influence on the whole process of household formation (see above, p. 493). Second, there is the impact on the age structure of a population of changes in fertil-

---

[25] The enumeration schedules of the mid-nineteenth-century censuses have been extensively analysed, but, as much of the work has been uncoordinated, it is often impossible to make direct comparisons between one study and another. It is the intention of the SSRC Cambridge Group to select a set of schedules representative of communities of diverse type and subject them to a standard analysis using the model tables to which Peter Laslett refers in ch. 17.

[26] Wall (1977): 94 shows that the proportion of households headed by women fell from 18.3% to 13.9%, while the proportion of households headed by non-married men rose from 11.5% to 13.4%. Other figures are subject to the slight discrepancies mentioned above (nn. 9, 12). For example, it was stated in 1977 that for the period 1650–1749 children constituted 37.6% of the total population; servants, 18.4%; and kin, 3.2%, whereas table 16.3 above suggests 39.9%, 13.8%, and 3.6% respectively.

ity, themselves the result primarily of the increase in nuptiality during the eighteenth century.[27] In 1696, approximately the midpoint of the earlier period of listings, fertility was low, and it has been calculated that some 9% of the population was over the age of 60 and 31% under age 15. In 1786, the approximate mid-point of the second period of listings, after several years of rising fertility, the proportion over age 60 was little changed at just under 8%, but the under-15-year-olds now made up some 35% of the population; and the age structure was to become even more youthful and remain so for much of the nineteenth century.[28] Since the type of household in which one lives and one's relationship to the head of that household are very much conditioned by age, it is to be expected, on the basis of these figures alone, that households of the late eighteenth century would differ in composition from those of the late seventeenth, and, most obviously, that there would be a rise in the number of children in the household. This, of course, is exactly what is recorded by the listings evidence. Beyond this, however, the alteration in age structure helps one to understand some of the other changes that have occurred to the structure of households. For example, it was reported above that the proportion of households headed by women fell by 4.4% between the late seventeenth and late eighteenth centuries (n. 26). This was primarily caused by a decline in the proportion of households headed by widows (from 14.6% to 10.8% of all households), and it would be easy to jump to the conclusion that this followed from a reduced risk of prolonged widowhood because of a decline in mortality amongst younger adults.[29]

[27] Nuptiality rose because age at marriage fell and the proportion ever marrying increased, as did illegitimate fertility. The relative importance of these three factors in raising fertility in the eighteenth century is calculated in Wrigley and Schofield (1981): 267, table 7.29. Two other factors can be largely discounted. Changes in mortality have a much less significant impact than changes in fertility on the age structure of a population (*ibid.* 443 n. 84), and the level of marital fertility changed very little between the late sixteenth and later eighteenth centuries (*ibid.* 254).

[28] *Ibid.* 217 and appendix 3.1.

[29] The reconstitution evidence on this point is somewhat equivocal, suggesting between the late seventeenth century and the late eighteenth only a modest improvement in male survivorship chances in early adulthood, although there was a more marked improvement for women. However, estimates of adult mortality from reconstitution studies are bedevilled both by the small number of individuals in observation and by the fact that the period of observation is arbitrarily curtailed by the termination of reconstitutions in 1812 or 1837, and it is thought that the existing tabulations underestimate survivorship, particularly for the period 1750–99.

However, the information that is now available from changes in the age structure of a population makes it clear that even without a fall in mortality the proportion of widows heading households would have fallen (other factors remaining constant) because of the declining share of those over the age of 45 in the total adult population.[30]

Of course, in reality other factors may well have played a role. For example, the Poor Law authorities might have modified their attitude towards paying maintenance to widows in their own households, or the economic situation might have changed in a way that made households headed by widows less viable or gave widows a role to play in other households, perhaps as child-minders.[31]

So far it has proved possible to identify three different links between changes in the demographic situation prompted by the level of the real wage and the structure of the household. Thus it was argued that earlier marriage promoted earlier household formation, while higher fertility led to an expansion of the child population and to a reduction in the proportion of households headed by widows, though the latter reflected also the fall in mortality, a trend less clearly linked to the level of the real wage.[32] To these can be added a fourth, but indirect, link: the decline in farm service that was discussed above. It has to be said, though, that these links are suggested rather than proved, since the only evidence put forward is that the upward movement in population and the changes in household composition occurred at approximately the same time. A much more precise statement of the relationship is required, for which it will be necessary to develop models of household structure to show how variations in nuptiality, fertility, and mortality within the range of the English experience might have produced various proportions of children, widowers, and widows in households, when children went into service in large numbers only from the age of 15 and two out of three widows lived with at least one other person (not counting

---

[30] Unpublished estimates of the age structure of England produced for Wrigley and Schofield (1981) suggest that of the population over the age of 25, those over age 45 were 47.6% in 1696, 43.8% in 1786, and 40.2% in 1851.
[31] See Anderson, *Family structure in nineteenth century Lancashire* (1971): 141, and cf. Thomson, 'Provision for the elderly in England' (1980): 350f for a demonstration of the extent to which changes in the operation of the Poor Laws during the nineteenth century affected family patterns.
[32] Wrigley and Schofield (1981): 414–15.

lodgers).[33] Previous modelling of pre-industrial households has focused almost exclusively on variations in kin composition in relation to a variety of inheritance strategies.[34]

On theoretical grounds, too, one might well want to argue that the real wage exerted only a limited influence on the composition of the household. Admittedly, real income, as experienced in the parental household or indeed in service, in conjunction with any norms about ideal households,[35] might have given rise to certain expectations about the type of household in which an individual would want to live in later life. Further, real incomes, provided the younger generation were able to retain the profit of their labour, yielded the economic wherewithal to establish such households. However, whether the households would be formed in precisely the way intended depended on circumstances that could be outside the control of the individual, such as the number of openings in the village economy or other structural economic constraints. There is a classic example just after the end of the Second World War, when there was insufficient housing to satisfy demand.[36] This provides a more convincing explanation of why so many kin were present in the household in 1947 than the argument that the population had formed expectations during the war years or earlier as to the sorts of household it would be preferable to form. At such times, tensions between generations could become particularly acute if what had seemed realistic expectations in terms of the real wage were unexpectedly thwarted. Periods when this seems most likely occurred at the end of the First World War (a housing crisis again)[37] and in the last years of the eighteenth century, when a considerable number of houses seem to have been subdivided to accommodate the unprecedented growth in population, although households themselves were

[33] Wall, 'The age at leaving home' (1978): 190–1, tables 2, 3; and for the household position of widowed persons, Wall (1981), table 4. In any modelling exercise it would be necessary to allow for the considerable variations in the age at leaving home according to the sex of the child and occupation and marital status of the parent.

[34] For example, see Wachter with Hammel and Laslett (1978).

[35] This issue is discussed above in ch. 1, p. 28.

[36] Hole and Pountney (1971): 26, who argue, however, that the shortage of housing was less severe in 1951 than after the First World War; and see Wall (1982a). It might also be argued that experiences of the war years, when family members might be separated as a result of war service or evacuation, fostered a feeling for 'family togetherness' that persisted into the immediate post-war period when demobilization of the armed forces had not yet been completed. For this interesting suggestion I am grateful to Jean Robin.

[37] Hole and Pountney (1971): 25.

no smaller—were, indeed, somewhat larger (see above) than they had been previously.[38] In general, however, it is probably correct to think of such tensions as affecting individuals more often than they affected whole communities, and local communities more often than society as a whole. Of the 10 communities that appear in table 16.1, in 2 only, Ringmore, enumerated in 1698, and Ardleigh, enumerated in 1796, were there in the age group 20–9 more married men than there were heads of households.

Another possibility is that the rise in the number of relatives between the eighteenth and nineteenth centuries was caused because the division of existing houses failed to create sufficient additional accommodation for independent household units. Certainly there is no reason why one should have predicted an increase in the number of resident kin from the trends in population and overall real wages. It would be otherwise if it could be shown that the increase was limited to grand-children or nephews or nieces who would, in most cases, be of those age groups that during the course of the eighteenth century expanded their share of the total population; but, as is clear from table 16.4, there was an increase in almost all types of relative. Only part of the increase in the size of the kin group could, therefore, be ascribed to changes in the age structure of the population, leaving the rest to be explained by an increase in communal living as household formation failed to keep pace with the expansion of the population. However, one should bear in mind also a point made in the introduction (p. 35 above), that some of the increase in kin may be more apparent than real, occasioned by a change in the basis of censuses from 'ideal' to 'real', that is from a description of where people usually resided to a description of where they were located on census night. This change was particularly likely to affect the recording of kin who might well be present in a household for a short period of time, for example after a bereavement or at a time of childbirth.

At this point it is useful to introduce a final table, on the subject of kin. It was admitted above that, until the census of 1851, the evidence on the structure of the household has to come from listings of individual communities, and this imposes limitations on the analysis of the English household. The listings can be divided, as above, into broad time periods to provide an impression of change or stability, but since no community is listed in detail in both the

[38] Wall, 'Mean household size in England' (1972): table 5.8.

seventeenth and the eighteenth century, there is always the danger that any variation (or lack of it) between periods has arisen because the comparison involved two quite distinct groups that would have differed in terms of household composition even if it had been possible to examine them at a single point in time. The fewer the listings that are selected for analysis, in order to increase the precision with which the household can be portrayed, the greater the danger that the set of communities will be atypical in some way. As far as change between the seventeenth and eighteenth centuries is concerned, there is no immediate solution,[39] but it is possible to sidestep the problem for the period between the eighteenth and nineteenth centuries by selecting for analysis in 1851 the same communities for which listings survive from the eighteenth century. Such a selection has been used in the analysis of the composition of the kin group in table 16.4, and it indeed confirmed the increase in kin that was observed when comparisons involved different sets of communities.[40] One is, of course, still left with the problem of whether the few communities one can follow through time are representative of the general experience.

In table 16.5 the analysis is taken a stage further by measuring the variation in the proportion of multiple and extended households[41] between the eighteenth and mid-nineteenth centuries for the same group of communities and for the same occupational groups. The result is something of a surprise in that almost all social groups seem to have experienced an increase in the proportion of households that were complex in structure: from gentry and yeomen at the top of the social pyramid to labourers and paupers at the bottom.[42] The

[39] One might perhaps say a problem without any solution, unless many further listings can be located. Even if it were to emerge that the settlements enumerated before 1750 and after 1750 were similar in character at the time of the 1851 census, it would be dangerous to infer that this had been true at earlier times.

[40] The values, though, are a little different: from 18 (1750–1821) to 32 per 100 households in 1851 when the communities were the same, compared with 22 (1750–1821) to 31 (1851) when different communities were used for 1750–1821 and a random sample of schedules in 1851; cf. table 16.2 above, but averaging the figures for urban and rural areas in 1851.

[41] These are most but not all of the households that contained kin. Excluded are relatives in households without a conjugal family (for example co-resident siblings) and some in simple-family households (for example where a windowed parent co-resided with a son or daughter but was not herself the household head).

[42] There are problems in defining occupational groups which are sufficiently flexible to cope with the degree of social change experienced during the late eighteenth and early nineteenth centuries. First, certain terms such as 'husbandman' disappear without being replaced by any other term of equivalent status. Whether this represents a real

Table 16.5. *Complex households by occupational group of household head*

Occupational group of household head	1750–1821		1851	
	Total households	Complex[a] (%)	Total households	Complex[a] (%)
Gentry and clergy	40	10.0	108	15.8
Yeomen and farmers	185	18.4	298	24.8
Intermediate agriculture[b]	137	17.5	43	9.3
Tradesmen and craftsmen	395	12.1	478	16.3
Labourers	415	10.4	854	16.6
Paupers	18	11.2	56	17.9
Widows without specified occupation	116	10.3	63	26.9
Not classified and not given	64	14.0	64	12.5
All	1,370	12.9	1,964	17.8

[a] Extended and multiple (types 4 and 5) in the Laslett-Hammel classificatory system: see ch. 1 n. 33 for a brief description, and for a fuller account, P. Laslett and Wall (eds.) (1972): 28–31.
[b] Gardeners and husbandmen except for the parish of Ardleigh, where husbandmen have been classed as labourers, no labourers as such being listed in 1796.
Sources:
1750–1821 Cambridge Group listings; Littleover, Derby. (1811); Mickleover, Derby. (1811); Corfe Castle, Dorset (1790); Ardleigh, Essex (1796); Forthampton, Gloucs. (1752); Barkway and Reed, Herts. (1801); Bampton, Barton, Hackthorpe, Kings Meaburn, Lowther, Morland, Newby, and Great Strickland, Westmor. (1787).
1851 Enumerators' schedules for same settlements as 1750–1821.

similarity in trend does not, of course, mean that the causes of that trend are necessarily the same. The increase in kin residing in the household could even be seen as the product of three quite different processes: changes to the age structure of the population; various

change (the disappearance of a particular class of person) or is simply a change of nomenclature is unclear, for differences within the group of labourers (the natural successors to husbandmen) can sometimes be discerned; cf. Wall, 'Real property, marriage and children' (1982b) on households and marriage patterns of two groups of labourers (occupiers of property above or below a certain value) in Colyton, Devon in the nineteenth century. The second major problem is that there is no guarantee that the same terms are used consistently in listings of similar date. The identification of gentry in particular is something about which opinions could differ, and the Rector of Ardleigh in drawing up the listing of 1796 seems to have used the term 'husbandman' in a different sense from that of other listmakers. In the latter case an appropriate correction has been made (cf. note to table 16.5), but detailed work on other parishes might bring to light other discrepancies.

attempts by the population to offset the effects of demographic expansion, for example when parents placed out one of their children with their own parents or took in a daughter's illegitimate child;[43] and a modification of familial and migration patterns as old employments decayed and new ones opened in areas where individuals could not immediately establish their own homes.[44] Much more detail on household patterns within particular occupational groups is required before the exact pattern of change can be established, but this combination of processes provides a credible interpretation of trends in the numbers of kin. Moreover, it would appear more convincing than the assertion of a general link between the increase in kin and urbanization or industrialization, whether attributed to the emergence of a new calculative element in attitudes towards helping others such as Michael Anderson associated with family relationships in mid-nineteenth-century Preston or, more simply, through the expansion of sectors of society where co-residence with a relative had always been above the average.[45]

However, the general relevance for household forms of the social and economic changes of the late eighteenth and early nineteenth centuries does merit further consideration. Indeed, it would be odd if the developments that characterized this period were without impact on the pace of household formation and the types of household that were created. In the middle of the nineteenth century the composition of households in urban areas was not the same as those in rural areas, as table 16.2 makes clear. Urban households were, generally, smaller. They were less likely to be headed by a married couple, and they contained fewer children and fewer relatives and servants. This last is something of a surprise, given that domestic service in the nineteenth century is often considered to have been the mechanism by which people were channelled into towns.[46] However, apart

[43] A study of nineteenth-century enumerators' schedules shows that a number of three-generational-family households arose through the presence of an illegitimate child. Given the rise in illegitimacy during the late eighteenth century and the possibility of a further rise between the 1830s and the 1850s (Laslett, Oosterveen, and Smith (eds), *Bastardy and its comparative history* (1980): 18), it seems likely that this type of household will also have become more frequent over the same period.

[44] Judging from Preston in mid-nineteenth century, migrants usually went into lodgings rather than to kin, possibly because in many instances they had no kin with whom they could live. See Anderson (1971): 52. My argument is, however, that migrant kin would be 'extra' to any other households with kin that might be formed.

[45] Anderson (1971): 170f.

[46] Cf. McBride, *The domestic revolution* (1976): 34; Ebery and Preston, *Domestic service in late Victorian and Edwardian England* (1976): 77.

from the question of servants and the presence in towns of many more lodgers, the difference between urban and rural households is not large, and urbanization could not be said to have altered the general shape of the household. It has recently been claimed that there is no evidence in England to associate a particular mode of production with a particular nuptiality and fertility pattern.[47] Should one now go further and disclaim any association of a particular household type with either urbanization or industrialization?

From one perspective, the case is a strong one. Much of the temporal change in the composition of English households can be plausibly associated, either directly or indirectly, with demographic factors, responding in turn to variations in the level of the real wage, with a suitable allowance made for disjunctures in the local economy. Such an argument, however, ignores the considerable variation in household structure that is known to have existed among communities. For example, in the period 1750–1821 10% of settlements had a mean household size of 4.27 or less, while in another 10% it was more than 5.41. A similar situation arises in the case of kin: in a quarter of settlements, under 5% of all households spanned three generations, while in another quarter at least 10% were three-generational households. Other examples could be cited involving servants or children.[48] Admittedly the statistical modelling of household processes has still to be completed in order to reveal how much of such differences could be attributed to chance variation in small populations enumerated on one occasion (see n. 34 above), but it is possible, and perhaps more likely, that variation on this scale reflects the fact that particular communities operated within very distinct demographic and economic contexts.[49] Of the demographic factors,

[47] R. M. Smith (1981b): 614.
[48] These examples are from Wall (1977): 97, table 4.4.
[49] Whether one takes this degree of variation as large or small is a matter of the perspective from which one views it. There is unfortunately no tabulation by district of all the households containing kin in contemporary England, but a very crude comparison can be made using the data on the proportion of households containing two or more families, since in the vast majority of cases it is known that such families were related in direct descent (Wall 1982a). This comparison indicates rather greater variability in the proportion of households that were three-generational in England in 1750–1821 than in the proportion of households containing two or more families in England and Wales in 1971 (15% of settlements within 10% of the median, range 0%–16% for England in 1750–1821; 23% within 10% of the median, range 0%–2.9% for England in 1971). Against Austrian experience in the past, the variation in household composition in late eighteenth to early-nineteenth-century England looks more modest: in England in 1750–1821 kin formed between 0% and 10% of the population within households,

mortality was subject to most local variation (as a function of density and location), then nuptiality (reflecting differences in economic opportunities), while the variation in marital fertility among communities was relatively less well marked.[50] It does not necessarily follow, however, that it will be the variation in mortality that will have most impact on the household, since a modest variation in nuptiality will alter the pace at which new households are formed. Of the economic factors, access to land and the nature of the labour market were critical, but neither their influence nor the forms of household they helped to produce were constant over time. The fact that the relationship between economic change and household structural change has not been more visible is because the attempt to understand the transformation in economic relationships has so far been rather schematic, relying on generalized concepts, such as industrialization and proto-industrialization, that have somewhat obscured the intricacies of the changes that occurred within individual communities. The construction of a more refined set of concepts for the analysis of economic opportunities and developments at the local level will, it is anticipated, permit a fuller assessment of the role of economic combined with demographic factors in promoting the modification of the structure of the English household between the seventeenth and nineteenth centuries.

and proportions in a third of settlements were within 10% of the median, whereas in Austria the range was 0.8%–17.9%, and proportions in only 15% of settlements were within 10% of the median. The figures for England and Wales in 1971 relate to the proportions of households containing two or more families in a random sample of county and municipal boroughs and urban and rural districts selected from *Census of England and Wales 1971: household composition tables* (1975): III, table 32. The sample N corresponds to the number of settlements for which information on three-generational households was available during the period 1750–1821; cf. Wall (1977): 94, table 4.3, and n. 9 above. Data on Austria are from Schmidtbauer, 'Daten zur historischen Demographie und Familienstruktur' (1977).

[50] The weighting of these three factors was suggested by Roger Schofield. See also n. 7 above, and for proportions of men married in the age group 20–9, table 16.1.

7

Anthropology and ethnohistorians

In the second half of the nineteenth century there were many parallels between the disciplines of history and anthropology. Both employed an empiricist methodology, and while historians charted the rise of nations, anthropologists traced the cultural and social evolution of mankind. Central to anthropological study was the concept of human culture, defined in the late nineteenth century by Edward Burnett Tylor, often regarded as 'the founder of academic anthropology in the English-speaking world':

> Culture . . . taken in its wide ethnographic sense is that complex whole which includes knowledge, belief, art, morals, law, custom and any other capabilities and habits acquired by man as a member of society.[1]

From the 1860s anthropological interpretation of diverse human cultures was based upon a specific conceptual framework: the evolutionary trajectory of human progress, of which the institutions and values of Europe were the apotheosis. Societies and cultures were slotted into appropriate stages along the path of human development from savagery and barbarism to civilization.

After the First World War the premises of evolutionary anthropology were challenged and alternative perspectives and distinctive methods began to take shape. In terms of the latter, fieldwork and participant observation became the hallmarks of the professional anthropologist following the publication of *Argonauts of the Western Pacific* by Bronislaw Malinowski in 1922. New interpretative approaches to the study of human culture also developed, and while adherents could be found on both sides of the Atlantic, two schools of thought emerged in Britain and the United States. These were characterized respectively as social anthropology and cultural anthropology. The first sought evidence in human culture of social patterns, while the second preferred to interpret culture at the level of ideas learned by individuals. While the British focused upon the social structure, and the

Americans upon a more autonomous concept of culture, both came to adopt a position of cultural relativism. Anthropologists took the lead in replacing the normative values implicit within the evolutionary model of human history and culture. In the United States, Franz Boas led the way in establishing that race, culture and language were separate aspects of human existence. In so doing, he demolished the 'Social Darwinist position that biological and cultural evolution were part of a single process'.[2]

One of the key influences upon the development of the British anthropology in the early twentieth century was Émile Durkheim. Born in France in 1858, Durkheim devoted his life to establishing a science of society as the basis for the discipline of sociology.[3] For Durkheim, study of the social group or community took precedence over the individual. He believed that human behaviour is fundamentally shaped by the moral, religious and social society in which the individual lives. The social cohesion of any society is achieved through communal rituals and ceremonies, and these therefore fulfil important functions in that society. The British school of social anthropology was heavily influenced by Durkheim, and the concept of functionalism, until at least the 1970s.[4] Functionalism was not new: nineteenth-century social scientists from a wide range of disciplines had drawn analogies between society and organic bodies or machines. Malinowski's study of the Trobriand islanders in Melanesia, mentioned above, focused upon patterns of behaviour such as kinship, exchange and magic, and argued that these fulfilled biological and psychological needs, thereby contributing towards the successful functioning of that society. From the 1940s onwards A. R. Radcliffe-Brown combined functionalism with a structural perspective; social institutions and relationships were perceived as mechanisms which ensured the survival and stability of the social system as a whole. The emphasis within structural-functionalism upon the means by which society preserved continuity and stability did not fit well with conventional historical interest in the causes of political and social change.

Under the influence of functionalism the work of British anthropologists became largely synchronic, that is, societies were investigated at a given moment in time. While Susan Kellogg has argued that 'anthropologists were never as indifferent to history as it now seems fashionable to assume', she accepts that, regardless of their specific focus, most anthropologists did not inject a truly historical dimension into their work until the late 1970s.[5] Functionalism also challenged orthodox historical practice in another way. The organic metaphor underpinning functionalism suggested that all aspects of society were interrelated and therefore society should be studied as a whole. This led anthropologists to adopt a holistic interpretative approach, contrary to the historians' practice of separating different aspects of the past (political, social, economic history) into discrete areas of study.

The value of the holistic approach, of studying 'topics in relation to society as a whole', was emphasized by British historian Keith Thomas in an influential article published in 1961.[6] However, anthropological studies tended to investigate small, relatively homogeneous societies and Thomas later suggested that a holistic approach could be more difficult in the context of a larger, much more diverse society.[7] Indeed, many historians influenced by the anthropological approach have favoured microhistory, placing small communities, single events or even one individual under minute scrutiny.[8] Two highly regarded studies of this genre are Carlo Ginzburg's exploration of the beliefs of an Italian miller to illuminate sixteenth-century popular culture, and Natalie Zemon Davis' account of the French peasant who deserted his family and was replaced by an imposter.[9]

Keith Thomas also drew attention to the importance in anthropology of everyday life, wryly concluding that 'domestic and community relations form the very stuff of social anthropology and, for that matter, of most people's lives, but one would never deduce this from the subject-matter of most historical enquiry'.[10] In this sense, anthropology was to become immensely influential in redirecting historians' attention away from the public, political sphere of human action towards private, daily life. Rediscovering old sources, including oral history and oral tradition, and re-reading others, historians began to investigate sexuality, marriage and childhood, as well as magic, myth and ritual. The importance of magic is central to Keith Thomas' 1971 study of theological and supernatural belief in early modern England.[11] Thomas linked the material conditions of existence in sixteenth- and seventeenth-century England to popular beliefs and practices. Fighting for ascendancy in the popular mind were the theological beliefs of the Church and the magic of astrologers, cunning men and witches: who could provide the most convincing explanation for lives dominated by dearth, disease and death?

Writing from the perspective of an anthropologist, Hildred Geertz criticized Thomas for failing to understand that anthropology sought to understand human behaviour, for example magic rituals, in non-judgemental terms, and as part of coherent and complex systems of belief.[12] 'As Thomas sees them', Geertz argues, 'magical beliefs and practices do not present or derive from a coherent, comprehensive, and general view of the world, although religious ones do.' In seeing magic as 'not-religion', and 'not-reasonable' and 'not-effective', Geertz suggests that Thomas is employing the ideological perspective of the foes of magic. Consequently he fails to illuminate the wider conceptual framework of those who engaged in such practices. Yet even within Thomas' own account, Geertz shows, the broader cognitive matrix within which magical beliefs were embedded is apparent: '[t]he universe was alive, teeming with active, intelligent, and purposeful agents who were both human and non-human'. But in contrast to religion, which was the subject of fierce debate among the literate, she suggests that the philosophical underpinnings of magic were 'neither consciously articulated nor critically elaborated by intellectuals of the time'. While Geertz's critique draws our attention to the perils inherent in an interdisciplinary approach, *Religion and the Decline of Magic* precipitated a great deal of historical research into the popular culture of early modern Britain.

In the 1950s historians working in the field of American Indian history were also becoming interested in anthropology, and the engagement has been very fruitful. This sudden turn to interdisciplinary co-operation arose in part out of the creation of the United States Indian Claims Commission in 1946 which commissioned research and expert testimony 'and collaboration became a requirement of the circumstances'.[13] By the end of the decade anthropologists and historians came together to combine the strengths of both disciplines, and founded the journal *Ethnohistory*. Their new field was defined by W. C. Sturtevant as '[the study of] the history of the peoples normally studied by anthropologists'.[14] James Axtell, one of the major historians in this field, defined ethnohistory as 'a union of history and ethnology, whose purpose is to produce scholarly offspring who bear the diachronic dimensions of history and the synchronic sensitivity of ethnology'.[15] Ethnohistory encompasses archaeology, ethnology, history and linguistics, and the source materials available to the ethnohistorian include folklore, oral tradition, maps, paintings and artefacts, as well as written sources.

While some anthropologists and historians confine their study to one society or culture, other American ethnohistorians work at the point of contact between two or more. This, of course, places ethnohistorians in the crucible of colonial conflict. The result has been a powerful challenge to the orthodox narratives of colonial history, particularly through the 'startling' work of Francis Jennings.[16] In *The Invasion of America: Indians, Colonialism, and the Cant of Conquest*, Jennings employs the tools of ethnohistory to test, and reject, the justificatory myths and propaganda which accompanied the brutal violence of Puritan conquest. However, it is more common for ethnohistorians to eschew such explicit moral judgements, and to present all those engaged in culture contact as active agents who jointly determine the outcome.[17] This was a major advance from the previously dominant perspective which portrayed Native Americans as the objects of European actions or policies; historians had largely discounted 'the inclusion of a Native American viewpoint as speculative since such a perspective could not be documented by traditional means'.[18]

A good example of the new ethnohistory may be seen in an essay by James Axtell which seeks to understand how the Indian tribes perceived the European invaders.[19] Such a project is fraught with difficulty: the Indians of North America had no 'writing systems, [and] they have left us virtually no first-hand accounts of their early perceptions of white men'. Axtell proceeds to examine the records written by the Europeans including the descriptions of early explorers, and later accounts of Indian oral tradition. In so doing, we see the historian reading sources against the grain, in the attempt to bring the Indian into focus. For an example of the way in which this is done, Axtell draws our attention to the names given to Europeans as 'a valuable index to native images and values'. The names assigned to the Europeans with whom Indians came into contact nearly all make reference to their technology: 'the Narragansetts of Rhode Island called all Europeans "Coatmen" or "swordmen". The Mohawks of New York referred to the Dutch as "Iron-workers" or "Cloth makers", while the Hurons called the French *Agnonha*, "Iron People"'. Axtell had earlier reminded us that weapons were extremely important in the context of 'feuding native polities', and the newcomers' technological superiority contributed to the 'Indians' initially exalted opinion of the white strangers'.

While much of the scholarship has become more indigenous-centred, there remains a debate over whether the voice of the Native American has really been integrated into historical accounts. R. David Edmunds points out that when historians examine Native American history on the plains in 1833, they concentrate upon events such as 'inter-tribal warfare, the fur trade, a cholera epidemic'. However, 'pictographic calendars recorded by the Great Plains tribes for 1833 focus primarily on a spectacular shower of meteors that fell to earth . . . and the plains people remember this time as "the winter that the stars fell"'.[20] It is, perhaps, this enduring problem of perspective, between that of the emic (the insiders' viewpoint) as opposed to the etic (the outsiders'), that has led to the development of a postcolonial history.

By the 1980s historians in a wide range of fields were following the lead of those drawing upon anthropology to widen and enrich the study of history. The American historian Natalie Zemon Davis suggested that there were four specific features of anthropological work from which historians could learn: the 'close observation of living processes of social interaction; interesting ways of interpreting symbolic behaviour; suggestions about how the parts of a social system fit together; and material from cultures very different from those which historians are used to studying'.[21] The last three features, in particular, have been utilized by historians to illuminate different aspects of both European and American history.

A good example of the way in which anthropological insights can be put to use in the interpretation of symbolic behaviour may be found in Robert Darnton's essay 'Workers' Revolt: The Great Cat Massacre of the Rue Saint-Séverin'.[22] Darnton has acknowledged his intellectual debt to the American anthropologist Clifford Geertz, whose semiotic interpretation of culture ascribes primary importance to the signs (which may be language, clothes, or gestures) by which people communicate with each other.[23] In order to understand these signs, Geertz pioneered an approach called 'thick description'. Using the example of a wink, Geertz illustrated the many layers of meaning such a simple act may convey. Without understanding the conceptual structures and imaginative universe within which our subjects lived, Geertz argues, it is impossible to reconstruct the possible meaning of a wink. The goal is to get beneath surface behaviour to reach an emic (insiders') understanding, 'cast in terms of the interpretations to which the persons . . . subject their experience'.[24]

This is precisely the goal of Robert Darnton, who applies Geertz's approach to an unusual, and unpleasant, account of the massacre of cats by printing apprentices in Paris during the late 1730s.[25] Darnton's interpretation of the story is derived from an account written thirty years after the event by one of participants, who described the massacre as the most hilarious event of his career. Darnton suggests that 'by getting the joke of the great cat massacre, it may be possible to "get" a basic ingredient of artisanal culture under the Old Regime'.[26] All the ingredients of the tale are subject to the detailed contextual analysis of 'thick description', from the symbolic significance of cats in French culture to the ceremonial cycles of carnival, when the conventional rules of behaviour were turned upside down. By focusing upon the cultural context, and the multiple meanings attributed to cats, Darnton proposes that the cat massacre represented the revolt of apprentices against poor treatment by their masters. 'The workers found the massacre funny because it gave them a way to turn the tables on the bourgeois' in the only way possible – on a symbolic level.[27]

Darnton's essay has fomented debate, most of which concentrates upon the use of symbolic interpretation. The first critique challenges the fixed relationship between symbols and that which they purport to represent, arguing that the meaning of symbols is not as transparent as Darnton's interpretation suggests.[28] Another finds *The Great Cat Massacre* 'overdetermined' in the sense of a hermeneutically coherent narrative, leaving little room for contestation or alternative readings.[29] A third asks what has happened to the second half of the original text upon which Darnton's interpretation is based; this, it is suggested, offers the possibility of a quite different conclusion.[30] These critiques raise the unresolved problem of how to assess the validity of symbolic interpretation. Historians may be less than satisfied with Geertz's assertion that '[c]ultural analysis is (or should be) guessing at meanings, assessing the guesses, and drawing explanatory conclusions from the better guesses'.[31]

What then has been the legacy of anthropology to the study of history over the past thirty years? Perhaps the most important has been the inclusion of 'the people without history' within the written historical record.[32] This is particularly true in the North American context of cultural encounter between indigenous Native Peoples and Europeans. Anthropology has also drawn the attention of historians to the need for careful synchronic analysis, a product of its holistic approach to the study of society, and the importance of understanding the social structures within which individuals play out their lives. A greatly enriched historiography of daily life, family, myth, and ritual is also a consequence of paying attention to anthropology's concerns. While historians have been aware of the importance of understanding the past from the perspective of the historical actors, anthropologists have drawn out the tension between, and implications of, emic and etic perspectives.

Those are the strengths that anthropology has brought to the study of history. The problems derive, as they so often do, from the methods employed to make the most of the limited source material. Ethnohistorians and those researching popular culture must often work with scraps of evidence, frequently those written or compiled by the dominant party. Anthropologists have pioneered reading such materials 'against the grain', or for silences and suppression, as a means to recover voices from the past. A more recent idea is that of 'controlled speculation'. Where the evidence is inadequate, researchers employ 'comparative material from other cultural or historical situations to infer crucial information that may be missing or obscured in the historical record of a particular situation'.[33] Historians may be very reluctant to embrace a method as potentially loose as this, but the carefully controlled application of contextual knowledge can yield rewarding results. In 1983 Natalie Zemon Davis included contextual historical knowledge to flesh out the lives of the main actors in *The Return of Martin Guerre*:

> [W]hen I could not find my individual man or woman . . . then I did my best through other sources from the period and place to discover the world they would have seen and the reactions they might have had. What I offer you here is in part my invention, but held tightly in check by the voices of the past.[34]

The reading which follows is by Inga Clendinnen, an Australian historian whose research has explored the world of the Aztecs and cultural encounter in sixteenth-century Mexico. Clendinnen has identified both Clifford Geertz and E. P. Thompson as sources of inspiration and this article, which explores the impact of Spanish colonial conquest upon the native women of Yucatan, illustrates the richness of the anthropological heritage for historical writing. What specifically does Clendinnen focus upon in order to make women's roles in this society visible? What does she suggest that this evidence reveals about women's status? Can you find examples where Clendinnen takes the main sources for this study, the records of Spanish missionaries, and reads them 'against the grain' to provide glimpses into the lives of Yucatec Maya women? Do you find her argument that, despite women's exclusion from the production of maize, their role in its preparation for food was equally sacred? Are

Clendinnen's judgements based upon an emic or etic perspective?
Finally, why does she conclude that the Spanish conquest resulted in
a loss of status and dignity for Yucatec Maya women?

Notes

1 Cited in Marvin Harris, *Cultural Anthropology* (3rd edn, New York, 1991), p. 9.
2 Marvin Harris, *Culture, People, Nature* (6th edn, New York, 1993), p. 476. See also Eric R. Wolf, 'Perilous Ideas: Race, Culture, People', *Current Anthropology*, 35 (1994), pp. 1–12.
3 Greater elaboration of Durkheim's ideas may be found in Randall Collins, *Four Sociological Traditions* (Oxford, 1994), especially pp. 203–4.
4 See Adam Kuper, *Anthropology and Anthropologists: The Modern British School* (rev. edn, London, 1983).
5 Susan Kellogg, 'Histories for Anthropology: Ten Years of Historical Research and Writing by Anthropologists, 1980–1990', *Social Science History*, 15 (1991), pp. 418–19.
6 Keith Thomas, 'History and Anthropology', *Past and Present*, 24 (1963), pp. 3–24.
7 Keith Thomas, *Religion and the Decline of Magic* (Harmondsworth, 1971), p. 5.
8 See Peter Burke, *History and Social Theory* (Cambridge, 1992), pp. 38–43.
9 Carlo Ginzburg, *The Cheese and the Worms: The Cosmos of a Sixteenth-century Miller*, trans. John and Anne Tedeschi (London, [1976] 1992); Natalie Zemon Davis, *The Return of Martin Guerre* (Cambridge, Mass., 1983).
10 Thomas, 'History and Anthropology', p. 15.
11 Thomas, *Religion and the Decline of Magic*.
12 Hildred Geertz, 'An Anthropology of Religion and Magic, I', *Journal of Interdisciplinary History*, 6, I (1975), pp. 71–89.
13 Francis Jennings, 'A Growing Partnership: Historians, Anthropologists and American Indian History', *Ethnohistory*, 29, 1 (1982), p. 21.
14 Shepard Krech III, 'The State of Ethnohistory', *Annual Review of Anthropology*, 20 (1991), p. 348. Krech discusses the criticisms of the term ethnohistory. For another critic, see James H. Merrell, 'Some Thoughts on Colonial Historians and American Indians', *William and Mary Quarterly*, 46 (1989), pp. 114–15.
15 James Axtell, 'Ethnohistory: A Historian's Viewpoint', in Axtell, *The European and the Indian: Essays in the Ethnohistory of Colonial North America* (Oxford, 1981), p. 5.
16 Francis Jennings, *The Invasion of America: Indians, Colonialism, and the Cant of Conquest* (Chapel Hill, 1975); the description is taken from Bruce G. Trigger, 'Ethnohistory: The Unfinished Edifice', *Ethnohistory*, 33, 3 (1986), p. 258.
17 For examples, see Bruce Trigger, *Natives and Newcomers: Canada's 'Heroic Age' Reconsidered* (Kingston, 1985); Richard White, *The Middle Ground: Indians, Empires, and Republics in the Great Lakes Region, 1650–1815* (Cambridge, 1991).
18 R. David Edmunds, 'Native Americans, New Voices: American Indian History, 1895–1995', *American Historical Review*, 100 (1995), pp. 720, 725.
19 James Axtell, 'Through Another Glass Darkly: Early Indian Views of Europeans', in Axtell, *After Columbus: Essays in the Ethnohistory of Colonial North America* (Oxford, 1988), pp. 125–43. All quotations are taken from this essay.
20 Edmunds, 'Native Americans, New Voices', p. 737; see also Daniel Richter, 'Whose Indian History?', *William and Mary Quarterly*, 50 (1993), pp. 379–93.
21 Natalie Zemon Davis, 'Anthropology and History in the 1980s', in Theodore Rabb and Robert Rotberg (eds), *The New History: The 1980s and Beyond* (Princeton, 1982), p. 267.
22 Robert Darnton, *The Great Cat Massacre and Other Episodes in French Cultural History* (New York, 1985).

23 Clifford Geertz, *The Interpretation of Cultures* (London, 1975): see ch. 1 'Thick Description: Toward an Interpretive Theory of Culture'. For a recent evaluation of the contemporary significance of Geertz, see the special issue of *Representations*, 59 (1997). In Pacific ethnohistory, the major influence has been Marshall Sahlins: see *Islands of History* (Chicago, 1985).
24 Geertz, *The Interpretation of Cultures*, p. 15.
25 Darnton, *The Great Cat Massacre.*
26 *Ibid.*, pp. 77–8.
27 *Ibid.*, p. 100.
28 Roger Chartier, 'Text, Symbols and Frenchness', *Journal of Modern History*, 57 (1985), pp. 682–95. For Darnton's response, see 'The Symbolic Element in History', *Journal of Modern History*, 58 (1986), pp. 218–34.
29 Dominick LaCapra, 'Chartier, Darnton, and the Great Symbol Massacre', *Journal of Modern History*, 60 (1988), p. 103.
30 Harold Mah, 'Suppressing the Text: The Metaphysics of Ethnographic History in Darnton's Great Cat Massacre', *History Workshop Journal*, 31 (1991), pp. 1–20.
31 Geertz, *The Interpretation of Cultures*, p. 20.
32 The term is taken from Eric R. Wolf, *Europe and the People without History* (Berkeley, 1982).
33 Frederic W. Gleach, 'Controlled Speculation: Interpreting the Saga of Pocahontas and Captain John Smith', in Jennifer Brown and Elizabeth Vibert (eds), *Reading Beyond Words: Contexts for Native History* (Peterborough, Ont., 1996), p. 22.
34 Davis, *The Return of Martin Guerre*, p. 5.

Additional reading

Axtell, James, The *European and the Indian: Essays in the Ethnohistory of Colonial North America* (New York, 1981).

Clendinnen, Inga, *Aztecs: An Interpretation* (Cambridge, 1991).

Darnton, Robert, 'Workers Revolt: The Great Cat Massacre of the Rue Saint-Séverin', in *The Great Cat Massacre and Other Episodes in French Cultural History* (New York, 1985).

Darnton, Robert, 'The Symbolic Element in History', *Journal of Modern History*, 58 (1986), pp. 218–34.

Davis, Natalie Zemon, *The Return of Martin Guerre* (Cambridge, Mass., 1983).

Geertz, Clifford, 'Thick Description: Toward an Interpretive Theory of Culture', in *The Interpretation of Cultures* (London, 1975).

Ginzburg, Carlo, *The Cheese and the Worms: The Cosmos of a Sixteenth-century Miller*, trans. John and Anne Tedeschi (London, [1976] 1992).

Jennings, Francis, *The Invasion of America: Indians, Colonialism, and the Cant of Conquest* (Chapel Hill, 1975).

Krech III, Shepard, 'The State of Ethnohistory', *Annual Review of Anthropology*, 20 (1991), pp. 345–75.

Rabb, Theodore and Robert Rotberg (eds), *The New History: The 1980s and Beyond* (Princeton, 1982), chapters on Anthropology and History in the 1980s.

Thomas, Keith, 'History and Anthropology', *Past and Present*, 24 (1963), pp. 3–24.

Thomas, Keith, *Religion and the Decline of Magic* (Harmondsworth, 1971).

White, Richard, *The Middle Ground: Indians, Empires, and Republics in the Great Lakes Region, 1650–1815* (Cambridge, 1991).

YUCATEC MAYA WOMEN AND THE SPANISH CONQUEST: ROLE AND RITUAL IN HISTORICAL RECONSTRUCTION
Inga Clendinnen

Over the last several years historians of different places and periods have been engaged in the search for the 'common man.' There have been notable successes, achieved in part by more intensive exploitation of recognized sources, in part by the identification as sources of previously unconsidered survivals.[1] The quest for the common woman, pursued with at least equal passion, has not fared well. Latin America exhibits the difficulties in dramatically stark form. For the immediate past, where statistics give some opportunity to establish the external conditions of women's lives, and where researchers armed with tape recorders can seek to grasp something of particular women's experience, the yield has been substantial. For earlier periods, the sharpness of social and ethnic divisions, the poverty and illiteracy of the mass of the population, and the strength of the cultural habit of identifying the male as fully representative of his female kin, have effectively excluded the ordinary woman from the historical record.[2]

There are ways, however, by which we may seek to learn something of the patterns of existence and experience of women, even for so early a period as those crucial decades of the sixteenth century which saw the shaping of European-Indian relations. In what follows I want to retrieve what I can of the impact of Spanish conquest and colonization on the native women of Yucatán. The sources are overwhelmingly Spanish, and exclusively male.[3] From the native side we

---

As always, I have to thank my colleagues June Philipp, Rhys Isaac and Tony Barta for their penetrating and precise criticisms of earlier drafts.

[1] The work of E. P. Thompson and his colleagues is exemplary on both counts. See esp. Douglas Hay et al., *Albion's Fatal Tree* (New York, 1975).

[2] Asunción Lavrín (ed.), *Latin American Women: Historical Perspectives*, Contributions in Women's Studies, Number 3 (Westport, CT, 1978), Intro., p. 4. For a recent bibliographical survey, see Meri Knaster, *Women in Spanish America: An Annotated Bibliography from Pre-Conquest to Contemporary Times* (Boston, 1977).

[3] The statistical materials so profitably exploited by social historians elsewhere to reconstruct population shifts and local demographic profiles are lacking for the peninsula; all we have are estimates of absolute populations, and crude indicators of differ-

have little more than the compilations of invocations, prophecies, histories and calendrics to which scholars have given the generic title of the 'Books of Chilam Balam.' Being concerned with high, sacred and therefore male matters, they mention women only glancingly.[4] The Spanish writings have the usual defects of 'outsider' accounts: alien conquerors rarely make good ethnographers. As males, they were doubly distanced from the lives of the women of their defeated enemies.

Sources need not bear directly or even obliquely on women to be revealing of their situation. By reconstructing the boundaries drawn around male activities, we may infer the definition of complementary female activity. But to establish the boundaries, the content and even the associated demeanours of gender roles is not to understand how those roles were experienced and valued by those who acted them out. For that, we must turn to those occasions where the 'unarticulated concepts that inform the lives and cultures of . . . peoples' are most formally expressed, and so rendered more accessible to the observer: the world of ritual action.[5] What we need, then, are detailed

ential losses between regions. See Woodrow Borah and Sherburne F. Cook, *Essays in Population History: Mexico and the Caribbean* (Berkeley, 1971–79), 3 vols, vol. 2, 1974, chapter 1. See also Peter Gerhard, *The Southeast Frontier of New Spain* (Princeton, 1979). For an impressive attempt to identify the cultural dynamics of population movements in the peninsula during the colonial period, see Nancy M. Farriss, 'Nucleation versus Dispersal: The Dynamics of Population Movement in Colonial Yucatán,' *Hispanic American Historical Review* 58 (1978): 187–216. For early secular Spanish accounts, see Henry Raup Wagner (ed.), *The Discovery of Yucatán by Francisco Hernandez de Cordoba* (Berkeley, 1942) and his *The Discovery of New Spain in 1518 by Juan de Grijalva* (Berkeley, 1942). For the experiences of Jeronimo de Aguilar, 'enslaved' by the Maya, see Cervantes de Salazar, *Crónica de la Nueva España* bk. 2, chs. 25–29. An English translation of the relevant passages appears as Appendix D in Alfred M. Tozzer (ed.), *Landa's Relación de las cosas de Yucatán: A Translation* (Cambridge, Mass., 1941). Also important are the *Relaciónes* from Yucatán, (1579–81), published as volumes 11 and 13 of the *Colección de documentos inéditos relativos al descubrimiento, conquista y organización de los antiguas posesiones españolas de Ultramar* 25 vols (Madrid, 1885–1932). Hereinafter *RY* I and *RY* II.
  [4] For the most accessible example, see Ralph L. Roys (trans & ed.), *The Book of Chilam Balam of Chumayel* first published 1933 (new edition Norman, 1967). For a full listing of the books of Chilam Balam, and other Lowland Maya sources, see Charles Gibson and John B. Glass, 'A Census of Middle American Prose Manuscripts in the Native Historical Tradition,' in *Handbook of Middle American Indians* vol. 15, ed. Howard F. Cline (Austin, 1975).
  [5] Clifford Geertz, 'On the Nature of Anthropological Understanding,' *American Scientist* 63 (1975): 47. Geertz's conceptualization of 'culture' is I think indispensable to the ethnohistorian—or any other historian, for that matter. See especially 'Thick Description: Toward an Interpretive Theory of Culture,' in his *The Interpretation of Cultures* (New York, 1973), pp. 2–30. An essential chart for the particular waters of women's studies is provided by Susan Carol Rogers, 'Women's Place: A Critical Review of Anthropological Theory,' *Comparative Studies in Society and History* 20 (1978): 123–162.

descriptions of actions. And we have them. Some Spanish missionaries, professionally determined to discern the social ethics moulding familial and communal interaction, took pains to record the mundane routines of native life. They were even more intent on describing those performances they identified as belonging to the forbidden world of native ritual.[6] Of course, they 'saw' only what they took to be significant, but their reports are sufficiently rich to provide the essential basis for this study. Tracking between role and ritual— and noting other paths, and other pitfalls, along the way—we may retrieve not only what sixteenth-century Yucatec Maya women did, and what was done to them, but what they made of those experiences.

If we are to trace the impact of conquest, we must first locate women within the traditional world.[7] it would be easy to read male-female relations in pre-conquest Yucatán as yet another chapter in the overlong book of female subjugation. Gender roles were sharply differentiated, women and girls being confined to what we would call the domestic sphere, and to a rigorously modest demeanor. Women had no jural role; no right to inherit property or position. A young man 'earned' control over his wife and her issue by coming to live in her father's house and serving him for two or three years.[8] If monogamy was the rule among commoners, the lords maintained numerous secondary wives and concubines, and all men assumed their right to the sexual use of their female slaves. Women were excluded from the most sacred rituals,[9] and from making offerings of their blood to the

[6] The most important single source is the 'Account of the Things of Yucatán' written in Spain by the Franciscan Diego de Landa in 1566, drawing on fifteen years' experience in the peninsula. See n. 3 above. See also Diego López de Cogolludo, *Historia de Yucatán* (Mérida, 1867–8). Hereinafter Cogolludo, *Historia*. Other missionary accounts are scattered through F. V. Scholes, C. R. Menendez, J. I. Rubio Mañé and E. B. Adams (eds), *Documentos para la historia de Yucatán* 3 vols (Compañía Tipográfica Yucateca, 1936–38); F. V. Scholes and E. B. Adams, *Don Diego Quijada, alcalde mayor de Yucatán, Campeche y Tabasco* 3 vols (Mexico City, 1942). There is also significant Yucatecan material in *Cartas de Indias* (Madrid, 1877), and Mariano Cuevas (ed.), *Documentos inéditos del siglo xvi para la historia de Mexico* (Mexico City, 1946–47).

[7] Most of the information in this section is derived from Landa, *Landa's Relación*, *passim*, but especially pp. 85–133.

[8] Tomas Lopez Medel, 'Ordenanzas,' in Cogolludo, *Historia* bk. 5, ch. 17.

[9] The 'virgin' water required for certain rituals was fetched from places so remote it could not have been contaminated by women. J. Eric Thompson, intro., to reprinted edition of Henry C. Mercer, *The Hill Caves of Yucatán* (Teaneck, N.J., 1973), pp. xv–xxii; Landa, *Relación* p. 103, p. 153, n. 468. See also J. Eric Thompson, *Maya History and Religion* (Norman, 1970), pp. 185–185 [sic].

gods.[10] Only pre-pubescent girls died bloodily in sacrifice; only old women safely past menopause were permitted to enter the temple and dance before the images.[11] Aspects of male ritual behavior could also be read as inimical to women, or at least to sexuality. Abstention from sexual intercourse is a common enough preparation for ritual activity, but the Yucatec Maya imposed abstinence for quite uncommonly long periods.[12] Throughout Middle America penis laceration was performed as an act of auto-sacrifice, but while in Mexico the practice was restricted to celibate priests, in Yucatán the ritual was open to all males, and was practised with competitive intensity.[13]

On this selection of evidence it could seem that Yucatec Maya women were regarded as chattels in their own society, and as unclean chattels at that. But this bleak view is challenged by other glimpses we have of Indian behavior, which imply an amiable mutual acceptance. Spaniards—who shocked the Indians by their overt lasciviousness—were shocked in their turn to see how casually men and women bathed in the water holes, the men troubling to conceal no more than 'a hand would cover.'[14] Girls were not secluded at the onset of menstruation nor is there any evidence of avoidances being

[10] For the tabu on female voluntary offerings of blocd, see Landa, *Landa's Relación*, pp. 114, 128. The restrictions are the more interesting in that they appear to be local to the peninsula, and to represent a break at some point with traditional practice. We have clear evidence that Lowland Maya women made blood offerings in the Classic Maya period 'performing the bloodletting rite, and even assisting at the arraignment of prisoners after a raid.' Tatiana Proskouriakoff, 'Portraits of Maya Women in Maya Art,' in Samuel K. Lothrop (ed.), *Essays in Pre-Columbian Art and Archaeology* (Cambridge, Mass., 1964), pp. 90–1. Joyce Marcus, arguing from epigraphic and iconographic evidence, suggests that women have come to enjoy 'new roles and recognition' during cycle 9 of the Classic Period, with women from dynasties ruling at capital centers perhaps exercising authority at lesser dependent centers. Joyce Marcus, *Emblem and State in the Classic Maya Lowlands*, (Washington, D.C., 1976). She notes that during Cycle 10 (A.D. 830–909) women cease to be represented on monuments. Marcus, *Op. Cit.*, pp. 192–193.
[11] Despite popular fantasies, there is nothing to suggest that the Sacred Cenote would accept only beautiful female virgins—and its victims died by drowning. Earnest A. Hooton, 'Skeletons from the Cenote of Sacrifice at Chichén Itzá,' in Alfred M. Tozzer (dedicated to), *The Maya and their Neighbours* (New York, 1962), (2nd ed.), pp. 272–280. See also RY II, 24–26. In Landa's account as we have it he refers to a 'man or woman' victim in the arrow sacrifice. Landa, *Landa's Relación* p. 118. However, as the arrow sacrifice was firmly identified with the warrior cult, I take this to be a slip, either on the part of Landa, or a later scribe.
[12] For example, the man chose as Nacom or war captain was to abstain from sexual intercourse for the full three years of his term. Landa, *Landa's Relación* pp. 122–3.
[13] Landa, *Landa's Relación* p. 114.
[14] Landa, *Landa's Relación* pp. 89, 126.

practised during its recurrence.[15] Childbirth was the business of women, but there is no record of post-parturition rituals of purification. Both sexes spent long hours in considerable discomfort making their bodies pleasing to sight, touch and smell with tattoos, paint and sweetly scented unguents. The sexual act itself seems to have been treated matter-of-factly. While a bride was certainly expected to be a virgin, there was no exaggerated concern with the signs of virginity: the young couple were bedded on the wedding night with minimal formality, the serious business of the evening being the feasting of the kin. Should the marriage break down before bride service was completed there is no suggestion that the girl's father found her more difficult to rematch when she was no longer a virgin, and possibly even a mother. Widows and widowers could remarry, but they more commonly entered into informal sexual liaisons, which appear to have concerned no one but themselves. Certainly displays of lasciviousness were regarded with distaste, but distaste was elicited by all lapses from a high standard of dignity and self control.[16]

[15] Here we must face the disquieting possibility that menstrual seclusions and avoidances were practised, but were either not mentioned to later investigators, or were deleted as irrelevant or indecent.

[16] Indeed, a lapse in sexual control was dangerous precisely because it opened the way to more serious disorders. Here is an account, from one of the books of Chilam Balam, of the process of disintegration initiated in the 'invasion' year Katun 7 Ahau, where the lasciviousness of the 'wise men,' whose responsibility it is to maintain order, dissolves that order. (The *plumería* is our frangipani. The Yucatec Maya always associated it, not always negatively, with sexuality.)

> Katun 7 Ahau is the third katun . . . the Plumería is its bread, the Plumería is its water, the burden of the katun. Then begins the lewdness of the wise men, the beckoning of carnal sin, the beckoning of the katun. . . . They twist their necks, they twist their mouths, they wink the eye, they slaver at the mouth, at men, women, chiefs, justices, presiding officers, clerks, choirmasters, everybody both great and small. There is no great teaching. Heaven and earth are truly lost to them; they have lost all shame. Then the head-chiefs of the towns, the rulers of the towns, the prophets of the towns, the priests of the Maya men are hanged. Understanding is lost; wisdom is lost. Prepare yourselves, Oh Itza! Your sons shall see the mirth of the katun, the jesting of the katun. Dissolute is the speech, dissolute the face of the rogue to the rulers, to the head-chiefs . . .

Roys, *The Book of Chilam Balam of Chumayel* p. 151. See also pp. 105–106; 169. The books of Chilam Balam, written down as they were in the period of European domination, are (as the cited passage demonstrates) touched by Christian influence, but the cosmology they celebrate is traditional. See Inga Clendinnen, 'Landscape and World View: the Survival of Yucatec Maya Culture under Spanish Conquest,' *Comparative Studies in Society and History* 22 (1980): 374–393. There is the possibility that promiscuous sexual activity occurred on occasions of ritual drunkenness. The *encomendero* Diego de Contreras reported that when drunk '[the Indians] . . . used to worship idols and had carnal knowl-

Marriage need not have been experienced as an oppressive institution. If the woman possessed no formalised 'rights,' she nonetheless enjoyed significant protection. During the first uncertain years
while she and her new husband came to understand the terms of
their relationship she continued to live with her closest kin and to
enjoy the security of familiar routines and surroundings. She probably bore her first child in that same secure setting. When the time
came for the transition to her husband's father's household, she
could make the move with her role and reputation as a matron
already acknowledged. Nor was she physically distanced from her
kin. In the multiple-family, multiple-generational households of
Yucatán, 'society,' the example and possible intervention of others
must have been very much present in all relationships. The clarity
of the prescriptions for proper conduct in marriage suggest that each
spouse was well protected from arbitrary treatment by the other.
There are indications that the completion of brideservice marked the
transition to full social maturity for each spouse. Matrons were freed
from the tight social and physical restrictions which had hedged
their earlier years, as were the young men who, having quit the
warrior house and the black body paint of bachelorhood for the
tattoos and increased independence of the married state, then grad-
uated to a position where they could become head of their own
household. Naming practices add their testimony: women retained
their names after marriage, and among the names borne by each
individual was a teknonym derived from the mother.[17] It is possible

edge of their sisters and daughters and female kin.' Landa himself claimed that when
drunk the Indians would 'violate the conjugal rights of each other, the poor women
thinking they were receiving their husbands...' Landa, *Landa's Relación* p. 91. Yet
nowhere else in his great *Relación* does he return to the charge of drunken promiscuity—
not even in his account of the violence and drunkenness which attended the celebra-
tory period of the last three months of the Maya year. Landa, *Landa's Relación* p. 166.
Through most of his work he emphasized the high value placed on chastity, and the
stringency of the laws governing sexual activities, eg. Landa, *Landa's Relación* pp. 32,
123–124, 127. See also Pedro García, *RY* I, 149.

[17] Ralph Roys believes this name to have been derived from the mother's matronymic,
'which she could have inherited only from a female line of maternal ancestors.' Ralph
Roys, 'Personal Names of the Mayas of Yucatán,' *Contributions to American Anthropology
and History* Vol. 6 (Washington, D.C., 1940), pp. 37–8. Roys suspected that 'there was some
kind of matriarchal organization in Maya society which has never been brought to light
in the literature on the subject.' Ralph L. Roys, 'Literary sources for the History of
Mayapan,' *Mayapan Yucatán Mexico* ed. H. E. D. Pollock, Ralph L. Roys, T. Proskouriakoff,
A Ledyard Smith, Pub. No. 609, (Washington, D.C., 1962), p. 63, and 'Personal Names of
the Mayas of Yucatán,' p. 38. Though the evidence is confused on the matter, Roys' judgment as always compels respect. For a discussion of the evidence, see William A. Haviland, 'Rules of descent in sixteenth century Yucatán,' *Estudios de cutura Maya IX* (1973),

that women had their own exclusive ritual occasions, concealed from us by the slant of the sources. They certainly had their own place: if men found the locus of their sociability in the public spaces around the warrior house and the dwellings of the priests and the lords, the houseyards were women's territory, where they could gather in the fruit-trees' shade to talk, to watch the children, and to help each other with the endless elaborations of their weaving.

A more systematic investigation of the world of ritual reveals that despite concern to keep sexually mature women away from the most sacred places and moments, they were not excluded from all, or even most, religious occasions. Women were the chief custodians of the domestic shrines housing the gods of the lineage and the household which probably commanded the greater part of Indian devotions.[18] For the more public ceremonies held in the courtyards of the temples and the houses of the lords, men brewed the mead-like *balché*, but women were responsible for most of the ritual fare, and—seated separately from the men—participated in the feasting and drinking at the ceremonies' end. They also had modes of expression distinctive to themselves, yet valued by the whole society. Their weaving skills were essential to the sustaining of ceremonial display. Extra-peninsula trading was the prerogative of the lords, who consumed most of the imported luxuries in the public manifestations of their social authority. A major and specially prized export item was the fine cotton garments woven by the women of Yucatán. While some of the mantles and breechclouts for that external trade were perhaps offered as a tribute, there can be little doubt that most were woven in the 'domestic factory' environment of the lords' households, where the cooperative dimension of female labor already noted in commoner households could develop into expert specialization.[19] And always women's handiwork decked the leading participants in the great theatre of ritual.

135–150. Haviland claims that while descent was ideally patrilineal, in reality, in response to the need for flexibility in troubled times, it was ambilineal.

[18] Tozzer, *Landa's Relación* p. 18, n. 105.

[19] For pre-conquest trade, see France V. Scholes and Ralph L. Roys, *The Maya-Chontal Indians of Acalan-Tixchel* 2nd ed. (Norman, 1968), esp. chapter 2; Anne C. Chapman, 'Port of Trade Enclaves in Aztec and Maya Civilizations,' in Karl Polanyi, Conrad M. Arensberg, Harry W. Pearson (eds), *Trade and Market in the early empires; economics in history and theory* (New York, 1957), pp. 144–153. See also Ralph L. Roys, *The Indian Background of Colonial Yucatán* second ed. (Norman, 1972) esp. chapter 8. For pre-conquest tribute levels, see n. 29 below.

Feminine skills were ritually honoured as often and equally with men's: in the annual 'blessing of the occupations' ceremony, 'all the appliances of all pursuits,' from the paraphernalia of the priests to the spindles of the women, were anointed with the sacred blue bitumen, and all the children of the town, boys in one group and girls in another, were lightly struck upon the hands, to make those hands skillful in their appropriate occupations.[20] (That ceremony, it is worth noting, was performed by an old woman.) When the male specialists of the community gathered in one of their houses for the annual celebration of their profession, their wives were present also, as participants, and as partners.[21] Nor, despite emphasis on prolonged periods of sexual abstinence, were priests required to remain celibate: for them, as for others, marriage marked social maturation, and they were expected to pass on their esoteric knowledge to their sons.

In the raising and use of maize, that central activity—central in its importance for subsistence, in the hours spent in its production, and in its sacred significance—the interdependence of male and female, husband and wife, was again demonstrated. The Franciscan Francisco Vásquez, writing of the *milperos* in the highlands of Guatemala in the early years of the eighteenth century, saw the maize cycle as an exclusively masculine affair:

> Everything they did and said so concerned maize they almost regarded it as a god. The enchantment and rapture with which they look upon their *milpas* is such that on their account they forget children, wife, and other pleasure, as though the *milpas* were their final purpose in life and source of all their felicity.[22]

In Yucatán, as in Guatemala, the planting, tending and cropping of maize was a masculine privilege. At most, women might help to transport the harvested maize back to the village. While the Mexicans were prepared to conceive of the maize as female at some stages of its growth, Maya maize god personifications were unequivocally male, and women were permitted to play no part in the *milpa* rituals to aid the maize growth. But the notion that women were excluded from that central activity can be sustained only if we stop the enquiry at what we would designate 'the end of the production cycle': if we continue to trace through the whole cycle of production and con-

[20] Landa, *Landa's Relación* p. 159.
[21] Landa, *Landa's Relación* pp. 154–155.
[22] Fray Francisco Vásquez, 'Croníca de la provincia de Santísimo nombre de Jesús de Guatemala de la Orden de nuestro seráfico Padre San Francisco,' quoted Thompson, *Maya History and Religion* p. 287.

sumption, the interdependence of male and female activities, the complementarity of husband and wife, is again made manifest. It was the women's part to control and care for the maize once it was in the village, and to prepare it with the attentiveness and respect appropriate to the handling of sacred materials: casual waste of the grains, or the thoughtless disposal of the husks, would bring retribution on the whole community. The three-stone fireplace was a sacred place, and the hours spend grinding and cooking the corn were as much permeated with sacred significance as were the hours of labor the men had spent in the *milpa*, (which reminds us just how artificial the necessary analytic distinction between 'role' and 'ritual' is). As the number four was associated with the male, symbolizing the four-sided *milpa* in which he would spend most of his days, the number three, signifying the three stones of the cooking fire, represented the woman who would spend so much of her life close by the domestic hearth. Even the penis laceration ceremony—so disturbing to us, steeped in Christian notions of the mortification of the sinful flesh—might well have celebrated the same interdependence. Peter Furst has argued persuasively that when Maya priests and rulers of the Classic Period drew blood from their penes—blood thought to have extraordinary fertilizing power—they were giving expression to 'certain basic assumptions of the Mesoamerican world about the interdependence of complimentary [sic] opposites—in this case male and female . . . ,' male genital blood being identified with menstrual blood.[23] We would certainly not be justified in reading the ritual as inimical to women.

It will not do to sentimentalize pre-contact Yucatán into some dewy 'world we have lost' of social and sexual harmony: to romanticize the past is to abdicate our obligation to understand it. War captives labored sullenly in the villages, and in times of famine the

[23] Peter T. Furst, 'Fertility, Vision Quest and Auto-Sacrifice: Some Thoughts on Ritual Blood-Letting Among the Maya,' in Merle Greene Robertson (ed.), *The Art, Iconography and Dynastic History of Palenque Part III*, (Pebble Beach, Calif., 1976), p. 183. For the fertilizing power of genital blood, see David Joralemon, 'Ritual Blood-Sacrifice among the Ancient Maya: Part I,' in Merle Greene Robertson, ed., *Primera Mesa Redonda de Palenque: Part II*, (Pebble Beach, Calif., 1974) pp. 59–75. Ought we to seek for more strands of this shadowy web of meaning in myth and in the characteristics attributed to the female deities? In my hands, that clue breaks: what I discern in the dominant myths and personae of the deities (in so far as they are projections of 'the human' at all) is the straightforward replication of conventional female roles. See J. Eric Thompson, *Maya History and Religion* esp. 214–219. The X-Tabai, malignant female spirits who take on the shapes of beautiful girls to lure men to their doom, are a modern invention. Robert Redfield and Alonso Villa R., *Chan Kom: A Maya Village* (Washington, D.C., 1934), p. 122.

desperate poor sold themselves into slavery, while the gods took their toll of human hearts and blood. Order was sought and cherished because it was a fragile thing. But if romanticism is easy, it is even easier for our capacity for understanding to be obstructed by the most obstinate because most taken-for-granted ethnocentrism, the Western conceptualization of the 'person,' with its concomitant notions of 'individualism' and 'autonomy,'[24] and to be clouded by our own—justified—sensitivity to the political dimension of relations between the sexes. Yucatec Maya women certainly remained separate from men, and were subordinate to them. Males systematically took precedence over females: males controlled public ritual activity and the whole public sphere, while women moved in what we designate the domestic zone. But to say women were separate and subordinate is not at all the same thing as to say they were segregated and subjugated, and were regarded, and regarded themselves, as inferior. Males were equally if differently bound, by the duty of the younger to the older, of the lower to the higher rank. Nor did social authority enhance 'independence': lords were doubly bound by their duty to commoners and priests, priests by their duty to men and to the gods. Within that conceptualization of the world differentiation of function, as of status, was understood in terms of interdependence. Men and women moved in largely separate zones, but those zones were linked by multiple bridges of mundane and ritual action expressive of that interdependence, and within them each group could move with equal assurance.

The first devastation the Yucatec Maya suffered in consequence of the Spanish presence in the New World preceded military action: smallpox, perhaps carried from Darien, swept the peninsula some time before 1517, the year of Yucatán's official 'discovery.' The first Spanish assaults, launched in 1527, probably affected only particular communities. The threat of the dense gray forest, and the high risk of ambush along the narrow twisting paths, discouraged venturesomeness among the would-be conquerors, and when they stumbled upon a village the inhabitants usually had been sufficiently warned by the noise of their approach to take refuge in the bush. The Spaniards found so little attractive in the stony land that in 1535, lured by stories of golden Peru, they quit the peninsula. Those who returned in 1540 came with a new determination to make sure of

[24] Clifford Geertz puts the point and sounds the warning with his usual lucid grace in 'On the Nature of Anthropological Understanding,' *American Scientist* 63 (1975): 47–53.

their prize, poor as they knew it to be. They found a transformed landscape: during the interregnum, the Indians had suffered savage internal wars, drought, and then famine, as locusts swarmed over the land. During those desolate days the people, we are told, 'fell dead on the roads, and the returning Spaniards no longer recognized the country.'[25] Despite these ravages, several provinces resisted desperately, and the last campaigns were fought with a terrible bitterness on both sides. In this final phase, few villages escaped unscathed, and whole regions were devastated: the once-populous province of Uaymil-Chetumal, when the fighting finally stilled, had become an empty place haunted by only a few survivors. There and elsewhere communities abandoned their villages and their cornplots and lived as best they could scattered through the forest.

The Indians had fought hard, but without sufficient understanding of their opponents. Native women and children, as well as men, were chained by the neck to make the long lines of captives the conquerors dragged behind them. When Gaspar Pacheco, having seized a town and requiring carriers, found the men had fled, he had the women rounded up and forced to carry—a solution the Indians had not conceived of.[26] Women also suffered the usual appalling sexual abuse at the hands of the Spaniards and their Mexican allies. There are the standard horror stories, which we unfortunately have no reason to doubt, of women hanged, with their children hanging from their feet; of sexual mutilations; of 'uncooperative' women torn apart by the great dogs which were feared more than the Spaniards themselves. Those women who escaped direct physical encounter with the invaders must still have suffered from hunger and exposure; the rigid division of labor between the sexes bore heavily on each when old patterns of life were disrupted.

The outcome

With the 'peace' which came, through the defenders' exhaustion, in 1546, the land was divided into tributary zones and left to recover.

The survivors lived in a changed world, most obviously because of what we know to have been a great reduction in population, the

[25] Landa, *Landa's Relación* p. 55.
[26] The key source on the Pachecos's campaigns is Fray Lorenzo de Bienvenida to the Crown, Mérida, 10 February 1548, *Cartas de Indias* pp. 70–82. For the carriers episode, see p. 80. For the whole conquest, the best treatment remains that of Robert S. Chamberlain, *The Conquest and Colonization of Yucatán, 1517–1550* (Washington, D.C., 1948).

precise dimensions of which remain obscure. The most that can be said with any confidence is that the population of the peninsula, already much reduced, was more than halved by the twenty years of the conquest, and that the provinces of the east and south, populous before the coming of the Spaniards, had been effectively depopulated.[27] Then within a decade came a forced nucleation of remaining Indian settlements, carried through (in face of bitter opposition from both lay Spaniards and Indians) by the missionary friars, and again at a high cost in Indian lives. We glimpse the survivors' anguish and psychic shock at being driven from their homes to be relocated in an unfamiliar place of the friars' choosing through the tough old colonist Giraldo Diaz, who recalled that while many of the people herded into the new settlements died of hunger and exposure, some died from 'the great sadness in their hearts.'[28] For the rest of the century, the few indicators we have point to a continuing, if less dramatic, decline, in part due to the 'natural' disasters of epidemic disease, of famines (exacerbated, of course, by the relocations), and perhaps in part to changes in child-bearing patterns.

The economic demands made upon the defeated Indians by their conquerors were, broadly, familiar. There was no mineral wealth in Yucatán, nor, as the Spaniards quickly found, any other commercially viable product which could be raised in the arid land. Had the peninsula been conquered more quickly, it is likely its human population would have become its commercial resource, to be shipped out to the labor-hungry mines of the mainland and the islands, but by the mid fifteen-forties the Crown had firmly set its face against such casual expenditure of its vassals, and that way to profit was closed. There was nothing to attract later adventurers to the poverty-stricken province, and the Spaniards who had fought so long and hard had to content themselves with the modest reward of living in one of the four Spanish towns, and relying on the chiefs of their allotted towns for tribute in the traditional native products of cotton mantles, honey and wax, salt, maize and beans and of introduced chickens; and for the organization of labor drafts for largely domestic needs.

These demands were not new to Maya men. While it is impossible to establish with any confidence the precise levels of pre-conquest

[27] Borah and Cook estimate the peninsula's population in 1527, the first year of the military campaign, and after the smallpox epidemic, at 800,000, and in 1546 at about 350,000. For a list of the major 'natural' disasters of the second half of the sixteenth century see their *Essays in Population History* II, pp. 62–63, 176–177.

[28] Giraldo Diaz, *RY* II, 209–210.

tribute paid to the lords,[29] they had customarily been offered a share in local produce, and had drawn on the labor services of men and, less certainly, of women. For the men, the post-conquest mode of agricultural production—techniques, social groups and locations—remained familiar, even if the amount of tribute demanded and its ultimate use were novel. For women, the imposed change was very much greater. While Spanish tribute requirements passed through a series of adjustments, one demand remained constant: each tributary, however, defined, had to supply each year a substantial length of plain cotton cloth.[30] Women had always woven cotton in Yucatán, for their own use and, as we have seen, to supply the luxury market in external trade, but the weaving of the heavy, wide, unadorned *mantas* as specified by the Spaniards was an unfamiliar and tedious task. Further, their labor obligation committed women to domestic service in Spanish towns, and military habits die hard: in 1561 an ultimately successful argument advanced for the abolition of women's tributary labor was that the women could not otherwise be protected from sexual molestation.[31] (It was on this occasion that the Franciscans urged, with the pragmatism so shocking to the tender-minded secularist, that 'vagabond' women causing 'trouble' in the villages be rounded up and forced to serve in the Spaniards' houses, presumably on the grounds that, having already fallen, they could fall no further).[32]

For casual sexual encounters there remained the 'lewd houses' operating in Mérida, presumably largely staffed by Indian girls,[33] but most Spaniards preferred more permanent liaisons. There were in Yucatán few Indian women of a rank to tempt Spaniards into marriage, though a handful of conquerors, and more artisans, took

---

[29] Eg., Landa, *Landa's Relación* p. 87; Juan Bote, *RY* I 287–288; Pedro de Santillana, *RY* I, 254–255; Juan de Magaña, *RY* I 187. Much of the relación material relating to tribute levels has been handily assembled in Robert S. Chamberlain, *The Pre-Conquest Tribute and Service System of the Maya as a Preparation for the Spanish Repartimiento-Encomienda in Yucatán* (Coral Gables, 1951).

[30] The 1549 tribute required each married man, or more properly each married couple, to present one cotton *manta* of about ten square yards or twelve square *varas*, and a number of European hens, together with maize, beans, beeswax and honey. For an estimation of the value of the *manta* in *reales*, and an astute assessment of the oppressiveness of requirements, see Scholes and Roys, *The Maya-Chontal Indians of Acalan Tixchel* pp. 151–153. See also p. 470, n. 1.

[31] Don Diego Quijada to the Crown, 6 October, 1561, *RY* II, 260–261.

[32] Don Diego Quijada to the Crown, 6 October, 1561, *RY* II, 260.

[33] Fray Francisco de Toral to the Crown, 20 April 1567, *Cartas de Indias* XLII; Petition of Joaquín de Leguizamo, n.d., Scholes and Adams, *Don Diego Quijada* II, 207–208.

Indian wives.[34] Concubines were another matter. In 1552 Tomas Lopez Medél, a visiting royal judge, had done what he could to force Spaniards to disband 'their houses filled with women,'[35] but in 1579 Giraldo Diaz could still nonchalantly comment on the fetching ways of those Indian girls who were the special *amigas* of Spaniards. (He then waspishly complained that native women were becoming 'bigger whores every day,' which would seem to be a case of the fire blaming the kettle for turning black.)[36] Unhappily we know nothing of the fate of these women or of their offspring, though it is possible that, as Lockhart has shown for Peru, some children of informal alliances were accepted by their Spanish fathers and granted some place in Spanish society.

Such women had been shaken out of the traditional fabric by the dislocations of war and by the conquerors' sexual demands. But the great majority of women remained in the villages. Those villages had been relocated and restructured by the missionary friars in the clear determination to destroy the traditional patterns and the traditional relationships of native life. The friars saw the old multiple-family, multi-generational households of the commoners, which had nurtured female work-sharing and mutual support, as incitements to sexual promiscuity and social confusion; by the last decade of the century such houses survived only in remote areas, far from Spanish surveillance.[37] The households of the lords, with their entourages of women, they saw as temples of lechery. Each lord, they insisted, must restrict his sexual interest to his principal 'legitimate' wife, and any other woman living and serving in the house must be paid for her labor. The 'monogamous' marriages of the commoners did not escape attention. Brideservice was seen as the selling of women. Christian life required, they insisted—averting their eyes from Spanish examples—that each married couple live with their issue in a single and

[34] Juan Francisco Molina Solis, *Historia del Descubrimiento y conquista de Yucatán* (Mexico, D.F.: 1943), 2 vols II, pp. 384–385.

[35] Tomas Lopez Medél, 'Ordenanzas,' in Cogolludo, *Historia* bk 5, chs. 16–19.

[36] Giraldo Diaz, *RY* II, 212. Landa records that old men lamented the decline of the chastity of their women since they had come into contact with Spaniards. Landa, *Landa's Relación* p. 71.

[37] Lopez Medél, 'Ordenanzas'; Giraldo Diaz, *RY* II, 209–210. Fray Lorenzo de Bienvenida to the Crown, Mérida, 10 February 1548, in *Cartas de Indias* p. 78; France V. Scholes, Ralph L. Roys and E. B. Adams, 'Report and Census of the Indians of Cozumel, 1570,' *Contributions to American Anthropology and History* Vol. 6, (Washington, D.C., 1940), pp. 5–29; Ralph L. Roys, France V. Scholes and Eleanor B. Adams, 'Census and Inspection of the Town of Pencuyut, Yucatán, in 1583 by Diego Garcia de Palacio, *oidor* of the Audiencia of Guatemala,' *Ethnohistory*, 6, no. 3 (Summer 1959): 195–225.

separate dwelling. Women's kin were no longer to interfere in marriages, for marriage was not an alliance between families but a solemn sacrament between individuals, transforming them into one flesh, binding each to each in Christian duty.[38]

All pagan rituals were of course forbidden. Nor were any Indians to be trusted with Christian paraphernalia in their houses: the church, and only the church, was designated the sacred locus in the village, where sacred objects were to be housed, and reverent behavior displayed. But women equally with men were required to attend the church, and in the 'Christian' schools run by native schoolmasters under the supervision of visiting friars little girls, called out of the seclusion of their mother's care, stumbled together with little boys through the strange prayers and gestures of the new order.

That new order could seem to have offered Yucatec women some increase in security and position. Economic theorists have hopefully assured us that women's status increases proportionately to their non-domestic input, and women's economic role had expanded: the women now supplied the mantles and chickens which comprised a major part of the obligatory tribute. Landa recorded that the nobles of Yucatán had laughed at the friars 'because they gave ear to the poor and the rich without distinctions.'[39] The lords knew the natural, real and proper order of the world was based on distinctions and the ordering of those distinctions; on the superordination of the noble, the male and the elder and the subordination of the common, the female and the younger. The friars, wittingly, strove to subvert that order, and to win acceptance for their own more egalitarian account of the world. Women were urged to turn to the friars for redress of what the frairs defined as 'injustices,'[40] and for protection of what the friars defined as their 'rights.' They were taught in the new faith that men and women, equally sinners, were equally equipped for sal-

[38] This intervention in the lords' polygamous relationships must have ejected a number of women (and children) from lowly but secure niches in the social order into a social void. In a period of general dislocation, after war, and with death striking so often, we cannot blame the friars' experiments in social engineering for all the displaced persons who wandered through the villages, but their legislation must have been responsible for many of those 'vagabond Indian women, unmarried and evil living' complained of in 1561.

[39] Landa, *Landa's Relación* p. 97.

[40] Eg., Landa noted that in the early days of the conversion campaign enthusiastic young boys, trained in the special schools for the sons of nobles attached to the monasteries, 'urged the divorced women and the orphans if they had been reduced to slavery, to complain to the friars.' Landa, *Landa's Relación* p. 73. Landa also records the case of a married woman who came to him to ask his protection after a man had attempted first to seduce and then to rape her, p. 127.

vation, and they saw a gentle mother called Mary venerated, and were told she was a potent force in human and divine affairs. The task now is to see how far women's traditional relationships and traditional self-perceptions were altered, wittingly or unwittingly, by the new rulers' interventions.

In one crucial area there was significant change: where before the conquest girls had married at twenty, two decades later they were marrying at twelve or fourteen—partly in response to Franciscan pressure, partly, perhaps, in response to the miserable uncertainty of the times.[41] Earlier marriage, and the emphasis on monogamy, led to earlier and more frequent pregnancies: Fray Diego de Landa noted the girls were 'very productive,' and had children 'very early.'[42] In societies today where missionary insistence on monogamy has led to the early resumption of sexual relations after child-birth the outcome has too often been serious protein deficiencies in both mothers and children, with significant increases in difficulties in carrying to full term, successful delivery and infant survival. Fragments of evidence point in that direction in Yucatán: one colonist reported that while many Indian children were born, not all grew up,[43] and when Bishop Toral drew up an *aviso* for his curates in the fifteen-sixties he gave detailed instructions for the procedures to use when baptizing an infant which could not be properly delivered.[44] On the other hand, Landa remarked upon the vigor of the 'marvellously pretty and plump' babies, putting their liveliness down to their mother's abundant milk and the continuation of breastfeeding for three or four years.[45] It is possible that this customary prolonged lactation, combined with the formidable resources of native herbal knowledge, inhibited too frequent conception. Further, the dietary effects of the Spanish presence were not all deleterious. While both game and the time to pursue it must have been much reduced, and less salted fish was being brought in from the coast, fast-breeding European chickens soon scratched and squawked around most Indian huts, and if their owners were unready to eat the birds, except in case of sickness or to mark some festive occasion, chickens being a tributary item,

[41] Landa, *Landa's Relación* p. 100.
[42] Landa, *Landa's Relación* p. 128.
[43] Juan Bote, *RY* I, 289.
[44] 'Avisos del muy illustre y reverendísimo señor don Fray Francisco de Toral, primer obispo de Yucatán, Cozumel y Tabasco . . . para los padres curas y vicarios de este obispado y para los que en su ausencia quedan en las iglesias,' n.d., Scholes, Menendez, Rubío Mané, Adams (eds), *Documentos para la Historia de Yucatán* II, 27.
[45] Landa, *Landa's Relación* pp. 125, 128.

the eggs must have added to protein intake. Pork was, very occasionally, available, to supplement the meat from the little dogs the Indians continued to breed for food. The introduction of Spanish wells into many villages increased the accessibility of that most necessary yet scarce resource, water, and significantly reduced heavy lifting and carrying, with the attendant risks of miscarriage.[46]

Child-birth itself was still attended by skilled local women, together with close female kin. Spanish friars could burn the old multiple-family houses, and preach that marriage was an affair of individuals only, but in those small face-to-face communities kin could not easily be persuaded that the old relationships and the old responsibilities were at an end. Bishop Toral warned his curates to be sure that couples presenting themselves for marriage did so voluntarily, without pressure from parents or 'those old marriage brokers they used to have in some villages,' and to instruct the couple in the duties of marriage, making clear that they must live, sleep and eat together, and quit their own families.[47] We do not know if bride-service was still exacted in some modified form: the Spaniards took no cognizance of what went on in the *milpas*. Elaborate reciprocal feasting (with the traditional separation of the sexes) certainly continued, despite missionary disapproval. The village plaza appears to have replaced the warrior house as the venue for those masculine meetings still held within the village. There is nothing to suggest that the men spent any more time in the domestic zone after the conquest than before it, and the lives of boys and girls still diverged radically after the toddler stage, despite their forced physical proximity in the school.

There are indications of some new strains in the newly-private husband-wife relationship: Landa noted regretfully that repudiation of wives, once rare, had become common, and that Indian men, observing Spanish behavior towards unfaithful women, had begun to maltreat their erring wives, or even to kill them. Despite their usual gentleness, the women seemed little inclined to accept a double standard, and were also violent in jealousy, usually assaulting the other woman, but sometimes turning on their husbands, tearing their hair 'no matter how few times they had been unfaithful.'[48] But if female solidarity did not always overcome sexual competitiveness, it did work to render conditions of women's tribute labor more

[46] Juan Bote, *RY* I, 290.
[47] Bishop Toral, 'Avisos,' 31.
[48] Landa, *Landa's Relación* pp. 100, 127.

tolerable. With the dissolution of the lords' households the 'domestic factory' situation which these complex households had sustained was also dissolved, and we must assume that specialist weavers lost both the pleasure in the exercise of their skill and the status their expertise had brought them. For the commoner women too the weaving of the great plain mantles must have threatened to be a weary task, especially had the friars succeeded in penning each woman into her individual domestic prison. But the old houseyard sociability maintained itself: women still spent most of their time in company with other women, working at their shared pursuits, and casually assisting each other.

Not all their weaving time was taken up working on their tribute mantles. Although the Indians' own domestic consumption of cloth declined from pre-conquest levels, largely because men's clothing had been reduced to the new simplicity of unadorned shirts and loose trousers, women's dress remained highly expressive, as did their modes of decoration and presentation of self.

Despite the flinching of sensibilities bruised by modern advertising, this is no trivial matter; after all, a people displays itself in its notions of 'the beautiful' quite as much as it does in its notions of 'the good,' and in the preferences of the Indian women we have some chance of gauging their evaluation and response to Spanish conceptualizations of female beauty. The delicate tattooing and tooth filing so prized in pre-conquest times had fallen into disuse at least by the fifteen sixties. Tattooing had been outlawed by Lopez Medél in 1552, but it seems that tooth filing, along with body painting, had lapsed not because of regulations but through a combination of Spanish disdain, and a decrease in the time for their creation and the occasions for their appropriate display. Yet there is no indication of mimicry of Spanish notions of female elegance; despite ample opportunity to observe and learn Spanish preferences and techniques in their periods of service in Spanish houses, Yucatec Maya women rejected Spanish women's facial cosmetics as immodest, and continued to wear their long and carefully tended hair in the traditional styles.[49] Their dress, too, remained essentially traditional. Certainly, after the conquest as before, women's festival garments continued to be silent statements of their wearers' weaving skills, aesthetic sense and, doubtless, for those versed in the esoteric language of decorative motif, preferred self-image, being richly adorned with elaborate

[49] Landa, *Landa's Relación* pp. 126–127.

figured borders of coloured yarns, with duck feathers interworked. Even to the uninstructed eye of Giraldo Diaz, they 'looked good.'[50] The bright woollen yarns women incorporated into the designs, or twisted through their braided hair, were a novelty, imported from Mexico, and testify that the women were able to accumulate enough small monies from their bartering in local markets, and had the independence, to buy a few desired objects from the itinerant peddlars who trotted from village to village, in defiance of somewhat lackadaisical Spanish attempts to legislate them out of existence.[51]

For all the dislocations of conquest, and the vigor and precision of the friars' campaign, it would seem that the powerful rhythms of traditional routines and traditional roles contrived to reassert themselves. But not all indicators point to continuity or controlled innovation. Despite their energy, the friars were too remote from the villages, both physically and culturally, to offer a serious alternative to traditional ways of thinking and traditional authority structures. But their deliberate assault on the performances identified with the native religion did have an unintended consequence: that intervention fractured the ritual nexus which had bound the worlds of men and of women together.

In the great idolatry trials of 1562 a number of women were put to the torture, presumably because they were thought to have some knowledge of illicit ceremonies as, given the narrow boundaries of the village world, they probably had. But in none of the extorted testimonies which survive is there any mention of female presence or auxilliary participation save that some of the sacrificial victims are identified as pre-pubescent girls.[52] We would perhaps understand the exclusion of women from the ceremonies held within the village church, where the church could be identified with the pre-conquest temple. Again, we would not expect women to be present at rituals conducted in the forest, at caves or hidden water-holes: those locations had always been the preserve of men. But some ceremonies, we are told, were performed in the churchyards or in the cemeteries

[50] *RY* II 212.

[51] For the woollen yarns, see above, and also the *relación* de Mérida, *RY* I, 70–71. For an early attempt to outlaw the pedlars, see Lopez Medél, 'Ordenanzas,' nos 9 and 33.

[52] Report of Sebastian Vásquez, 25 March 1565, Scholes and Adams, *Don Diego Quijada* II, 213–214. For pre-pubescent female victims see e.g., Testimony of Juan Tzabnal, 5 September 1562, *Don Diego Quijada* I, 152. I have argued elsewhere that the extracted testimonies cannot be read as directly descriptive of actual events, but the social context casually revealed may be accepted as accurately represented.

attached to the churches,[53] and there, given pre-conquest practice, we would expect women to be present, if only as attentive audience. Yet, it seems, they were not. It is likely that the enforced secrecy of the performances, and the high risk attached to them—their being, in a sense, a continuation of war—identified them as inappropriate to women, and as exclusively male.

The friars' punitive campaign did not stop idolatry; through the rest of the century and beyond there are reports of idols concealed even in the village schools, and of the continued involvement of 'Christian' schoolmasters, lords and commoners in pagan rituals.[54] But constant pressure led to a sharpening distinction between traditional and Catholic activities, and the displacement of the former from the arena of the village. Through the rest of the colonial period Indian prayer-leaders and schoolmasters taught their version of Christianity within the villages, but the *milpa* rituals, the most enduring of the traditional ritual round, were conducted in the forest, where women could not follow. Women could perhaps prepare some of the ritual fare, but then it was borne away, beyond their ken, to what had become exclusively male excitements and solemnities. The impoverished villages could not sustain those specialists whose wives' part in sustaining their skills has been regularly and publicly acknowledged. Women could no longer tend the gods of the household, and so proclaim their identification with the lineage, nor were they able to display the importance of their contributions in more public modes of worship. A woman's handicrafts no longer decked the image of a god or the person of a great lord as an integral and essential component of the theatre of ritual. The wide plain cotton pieces which now consumed most of her weaving time were simply collected and taken away, for unknown uses and destination (alienation is not an experience restricted to the industrialized world). Her more elaborate skills had come to serve merely personal adornment.

It is one thing to observe behavior and very much another to claim to understand its meaning for the people we are observing. Nonetheless it is clear that the Spanish presence, little as it touched so many of the routines of the lives of women—their 'gender roles,'

[53] Eg., Petition by Fray Diego de Landa to Diego Quijada, 4 July 1562, *Don Diego Quijada* I, 69; Indictment against the Indians of Sotuta province, 11 August 1562, *Don Diego Quijada* I, 71–72.

[54] Scholes and Adams, *Don Diego Quijada* I, 114; *RY* II, 28, 147, 190, 213; Pedro Sanchez de Aguilar, 'Informe contra idolorum cultores del Obispado de Yucatán,' in Francisco del Paso y Troncoso, *Tratado de las Idolatrías, supersticiones, dioses, ritos, hechicerias y otras constumbres gentílicas de las razas aborigenes de Mexico* (Mexico City, 1953), Tomo II, *passim*.

in that restricted sense—had reduced severely those religious and social occasions through which female occupations had been publicly validated and the complementarity of male and female roles celebrated. Most of men's laboring hours had always been spent outside the village; in response to Spanish interventions, much of their social and most of their religious life, once centered on the village and integrated with the social and religious life of the women, migrated to their place of labor. Caught in the shrunken worlds of the villages women were reduced to constructing their social lives among themselves, and to making what religious accommodations they could within the male-led structures of the Roman Catholic Church.[55] Rituals establish reality, as well as confirm it. We may infer that one outcome of the Spanish conquest was a subtle but real diminution in the status of the women of Yucatán.

[55] Eg., see Thompson, *Maya History and Religion*, pp. 248–9 and Irwin Press, *Tradition and Adaptation: Life in a Modern Yucatán Village* (Westport, LT, 1975). Press claims that in Pustunich Catholicism is 'a women's religion,' and that 'boys' attendance at the Church begins to wane at roughly the same time their *milpa* activities increase,' p. 184. Women are permitted to observe the *milpa* rituals, and to consume a portion of the key ritual offerings, but only at a discreet distance from the altar. Press, *Tradition and Adaptation* p. 189. The Yucatan Maya solution is very different from that of Highland Maya communities, where an elaborated civil-religious hierarchy within the village provides the focus for masculine religious and social energies, with women in subordinate but essential supportive roles. For a close analysis of one such system, see Evon Vogt, *Zinacantán: A Maya Community in the Highlands of Chiapas* (Cambridge, Mass., 1969).

8

The question of narrative

Story-telling is generally perceived as one of the important functions of writing history. Some historians have suggested that this is the defining feature of the discipline; François Furet, for example, argues that '[h]istory is the child of narrative' – that history is defined by its 'type of discourse' rather than its object of study.[1] Central to story-telling is the construction of a narrative that has a beginning, middle and end, and which is structured around a sequence of events that take place over time. The following definition of narrative, by Lawrence Stone, might be taken as representative of the conventional understanding of narrative:

> Narrative is taken to mean the organisation of material in a chronologically sequential order and the focusing of the content into a single coherent story, albeit with sub-plots. The two essential ways in which narrative history differs from structural history is that its arrangement is descriptive rather than analytical and that its central focus is on man not circumstances. It therefore deals with the particular and specific rather than the collective and statistical. Narrative is a mode of historical writing, but it is a mode which also affects and is affected by the content and method.[2]

There are two key phrases in this definition which require elaboration. The first concerns the idea that narrative is a single, coherent story, and the second is the suggestion that narrative is inherently descriptive, not analytical. Narratives require a high degree of coherence to work as a story. However, the scale of the narrative may entail quite distinct levels of conceptual coherence. Drawing upon Allan Megill's categorization, these levels range from the micro-narrative of a particular event; a master narrative which seeks to explain a broader segment of history; a grand narrative 'which claims to offer the authoritative account of history generally'; and finally a metanarrative which draws upon some particular cosmology or metaphysical foundation, for example, Christianity.[3]

Robert Berkhofer suggests that 'great stories' continue to exert considerable appeal for both historians and their readership. Taking the example of the five hundredth anniversary of Christopher Columbus, Berkhofer showed the highly contested nature of a particular master narrative. Was the Columbus story 'a discovery, an invasion, a conquest, an encounter, an interaction, an intervention or something else'?[4] In terms of grand narratives, Megill argues that most twentieth-century historians have retained a commitment to a single history of humankind, but only as it exists 'ideally, . . . the unreachable end of an autonomous discipline. Coherence is now located not in the told or anticipated Story, but in the unified mode of thinking of the discipline'.[5] This compromise, he argues, has enabled historians to keep the idea of coherence embedded in the methods and aims of the historical profession.

How, then, have historians gone about the process of constructing coherent narratives from the mass of empirical evidence? Let us begin with an argument which supports Stone's thesis that historical narrative is primarily descriptive, not analytical. One contribution to this debate by M. C. Lemon states the case for traditional empiricism by arguing that it is possible for a narrative to simply 'inform the reader of "what happened"'.[6] Lemon rejects the idea that narratives invariably have a persuasive or rhetorical purpose, and is highly critical of those written from a particular perspective. Recognizing that historians must engage in a process of selection among the available facts in order to construct a narrative, Lemon suggests that the way in which these choices are made rests upon the requirements for coherence and intelligibility, in which prior and subsequent events are cemented together by a 'conventionally acceptable contiguity'.[7] In terms of narrative's explanatory power, Lemon argues that 'it seems to offer an understanding in the sense that the reader can see an action as an appropriate response by an agent'. Lemon agrees that narrative 'assumes a general theory about human conduct . . . a set of assumptions about how people behave and how the world works'.[8] However, contrary to Abrams' critique of unexamined concepts in the writing of narrative history, referred to earlier in the context of Elton's work, Lemon sees this as the strength of a narrative approach.[9] He concludes:

> that this mode of explanation does not need articulating on each occasion through explanatory and analytic discourse but is actually embedded in a *form* of discourse exclusive to itself (viz. narrative), suggests that narrative explanation is sophisticated rather than naive.[10]

Lemon draws a firm line between historical narratives, based upon fact, and fictional narratives, utilizing imagination. However, this distinction has been challenged in the late twentieth century as the essentially constructed nature of historical narrative has been subjected to closer, and critical, scrutiny. Historians must now consider the assertion that our representation of the past has no greater claim to truth than that of novelists and poets, and that our narratives are literary artefacts, produced according to the rules of genre and style. This challenge has come from Hayden White, who argues that 'in general there has been a reluctance to consider historical narratives as what they manifestly are – verbal fictions, the contents of which have more in common with their counterparts in literature than they have with those in the sciences'.[11]

In a widely read essay entitled 'The Burden of History' published in 1966, White criticized what he perceived as the disingenuous way in which historians claimed that their work 'depend[ed] as much upon intuitive as upon analytical methods', while their professional training focused almost entirely upon the latter.[12] He argued that historians had lost sight of the value of 'historical imagination' for understanding the human condition, and he pointed to 'history's golden age' between 1800 and 1850 when 'the best representatives of historical thought' actively engaged historical imagination to illustrate 'man's responsibility for his own fate'.[13] White pursued this theme further when he published a major analysis of the narrative modes employed by major philosophers and historians during 'history's golden age'. The writings of four leading European historians: Michelet, Ranke, Tocqueville and Burckhardt; and four philosophers of history: Hegel, Marx, Nietzsche and Croce, form the basis for White's theory of 'historical imagination'.[14]

White's central point is that language, and linguistic protocols, fundamentally shape the writing of history. They do so in two ways: in the choice of the theoretical concepts and narrative structures employed by historians to analyse and explain historical events, and secondly, through the linguistic paradigm 'by which historians prefigure their field of study'. It is the latter that White defines as the metahistorical element in all historical writing:

> Histories combine a certain amount of 'data', theoretical concepts for explaining these data, and a narrative structure for their presentation. . . . In addition, I maintain, they contain a deep structural content which is generally poetic, and specifically linguistic in nature, and which serves as the

precritically accepted paradigm of what a distinctively 'historical' explanation should be. This paradigm functions as the 'metahistorical' element in all historical works that are more comprehensive in scope than the monograph or archival report.[15]

The metahistorical element in historical writing is determined right from the start. The historian must '*pre*figure the field – that is to say, constitute it as an object of mental perception'.[16] This mental process takes place first, and underpins every other aspect of research and writing. White describes it as a 'poetic act which precedes the formal analysis of the field, [in which] the historian both creates his object of analysis and predetermines the modality of the conceptual strategies he will use to explain it'.[17] To understand the metahistorical aspect of history writing, White turns to the theory of tropes. Tropes are the underlying linguistic structures of poetic or figurative language. The way in which the historian conceptualizes his or her research is, he argues, constrained by these linguistic structures. White suggests that there are four tropes which shape the 'deep structural forms of the historical imagination', and these are as follows:[18]

The theory of tropes

metaphor	one thing is described as being another thing, thus 'carrying over' all its associations
metonymy	the substitution of the name of a thing by the name of an attribute of it, or something closely associated with it
synecdoche	a part of something is used to describe the whole, or vice versa
irony	saying one thing while you mean another

Through the concept of tropes, White transforms figures of speech into deep structures of thought which predetermine the kind of narrative the historian will construct. Two critiques of this proposition may concern us here. In practice historians may employ more than one trope. White's own study of nineteenth-century historians illustrates that each one employed multiple tropes, for example, Tocqueville alternates between 'two modes of consciousness, Metaphorical and Metonymical', mediated through Irony.[19] On a more fundamental level, empirically minded historians have rejected the elevation of tropes to a determining role in historical narrative. Windschuttle, for example, claims that '[t]ropes are not deep foundations that determine the whole structure. Rather, they are relatively minor stylistic devices used *within historical accounts.* . . .

White has mistaken the surface for the substance, the decoration for the edifice'.[20]

Once the historian has commenced research, White argues that he or she must choose specific theoretical concepts and narrative structures to make sense of the evidence. White suggests that historians have three strategies that may be used for historical explanation: emplotment, formal argument and ideological implication, and each of these have four alternative modes of articulation:[21]

Mode of emplotment	Mode of argument	Mode of ideological implication
Romantic	Formist	Anarchist
Tragic	Mechanistic	Radical
Comic	Organicist	Conservative
Satirical	Contextualist	Liberal

The particular combination of emplotment, argument and ideological implication chosen by a historian determines his or her historiographical style. But that choice is not entirely free. White suggests that there are 'elective affinities' among the various modes and these are represented on the horizontal plane in the table above.[22]

Let us take Leopold von Ranke, one of the historians examined in *Metahistory*, to see how the theory works in practice. Ranke was among the foremost nineteenth-century historians writing about the history of peoples and nations. White suggests that most of Ranke's work employs the comic, organicist and conservative modes of emplotment, argument and ideology. Historians emplot their narratives in particular ways, and these may themselves provide a form of explanation. After all, the sources do not tell historians when to begin their narrative, or when to end it. White argues that Ranke employs a comic emplotment, a model in which men may triumph over their divided state, even if temporarily, and achieve reconciliation and harmony. Secondly, the organicist argument, as the name suggests, employs an organic metaphor for explanation. Individuals and entities are component parts of a whole, and the result is 'integrative in intent'. Finally, the conservative ideological implication is also consistent with an organic metaphor. Change is best undertaken slowly, and should be a gradual adaptation of prevailing institutions and structures. These three aspects, according to White, are integral to Ranke's accounts of the rise of the nation. Ranke's narrative, like the definition of comedy above, moves 'from a condition of apparent peace, through the revelation of conflict, to the resolution of conflict in the establishment of a genuinely peaceful social order'.[23]

The narrative strategies of emplotment, argument and ideology Ranke employs in his narratives are, according to White, derived from the 'metahistorical' element, the 'tropological explanation' with which he began. Ranke's work illustrates the 'trope' of synecdoche, that is, his characterization of European history 'provides the reader with the sense of succession of formal coherencies through which the action moves in such a way as to suggest the *integration* of the parts with the larger historical whole'.[24] White does not suggest why Ranke would choose this trope over the alternatives, and this has been the source of one critique.

Hans Kellner accepts that White posits a profoundly moral dimension to the rhetorical and linguistic choices made by historians, but argues that White provides no explanation of how these choices are made. 'Since history cannot begin with documents (the process is already well under way before a document is confronted), what is at the bottom of White's system? Where is its *beginning*?'[25] At no stage does White suggest that the choice of trope may be influenced by the historians' own biographical or historical environment.[26] It has been argued that White's 'lack of psychological theory deprives his concept of style of a fully explicated, active, synthetic principle'.[27] This leads, according to Kellner, to contradictory tenets in White's thought:

> If language is irreducible, a 'sacred' beginning, then human freedom is sacrificed. If men are free to choose their linguistic protocols, then some deeper, prior, force must be posited. White asserts as an existential paradox that men *are* free, and that language is irreducible.[28]

A second common critique concerns White's relativism. White asserts that there is no necessary relationship between the structure of the narrative and the historical evidence, and therefore there are no grounds upon which a historian can claim greater authority for one interpretation over another.[29] In an essay concerning the historical representation of Nazism, White reiterated that '[t]here is an inexpungeable relativity in every representation of historical phenomena'.[30] Many empirical historians would not accept that the narrator's subjectivity entirely determines an historical text.[31] Furthermore, such a position 'leaves no basis for a responsibility to the subject'.[32] However, in his essay referred to above, White appears to qualify his relativism. In the context of Nazism, White suggests that complete freedom of choice in linguistic protocols, for example, the choice of a comic mode, would be rejected by an appeal to 'the facts'. As Wulf Kansteiner points out, this contradiction in White's theory 'leaves the reader in a state of methodological uncertainty'.[33]

The response by historians to the central propositions of *Metahistory* frequently reflect their own receptiveness to the concepts of poststructuralism (see chapter 12). Dominick LaCapra, for example, extols the way in which White has challenged the unreflective use of narrative in the writing of history: '[n]o one writing in this country at the present time has done more to wake historians from their dogmatic slumber'.[34] More common, however, is the argument that while White's insights have relevance for nineteenth-century historians they are not applicable to the contemporary diversity of history writing.[35] However, White has applied his tropological model to E. P. Thompson's *The Making of the English Working Class*, an extract from which forms the reading for the chapter on Marxist historians. White perceives a correspondence between the four 'master tropes of figuration' and the four explicit divisions in Thompson's book. The first section, entitled 'The Liberty Tree', White describes as metaphorical, 'in which working people apprehend their differences from the wealthy and sense their similarity to one another, but are unable to organize themselves except in terms of the general desire for an elusive "liberty" '.[36] The subsequent sections move through metonymic, synecdochic and ironic modes, and White concludes that '[t]he pattern which Thompson discerned in the history of English working-class consciousness was perhaps as much imposed upon his data as it was found in them . . . a pattern long associated with the analysis of processes of consciousness in rhetoric and poetics'.[37]

François Furet, among other historians, has argued that narrative has lost ground to 'problem-oriented' history in the twentieth century.[38] This development in history writing has not been without its critics.[39] In the late 1970s, Lawrence Stone deplored that the 'story-telling function has fallen into ill-repute among those who have regarded themselves as in the vanguard of the profession, the practitioners of the so-called "new history" of the post-Second-World-War era'. He attributed the decline to, among others, Marxist and *Annales* historians, and 'their attempt to produce a coherent and scientific explanation of change in the past'.[40] These attempts having failed, Stone more cheerfully reported, narrative was once again back on the agenda. However, some of the histories Stone identified as evidence of this new trend, for example, Carlo Ginzburg's *The Cheese and the Worms*, sit very uneasily with his own unitary, chronological definition of narrative (with which we began this chapter).[41]

The answer may lie in a more flexible definition of narrative, which takes into account the contemporary focus upon social groups for which the historical record is patchy and incomplete.[42] To what extent narrative can expand without losing the coherence of a story remains one of the central problems of writing history.[43] David Hackett Fischer called some years ago for a 'braided narrative [which] interweaves analysis with storytelling', and innovative attempts to achieve this goal have been made.[44] But the effort to enhance story-telling techniques should include active consideration of the rhetorical and linguistic aspects of narration to which White has drawn our attention. Historians do not 'simply . . . explain, as some contend. On the contrary, they first of all recount, in delight, or fascination or horror or resignation.'[45] It is essential, therefore, that historians fully understand the implications of their own narrative choice.[46]

The following essay is by the American historian Hayden White whose most influential work has focused, as we have previously explained, upon the application of concepts derived from literary theory to major historical texts. Consider the extent to which he suggests that 'the discourse of the historian' and fictional writing share common features. What precisely are these common aspects? In what ways did the eighteenth-century view of historical writing, as defined by White, differ from the scholarly aspirations of nineteenth-century historians? Does the writing of history invariably entail utilizing the persuasive skills of rhetoric? Allan Megill has suggested that it is desirable to make a distinction between the literary and fictive aspects of writing; by this he means between literary rhetorical devices and the concepts and typologies employed by historians.[47] Is the narrative historian using poetic imagination to fuse and fashion the fragments of the past, as White suggests; how is this different from the application of clearly defined theoretical concepts and paradigms to make sense of human history? Finally, do you think that novelists and historians share the same goals, and are engaged in fundamentally the same enterprise?

Notes

1 François Furet, 'From Narrative History to Problem-oriented History', in *In the Workshop of History*, trans. Jonathan Mandelbaum (Chicago, 1984), p. 54.

2 Lawrence Stone, 'The Revival of Narrative: Reflections on a New Old History', in *The Past and the Present Revisited* (London, 1987), p. 74.

3 Allan Megill, '"Grand Narrative" and the Discipline of History', in Frank Ankersmit and Hans Kellner (eds), *A New Philosophy of History* (Chicago, 1995), pp. 152–3.

4 Robert Berkhofer, Jr., *Beyond the Great Story: History as Text and Discourse* (Cambridge, Mass., 1995), p. 45.

5 *Ibid.*, p. 160.

6 M. C. Lemon, *The Discipline of History and the History of Thought* (London, 1995), p. 48.

7 *Ibid.*, p. 49.

8 *Ibid.*, p. 53.

9 Philip Abrams, *Historical Sociology* (Shepton Mallet, 1982), pp. 309–10.

10 *Ibid.*, pp. 53–4.

11 Hayden White, 'The Historical Text as Literary Artefact', in Robert Canary and Henry Kozicki (eds), *The Writing of History: Literary Form and Historical Understanding* (Madison, 1978), p. 42.

12 Hayden White, 'The Burden of History', *History and Theory*, 2 (1966), p. 111.

13 *Ibid.*, p. 132.

14 Hayden White, *Metahistory: The Historical Imagination in Nineteenth-century Europe* (Baltimore, 1973). See 'Introduction: The Poetics of History', pp. 1–42, for a detailed elaboration of White's theory.

15 *Ibid.*, p. ix.

16 *Ibid.*, p. 30.

17 *Ibid.*, p. 31.

18 *Ibid.*, pp. 31–8; the definitions are taken from Martin Gray, *A Dictionary of Literary Terms* (2nd edn, Harlow, 1992). White's use of four tropes is unlike the binary dyad of structuralist Claude Lévi-Strauss: see Hans Kellner, 'A Bedrock of Order: Hayden White's Linguistic Humanism', *History and Theory Beiheft* 19 (1980), p. 5.

19 White, *Metahistory*, p. 203.

20 Keith Windschuttle, *The Killing of History* (Sydney, 1994), p. 241.

21 White, *Metahistory*, p. 29.

22 The problems with the concept of 'elective affinities' are discussed in Philip Pomper, 'Typologies and Cycles in Intellectual History', *History and Theory Beiheft* 19 (1980), p. 32.

23 White, *Metahistory*, p. 177.

24 *Ibid.*

25 Kellner, 'A Bedrock of Order', p. 14.

26 Pomper, 'Typologies and Cycles', p. 33.

27 *Ibid.*, p. 32.

28 Kellner, 'A Bedrock of Order', p. 23.

29 White, *Metahistory*, p. xii.

30 White, 'Historical Emplotment and the Problem of Truth', in S. Friedlander (ed.), *Probing the Limits of Representation: Nazism and the 'Final Solution'* (Cambridge, Mass., 1992), p. 37.

31 See the discussion in Maurice Mandelbaum, 'The Presuppositions of *Metahistory*', *History and Theory Beiheft* 19 (1980), pp. 44–5.

32 Kellner, 'A Bedrock of Order', p. 14.

33 Wulf Kansteiner, 'Hayden White's Critique of the Writing of History', *History and Theory*, 32 (1993), p. 293.

34 Dominick LaCapra, *Rethinking Intellectual History: Texts, Contexts, Language* (Ithaca, 1983), p. 72.

35 Michael Stanford, *The Nature of Historical Knowledge* (Oxford, 1986), p. 137.

36 Hayden White, *Tropics of Discourse: Essays in Cultural Criticism* (Baltimore, 1978), pp. 15–17.

37 *Ibid.*, p. 19.

38 Furet, 'From Narrative History to Problem-oriented History'.

39 See the debates in *Past and Present*, 85 (1979), 86 (1980) and 87 (1980). Also W. Dray, 'On the Nature and Role of Narrative in Historiography', *History and Theory*, 8 (1971), pp. 153–71.

40 Stone, 'The Revival of Narrative', pp. 74, 91.

41 See the discussion in Mark Phillips, 'The Revival of Narrative: Thoughts on a Current Historiographical Debate', *University of Toronto Quarterly*, 53 (Winter 1983/84), p. 149.

42 *Ibid.*, p. 153.

43 See the issue of *Critical Inquiry* devoted to the question of narrative: 7 (1980).

44 David Hackett Fischer, *Albion's Seed* (Oxford, 1989), p. xi. For a good discussion of alternative narrative structures, see Peter Burke in *New Perspectives on Historical Writing* (Cambridge, 1991), ch. 11.

45 Allan Megill, 'Recounting the Past: "Description", Explanation, and Narrative in History', *American Historical Review*, 94 (1989), pp. 652–3.

46 Phillips, 'The Revival of Narrative', p. 162.

47 Megill, '"Grand Narrative" and the Discipline of History', p. 171.

Additional reading

Berkhofer, Robert F., Jr., 'Narratives and Historicization', in *Beyond the Great Story: History as Text and Discourse* (Cambridge, Mass., 1995).

Burke, Peter, 'History of Events and the Revival of Narrative', in *New Perspectives on Historical Writing* (Cambridge, 1991).

Canary, Robert and Henry Kozicki (eds), *The Writing of History: Literary Form and Historical Understanding* (Madison, 1978).

Easthope, Antony, 'Romancing the Stone: History-writing and Rhetoric', *Social History*, 18, 2 (1993), pp. 235–49.

Kansteiner, Wulf, 'Hayden White's Critique of the Writing of History', *History and Theory*, 32 (1993), pp. 273–95.

Kellner, Hans, *Language and Historical Representation: Getting the Story Crooked* (Madison, 1989).

Megill, Allan, 'Recounting the Past: "Description", Explanation, and Narrative in History', *American Historical Review*, 94 (1989), pp. 627–53.

Megill, Allan, '"Grand Narrative" and the Discipline of History', in Frank Ankersmit and Hans Kellner (eds), *A New Philosophy of History* (Chicago, 1995).

'Metahistory: Six Critiques', *History and Theory Beiheft* 19 (1980).

Stone, Lawrence, 'The Revival of Narrative: Reflections on a New Old History', *Past and Present*, 85 (1979), pp. 3–24.

'The Representation of Historical Events', *History and Theory Beiheft* 26 (1995).

White, Hayden, 'The Burden of History', *History and Theory*, 5 (1966), pp. 111–34.

White, Hayden, *Metahistory: The Historical Imagination in Nineteenth-Century Europe* (Baltimore, 1973).

White, Hayden, 'Historical Emplotment and the Problem of Truth', in S. Friedlander (ed.), *Probing the Limits of Representation: Nazism and the 'Final Solution'* (Cambridge, 1992).

THE FICTIONS OF FACTUAL REPRESENTATION
Hayden White

In order to anticipate some of the objections with which historians often meet the argument that follows, I wish to grant at the outset that *historical events* differ from *fictional events* in the ways that it has been conventional to characterize their differences since Aristotle. Historians are concerned with events which can be assigned to specific time-space locations, events which are (or were) in principle observable or perceivable, whereas imaginative writers—poets, novelists, playwrights—are concerned with both these kinds of events and imagined, hypothetical, or invented ones. The nature of the kinds of events with which historians and imaginative writers are concerned is not the issue. What should interest us in the discussion of 'the literature of fact' or, as I have chosen to call it, 'the fictions of factual representation' is the extent to which the discourse of the historian and that of the writer of imaginative fictions overlap, resemble, or correspond with each other. Although historians and writers of fiction may be interested in different kinds of events, both the forms of their respective discourses and their aims in writing are often the same. In addition, in my view, the techniques or strategies that they use in the composition of their discourses can be shown to be substantially the same, however different they may appear on a purely surface, or dictional, level of their texts.

Readers of histories and novels can hardly fail to be struck by their similarities. There are many histories that could pass for novels, and many novels that could pass for histories, considered in purely formal (or, I should say, formalist) terms. Viewed simply as verbal artifacts histories and novels are indistinguishable from one another. We cannot easily distinguish between them on formal grounds unless we approach them with specific preconceptions about the kinds of truths that each is supposed to deal in. But the aim of the writer of a novel must be the same as that of the writer of a history. Both wish to provide a verbal image of 'reality.' The novelist may present his notion of this reality indirectly, that is to say, by figurative techniques, rather than directly, which is to say, by registering a series of propositions which are supposed to correspond point by point to some extra-textual domain of occurrence or happening, as the historian claims to do. But the image of reality which the novelist thus constructs is meant to correspond in its general outline to some domain of human experience which is no less 'real' than that referred to by the historian. It is not, then, a matter of a conflict between two kinds of truth (which the Western prejudice for empiricism as the sole access to reality has foisted upon us), a conflict between the truth of correspondence, on the one side, and the truth of coherence, on the other. Every history must meet standards of coherence no less than those of correspondence if it is to pass as a plausible account of 'the way things *really* were.' For the empiricist prejudice is attended by a conviction that 'reality' is not only perceivable but is also coherent in its structure. A mere list of confirmable singular existential statements does not add up to an account of reality if there is not some coherence, logical or aesthetic, connecting them one to another. So too every fiction must pass a test of correspondence (it must be 'adequate' as an image of something beyond itself) if it is to lay claim to representing an insight into or illumination of the human experience of the world. Whether the events represented in a discourse are construed as atomic parts of a molar whole or as possible occurrences within a perceivable totality, the discourse taken in *its* totality as an image of some reality, bears a relationship of correspondence to that *of which* it is an image. It is in these twin senses that all written discourse is cognitive in its aims and mimetic in its means. And this is true even of the most ludic and seemingly expressivist discourse, of poetry no less than of prose, and even of those forms of poetry which seem to wish to illuminate only 'writing' itself. In this respect, history is no less a form of fiction than the novel is a form of historical representation.

This characterization of historiography as a form of fiction making is not likely to be received sympathetically by either historians or literary critics who, if they agree on little else, conventionally agree that history and fiction deal with distinct orders of experience and therefore represent distinct, if not opposed, forms of discourse. For this reason it will be well to say a few words about how this notion of the *opposition* of history to fiction arose and why it has remained unchallenged in Western thought for so long.

Prior to the French Revolution, historiography was conventionally regarded as a literary art. More specifically, it was regarded as a branch of rhetoric and its 'fictive' nature generally recognized. Although eighteenth-century theorists distinguished rather rigidly

(and not always with adequate philosophical justification) between 'fact' and 'fancy,' they did not on the whole view historiography as a representation of the facts unalloyed by elements
of fancy. While granting the general desirability of historical
accounts that dealt in real, rather than imagined events, theorists
from Bayle to Voltaire and De Mably recognized the inevitability of
a recourse to fictive techniques in the *representation* of real events
in the historical discourse. The eighteenth century abounds in
works which distinguish between the 'study' of history on the one
side and the 'writing' of history on the other. The 'writing' was a
literary, specifically rhetorical exercise, and the product of this
exercise was to be assessed as much on literary as on scientific
principles.

Here the crucial opposition was between 'truth' and 'error,' rather
than between 'fact' and 'fancy,' with it being understood that many
kinds of truth, even in history, could only be presented to the reader
by means of fictional techniques of representation. These techniques
were conceived to consist of rhetorical devices, tropes, figures, and
schemata of words and thoughts, which, as described by the classical and Renaissance rhetoricians, were identical with the techniques
of poetry in general. 'Truth' was not equated with 'fact,' but with a
combination of fact and the conceptual matrix within which it was
appropriately located in the discourse. The imagination no less than
the reason had to be engaged in any adequate representation of the
truth; and this meant that the techniques of fiction-making were as
necessary to the composition of a historical discourse as erudition
might be.

In the early nineteenth century, however, it became conventional,
at least among historians, to identify truth with fact and to regard
fiction as the opposite of truth, hence as a hindrance to the understanding of reality rather than as a way of apprehending it. History
came to be set over against fiction, and especially the novel, as the
representation of the 'actual' to the representation of the 'possible'
or only 'imaginable.' And thus was born the dream of a historical
discourse that would consist of nothing but factually accurate statements about a realm of events which were (or had been) observable
in principle, the arrangement of which in the order of their original
occurrence would permit them to figure forth their true meaning or
significance. Typically, the nineteenth-century historian's aim was to
expunge every hint of the fictive, or merely imaginable, from his discourse, to eschew the techniques of the poet and orator, and to forego

what were regarded as the intuitive procedures of the maker of
fictions in his apprehension of reality.

In order to understand this development in historical thinking, it
must be recognized that historiography took shape as a distinct
scholarly discipline in the West in the nineteenth century against a
background of a profound hostility to all forms of myth. Both the
political Right and the political Left blamed mythic thinking for the
excesses and failures of the Revolution. False readings of history, mis-
conceptions of the nature of the historical process, unrealistic expectations about the ways that historical societies could be
transformed—all these had led to the outbreak of the Revolution in
the first place, the strange course that Revolutionary developments
followed, and the effects of Revolutionary activities over the long
run. It became imperative to rise above any impulse to interpret the
historical record in the light of party prejudices, utopian expectations, or sentimental attachments to traditional institutions. In order
to find one's way among the conflicting claims of the parties which
took shape during and after the Revolution, it was necessary to locate
some standpoint of social perception that was truly 'objective,' truly
'realistic.' If social processes and structures seemed 'demonic' in their
capacity to resist direction, to take turns unforeseen, and to overturn
the highest plans, frustrating the most heartfelt desires, then the
study of history had to be de-mythified. But in the thought of the
age, de-mythification of any domain of inquiry tended to be equated
with the de-fictionalization of that domain as well.

The distinction between myth and fiction which is a commonplace in the thought of our own century was hardly grasped at all by
many of the foremost ideologues of the early nineteenth century.
Thus it came about that history, the realistic science par excellence,
was set over against fiction as the study of the real versus the study
of the merely imaginable. Although Ranke had in mind that form of
the novel which we have since come to call 'Romantic' when he castigated it as mere fancy, he manifested a prejudice shared by many
of his contemporaries when he defined history as the study of the
real and the novel as the representation of the imaginary. Only a few
theorists, among whom J. G. Droysen was the most prominent, saw
that it was impossible to write history without having recourse to the
techniques of the orator and the poet. Most of the 'scientific' historians of the age did not see that for every identifiable kind of novel,
historians produced an equivalent kind of historical discourse.
Romantic historiography produced its genius in Michelet, Realistic

historiography its paradigm in Ranke himself, Symbolist historiography produced Burckhardt (who had more in common with Flaubert and Baudelaire than with Ranke), and Modernist historiography its prototype in Spengler. It was no accident that the Realistic novel and Rankean historicism entered their respective crises at roughly the same time.

There were, in short, as many 'styles' of historical representation as there are discernible literary styles in the nineteenth century. This was not perceived by the historians of the nineteenth century because they were captives of the illusion that one could write history without employing any fictional techniques whatsoever. They continued to honor the conception of the opposition of history to fiction throughout the entire period, even while producing forms of historical discourse so different from one another that their grounding in aesthetic preconceptions of the nature of the historical process alone could explain those differences. Historians continued to believe that different interpretations of the same set of events were functions of ideological distortions or of inadequate factual data. They continued to believe that if one only eschewed ideology and remained true to the facts, history would produce a knowledge as certain as anything offered by the physical sciences and as objective as a mathematical exercise.

Most nineteenth-century historians did not realize that, when it is a matter of trying to deal with past facts, the crucial consideration for him who would represent them faithfully are the notions he brings to his representation of the ways parts relate to the whole which they comprise. They did not realize that the facts do not speak for themselves, but that the historian speaks for them, speaks on their behalf, and fashions the fragments of the past into a whole whose integrity is—in its *re*presentation—a purely discursive one. Novelists might be dealing only with imaginary events whereas historians are dealing with real ones, but the process of fusing events, whether imaginary or real, into a comprehensible totality capable of serving as the *object* of a representation, is a poetic process. Here the historian must utilize precisely the same tropological strategies, the same modalities of representing relationships in words, that the poet or novelist uses. In the unprocessed historical record and in the chronicle of events which the historian extracts from the record, the facts exist only as a congeries of contiguously related fragments. These fragments have to be put together to make a whole of a particular, not a general, kind. And they are put together in the same ways that novelists use to put together figments of their imaginations to display an ordered world, a cosmos, where only disorder or chaos might appear.

So much for manifestos. On what grounds can such a reactionary position be justified? On what grounds can the assertion that historical discourse shares more than it divides with novelistic discourse be sustained? The first ground is to be found in recent developments in literary theory—especially in the insistence by modern Structuralist and text critics on the necessity of dissolving the distinction between prose and poetry in order to identify their shared attributes as forms of linguistic behavior that are as much constitutive of their objects of representation as they are reflective of external reality, on the one side, and projective of internal emotional states, on the other. It appears that Stalin was right when he opined that language belonged neither to the Superstructure nor the Base of cultural praxis, but was, in some unspecified way, *prior to both*. We don't know the origin of language and never shall, but it is certain today that language is more adequately characterized as being neither a free creation of human consciousness nor merely a product of environmental forces acting on the psyche, but rather the *instrument of mediation* between consciousness and the world that consciousness inhabits.

This will not be news to literary theorists, but it has not yet reached the historians buried in the archives hoping, by what they call a 'sifting of the facts' or 'the manipulation of the data,' to *find* the form of the reality that will serve as the object of representation in the account that they will write when 'all the facts are known' and they have finally 'got the story straight.'

So, too, contemporary critical theory permits us to believe more confidently than ever before that 'poetizing' is not an activity that hovers over, transcends, or otherwise remains alienated from life or reality, but represents a mode of praxis which serves as the immediate base of all cultural activity (this an insight of Vico, Hegel, and Nietzsche, no less than of Freud and Lévi-Strauss), even of science itself. We are no longer compelled, therefore, to believe—as historians in the post-Romantic period had to believe—that fiction is the antithesis of fact (in the way that superstition or magic is the antithesis of science) or that we can relate facts to one another without the aid of some enabling and generically fictional matrix. This too would be news to many historians were they not so fetishistically enamored of the notion of 'facts' and so congenitally hostile to 'theory' in any form that the presence in a historical work of a formal theory used to explicate the relationship between facts and concepts is enough to earn them the charge of having defected to the despised 'sociology' or of having lapsed into the nefarious 'philosophy of history.'

Every discipline, I suppose, is, as Nietzsche saw most clearly, constituted by what it *forbids* its practitioners to do. Every discipline is made up of a set of restrictions on thought and imagination, and none is more hedged about with taboos than professional historiography—so much so that the so-called 'historical method' consists of little more than the injunction to 'get the story straight' (without any notion of what the relation of 'story' to 'fact' might be) and to avoid both conceptual over-determination and imaginative excess (i.e., 'enthusiasm') at any price.

Yet the price paid is a considerable one. It has resulted in the repression of the *conceptual apparatus* (without which atomic facts cannot be aggregated into complex macro-structures and constituted as objects of discursive representation in a historical narrative) and the remission of the *poetic moment* in historical writing to the interior of the discourse (where it functions as an unacknowledged—and therefore uncriticizable—*content* of the historical narrative).

Those historians who draw a firm line between history and philosophy of history fail to recognize that every historical discourse contains within it a full blown—if only implicit—philosophy of history. And this is as true of what is conventionally called 'narrative' (or diachronic) historiography as it is of 'conceptual' (or synchronic) historical representation. The principal difference between history and philosophy of history is that the latter brings the conceptual apparatus by which the facts are ordered in the discourse to the surface of the text, while 'history proper' (as it is called) buries it in the interior of the narrative, where it serves as a hidden or implicit shaping device, in precisely the same way that Professor Frye conceives his *archetypes* to do in narrative fictions. History does not therefore stand over against myth as its cognitive antithesis, but represents merely another, and more extreme form of that 'displacement' which Professor Frye has analyzed in his *Anatomy*. Every history has its myth; and if there are different fictional modes based on different identifiable mythical archetypes, so too there are different historiographical modes—different ways of hypotactically ordering the 'facts' contained in the chronicle of events occurring in a specific time-space location, such that events in the same set are capable of functioning differently in order to figure forth different *meanings*, moral, cognitive, or aesthetic, within different fictional matrices.

In fact, I would argue that these mythic modes are more easily identifiable in historiographical than they are in 'literary' texts. For historians usually work with much less *linguistic* (and therefore less *poetic*) self-consciousness than writers of fiction do. They tend to treat language as a transparent vehicle of representation that brings no cognitive baggage of its own into the discourse. Great works of fiction will usually—if Roman Jakobson is right—not only be *about* their putative subject-matter, but also *about* language itself and the problematical relation between language, consciousness, and reality— including the writer's own language. Most historians' concern with language extends only to the effort to speak plainly, to avoid florid figures of speech, to assure that the persona of the author appears nowhere identifiable in the text, and to make clear what technical terms mean, when they dare to use any.

This is not, of course, the case with the great philosophers of history—from Augustine, Machiavelli, and Vico to Hegel, Marx, Nietzsche, Croce, and Spengler. The problematical status of language (including their own linguistic protocols) constitutes a crucial element in their own *apparatus criticus*. And it is not the case with the great classic writers of historiography—from Thucydides and Tacitus to Michelet, Carlyle, Ranke, Droysen, Tocqueville, and Burckhardt. These historians at least had a rhetorical self-consciousness that permitted them to recognize that any set of facts was variously, and equally legitimately, describable, that there is no such thing as a single correct original description of anything, on the basis of which an interpretation of that thing can *subsequently* be brought to bear. They recognized, in short, that all original descriptions of any field of phenomena are *already* interpretations of its structure, and that the linguistic mode in which the original description (or taxonomy) of the field is cast will implicitly rule out certain modes of representation and modes of explanation regarding the field's structure and tacitly sanction others. In other words, the favored mode of original description of a field of historical phenomena (and this includes the field of literary texts) already contains implicitly within it a limited range of modes of emplotment and modes of argument by which to disclose the meaning of the field in a discursive prose representation. If, that is, the description is anything more than a random registering of impressions. The plot-structure of a historical narrative (*how* things turned out as they did) and the formal argument or explanation of *why* 'things happened or turned out as they did' are *pre*figured by the original description (of the 'facts' to be explained) in a given dominant modality of language use: metaphor, metonymy, synecdoche, or irony.

Now, I want to make clear that I am myself using these terms as metaphors for the different ways we construe fields or sets of phenomena in order to 'work them up' into *possible objects of narrative representation* and *discursive analysis*. Anyone who originally encodes the world in the mode of metaphor, will be inclined to decode it— that is, narratively 'explicate' and discursively analyze it—as a congeries of individualities. To those for whom there is no real resemblance in the world, decodation must take the form of a disclosure, either of the simple *contiguity* of things (the mode of metonymy) or of the *contrast* that lies hidden within every apparent resemblance or unity (the mode of irony). In the first case, the narrative representation of the field, construed as a diachronic process, will favor as a privileged mode of emplotment the archetype of Romance and a mode of explanation that identifies knowledge with the appreciation and delineation of the particularity and individuality of things. In the second case, an original description of the field in the mode of metonymy will favor a tragic plot-structure as a privileged mode of emplotment and mechanistic causal connection as the favored mode of explanation, to account for changes topographically outlined in the emplotment. So too an ironic original description of the field will generate a tendency to favor emplotment in the mode of satire and pragmatic or contextual explanation of the structures thus illuminated. Finally, to round out the list, fields originally described in the synecdochic mode will tend to generate comic emplotments and organicist explanations of why these fields change as they do.[1]

Note, for example, that both those great narrative hulks produced by such classic historians as Michelet, Tocqueville, Burckhardt, and Ranke, on the one side, and the elegant synopses produced by philosophers of history such as Herder, Marx, Nietzsche, and Hegel, on the other, become more easily relatable, one to the other, if we see them as both victims and exploiters of the linguistic mode in which they originally describe a field of historical events *before* they apply their characteristic modalities of narrative representation and

[1] I have tried to exemplify at length each of these webs of relationships in given historians in my book *Metahistory: The Historical Imagination in Nineteenth-Century Europe* (Baltimore & London: The Johns Hopkins Univ. Press, 1973).

explanation, that is, their 'interpretations' of the field's 'meaning.' In addition, each of the linguistic modes, modes of emplotment, and modes of explanation has affinities with a specific ideological position: anarchist, radical, liberal, and conservative respectively. The issue of ideology points to the fact that there is no value-neutral mode of emplotment, explanation, or even description of any field of events, whether imaginary or real, and suggests that the very use of language itself implies or entails a specific posture before the world which is ethical, ideological, or more generally political: not only all interpretation, but also all language is politically contaminated.

Now, in my view, any historian who simply described a set of facts in, let us say, metonymic terms and then went on to emplot its processes in the mode of tragedy and proceeded to explain those processes mechanistically, and finally drew explicit ideological implications from it—as most vulgar Marxists and materialistic determinists do—would not only not be very interesting but could legitimately be labelled a *doctrinaire* thinker who had 'bent the facts' to fit a preconceived theory. The peculiar dialectic of historical discourse—and of other forms of discursive prose as well, perhaps even the novel—comes from the effort of the author to mediate between alternative modes of emplotment and explanation, which means, finally, *mediating between alternative modes of language use* or *tropological* strategies for originally describing a given field of phenomena and constituting it as a possible object of representation.

It is this sensitivity to alternative linguistic protocols, cast in the modes of metaphor, metonymy, synecdoche, and irony, that distinguishes the great historians and philosophers of history from their less interesting counterparts among the technicians of these two crafts. This is what makes Tocqueville so much more interesting (and a source of so many different later thinkers) than either his contemporary, the doctrinaire Guizot, or most of his modern liberal or conservative followers, whose knowledge is greater than his and whose retrospective vision is more extensive but whose dialectical capacity is so much more weakly developed. Tocqueville writes about the French Revolution, but he writes even more meaningfully about the difficulty of ever attaining to a definitive *objective characterization* of the complex web of facts that comprise the Revolution as a graspable totality or structured whole. The contradiction, the *aporia*, at the heart of Tocqueville's discourse is born of his awareness that alternative, mutually exclusive, original descriptions of what the Revolution *is* are possible. He recognizes that *both* metonymical and synecdochic linguistic protocols can be used, equally legitimately, to describe the field of facts that comprise the 'Revolution' and to constitute it as a *possible object* of *historical discourse*. He moves feverishly between the two modes of original description, testing both, trying to assign them to different mental sets or cultural types (what he means by a 'democratic' consciousness is a metonymic transcription of phenomena; 'aristocratic' consciousness is synecdochic). He himself is satisfied with neither mode, although he recognizes that each gives access to a specific aspect of reality and represents a possible way of apprehending it. His aim, ultimately, is to contrive a language capable of mediating between the two modes of consciousness which these linguistic modes represent. This aim of mediation, in turn, drives him progressively toward the ironic recognition that any given linguistic protocol will obscure as much as it reveals about the reality it seeks to capture in an order of words. This *aporia* or sense of contradiction residing at the heart of language itself is present in *all* of the classic historians. It is this linguistic self-consciousness which distinguishes them from their mundane counterparts and followers, who think that language can serve as a perfectly transparent medium of representation and who think that if one can only find the right language for describing events, the meaning of the events will *display itself* to consciousness.

This movement between alternative linguistic modes conceived as alternative descriptive protocols is, I would argue, a distinguishing feature of all of the great classics of the 'literature of fact.' Consider, for example, Darwin's *Origin of Species*,[2] a work which must rank as a classic in any list of the great monuments of this kind of literature. This work which, more than any other, desires to remain within the ambit of plain fact, is just as much about the problem of classification as it is about its ostensible subject matter, the data of natural history. This means that it deals with two problems: how are events to be described as possible elements of an argument; and what kind of argument do they add up to once they are so described?

Darwin claims to be concerned with a single, crucial question: 'Why are not all organic things linked together in inextricable chaos?' (p. 453). But he wishes to answer this question in particular terms. He does not wish to suggest, as many of his contemporaries held, that all systems of classification are arbitrary, that is, mere products of the minds of the classifiers; he insists that there is a *real* order

[2] References in the text to Darwin's *Origin of Species* are to the Dolphin Edition (New York: Doubleday, n.d.).

in nature. On the other hand, he does not wish to regard this order as a product of some spiritual or teleological power. The order which he seeks in the data, then, must be manifest in the facts themselves but not manifested in such a way as to display the operations of any transcendental power. In order to establish this notion of nature's plan, he purports, first, simply to entertain 'objectively' all of the 'facts' of natural history provided by field naturalists, domestic breeders, and students of the geological record—in much the same way that the historian entertains the data provided by the archives. But this entertainment of the record is no simple reception of the facts; it is an entertainment of the facts with a view toward the discrediting of all previous taxonomic systems in which they have previously been encoded.

Like Kant before him, Darwin insists that the source of all error is semblance. Analogy, he says again and again, is always a 'deceitful guide' (see pp. 61, 66, 473). As against analogy, or as I would say merely metaphorical characterizations of the facts, Darwin wishes to make a case for the existence of real 'affinities' genealogically construed. The establishment of these affinities will permit him to postulate the linkage of all living things to all others by the 'laws' or 'principles' of genealogical descent, variation, and natural selection. These laws and principles are the formal elements in his mechanistic explanation of why creatures are arranged in families in a time series. But this explanation could not be offered as long as the data remained encoded in the linguistic modes of either metaphor or synecdoche, the modes of qualitative connection. As long as creatures are classified in terms of either semblance or essential unity, the realm of organic things must remain either a chaos of arbitrarily affirmed connectedness or a hierarchy of higher and lower forms. Science as Darwin understood it, however, cannot deal in the categories of the 'higher' and 'lower' any more than it can deal in the categories of the 'normal' and 'monstrous.' Everything must be entertained as what it manifestly *seems to be*. Nothing can be regarded as 'surprising,' any more than anything can be regarded as 'miraculous.'

There are many kinds of facts invoked in *The Origin of Species*: Darwin speaks of 'astonishing' facts (p. 301), 'remarkable' facts (p. 384), 'leading' facts (pp. 444, 447), 'unimportant' facts (p. 58), 'well-established' facts, even 'strange' facts (p. 105); but there are no 'surprising' facts. Everything, for Darwin no less than for Nietzsche, is just what it appears to be—but what things appear to be are data inscribed under the aspect of *mere contiguity in space* (all the facts gathered by naturalists all over the world) *and time* (the records of domestic breeders and the geological record). As the elements of a problem (or rather, of a puzzle, for Darwin is confident that there is a solution to his problem), the facts of natural history are conceived to exist in that mode of relationship which is presupposed in the operation of the linguistic trope of metonymy, which is the favored trope of all *modern* scientific discourse (this is one of the crucial distinctions between modern and pre-modern sciences). The substitution of the name of a part of a thing for the name of the whole is pre-linguistically sanctioned by the importance which the scientific consciousness grants to mere contiguity. Considerations of *semblance* are tacitly retired in the employment of this trope, and so are considerations of *difference* and *contrast*. This is what gives to metonymic consciousness what Kenneth Burke calls its 'reductive' aspect. Things exist in contiguous relationships that are only spatially and temporally definable. This metonymizing of the world, this preliminary encoding of the facts in terms of merely contiguous relationships, is necessary to the removal of metaphor and teleology from phenomena which every *modern* science seeks to effect. And Darwin spends the greater part of his book on the justification of this encodation, or original description, of reality, in order to discharge the errors and confusion which a *merely* metaphorical profile of it has produced.

But this is only a preliminary operation. Darwin then proceeds to restructure the facts—but *only along one axis* of the time-space grid on which he has originally deployed them. Instead of stressing the mere contiguity of the phenomena, he shifts gears, or rather tropological modes, and begins to concentrate on differences—but two kinds of differences: *variations within species*, on the one side, and *contrasts between the species*, on the other. 'Systematists,' he writes, '. . . have only to decide . . . whether any form be sufficiently *constant* and *distinct* from other forms, to be capable of definition; and if definable, whether the differences be sufficiently important to deserve a specific name.' But the distinction between a species and a variety is only a matter of degree.

> Hereafter we shall be compelled to acknowledge that the only distinction between species and well-marked varieties is, that the latter are known, or believed, to be connected at the present day by intermediate gradation, whereas *species* were formerly thus connected. Hence, without rejecting the consideration of the *present existence* of intermediate gradations

between any two forms, we shall be led to weigh more carefully and to *value higher* the *actual amount of difference between them*. It is quite possible that forms now generally acknowledged to be merely varieties *may hereafter* be thought worthy of *specific names*; and in this case *scientific and common language will come into accordance*. In short, we shall have to treat species in the same manner as those naturalists treat genera, who admit that genera are merely artificial combinations made for convenience. This may not be a cheering prospect; but we shall at least be free from the vain search for the undiscovered and undiscoverable *essence* of the term species. (pp. 474–75; italics added)

And yet Darwin has smuggled in his own conception of the 'essence' of the term species. And he has done it by falling back on the geological record which, following Lyell, he calls 'a history of the world imperfectly kept, ... written in a changing dialect' and of which 'we possess the last volume alone' (p. 331). Using this record, he postulates the descent of all species and varieties from some four or five prototypes governed by what he calls the 'rule' of 'gradual transition' (pp. 180ff.) or 'the great principle of gradation' (p. 251). *Difference* has been dissolved in the *mystery of transition*, such that *continuity-in-variation* is seen as the 'rule' and radical discontinuity or variation as an 'anomaly' (p. 33). But this 'mystery' of transition (see his highly tentative, confused, and truncated discussion of the possible 'modes of transition'—pp. 179–82, 310) is nothing but the facts laid out on a time line, rather than spatially disposed, and treated as a 'series' which is permitted to '*impress* . . . the *mind* with the *idea of an actual passage*' (p. 66). All organic beings are then (gratuitously on the basis of both the facts and the theories available to Darwin) treated (metaphorically on the literal level of the text but synecdochically on the allegorical level) as belonging to families linked by genealogical descent (through the operation of variation and natural selection) from the postulated four or five prototypes. It is only his distaste for 'analogy,' he tells us, that keeps him from going 'one step further, namely, to the belief that all plants and animals are descended from some one prototype' (p. 473). But he has approached as close to a doctrine of organic unity as his respect for the 'facts,' in their original encodation in the mode of contiguity, will permit him to go. He has *transformed* 'the facts' from a structure of merely contiguously related particulars into a sublimated synecdoche. And this in order to put a new and more comforting (as well as, in his view, a more interesting and comprehensible) vision of nature in place of that of his vitalistic opponents.

The image which he finally offers—of an unbroken succession of generations—may have had a disquieting effect on his readers, inasmuch as it dissolved the distinction between both the 'higher' and 'lower' in nature (and by implication, therefore, in society) and the 'normal' and the 'monstrous' in life (and therefore in culture). But in Darwin's view, the new image of organic nature as an essential continuity of beings gave assurance that no 'cataclysm' had ever 'desolated the world' and permitted him to look forward to a 'secure future and progress toward perfection' (p. 477). For 'cataclysm' we can of course read 'revolution' and for 'secure future,' 'social status quo.' But all of this is presented, not as image, but as plain fact. Darwin is ironic only with respect to those systems of classification that would ground 'reality' in fictions of which he does not approve. Darwin distinguishes between tropological codes that are 'responsible' to the data and those that are not. But the criterion of responsibility to the data is not extrinsic to the operation by which the 'facts' are ordered in his initial description of them; this criterion is intrinsic to that operation.

As thus envisaged, even the *Origin of Species*, that *summa* of 'the literature of fact' of the nineteenth century, must be read as a kind of allegory—a history of nature meant to be understood literally but appealing ultimately to an image of coherency and orderliness which it constructs by linguistic 'turns' alone. And if this is true of the *Origin*, how much more true must it be of any history of human societies? In point of fact, historians have not agreed upon a terminological system for the description of the events which they wish to treat as facts and embed in their discourses as self-revealing data. Most historiographical disputes—among scholars of roughly equal erudition and intelligence—turn precisely on the matter of which among several linguistic protocols is to be used to *describe* the events under contention, not what explanatory system is to be applied to the events in order to reveal their meaning. Historians remain under the same illusion that had seized Darwin, the illusion that a value-neutral description of the facts, prior to their interpretation or analysis, was possible. It was not the doctrine of natural selection advanced by Darwin that commended him to other students of natural history as the Copernicus of natural history. That doctrine had been known and elaborated long before Darwin advanced it in the *Origin*. What had been required was a redescription of the facts to be explained in a language which would sanction the application to them of the doctrine as the most adequate way of explaining them.

And so too for historians seeking to 'explain' the 'facts' of the French Revolution, the decline and fall of the Roman Empire, the effects of slavery on American society, or the meaning of the Russian Revolution. What is at issue here is not: What are the facts? but rather: How are the facts to be described in order to sanction one mode of explaining them rather than another? Some historians will insist that history cannot become a science until it finds the technical terminology adequate to the correct characterization of its objects of study, in the way that physics did in the calculus and chemistry did in the periodic tables. Such is the recommendation of Marxists, Positivists, Cliometricians, and so on. Others will continue to insist that the integrity of historiography depends on its use of ordinary language, its avoidance of jargon. These latter suppose that ordinary language is a safeguard against ideological deformations of the 'facts.' What they fail to recognize is that ordinary language itself has its own forms of terminological determinism, represented by the figures of speech without which discourse itself is impossible.

9

Oral history

Oral history is usually referred to as a methodology, not a theory. But during the past decade oral historians have developed a number of interpretive theories about memory and subjectivity, and the narrative structures which provide the framework for oral stories about the past. While these have not yet coalesced into a single body of theoretical concepts, the directions are clear, and our understanding of both individual and collective memory has been greatly enhanced. Despite this, oral history is still regarded by the majority of historians as primarily a methodology. From this perspective, oral history often appears to be a more or less technical process in which the memories of the elderly are elicited through questions, recorded on tape machines and transcribed. The revival of interest in oral history from the 1960s onwards was not well received by conventional historians, who regarded oral testimonies as unreliable and tainted by personal subjectivity. Such sentiments were expressed by Eric Hobsbawm in an essay originally written in 1985. Describing oral history as 'a remarkably slippery medium for preserving facts', Hobsbawm called upon oral historians to work with psychologists to establish the parameters of memory.[1]

There are probably limits to the value of such an encounter between psychology and history. Daniel Schacter, Professor of Psychology at Harvard, argues that those events which we experience with the most intensity will be more elaborately encoded by a system of memory which ensures that we recall what is most important to us.[2] This is, therefore, unlikely to be the experiments carried out by psychologists in controlled tests! What is important will vary from individual to individual, and the British oral historian Paul Thompson cited an interesting instance in which an elderly Welshman was asked to recount the names of the occupiers of 108 farms in his district in 1900. When checked against the parish electoral list, he was found to be correct in 106 cases. Thompson concludes that the reliability of memory must rest partly on whether the question being asked interests the informant.[3] The memories of crucial experiences may be re-evaluated and re-contextualized throughout life, but they remain the basis upon which individual memory, and our sense of self-identity, is constructed.

The revival of oral history derived from a new generation of historians steeped in the politics of the New Left, civil rights and feminism. These university researchers, drawn from a much broader segment of the population than had been the case previously, wanted to include the experiences of marginalized or neglected social groups. Oral history was perceived as a means to empower women, the working class and ethnic minorities, allowing them to speak for themselves. We will return to this difficult question later. But there is no doubt that oral history has played a significant role in ensuring that many of the worst atrocities of the twentieth century against mankind are not forgotten, and that in some cases the perpetrators are brought to justice.[4] This aspect of oral history is celebrated in the new international award, Le Prix de la Mémoire, established in 1989 by the France-Libertés Foundation, to honour those who work to preserve collective memory. The prize grew out of the belief that 'the expression, transmission, and preservation of Human Memory is the most effective means of struggling against the recurrence of barbarism'.[5]

Until the 1970s oral testimonies were approached by historians in very much the same way as documentary sources, as a source of factual evidence. Michael Roper describes this period as 'oral history in the reconstructive mode'.[6] A great deal of valuable historical information was recorded and preserved, particularly in the areas of working lives. One of the largest oral history projects during this time was Paul Thompson's study of Edwardian Britain which sought to satisfy the traditional empirical requirements of a balanced sample producing representative results. Five hundred interviews were recorded with a cross-section of British society, exploring the dimensions of inequality and social structure. The interviews were structured around an interview schedule of some twenty pages, with the intention of generating comparable material. Thompson explicitly pointed out that the major strength of oral history lay in the 'particular facts and detailed accounts of everyday events'.[7]

But despite Thompson's efforts, establishing the empirical legitimacy of the source among professional historians remained elusive. Towards the end of the 1970s some historians sought to take oral history in a new direction, turning its perceived weakness, the subjectivity of individual memory, into a strength. Roper describes this turning point as 'oral history in the interpretive mode'.[8] In 1979 Italian historian Luisa Passerini published one of the most influential articles in the theory of oral history. Exploring the effects of Fascism upon the Italian working class in Turin, Passerini concluded that oral testimonies needed a far more sophisticated conceptual approach with which to understand the ways in which culture and psychology influenced memory. She argued that oral historians 'should not ignore that the raw material of oral history consists not just in factual statements, but is pre-eminently an expression and representation of culture, and therefore includes not only literal narrations but also the dimensions of memory, ideology and subconscious desires'.[9]

The role of female cultural norms, and subconscious resistance, have been central to Passerini's analysis of women's self-representation in oral testimonies. The following example illustrates the way in which Passerini locates individual stories within the matrix of cultural norms. Maddalena Bertagna gives an account of an occasion when she was part of a demonstration, and the soldiers opened fire (the actual event was in 1920). Maddelena attended the demonstration with a number of women and her young daughter. As the soldiers began to shoot, Maddalena ran away, holding the child by the hand. The following account includes both some of Maddalena's words (in italics) and Passerini's subsequent analysis:

> *I had her by the hand while running. She held onto Giambone's sister, the Giambone who they then killed at Martinetto. Well, his sister had her by the hand on one side and I had her on the other, and we were running to get away.*
> *When we stopped running, across that thing there was just by the arcades, just there her hat flew off her head, and to fetch the hat I let go of her [the daughter], she fell. I fell too, and the next moment we're heaped on top of one another.*
> This is the beginning of a sequence in which events are jumbled up together, recalled with accelerating pace in a loud, high-pitched voice, punctuated with laughter. Maddalena gets up, her hair loose and face dirty, her child with an injured arm. They pick up the hair-pins and take refuge in a janitor's lodge which is already full of people. The story emphasizes the things which transgress everyday norms – the women drink the water keeping the radishes cool and find it refreshing, they return home late, to find – in a reversal of roles – Maddalena's husband, who has been waiting

for some time, struggling with the soup she had put on the stove before leaving.[10]

Passerini draws our attention to the 'strong sexual connotations of the hair undone' and suggests that Maddalena's self-representation may best be understood as an unconscious manifestation of the older cultural figure of the disorderly woman, transgressing gender boundaries. This interpretation may have been fundamentally influenced by Passerini's own experience of psychoanalysis during this period.[11] An alternative reading of this narrative might have focused upon the rhetorical and performance aspects of story-telling, in which humour plays a central role. Indeed, Elizabeth Tonkin identifies the context in which the story is told as particularly important, for 'good storytellers are admired, and their genre gets critical and informed support. . . . But little academic attention is paid to the rhetorical skills of ordinary speakers.'[12]

Passerini's work also emphasizes other psychological dimensions of memory, 'including the un-said, the implicit, the imaginary, that . . . does not coincide with consciousness'.[13] She is probably best known for drawing our attention to the significance of silences in oral testimonies. One of the most striking features of her Turin study was the apparent excision of fascism from the memories of working-class men and women. Whole life histories were recounted without any mention of the years between 1925 and the outbreak of the Second World War. Passerini regards such silence as evidence of 'a scar, a violent annihilation of many years in human lives, a profound wound in daily experience'.[14] Many oral historians have been reluctant to actively employ the tools of psychology and psychoanalysis, and Jacqueline Rose has pointed out the risks of confusing an historical interview with a therapeutic psychoanalytic one, asking 'what are its objectives . . . what are the limits being placed on what can and cannot emerge?'[15]

Despite this concern, oral historians have increasingly followed Passerini's direction in seeking to understand the hidden, and often unconscious, structures which inform narratives about the past. In the United States Ron Grele, for example, drew attention in 1975 to the need for oral historians to grasp the 'underlying structure of consciousness which both governs and informs oral history interviews'.[16] Grele's initial contribution to this process was an in-depth analysis of two oral history interviews conducted as part of a larger project in New York. The two accounts, he argued, employed two different structural frameworks: the first a cyclical story of progress and decline, and the second, the binary opposition of two eternally opposing forces.[17] Historians, Grele suggested, needed to understand the way individuals constructed their life histories to create a 'usable past'.[18] This understanding of the need for individuals to construct a coherent account of their life history, with which they feel comfortable, is closely related to the concept of 'composure' developed in the reading by Alistair Thomson which follows this introduction.

Another way in which a 'usable past' is created is through adjusting the sequence of events to fit an overall narrative. In these cases, conflict between the oral and documentary record is a feature of oral history research, as Alessandro Portelli and John Bodnar discovered. Portelli recorded stories about the death of Luigi Trastulli in Terni, Italy when participating in a protest against the signing of the North Atlantic Treaty in 1949. However, in popular memory, the date of his death had shifted to 1953, in the context of conflict over the layoffs from the local steel factory.[19] Portelli sees this factually incorrect account not as the product of faulty memory, but as an active creation which gives us insight into the way in which experience is symbolically and psychologically incorporated into memory. In addition, Bodnar points to the importance of recognizing that oral accounts of the past are constructed in the present. Individual memories of working lives at the Studebaker automobile plant in Indiana were collectively constructed into a three-part narrative that did not always accord with the documentary evidence.[20] However, Bodnar argues that the perspective on each stage was inevitably informed by the final outcome, the closure of the plant, and 'that only from the perspective of the end do the beginnings and the middle of a narrative make sense'.[21] In both these cases the altered chronology entered collective memory, and became the dominant narrative for that group.

Increasingly oral historians have focused upon the role of imagination in story-telling. In 1987 a conference on 'myth and history' explored the importance of imaginative paradigms for the process of remembering. In this context myth was defined as:

> a metaphor for the symbolic order, or for the relationship between the imaginary and the real. We wanted to break down the opposition between the imaginary and the real, and to show for personal life narratives as anywhere else, that no statement that is made about one's past individually, is in any way innocent of ideology or of imaginative complexes.[22]

Two papers given at the conference, which were subsequently published, illustrate two different aspects of myth in oral history. Canadian anthropologist Julie Cruikshank showed how myth continued to play a critical role in oral tradition, the transmission of stories from generation to generation. She interviewed eight Athapaskan women who were born during or after the Klondike gold-rush of 1896–98.[23] Cruikshank's initial expectations of the content of the interviews, based around her knowledge of the disruptive effect of contact with prospectors, missionaries, traders and miners, was deflected by the women's determination to tell traditional stories. In the end Cruikshank recorded more than one hundred stories, many of which were almost identical to those described by early ethnographers in the late nineteenth century. Why did these stories persist as a way of explaining life experience? While Cruikshank acknowledges the implicit problems entailed by cross-cultural interpretation of oral traditions, she argues that the narratives were employed to convey ideas about social change to the next generation of young women. Myth was utilized as a bridge between past and present, and to explore the role of women within a culture suffering from painful dislocation. In this instance Cruikshank is deeply sensitive to Tonkin's point about the importance of the context in which stories are told.

However, myths are not confined to cultures in which the transmission of history remains primarily oral. Jean Peneff also drew attention to the pervasive elements of myth in the culture of capitalism.[24] In a study of Algerian entrepreneurs he explores the strength of the myth of the 'self-made man' for men who came from families of 'substantial privilege in colonial Algeria'. Peneff identified three elements to the story: the contrast of before and after in each individual story; a tendency to conceal any favourable social circumstances, and finally rarely any mention of familial support.[25] Peneff argues that it is essential for the oral historian to identify the myths employed within each story so that it is possible to evaluate the 'authenticity' of different aspects of a life history.

One consequence of the emphasis upon the value of subjectivity in oral testimonies has been a substantial shift away from older methods of interviewing towards a more subject-centred approach. While questionnaires are still utilized for social science research, oral historians increasingly employ techniques such as interactive interviewing in which as much control as possible over the direction of the interview remains with the interviewee.[26] In other words, advances in our understanding about the way in which our memories are constructed and narrated have begun to transform the methodology through which memories are elicited and preserved.

This has not, however, obviated the need for interviewers to interpret memories, and this is where major difficulties can arise. To some extent the new theory of oral history, which seeks to problematize memory and narratives about the past, runs contrary to the earlier democratic and empowering intentions of oral historians. This problem has been recognized, particularly in the area of women's history and feminist interpretation. In a perceptive account of an interview with her grandmother, Katherine Borland was forced to confront the very different understandings held by herself and her grandmother of a story about a day at the races.[27] Michael Frisch has argued that in the field of public history oral historians must share interpretative authority with those with whom they work.[28] It is not, however, always possible to put this into practice, and as Alistair Thomson has pointed out, 'a collective project which explores the relationships between personal and collective memories, and which challenges people's life stories, will almost inevitably generate difficulty and pain'.[29]

In conclusion, historians now argue that oral history has a different 'credibility' from the empirical evidence of documentary sources. Subjective and collective meaning is embedded in the narrative structures people employ to describe the past. All memory is valid, according to Passerini: 'the guiding principle should be that all autobiographical memory is true; it is up to the interpreter to discover in which sense, where, for which purpose'.[30] This means that every life history 'inextricably intertwines both objective and subjective evidence – of different, but equal value'.[31]

The powerful influence of myth and the unconscious in the process of remembering has undoubtedly undermined the initial optimism with which 'historians from below' embraced oral history as a means of rewriting history from the perspective of the marginalized or oppressed.[32] But in case we begin to lose sight of individual agency, and begin to perceive memory as over-determined, it is worth remembering the following conversation between Elizabeth and Darcy in *Pride and Prejudice*. 'You must learn some of my philosophy. Think only of the past as its remembrance gives you pleasure', Elizabeth tells Darcy. But he is unconvinced, and replies that 'painful recollections will intrude, which cannot, which ought not to be repelled'.[33]

The following article by Alistair Thomson explores the links between private and public memory for one Anzac (Australian and New Zealand Army Corps) soldier, Fred Farrall, a veteran of the First World War. Born and educated in Melbourne, Thomson's interest in the Anzacs arose out of his family history and the dominance of the myth in Australian culture. Thomson seeks to understand the extent to which national mythology about the Anzacs influenced Farrall's memories and the way in which he understood his experiences during the Great War. Consider the features of Thomson's theory of 'composure' and compare them with Farrall's memories. In this case, are the individual's memories adjusted to accord with the myth; has Farrall 'remade' his memories to achieve 'composure'? Do you think it is possible for the individual to retain oppositional memories in the context of powerful cultural myths? Where does the current direction of oral history, with its emphasis upon unconscious cultural norms and imaginative complexes in structuring our memories of the past, leave the active agency of individuals?

Notes

1 Eric Hobsbawm, *On History* (London, 1997), pp. 206–7.
2 Daniel L. Schacter, *Searching for Memory: The Brain, the Mind, and the Past* (New York, 1996), pp. 45–6. See also Steven Rose, *The Making of Memory: From Molecules to Mind* (London, 1992), p. 91.
3 Paul Thompson, *The Voice of the Past* (2nd edn, Oxford, 1988), p. 113.
4 See Luisa Passerini, *Memory and Totalitarianism* (Oxford, 1992).
5 Harvey J. Kaye, *Why Do Ruling Classes Fear History?* (New York, 1997), p. 61.
6 Michael Roper, 'Oral History', in Brian Brivati, Julia Buxton and Anthony Seldon (eds), *The Contemporary History Handbook* (Manchester, 1996), p. 346.
7 Paul Thompson, *The Edwardians* (St Albans, 1977), pp. 13–18.
8 Roper, 'Oral History', p. 347.
9 Luisa Passerini, 'Work Ideology and Consensus under Italian Fascism', *History Workshop Journal*, 8 (1979), p. 84.
10 Luisa Passerini, *Fascism in Popular Memory*, trans. Robert Lumley and Jude Bloomfield (Cambridge, 1987), pp. 20–1.
11 Susan A. Crane, 'Writing the Individual Back into Collective Memory', *The American Historical Review*, 102, 5 (December 1997), p. 1384.
12 Elizabeth Tonkin, *Narrating our Pasts: The Social Construction of Oral History* (Cambridge, 1992), pp. 53–4.
13 Cited in Karl Figlio, 'Oral History and the Unconscious', *History Workshop Journal*, 26 (1988), p. 128.
14 Passerini, 'Work Ideology and Consensus under Italian Fascism', p. 92.
15 Jacqueline Rose, 'A Comment', *History Workshop Journal*, 28 (1989), p. 150.
16 Ron Grele, 'Listen To Their Voices', *Oral History*, 7 (1979), p. 33.
17 *Ibid.*, p. 40.
18 *Ibid.*, p. 41.
19 Alessandro Portelli, *The Death of Luigi Trastulli and Other Stories* (New York, 1991), pp. 1–28.

20 John Bodnar, 'Power and Memory in Oral History: Workers and Managers at Studebaker', *Journal of American History*, 75 (1989), pp. 1201–21.

21 *Ibid.*, p. 1221.

22 Raphael Samuel, 'Myth and History: A First Reading', *Oral History*, 16 (1988), p. 15.

23 Julie Cruikshank, 'Myth as a Framework for Life Stories: Athapaskan Women Making Sense of Social Change in Northern Canada', in Raphael Samuel and Paul Thompson (eds), *The Myths We Live By* (London, 1990), pp. 174–83.

24 Jean Peneff, 'Myths in Life Stories', in Samuel and Thompson, *The Myths We Live By*, pp. 36–48.

25 *Ibid.*, p. 37.

26 Kathryn Anderson and Dana Jack, 'Learning to Listen: Interview Techniques and Analyses', in Sherna Berger Gluck and Daphne Patai (eds), *Women's Words: The Feminist Practice of Oral History* (New York and London, 1991), pp. 11–26.

27 Katherine Borland, 'That's Not What I Said', in Gluck and Patai, *Women's Words*, p. 64.

28 Michael Frisch, *A Shared Authority: Essays on the Craft and Meaning of Oral and Public History* (New York, 1990), p. xxii.

29 Alistair Thomson, Michael Frisch and Paula Hamilton, 'The Memory and History Debates: Some International Perspectives', *Oral History*, 25 (1994), p. 35.

30 Personal Narratives Group, *Interpreting Women's Lives: Feminist Theory and Personal Narratives* (Bloomington, 1989), p. 197.

31 Thomson, Frisch and Hamilton, 'The Memory and History Debates', p. 34.

32 See Samuel, 'Myth and History', pp. 16–17.

33 Jane Austen, *Pride and Prejudice* (Harmondsworth, [1813] 1972), p. 377.

Additional reading

Fraser, Ronald, *Blood of Spain* (London, 1979).

Gluck, Sherna, *Rosie the Riveter Revisited* (New York, 1987).

Gluck, Sherna Berger and Patai, Daphne, *Women's Words: The Feminist Practice of Oral History* (New York and London, 1991).

Grele, Ron (ed.), *Envelopes of Sound: The Art of Oral History* (New York, [1985] 1991).

Lagrand, James B., 'Whose Voices Count? Oral Sources and Twentieth-century American Indian History', *American Indian Culture and Research Journal*, 21:1 (1997), pp. 73–105.

Passerini, Luisa, 'Work Ideology and Consensus under Italian Fascism', *History Workshop Journal*, 8 (1979), pp. 82–108.

Passerini, Luisa, *Fascism in Popular Memory* (Cambridge, 1987).

Perks, Robert and Alistair Thomson (eds), *The Oral History Reader* (London, 1998).

Portelli, Alessandro, *The Death of Luigi Trastulli and Other Stories: Form and Meaning in Oral History* (New York, 1991).

Samuel, Raphael and Paul Thompson, *The Myths We Live By* (London, 1990).

Thompson, Paul, *The Voice of the Past* (2nd edn, Oxford, 1988).

Thomson, Alistair, *Anzac Memories: Living with the Legend* (Melbourne, 1994).

Vansina, Jan, *Oral Tradition as History* (Madison, 1985).

ANZAC MEMORIES: PUTTING POPULAR MEMORY THEORY INTO PRACTICE IN AUSTRALIA
Alistair Thomson

Australian soldiers of the Great War of 1914–1918 have been making regular appearances on British television and in the cinema in recent years. The Anzacs (named after the Australian and New Zealand Army Corps—the New Zealanders tend to be left out of Australian films) have swaggered across our screens in *Gallipoli*, *Anzacs* and *The Lighthorsemen*, and even made an honourable appearance in the controversial British series, *The Monocled Mutineer*. A feature of these films is their characterisation of the Australian soldier, and of Australian manhood in general, which can be summarised as follows. The digger, as he is also nick-named, is usually a bushman from the colonial frontier, strong, sun-tanned and resourceful. He's also a bit of a lad, a 'larrikin' in Australian slang, a boozer and gambler who's not too concerned with military spit and polish, and who despises the military discipline of the British army and the snobbishness of British officers. Of course there are no such tensions within the Australian Imperial Force (AIF), in which the ruling creed of mateship includes the Australian officers, who come from the ranks and thus from the same social background as their men. Respect for talent rather than status, and the encouragement of individual initiative, contrast sharply with British military and caste tradition, and make the diggers among the best fighters of the war and the AIF the most effective army.[1]

Australian war films are a product of a recent resurgence of this 'Anzac legend'. According to the legend, during the Great War Australian soldiers proved to themselves and to the rest of the world that the new breed of Anglo-Celtic men from the south was worthy to rank with the nations of the world. Gallipoli, where the Australians first went into battle on April 25 1915, was regarded as the baptism of fire of the new Australian Commonwealth, and the commemoration of Anzac Day on April 25 each year became the Australian equivalent of American Independence Day or Bastille Day in

---

[1] See Amanda Lohrey, 'Australian mythologies: *Gallipoli:* male innocence as a marketable commodity', *Island*, nos. 9 and 10, 1982, pp. 29–34.

France (without the revolutionary overtones). Like all commemorations, the meanings and forms of the Anzac legend have been contested since its inception, and it has many different variations. Recent Anzac films are simply the most powerful and popular representation of what Anzac means in Australia today. For a European audience they may have different meanings, especially because the manliness and military prowess of the Anzacs contrasts so markedly with the usual European imagery of western front soldiers as passive victims of modern warfare and military incompetence.[2]

This essay focuses on the life and memories of Fred Farrall, one of about twenty Melbourne working class veterans of the Great War whom I've interviewed over the last six years.[3] I don't pretend that Fred Farrall was a typical digger, far from it. The search for national character has been one of the obsessive dead ends of Australian history-writing, and in this essay I won't be analysing the extent to which the Anzac legend is an accurate representation of the 'typical' Australian soldier.[4] I'm more interested in the interactions between Anzac legend stereotypes and individual soldiers' identities, in the experience of difference as well as conformity, and in the ways that 'typical' can be oppressive. I want to assess the relationship between Fred Farrall's memory of the war and the national mythology which publicly defines his experience as a soldier, and to use his case study to make sense of the general relationship between individual memory and collective myth.

The theory of memory (and national myth) which informs this essay was developed by the Popular Memory Group at the Centre for Contemporary Cultural Studies in Birmingham. The group focused on the interactions between 'private' and 'public' memories, and used the following approach to individual memory. We compose our memories to make sense of our past and present lives. 'Composure' is the aptly ambiguous term used by the Popular Memory Group to

[2] See Robin Gerster, *Big-noting: The Heroic Theme in Australian War Writing*, Melbourne University Press, Melbourne 1987.

[3] I'd like to thank Fred Farrall for his assistance and cooperation, and for sharing his memories with me. The interviews with Fred were recorded in July of 1983 and April of 1987, and the tapes and transcripts of the interviews, together with others from the project, are available in the 'Australian Veterans of the Great War: Oral History Project' collection of the library of the Australian War Memorial. I am grateful for a Research Grant from the Australian War Memorial which paid for the transcription of the tapes.

[4] For such a critique see my chapter, 'Passing Shots at the Anzac Legend', in Verity Burgmann and Jenny Lee (eds), *A Most Valuable Acquisition: A People's History of Australia since 1788*, McPhee Gribble/Penguin, Melbourne 1988.

describe the process of memory making. In one sense we 'compose' or construct memories using the public language and meanings of our culture. In another sense we 'compose' memories which help us to feel relatively comfortable with our lives, which give us a feeling of composure. We remake or repress memories of experiences which are still painful and 'unsafe' because they do not easily accord with our present identity, or because their inherent traumas or tensions have never been resolved. We seek composure, an alignment of our past, present and future lives. One key theoretical connection, and the link between the two senses of composure, is that the apparently private process of composing safe memories is in fact very public. Our memories are risky and painful if they do not conform with the public norms or versions of the past. We compose our memories so that they will fit with what is publicly acceptable, or, if we have been excluded from general public acceptance, we seek out particular publics which affirm our identities and the way we want to remember our lives.[5]

Some critics of oral history have claimed that the fact that we compose our memories invalidates the use of memory by historians. That might be true for oral historians who have sought to use memory as a literal source of what happened in the past. But if we are also interested, as we must be, in the ways in which the past is resonant in our lives today, then oral testimony is essential evidence for analysis of the interactions between past and present, and between memory and mythology.

This approach to memory requires a review of interviewing technique. In my initial interviews with Melbourne war veterans I wanted to see how the experiences of working class soldiers contrasted with the Anzac legend, and used a chronological life story approach as the basis for questions. The interviews did reveal many differences between their lives and the legend, but I was also struck by the extent to which memories were entangled with the myth; for example, some men related scenes from the film *Gallipoli* as if they were their own. Therefore, guided by the ideas of the Popular Memory Group, I devised a new approach for a second set of interviews with some of the same men. In the new interviews I wanted to focus on how each

[5] Unfortunately the now defunct Popular Memory Group did not publish its most pioneering exploration of myth, memory and identity, though I'd like to thank Richard Johnson and Graham Dawson for letting me read various drafts. A relatively crude initial outline of their approach is 'Popular Memory: theory politics, method', in Richard Johnson, et al (eds), *Making Histories: Studies in history writing and politics*, Hutchinson, London 1982.

man composed and told his memories by exploring four key inter-actions: between public and private, past and present, memory and identity, and interviewer and interviewee. The personal information which I had already gained in the first interviews made it possible for me to tailor my questions specifically for each man in terms of his particular memories and identities. If I had not done the original interviews I would have needed to integrate the life story approach with the new approach.

To investigate the relationship between public and private mem-ories I made the public myth a starting point for questions: what was your response to various war books and films, past and present, and to Anzac Day and war memorials? How well did they represent your own experiences; how did they make you feel? We also focused on specific features of the legend: was there a distinctive Anzac charac-ter; how true was it for your own nature and experience? Were you so very different from the soldiers of other armies? I asked each man to define certain keywords in his own words—'digger', 'mateship', 'the spirit of Anzac'—and discovered that some of the men who seemed to be uncritical of the legend had contrary and even contra-dictory understanding of its key terms.

Another section of discussion focused on experience and personal identity: how did you feel about yourself and your actions at key moments (enlistment, battle, return)? What were your anxieties and uncertainties? How did you make sense of your experiences and how did other people define you? How were you included or excluded, what was acceptable and unacceptable behaviour (what was not 'manly'), and how and why were some men ostracised? Of course these memories, and the relative composure of memory, had shifted over time (the past/present interaction), so we discussed how postwar events—such as homecoming, the Depression and World War Two, domestic change and old age, and the revival of Anzac remembrance in the 1980s—affected identity and memory. The new interview approach showed me that what is possible to remember and to artic-ulate changes over time, and how this can be related to shifts in public perception.

Another related and difficult focus of the new interviews was upon the ways memories are affected by strategies of containment, by ways of handling frustration, failure, loss or pain. This required a sensitive balance between potentially painful probing and reading between the lines of memory. What is possible or impossible to remember, or even to say aloud? What are the hidden meanings of silences and sudden subject changes? What is being contained by a 'fixed' story? Deeply repressed experiences or feelings may be discharged in less conscious forms of expression, in past and present dreams, errors and Freudian slips, body language and even humour, which is often used to overcome or conceal embarrassment and pain. Discussion of the symbolic content and feelings expressed by war-related dreams suggested new understandings of the personal impact of the war, and of what could not be publicly expressed. And my interview notes about facial expression, body movements and the mode of talking were revealing about emotive meanings of memories which would not be apparent in interview transcripts.

This approach raised ethical dilemmas for me as an oral historian. Interviewing which approached a therapeutic relationship could be damaging for the interviewee as well as rewarding for the interviewer. It required great care and sensitivity, and a cardinal rule that the well-being of the interviewee always came before the interests of my research. At times I had to stop a line of questioning in an interview, or was asked to stop, because it was too painful. Unlike the therapist, as an oral historian I would not be around to help put together the pieces of memories which were no longer safe.

One partial response was to make the interview, and the interview relationship, a more open process. I tried to discuss how many questions affected remembering, and what was difficult to say to *me*. To encourage dialogue instead of monologue I talked about my own interests and role. In some ways this change in my role (limited by the fact that I never gave up my role as interviewer) affected the remembering. Sometimes it encouraged a man to open up to me and reconsider aspects of his life, though others resisted that opportunity. The explicit introduction of my attitudes into the interviews may have encouraged men to tell stories for my approval, though I usually felt that it facilitated discussion and provoked dissent as much as agreement. In Fred Farrall's case that was not such an issue, as by the time we met his memory of the war was relatively fixed. Although over the years we developed a close and trusting relationship, in which Fred's remembering was actively encouraged by my interest, he seemed to tell the same stories in the same ways to his various audiences, including me. Fred's war story had not always been so fixed, and I gradually realised that his memory of the war, and his identity as a soldier and ex-serviceman, had passed through three distinct phases, shaped by the shifting relationship between Anzac meanings and his own subjective identity.

Born in 1897, Fred Farrall grew up on a small farm in outback New South Wales. He didn't like farm work and, inspired by the patriotic fervour which swept the country after the Gallipoli landing, was glad to join a 'Kangaroo March' of rural recruits for the AIF. He enlisted in an infantry battalion and was sent to France and the Somme in 1916. By his own admission Fred was not much of a soldier. He was young, naive and under-confident, and wasn't very good at fighting and killing. Like many soldiers of all nationalities, he was terrified in battle and miserable in the trenches, and began to doubt his own worth and that of the war itself. His best mates were killed and mutilated at his side, and though Fred survived the war in one piece, he was a physical and emotional wreck:

> When I came home I was admitted to Randwick Hospital for six months to see what they could do with the trench feet condition, and the rheumatism and a nasal complaint that I contracted on the Somme. . . . I didn't realise this at the time, but I long since realised it. But I had neurosis, that was not recognised in those days, and so we just had it. You put up with it. And that developed an inferiority complex, plus, really, I mean extremely bad. . . . Well, I had reached a stage with it, where, when I wanted to speak I'd get that way that I couldn't talk. I would stammer and stutter and it seemed that inside me everything had got into a knot, and that went on for years and years and years.

From the fortunate, retrospective stance of a survivor who overcame his neurosis, Fred attributes his shell-shocked condition to the effect of constant bombardment on the Somme. He admits that he was unable to express his fear during and after the battle, and was discouraged from doing so: it was not manly or Australian. Many of Fred's stories contrast his own inadequacy with the supposed bravery of other Australians. The legend of the Australian soldier—the best fighter in the war—caused many diggers to repress their feelings, and worsened the psychological trauma of the war.[6]

Fred's condition, and his sense of personal inadequacy, was worsened by his return to Australia.

> I was something like pet dogs and cats that are turned out in the Dandenongs [a mountain range near Melbourne] . . . If anyone was to ask me now what I was like at that time, I would say that in some respects, it could truthfully be said, and I suppose this applied to many others, many

[6] For an analysis in these terms of the nature and effects of shell shock, see Elaine Showalter, 'Rivers and Sassoon: The Inscription of Male Gender Anxiety', in M.R. Higonnet, et al (eds), *Behind the Lines: Gender and the Two World Wars*, Yale University Press, New Haven 1987, pp. 61–9.

others, that we wouldn't be the full quid. In other words, we weren't what we were like when we went away. I don't know whether you've heard Eric Bogle's songs. Well he mentioned that in something he said about Vietnam. . . . And then when I got into civilian life, well this was something new, and to some extent it was, it was terrifying. You're out in the cold, hard world. Nobody to look after you now. You've got to get your own accommodation, your own meals. In short, you've got to fend for yourself.

For men like Fred who were teenagers when they enlisted, the social experience of repatriation was especially traumatic. Fred was lucky. Because of his ill-health he couldn't go back to work on the family farm, but a cousin and her digger husband gave him a room in their home in Sydney, and got him back on his feet. He enrolled in a government vocational training scheme to become an upholsterer, but the scheme was badly organised, and though the government subsidised trainees' wages, employers were not interested when the subsidy ended. Fred searched for work for almost two years before he got a job in a motor car factory. I asked him whether his war service badge helped him to get a job. It didn't, and he wouldn't wear it for many years:

Well, we didn't value it.
Why?
Well, it'd be hard to explain other than that first of all, we, of course, had been disillusioned. What we'd been told that the war was all about, didn't work out that way. What we'd been told that the government would do when the war was over, for what we'd done, didn't work out either.
In what ways?
Well, you see, the pensions in the 1920s, unless you had an arm off or a leg off or a hand off or something like that, it was almost as hard to get a pension as it would be to win Tatts [an Australian lottery]. There was no recognition of neurosis and other disabilities. . . . And anyway, the doctors that they had in those days, I suppose they were schooled in what, how they were to behave and so they treated the diggers as they interviewed them and examined them as though they were tenth rate citizens. Something like we look upon the aboriginals. There was great hostility between the diggers on one hand and the Repatriation officials on the other . . .

Fred felt that ex-servicemen were regarded as 'malingerers', and refused to use the Repat. until 1926, when he had a breakdown and had no choice.

Despite this hostility, the war remained a haunting memory for Fred. He chose to marry on the anniversary of his war wound, he named his house after the places where his two best mates were buried, he remembered (and still recites) in exact detail the places and dates where many friends were killed. These private forms of commemoration, which transformed grotesque experience into relatively safe lists and rituals, were Fred's way of coping with the past. Experiences and feelings which he could not cope with were unconsciously expressed in his dreams:

> Oh well, the dreams I had were dreams of being shelled, you know, lying in a trench, being in a trench or lying in a shellhole, and being shot at with shells. And being frightened, scared stiff. Here, to now, I didn't know there were so many others like me until I read this book on Pozieres.[7] That most of them had this fear, and when you come to think of it, well how could they be otherwise . . . You don't know when the next shell that is coming is going to blow you to pieces or leave you crippled in such a way that it'd be better if you had been blown to pieces. . . . [In the dream] you'd be going through this experience and you'd be scared stiff, you'd be frightened. You'd be frightened, and wakened up, probably, by the experience.

One reason why Fred could not come to terms with his wartime fears and feelings of inadequacy was because he could find no appropriate public affirmation of his experience as a soldier. He found that he could not talk about his war:

> Well, well it was a different atmosphere in the 1920s for instance, and the early 1930s. First of all those that were at the war were reluctant to talk about it, and those that were not at the war, didn't go to the war and the women and that, didn't seem to want to hear about it. So the war slipped into the background as far as the average person was concerned. . . . I never talked about it. Never. For years and years and years. Now just why that was I don't know. But, the soldiers, generally speaking, were not very enthusiastic about army life and were ever so pleased to get into civilian clothes again. . . . When we got back, there was a sort of hostility towards anything to do with the war, by a lot. . . . All they wanted to do was to distance themselves as far as they could from anything to do with the army, with the Repat., or the war.

Fred shut away his beautifully embossed discharge certificate in a dusty drawer, and he declined to wear his medals or to attend Anzac Day parades or battalion reunions. The nature of Anzac Day and of other public forms of commemoration, and the perceived neglect by the government, was partly to blame for Fred's inability to express or resolve his ambivalence about his war experience. This was not true for all diggers. Many of the men I interviewed describe how they

---

[7] Peter Charlton, *Pozieres; Australians on the Somme 1916*, Methuan Haynes, North Ryde 1980.

enjoyed the celebration of their digger identity on Anzac Day, and the humorous reminiscence of veterans' reunions. Public remembrance and affirmation helped these men to cope with their past, filtering out memories which were personally painful or which contradicted the legend. The nascent Anzac legend worked because many veterans wanted and needed to identify with it.

Fred's initial interview explanation of his non-participation is that Anzac Day was a drunken binge, and that he wasn't a drinker. He stresses his own sobriety and complains that the popular larrikin image of the digger—boozer, gambler and womaniser—has not accurately depicted his own experience and view of the AIF. I hadn't expected this response, but it shows how another aspect of the digger stereotype—larrikin as well as fighter—could misrepresent an individual's experience, exclude him from public affirmation rituals, and make him feel uncomfortable about his own identity. Several other old diggers expressed the same unease about the larrikin image which has featured prominently in recent Anzac films, and remembered that even during the war they were made to feel uncomfortable by this behaviour and reputation. Others revelled in the stereotype, which conjured up exciting memories of their own wild youth.

Fred also avoided Anzac Day because its patriotic rhetoric did not match his wartime doubts about the worth of Australian involvement, or the bitterness he felt about the postwar treatment of the soldiers. But the main reason for his non-participation in Anzac ritual was the extreme confusion and distress he felt about the war. The public celebration of Anzac heroes was a painful reminder of his own perceived inadequacy as a soldier and as a man, and Fred was unable to enjoy the solace and affirmation it offered to other returned servicemen.

Although Fred Farrall was traumatised by his memories and identity as an Anzac throughout the 1920s, he gradually found another life and identity in the labour movement, which in turn helped him to compose a sense of his war which he could live with more easily. Fred recalls that he was politically confused after the war, but that a work-mate persuaded him to join the Coachmaker's Union in 1923: 'that was the beginning of my active part in politics . . . [and] sowed the seeds for my socialism that I developed a few years after and have had all my life'. He became active in the union, joined the Labor Party in 1926 and then, unemployed and disillusioned with the Labour government of 1930, he joined the Communist Party. In the labour movement Fred found supportive comrades and gradually

regained his self-confidence. The new and empathetic peer group—
many of them were ex-servicemen—and eager reading of radical
tracts about the war, helped him to articulate and define his wartime
and postwar disillusionment. He believes that was true for many
other diggers, and cites the example of his friend Sid Norris:

> In that respect, the making of a big change politically speaking, Sid was
> but one of thousands of diggers who abandoned their prewar opinions of
> God, King and Empire being worthy of any sacrifice. The bitter experience
> of what wars were all about, the making of big profits for some people,
> was a lesson that changed the diggers' political ideas from conservatism
> to radicalism. And Alistair, this is one part, or side, of the Anzac legend
> that has never been dealt with by the writers of the Great War. Maybe you
> can give it some thought.

Although Fred had not himself made that recognition during the
war, in the late 1920s his new political understanding helped him to
emphasise particular senses of his experience as a soldier. Thus Fred
now ironically stressed the story of an Irish labourer on his father's
farm who had warned him not to go and fight in the rich men's war,
and he represented himself as an unwitting victim of an imperialist
war. He also stressed that the relationship between officers and men
in the AIF was not so very different to that between employers and
workers in peacetime Australia, and that the diggers were often rebellious towards authority (he recalled one incident in which he and
two mates planned, unsuccessfully, to kill an unpopular officer).
These understandings of the war were part of a more radical Anzac
tradition championed by some activists in the labour movement.[8] As
a proponent of this tradition Fred also articulated his disillusionment
about repatriation, and deduced that Anzac Day was 'a clever
manoeuvre' intended to bring the soldiers back together again and
stifle their anger about pensions and unemployment:

> Well I would say that if it wasn't for Anzac Day, the First World War would
> have probably been—met the same fate as the Eureka Stockade [an armed
> rebellion of gold miners in the 1850s]. That is, it wouldn't be recognised.
> It wouldn't be recognised. And whoever thought up celebrating Anzac Day,
> which was a—had nothing to recommend it in a way, first of all we were
> invading another country, Turkey. . . . Secondly, it finished in a defeat. So
> what was there to celebrate, looking at if from that angle? So they cele-
> brated it for another reason. That was to cultivate a spirit of war in the
> community. Of admiration or respect, or honour or something for war.

[8] L. F. Fox, *The Truth about Anzac*, Victorian Council Against War and Fascism, Melbourne 1936.

And that's all Anzac Day really does. But they had to do it in a certain way, and it was done in a way whereby they could get them together on a social basis. First of all they marched and paraded and showed themselves to the public. And then when that was over they got into their clubs or their pubs or whatever, and did what they wanted to do.

Fred also became sceptical of the returned servicemen's organisations which controlled Anzac Day. He recalls that the soldiers in the trenches talked about the need to organise for decent conditions after the war, and that he joined the Returned Sailors' and Soldiers' Imperial League of Australia (RSSILA—now the powerful RSL) on the day he was demobbed. But the RSSILA had been created and controlled by an alliance of citizen and ex-servicemen conservatives, and was granted government recognition as the official representative of returned servicemen 'in return for defending the powers that be' (who were frightened by the violence of dissatisfied diggers and the presence of more radical veterans' pressure groups).[9] In the early 1920s Fred's inner turmoil and physical handicaps had probably kept him away from RSSILA meetings, but this alienation was now confirmed by political suspicion:

> In other words it was the officers in somewhat the same position in civilian life as they were in the army. . . . It was not an organization in the best interests of the ordinary digger. . . . It was a political organization of the extreme right wing and there was no place in it for anyone that had any democratic principles.

By the end of the 1920s Fred Farrall had aligned himself against the RSSILA and was fighting with members of the communist-led Unemployed Workers' Movement in street battles against RSSILA club men and the proto-fascist New Guard movement. By 1937 he was a confident opponent of the official legend and its RSSILA organisers, and was arrested for distributing pacifist leaflets at an Anzac Day parade.

Ironically, by the time Fred had consolidated his radical view of the war, the RSSILA's more conservative Anzac legend, which celebrated the triumph of Australian manhood and the baptism of the nation, was well entrenched. Radicals did contest that version of the war—in Melbourne, for example, some ex-servicemen protested that the proposed Shrine of Remembrance would glorify war, and cam-

[9] See Marilyn Lake, 'The Power of Anzac', in M. McKernan and M. Browne (eds), *Australia: Two Centuries of War and Peace*, Australian War Memorial/Allen and Unwin, Canberra 1988.

paigned for the more utilitarian memorial of a veteran's hospital—but by 1930 radicals had lost the battle for the Anzac legend and the label 'radical digger' was a contradiction in terms. Fred Farrall gradually shed his identity as a returned serviceman and settled into the role of 'a soldier of the labour movement'.

Although the labour movement's version of the war did help Fred to feel relatively secure with an analysis of the war as imperial and business rivalry, and his sense of himself as a naive and then begrudging victim, it did not (maybe could not?) help him to express or resolve his traumatic personal feelings about the war. Theories about arms profiteers made him angry, but didn't help him to cope with memories of terror, guilt or inadequacy. Nor could he enjoy the wider public affirmation of Anzac Day, which helped other ex-servicemen feel proud of their war service. Thus, for many years Fred usually ignored his military past and tried to forget his painful memories.

There's a third phase in Fred Farrall's war story. Some time in the 1960s or early 1970s he started to read and talk outside of the labour movement about his war. He attended the annual Anzac Day ceremony and reunion of his old battalion. He pinned his war service badge back in his lapel, and retrieved his discharge certificate from its dusty hideaway and stuck it up on his living room wall (above a more recent photo of himself as the Mayor of the Melbourne municipality of Prahran). After years of silence he now talks eagerly and at length about the war to students, film makers and oral history interviewers. Why?

Fred explains the change in a number of ways. It's partly the renewed interest of an old man about his youth: 'I suppose as you get older you have some sort of feeling for what happened long ago'. He's also enjoying the respect, even veneration, which the few remaining Great War diggers receive, from people in the street who notice an AIF badge, and from Veterans' Affairs officials who tell them it is a 'badge of honour' and pay their increasing medical costs:

> Well, there was a time when it just didn't fit into that picture at all. . . . Well, we've never had much over the years of value from that sort of thing so if there is anything now, even to the extent of getting some respect, well I think it's worth doing.

Those comments hint at more general processes. In the resurgence of interest in the Anzacs, the specific and often contradictory experiences of individual veterans are being clouded by a generalised, almost nostalgic version of the diggers and their war. Furthermore, in this modern re-working of the legend aspects of their war experience which were once taboo are now publicly acceptable. The Vietnam War and the influence of the peace and anti-war movement have altered public perceptions of war so that the soldier as victim is a more acceptable character—though he still takes second place to the Anzac hero. Fred can now talk more easily about his experience of 'the war as hell', and of his own feelings of inadequacy as a soldier, because those aspects of the war are portrayed in the history books and films of the 1980s. He marvels at how well some recent Anzac historians and television directors depict the horror and degradation of trench warfare. The personal pleasure of having his experience as a soldier recognised and affirmed after years of alienation was vividly expressed when I asked Fred about his visit to the Australian War Memorial in Canberra (second only to the Sydney Opera House as a national tourist attraction):

> Nearly got a job there. I was there about eighteen months ago, you know, and oh gee, look here, I got the surprise of my life. . . . I was treated like a long lost cousin [and was asked to talk about the western front to other visitors]. 'Well', I said, 'I wouldn't mind doing that, but', I said, 'I'm a worker for peace and not for war'. 'Oh', the bloke said, 'you know this place was built as a Peace Memorial and so you're at liberty to express your opinions along those lines as you see fit'. . . . So up I went. Well I was there for two or three days really. It looked as though I was going to have, at eighty odd, as though I was going to get a permanent job.

No doubt Fred brought the old models to life with his stories of the misery of trench warfare—the rain, mud, rats, lice, shellfire, explosions, fear—and felt satisfied that at last his story of the war was being told. And he believed that he was making a message of peace.

Yet in this profoundly important reconciliation with his wartime past, and between his own memory and the public story of the Anzacs, Fred's political critique has been displaced. The War Memorial and war films admit that for the poor bloody infantry 'war is hell', yet they still promote the digger hero and the Anzac legend. Fred is so pleased with the new recognition that he doesn't see how other aspects of his experience are still ignored. He doesn't consider the absence of any depiction of tensions between officers and other ranks in the AIF, or of the postwar disillusionment of many diggers, or of the analysis of the war as a business, all important themes in his discussion with me. Fred assumes that any museum depicting the horror of the western front must be a 'peace memorial', but doesn't recognise the political ambiguity of a museum in which little boys clamber over tanks and want to grow up to be soldiers.

Fred's memory still has a radical cutting edge. He still condemns the artificial patriotism of Anzac Day and carries his war medals on Palm Sunday peace rallies, using the new interest in the Anzacs to make his own criticism of war and Australian society. But he doesn't direct that critique at the Anzac writers and film makers who are the most powerful mythmakers of our time. The effectiveness of the 1980s Anzac legend is that it convinces even radical diggers like Fred that their story is being told, while subtly reworking the conservative sense of the war, national character and Australian history into an appropriate form for the 1980s. This 'hegemonic' process seems similar to that undergone by the diggers who did join the RSSILA and Anzac Day back in the 20s. On each occasion individuals are included and their memories selectively affirmed by the public rituals and meanings of remembrance. That affirmation may be essential for individual peace of mind, but in the process contradictory and challenging memories are displaced or repressed.

Fred Farrall's case study highlights the dynamic relationship between individual memory and national myth, and suggests ways in which oral history can be more than just the 'voice of the past'. Oral history can help us to understand how and why national mythologies work (and don't work) for individuals, and in our society generally. It can also reveal the possibilities, and difficulties, of developing and sustaining oppositional memories. These understandings can enable us to participate more effectively as historians and in collective struggle for more democratic and radical verisons of our past and of what we can become.

10

Gender and history

Gender history arose from women's dissatisfaction with their historical invisibility, but subsequently expanded its scope to investigate specifically masculine history as well.[1] While historians such as Alice Clark, Ivy Pinchbeck, Eileen Power and Mary Beard had been researching women's lives from early this century, it was during the 1960s' women's liberation movement that women began actively working to redress the absence of their lives and experience from most historical writing. Lerner pointed out that '[w]omen's history is indispensable and essential to the emancipation of women'.[2] Indeed, '[t]o be without history is to be trapped in a present where oppressive social relations appear natural and inevitable. Knowledge of history is knowledge that things have changed and do change.'[3] This chapter concentrates on the analysis of women and the development of feminine identities in history. While it is fair to say that gender historians have mainly written from a woman-centred perspective, a considerable proportion of the research to date deals with both women and men, and the relationship between the two. Nevertheless, only recently has masculinity been addressed as a topic in its own right. We aim here to outline the main theoretical directions taken by gender history, and to show the huge diversity of research mainly concerning women in the past.

One traditional category used to divide humanity is sex, that is, the biological difference between women and men. Since sex is only rarely subject to change, it is not a useful concept for most historians. 'Gender' has proved to be central, however, in its two major definitions: 'the cultural definitions of behaviour defined as appropriate to the sexes in a given society at a given time', and 'a constitutive element of social relationships based on perceived differences between the sexes, and . . . a primary way of signifying relationships of power'.[4] If gender is a social construction, then gender has a history and we can ask the questions: who makes gender and by what means, and how does it endure and change? Including a dimension of power relations is also important, since history writing has long involved discussions of power, whether in terms of movers in the political sphere or concerning the participants in struggles over class and race. These definitions of gender, and the male/female and sex/gender dichotomies thus constituted, led to two strands of feminist analysis.

One thread of gender history reflects the course of the feminist movement in general. In the United States, activists lobbied for equal rights and historians tended to focus on examining women's status and experience in the past, sometimes writing about famous women. Labarge, for example, attempted 'to bring to light the not inconsiderable achievements of a number of women from all levels of medieval society in Western Europe between the twelfth and the fifteenth centuries'.[5] Other investigations proposed a radical re-working of the historical process, including the periodization traditionally used. Joan Kelly described her initial brush with Gerda Lerner and women's history which resulted in her essay 'Did Women Have a Renaissance?' In this ground-breaking work, Kelly examined the notion that 'events that further the historical development of men, liberating them from natural, social or ideological constraints, have quite different, even opposite, effects upon women'. She went on to argue that 'there was no renaissance for women – at least, not during the Renaissance'.[6] The historical analysis of patriarchy gave a political edge to the writing of women's history, and 'raised the consciousness' of the historical profession regarding the status of women's history and women historians.[7]

In Britain, the Marxist backgrounds of many early historians of women meant that they attempted to combine a gender dimension with an existing class analysis. Sheila Rowbotham's Hidden from History, for example, asks 'in what conditions have women produced and reproduced their lives, both through their labour and through procreation'?[8] In a wonderful essay, Sally Alexander discussed the sexual division of labour in relation to the class struggle and demonstrated the difference that a feminist perspective could make to analyses of the industrial revolution, long the stage of the working-class man.[9] Attempts to examine gender and class simultaneously, however, proved problematic: it seemed that some aspects of oppression and experience were common to women of all ranks despite the differences in their lives. And this oppression could be attributed to men, rather than to the specific economic system under which the women lived.

Radical feminism sought to explain the subordination of women by pointing to male control over women's sexuality, including reproduction, often arguing that all human oppression is rooted in the biological heterosexual family. From an historian's viewpoint, this can lead to a sense of gender relations as static across time, an ahistorical patriarchy. Bennett discusses the problems as well as the advantages she sees in the use of 'patriarchy', suggesting that to avoid this term is to depoliticize feminist history to an unacceptable degree.[10]

These early, generally North American approaches were mainly based on the premise that all women were essentially the same, and, that in effect, they shared the concerns of white middle-class women.[11] In retrospect this essentialism is manifestly incorrect, and was vociferously criticized from the late 1970s by women of colour. bell hooks, for example, wrote that '[t]here is much evidence substantiating the reality that race and class identity creates differences in quality of life, social status, and lifestyle that take precedence over the common experience women share – differences which are rarely transcended'.[12] Jones demonstrates the overwhelming importance of race to gender history in *Labor of Love, Labor of Sorrow*. Her chapter on black women's work during slavery picks apart the differences between black and white, women and men, and status differences in all these groups, setting them in an economic and cultural background, and showing how black women in their multiple working roles were agents in preserving their own culture against enormous odds.[13] Vron Ware and Catherine Hall have also examined the role of racial difference in the construction of white femininity.[14]

In a second set of approaches, the historical dichotomy between women and men has drawn attention to the analytic potential of a variety of other dichotomies: nature/culture, work/family and public/private.[15] For example, among the Carolingian aristocracy, running the domestic activities of a household was the wife's business, while a husband was often occupied with matters of state or war: thus some sense of separation of public and private seemed to exist. Nevertheless, when household management included its economy, a wife could exercise considerable power. A Carolingian queen, for instance, was in charge of the royal treasury, a 'domestic trifle' in the king's eyes. Similarly, much research concerning the sexual division of labour has shown that the value of women's work decreased when the workplace became separated from the home. Then men were seen as 'workers' while women were merely concerned with the family, an activity not labelled 'work'. Investigating nature and culture, Natalie Davis discussed how, in early modern France, women's disorderliness was thought to be rooted in their nature, while male transgressions related to nurture, that is, the culture in which they were raised or lived. Since women could not help their 'unruly' natures, men bent upon sedition and riot would often disguise themselves as females.[16] In the main, however, historians have found these dichotomies, mainly developed by early feminist anthropologists, restrictive: the Carolingian example shows how problematic is the assumed correlation between male/female, public/private and power/domesticity.[17]

Problems with the two approaches so far discussed led historians to seek more incisive theories. Even despite the addition of race as a category of investigation, using the 'Big Three', that is, liberal, socialist/Marxist and radical feminism, to describe feminist thinking and the writing of women's history seemed to have lost its usefulness. Maynard argues that such labelling leads to the stereotyping and homogenizing of theoretical positions, and the exclusion of research that does not fit into a category. In addition, theories tend to remain simple and have no space to change over time: that is, their historical dimension is missing. Maynard maintains that theory is most usefully formulated in conjunction with empirical research and feminist history can only benefit if theory is permitted its evolutionary nature.[18] As historians have become aware of the simplistic nature of the notion of 'women' implicit in these early theories, we have moved to de-essentialize 'woman' in two major ways.

Firstly, since the divisions of gender, class and race seem inadequate, historians have begun to categorize women of the past as well in terms of ethnicity, sexual orientations, age, marital status, religious affiliation, and mental and physical disability. We have thus studied more diverse groups of women. Strobel, for example, examined the intersection of religion, class and gender, ethnicity and the effects of colonialism on women in Mombasa. Judith Brown situated the life of Benedetta Carlini in the context of religious and social attitudes to lesbianism in Renaissance Italy.[19] Despite the proliferation of categories of women in a social and historical sense, the political assumption that all women can be represented by 'women' still remains.[20] Historians, therefore, are now moving to examine how feminism has historically constructed 'women'.

Secondly, theorists have suggested that an essential category 'woman' (singular) does not exist due to the fragmentary nature of identity: each woman's subjectivity is divided and conflicting. Psychoanalysis offers tools for uncovering and interpreting subjectivity, which can be viewed as made up of unconscious ideas, partly the internalized givens of our (patriarchal) society, coupled with experience. A psychoanalytic feminist historian like Sally Alexander argues that '[p]sychoanalysis offers a reading of sexual difference rooted not in the sexual division of labour (which nevertheless organizes that difference), nor within nature, but through the unconscious and language', and that it is 'psychic processes which give a political movement its emotional power'. Thus psychoanalysis contributes to the understanding of power relations in society. She uses an emphasis, in part derived from the work of the psychoanalyst Lacan, on the power of language to examine, for example, the role of femininity and masculinity in working class language in the nineteenth century, and to show that women could not speak within the terms of radical popular speech. This in turn helps her to offer a coherent explanation of the background to the emergence of nineteenth-century feminism. More recently Alexander has discussed the features in common between psychoanalysis and feminism, especially feminist history.[21]

Alexander also points out the movement away from a psychoanalytic understanding of sexual difference in the work of a theorist like Joan Scott. Scott takes a deconstructive approach which, like psychoanalysis, focuses on language and discourse. So, for example, she examines discourses (ways of speaking and writing) concerning women workers in the writings of nineteenth-century French political economists.[22] In these texts, the women 'served at once as an object of study and a means of representing ideas about social order and social organization'.[23] Here not the women but discourses concerning them are the object of Scott's study. We cannot know about the reality of women's work through these discourses because they construct women's situation (as marginalized) at the same time as they describe them. All we can do is examine the workings of the discourses. Since the subjects of the discourses (the authors) are divided and changing (as all selves are), the subjects are decentred (they possess no unitary self) and thus there can be no omniscient authorial voice. While this is problematic for historians, in that experience becomes obsolete, it is useful for feminist historians since the rational man producing these discourses is fragmented and can be deconstructed. Thus the power inherent in his apparently rational knowledge can be defused. Female subjects are similarly decentred in this approach, but Canning suggests that this can be dangerous from a political viewpoint, since the female subject is still being recovered and made visible in history. One may argue, however, that recovering a multiplicity of female identities can only enrich our history.[24]

Maynard and Canning suggest that deconstruction can be useful to feminist historians as long as the notion of hierarchies of power is not totally removed, and the idea of the real is not abandoned. Experience is thus important and can show the interaction of cultural discourses and material processes. Canning, therefore, in examining social reform in Germany in the late nineteenth century, investigates the emergence of discourses (not only the hegemonic) and their material and ideological consequences, thence restoring the voices of both the subjects and objects of reform. She found that women's embodied experience 'opened the way for the transformations of consciousness and subjectivities'.[25] Thus recent directions in feminist history offer exciting ways both of reading and politicizing research.

One of the recent debates in women's history concerns the issues of continuity and change, a 'tension' which Bennett labels 'perhaps the oldest and most productive of historical themes'.[26] She argues that women's historians have tended to focus on moments of change, usually fitting women into the traditional periodization of history, even if they have demonstrated, with Kelly, that the effects of change were different for men and women. Using women's work as an example, Bennett suggests that although there has been considerable change in women's experience since, say, 1200, the overall structure of women's work in relation to men's is still similar. Therefore, it could be useful to discuss women's history in terms of this paradigm: 'there has been much *change* in women's lives, but little *transformation* in women's status in relation to men'.[27] By this means, women's history could keep its political edge as part of the fight to achieve transformation.

This challenge provoked differing responses. Greene showed how dealing with the complex relationship of continuity and change had enriched African women's history almost from the start. Offen, however, argued that while Bennett's view might be an appropriate model for pre-industrial women's history, it did not work for the nineteenth and twentieth centuries. Her final sentence does point up the pervasive nature of the problem: 'the many changes for the better that have marked most women's lives even in the last 50 years tend to make us . . . very impatient with the necessity to confront continuity in women's history'.[28] Lerner tended to side with Bennett, citing her own experience of arguing for long-term patriarchy in the face of accusations of ahistoricity. She suggested that we need to analyse both continuity and change in a holistic framework, to 'refine and complicate our analysis by noticing that different aspects or structures in society change at a different pace and with different effects'.[29]

This debate over continuity and change in some respects echoes the arguments between Scott and her critics concerning the prioritization of analyses of discourses over discussion of what happened in a more material sense. Bennett wants to focus on the continuities of discourses of patriarchy, arguing that these are at least as basic to women's history as is material evidence of changing experience. It may be that the illusion of transformation produced by material change is part of the discourse itself. Her project is then perhaps along the lines of Canning's work, discussed earlier.

The move away from theorizing an essential feminine and the fragmenting of the subject has convinced some gender historians of the necessity of studying men and masculinity. Baron argues that 'gender is present even when women are not', and that if we only investigate women, then ' "man" remains the universal subject against which women are defined in their particularity'.[30] Tosh also remarks that encouraging a history of masculinity is a subversive act: '[m]aking men visible as gendered subjects has major implications for all the historian's established themes: for family, labour and business, class and national identities, religion, education, and . . . for institutional politics too'.[31] While the issue of the power of men over women sorely needs addressing in terms of masculinity, Baron reminds us that power differentials between men also deserve attention.[32]

The first work on men's history concerned gay men, and historians demonstrated that homosexual and heterosexual identities have changed over time.[33] The preoccupations and definitions of masculinity have also altered. We can now, for example, compare medieval European masculinity with that of nineteenth-century Britain and America.[34]

A recent article demonstrates the possibilities of a truly gendered history, combining ideas both of the feminine and the masculine. Who ran the dairies in Sweden between 1850 and 1950 turned on the degree of mechanization and consequent masculinization in contrast to the links made between milk and dairy maids previously seen as 'natural'. In this project, Sommestad links gender, labour and cultural history using a variety of methods to produce a subtle interpretation of the dairy industry.[35] Broad vistas open from such research.

Like many British feminist historians of her generation, Catherine Hall came to women's history through an earlier engagement with issues of Marxist history. Her work, moving from a study of the housewife to issues of gender interwoven with those of the working classes, is broadly in line with the development of British feminism, with her investigation of masculinity as part of gender and her inclusion of an important focus on race and ethnicity. Hall's article, which follows, demonstrates a number of the themes in gender history which we have discussed. She links class, femininity and masculinity, and the separation between the sexes by examining economics, politics and society, and the ideological framework of nineteenth-century Birmingham.

What historiographical gaps led Hall to write on this subject? Why, in her opinion, did these gaps exist? Hall argues that gender 'played an important part in unifying the middle classes'. What examples does she give to back up this view? Much of the argument in this article is structured around the public/private dichotomy. What does this tell us in practice about women's experience? How useful, in your opinion, is this dichotomy as an analytical tool? What other areas of gendered experience might Hall have examined?

Notes

1 Bennett discusses the implications of using the terms 'gender history', 'feminist history' and 'women's history', in Judith M. Bennett, 'Feminism and History', *Gender and History*, 1 (1989), pp. 251–72.
2 Gerda Lerner, *The Creation of Patriarchy* (Oxford, 1986), p. 3.
3 Glenn Jordan and Chris Weedon, *Cultural Politics: Class, Gender, Race and the Postmodern World* (Oxford, 1995), p. 187.
4 Lerner, *The Creation of Patriarchy*, p. 238; Joan Scott, 'Gender: A Useful Category of Historical Analysis', *American Historical Review*, 19 (1986), p. 1067.
5 Margaret Wade Labarge, *A Small Sound of the Trumpet: Women in Medieval Life* (Boston, 1986), p. xiv.
6 Joan Kelly, *Women, History and Theory: The Essays of Joan Kelly* (Chicago, 1984), pp. xii–xiii, 19.
7 Joan Scott, 'Women's History', in Peter Burke (ed.), *New Perspectives on Historical Writing* (Cambridge, 1992), p. 46.
8 Sheila Rowbotham, *Hidden from History: 300 Years of Women's Oppression and the Fight Against It* (3rd edn, London, 1977), p. ix.

9 Sally Alexander, 'Women's Work in Nineteenth-century London: A Study of the Years 1820–50', in Juliet Mitchell and Anne Oakley (eds), *The Rights and Wrongs of Women* (Harmondsworth, 1976), pp. 59–111.

10 Bennett, 'Feminism and History', p. 259 ff.

11 Note, however, the British Marxist feminists' careful attention to issues of class.

12 bell hooks, *Feminist Theory: From Margin to Centre* (Boston, 1984), p. 4. See also Catherine Hall's discussion and references in *White, Male and Middle Class: Explorations in Feminism and History* (Cambridge, 1992), pp. 18–21. Note, however, exceptions to this exclusion, such as Gerda Lerner, *Black Women in White America: A Documentary History* (New York, 1972), a very early collection, and those mentioned by Hall.

13 Jacqueline Jones, ' "My Mother Was Much of a Woman": Slavery', in *Labor of Love, Labor of Sorrow: Black Women, Work, and the Family from Slavery to the Present* (New York, 1985), pp. 11–43.

14 Vron Ware, *Beyond the Pale: White Women, Racism and History* (London, 1992); see Hall, *White, Male and Middle Class*.

15 See Gisela Bock, 'Challenging Dichotomies: Perspectives on Women's History', in K. Offen, R. R. Pierson and J. Rendall (eds), *Writing Women's History: International Perspectives* (Bloomington, 1991), pp. 1–5.

16 Suzanne Fonay Wemple, *Women in Frankish Society: Marriage and the Cloister 500–900* (Philadelphia, 1981), pp. 97–9; see, for example, essays in Mary Prior (ed.), *Women in English Society, 1500–1800* (London, 1985); Natalie Zemon Davis, 'Women on Top', in *Society and Culture in Early Modern France* (Stanford, 1975), pp. 124–51.

17 This is not to say that any of the examples given are unnuanced in this way.

18 Mary Maynard, 'Beyond the "Big Three": The Development of Feminist Theory into the 1990s', *Women's History Review*, 4 (1995), pp. 261–7, 276.

19 Margaret Strobel, *Muslim Women in Mombasa, 1890–1975* (New Haven, 1979); Judith C. Brown, *Immodest Acts: The life of a Lesbian Nun in Renaissance Italy* (New York, 1986).

20 See Judith Butler, *Gender Trouble: Feminism and the Subversion of Identity* (New York, 1990), pp. 1–6. Note that the dichotomy between sex and gender is also now seen as a problematic division: *ibid.*, pp. 6–7, 106–11; Henrietta L. Moore, *A Passion for Difference: Essays in Anthropology and Gender* (Cambridge, 1994), pp. 8–72. I am indebted to Catherine Kingfisher for the latter reference.

21 Sally Alexander, 'Women, Class and Sexual Difference', *History Workshop*, 17 (1984), pp. 125–49, and 'Feminist History and Psychoanalysis', *History Workshop*, 32 (1991), pp. 128–33. See also the useful discussion of recent works on psychoanalysis and feminism by Judith Kegan Gardiner and Michèle Barrett in *Signs*, 17 (1992), pp. 435–66.

22 Note that 'discourse' has been defined in different ways. Foucault, for example, views discourse as including the parameters of what can be said, and the conditions under which it can be said. See the following chapter on poststructuralism for more detail.

23 Joan Scott, ' "L'ouvrière! Mot impie, sordide . . .": Women Workers in the Discourse of French Political Economy, 1840–1860', in *Gender and the Politics of History* (New York, 1988), pp. 139–63.

24 The preceding discussion is drawn from Maynard, 'The Big Three', pp. 269–81 and Kathleen Canning, 'Feminist History after the Linguistic Turn: Historicizing Discourse and Experience', *Signs*, 19 (1994), pp. 368–404.

25 Canning, 'Feminist History'.

26 Bennett, 'Confronting Continuity', *Journal of Women's History*, 9, 3 (1997), p. 73. See p. 89, n. 4, for earlier debate on this issue.

27 *Ibid.*, pp. 73–94, esp. p. 88.

28 Sandra E. Greene, 'A Perspective from African Women's History: Comment on "Confronting Continuity" ', and Karen Offen, 'A Comparative European Perspective: Comment on "Confronting Continuity" ', *Journal of Women's History*, 9, 3 (1997), pp. 95–104, 105–13.

29 Lerner, 'A Perspective from European and U. S. Women's History: Comment on "Confronting Continuity"', *Journal of Women's History*, 9, 3 (1997), pp. 114–18.
30 Ava Baron, 'On Looking at Men: Masculinity and the Making of a Gendered Working-Class History', in Ann-Louise Shapiro (ed.), *Feminists Revision History* (New Brunswick, 1994), pp. 148–50.
31 John Tosh, 'What Should Historians do with Masculinity? Reflections on Nineteenth-century Britain', *History Workshop Journal*, 38 (1994), pp. 179–80; Michael Roper and John Tosh (eds), 'Introduction: Historians and the Politics of Masculinity', in *Manful Assertions: Masculinities in Britain since 1800* (London, 1991), p. 1.
32 Baron, 'On Looking at Men', pp. 154–7.
33 See, for example, John Boswell, *Christianity, Social Tolerance, and Homosexuality: Gay People in Western Europe from the Beginning of the Christian Era to the Fourteenth Century* (Chicago, 1980).
34 Clare A. Lees (ed.), *Medieval Masculinities: Regarding Men in the Middle Ages* (Minneapolis, 1994), Roper and Tosh, *Manful Assertions*, and Mark C. Carnes and Clyde Griffen, *Meanings for Manhood: Constructions of Masculinity in Victorian America* (Chicago, 1990).
35 Lena Sommestad, 'Gendering Work, Interpreting Gender: The Masculinization of Dairy Work in Sweden, 1850–1950', *History Workshop Journal*, 37 (1994), pp. 57–75.

Additional reading

Alexander, Sally, 'Feminist History and Psychoanalysis', *History Workshop Journal*, 32 (1991), pp. 128–33.

Burton, Antoinette, ' "History" is Now: Feminist Theory and the Production of Historical Feminisms', *Women's History Review*, 1 (1992), pp. 25–38.

Jones, Jacqueline, *Labor of Love, Labor of Sorrow: Black Women, Work, and the Family from Slavery to the Present* (New York, 1985).

Kelly, Joan, *Women, History and Theory: The Essays of Joan Kelly* (Chicago, 1984).

Lerner, Gerda, *The Majority Finds its Past: Placing Women in History* (Oxford 1979).

Maynard, Steven, 'Rough Work and Rugged Men: The Social Construction of Masculinity in Working-class History', *Labour/Le Travail*, 23 (1989), pp. 159–69.

Parr, Joy, 'Gender History and Historical Practice', *The Canadian Historical Review*, 76 (1995), pp. 354–76.

Roper, Michael and John Tosh (eds), *Manful Assertions: Masculinities in Britain since 1800* (London, 1991).

Scott, Joan Wallach, *Gender and the Politics of History* (New York, 1988).

Scott, Joan Wallach (ed.), *Feminism and History* (Oxford, 1996).

Shapiro, Ann-Louise (ed.), *Feminists Revision History* (New Brunswick, 1994).

Smith-Rosenberg, Carroll, *Disorderly Conduct: Visions of Gender in Victorian America* (New York, 1985).

Stansell, Christine, *City of Women: Sex and Class in New York, 1789–1860* (Urbana, 1986).

GENDER DIVISIONS AND CLASS FORMATION IN THE BIRMINGHAM MIDDLE CLASS, 1780–1850
Catherine Hall

The flowering of socialist historiography in the last fifteen years, of which the History Workshop is of course one very important instance, has seen an enormous development in working-class and people's history. This development has not been complemented by an equivalent amount of research going on into the dominant classes; the emphasis for socialist historians has been on cultures of opposition and resistance and on the mechanisms of control and subordination, rather than on the culture of the ruling class. The same point can be made about feminist history, which in England has been profoundly influenced by the particular way in which social history has developed. The vast majority of the work done so far has been on working-class women and the working-class family. This is entirely understandable, particularly in a period when the importance of our struggle has been stressed politically, as it has been, for example, in the women's movement. For most socialists it is clearly more attractive to work on material which offers some assertion and celebration of resistance rather than on material which documents the continuing power, albeit often challenged, of the bourgeoisie. This does leave us, however, with a somewhat unbalanced historiography. Any discussion on the 'making of the English middle class' for example, is infinitely less well documented and theorised than it is on the working class. John Foster's work on the bourgeoisie in the *Class Struggle and the Industrial Revolution* provides us with a starting point, but there is little else that is easily available.

The work that is available on the 'making of the middle class' in the late eighteenth and early nineteenth centuries is not for the most part placed within a socialist framework (for example Briggs or McCord)[1] but it also faces us with a second problem—the absence of gender. The middle class is treated as male and the account of the formation of middle-class consciousness is structured around a series of public events in which women played no part: the imposition of

---

[1] N. McCord, *The Anti-Corn Law League 1836–1848*, London 1958.

income tax, the reaction to the Orders in Council, the Queen Caroline affair, the 1832 reform agitation and the Anti-Corn Law League are usually seen as the seminal moments in the emergence of the middle class as a powerful and self-confident class. Yet when we come to descriptions of the Victorian family much emphasis is placed on the part which domesticity played in middle-class culture and on the social importance of the home. That is to say the class once formed is seen as sexually divided but that process of division is taken as given. Since eighteenth-century middle-class women did not, as far as we can tell, lead the sheltered and domestically defined lives of their Victorian counterparts it seems important to explore the relation between the process of class formation and gender division. Was 'the separation of spheres' and the division between the public and the private a given or was it constructed as an integral part of middle-class culture and self-identity? The development of the middle class between 1780–1850 must be thought of as gendered; the ideals of masculinity and femininity are important to the middle-class sense of self and the ideology of separate spheres played a crucial part in the construction of a specifically middle-class culture—separating them off from both the aristocracy and gentry above them and the working class below them.

Gender divisions appear also to have played an important part in unifying the middle class. The class is significantly divided, as Marx pointed out, between the bourgeoisie and the petit bourgeoisie. Foster uses this division and helps to extend its meaning as does R. J. Morris in his work.[2] The two groups are divided economically, socially and politically, and much of the political history of the period is concerned with the shifting alliances between these two factions and other classes—as for example in Birmingham over the reform agitation and the movement into Chartism. But one of the ways in which the middle class was held together, despite the many divisive factors, was by their ideas about masculinity and femininity. Men came to share a sense of what constituted masculinity and women a sense of what constituted femininity. One central opposition was that masculinity meant having dependants, femininity meant being dependent. Clearly the available ideals were not always ones which could be acted upon—petit-bourgeois men would often need their wives to work in the business, but they would often also

[2] R. J. Morris, 'The making of the British middle class', unpublished paper delivered at the University of Birmingham Social History seminar 1979.

aspire for that not to be so. Clearly, looking at gender divisions as having a unifying theme within the middle class is only one way of approaching the subject; it would be equally possible to examine the way in which it unites men across classes, or the way in which it creates contradictions within the middle class which led to the emergence of bourgeois feminism in the second half of the nineteenth century. For the moment it seems important to stress the class-specific nature of masculinity and femininity in this period; the idea of a universal womanhood is weak in comparison with the idea of certain types of sexual differentiation being a necessary part of class identity. This may help to explain the relative absence and weakness of feminism in the first half of the nineteenth century—*Jane Eyre*, for example, provides us with a very sensitive account of the limitations of middle-class femininity which leaves little space for the possibility of a cross-class alliance.

This general theme of the importance of a sharpened division between men and women, between the public and the private, and its relation to class formation can be illustrated by looking at the development of the Birmingham middle class between 1780–1850. The account that is being offered here is extremely sketchy, but can perhaps provide a framework for further discussion. Birmingham was a fast growing industrial town by the late eighteenth century—its population of only 40,000 in 1780 had grown to 250,000 by 1850. Its wealth was built on the metal industries and had been made possible by its strategic position in relation to coal and iron. The town has usually been taken, following Briggs, as one dominated by small masters with workshops but recent work, particularly that of Clive Behagg, has somewhat modified this view and suggested that factory production was better established by the 1830s and 1840s than has usually been thought. Although Birmingham had been gradually expanding since the seventeenth century the impression by the end of the eighteenth century is that the middle class within the town are only gradually coming to realise their potential strength and power. Consequently, Birmingham offers us a relatively uncomplicated account of the emergence of the middle class—uncomplicated by factors such as the struggle between the well-established merchant class of the eighteenth century and the new manufacturers, which took place in Leeds.

We can briefly examine the separation between the sexes as it took place in Birmingham in this period at three levels—that of the economic, the political and social, and the ideological. If we look first at the economic level it is important to stress from the beginning that the ideology of separate spheres has an economic effectivity. Clearly, the crucial problem which faces us is the question of what the relation is between the emergence of separate spheres and the development of industrial capitalism. Is there any relation at all? At this point it is only possible to say that women seem to be increasingly defined as economically dependent in our period, and that this economic dependence has important consequences for the ways in which industrial capitalism developed. That is to say, we cannot argue that industrial capitalism would not have developed without sexual divisions, but that the increasingly polarised form which sexual divisions took affected the forms of capitalist social relations and of capitalist accumulation.

The legal framework for this is provided by the centrality of the notion of dependence in marriage—Blackstone's famous dictum that the husband and wife are one person and that person is the husband. Married women's property passed automatically to their husbands unless a settlement had been made in the courts of equity. Married women had no right to sue or be sued or to make contracts. For working-class families the idea of the family wage came to encapsulate the idea of economic dependence—though we know that in reality few working-class families were in a position to afford to do without the earnings which a wife could bring in. For middle-class families there is no equivalent concept, since the men do not earn wages, but still the economic dependence of the wife and children was assumed. Amongst the aristocracy and gentry patrilineal rights to property had been established for a very long time, but although the middle class broke with their 'betters' at many other points the connection between masculinity and property rights was not broken. Two inter-related points need to be made here; first, the importance of marriage settlements in capital accumulation and second, the sexual specificity of inheritance practices. Neither of these are new developments—making an advantageous marriage had long been a crucial way of getting on in the world but whereas in the past the gentry and aristocracy had for the most part used money so acquired to enlarge their houses or consolidate their estates, small producers were now using it to build up their businesses. Archibald Kenrick, for example, a Birmingham buckle maker in the late 1780s who was caught up in the decline of the buckle trade, got married in 1790 and used his wife's marriage settlement to set up in business as an iron founder in 1791. Sometimes the capital would come from a mother rather than a wife, for amongst the wealthier bourgeoisie it was common practice to have a marriage settlement which protected the wife's property whereas amongst the petit bourgeoisie this would have been very unusual.[3] Richard and George Cadbury both inherited a substantial amount from their mother Candia Barrow at a time when the family business was doing rather badly and used the capital to re-organise and re-vitalise the business.[4] Marx noted that the bourgeoisie practised partible inheritance rather than primogeniture and widows and daughters were not disinherited, but the forms of female inheritance tended increasingly to be linked to dependence. In general boys would receive an education and training to enter a business or profession and then would be given either a share in the existing family business or capital to invest in another business. Thomas Southall, for example, who came to Birmingham in 1820 to set up in business as a chemist, had been educated and apprenticed by his father who had a mixed retailing business himself and set up each of his sons in one aspect—one as a draper, one as a vintner and one as a chemist.[5] Daughters, on the other hand, would either be given a lump sum as a marriage settlement (though it should be noted that as Freer has demonstrated they were sometimes not allowed to marry because of the impossibility of removing capital from the business) or they would be left money in trust, usually under the aegis of a male relative, to provide an income for them together with their widowed mothers. The money in trust would then often be available for the male relatives to invest as they pleased. It should be pointed out, however, that widows amongst the petit bourgeoisie often were left the business to manage—it might be a shop, for example—and this different pattern of inheritance marks an important division between the two groups in the middle class. Right of dower were finally abolished in 1833 but long before that it was accepted that men had a right to leave their property as they liked. Life insurance developed in the late eighteenth century as a way of providing for dependants, and this provides another instance of the ways in which sexual divisions structure the forms of capitalist development—insurance companies became important sources of capital accumulation which could not have existed without the notion of dependants.

[3] R. A. Church, *Kenricks in Hardware. A family business 1791–1966*, Newton Abbot 1969.

[4] A. G. Gardiner, *Life of George Cadbury*, London 1923.

[5] C. Southall, *Records of the Southall Family*, London, private circulation, 1932.

Meanwhile the kinds of businesses which women were running seem to have altered. An examination of the Birmingham Directories reveals women working in surprising trades throughout our period; only in very small numbers it is true, but still they survived. To take a few examples, there were women brass founders at the end of the eighteenth century, a bedscrew maker and a coach maker in 1803, several women engaged in aspects of the gun trade in 1812, an engine cutter and an iron and steel merchant in 1821, plumbers and painters in the 1830s and 1840s, burnishers and brushmakers in the 1850s. There are certain trades in which women never seem to appear as the owners—awl-blade making, for example, or iron founders. But although the percentage of women to men engaged in business goes up rather than down in the early nineteenth century, at least according to the evidence provided by the directories, there seems to be a significant shift towards the concentration of women in certain trades. In the late eighteenth century women were well represented among the button makers, and button making was one of the staple trades of Birmingham. Sketchley's Directory of 1767 described the button trade as

> very extensive and distinguished under the following heads viz. Gilt, Plated, Silvered, Lacquered, and Pinchback, the beautiful new Manufactures Platina, Inlaid, Glass, Horn, Ivory, and Pearl: Metal Buttons such as Bath, Hard and Soft White etc. there is likewise made Link Buttons in most of the above Metals, as well as of Paste, Stones, etc. in short the vast variety of sorts in both Branches is really amazing, and we may with Truth aver that this is the cheapest Market in the world for these Articles.

But by the 1830s and 1840s women were concentrated in what became traditional women's trades—in dressmaking, millinery, school teaching and the retail trade. Women were no longer engaged as employers in the central productive trades of the town in any number, they were marginalised into the servicing sector, though, of course, it should be clear that many working-class women continued as employers in, for example, the metal trades. G. J. Holyoake described in his own autobiography his mother's disappearance from business:

> In those days horn buttons were made in Birmingham, and my mother had a workshop attached to the house, in which she conducted a business herself, employing several hands. She had the business before her marriage. She received the orders; made the purchases of materials; superintended the making of the goods; made out the accounts; and received the money; besides taking care of her growing family. There were no 'Rights

of Women' thought of in her day, but she was an entirely self-acting, managing mistress. . . . The button business died out while I was young, and from the remarks which came from merchants, I learned that my mother was the last maker of that kind of button in the town.[6]

It is worth remarking that his mother became a keen attender at Carr's Lane Chapel where, as we shall see, John Angell James taught the domestic subordination of women from the pulpit for fifty years. Women increasingly did not have the necessary forms of knowledge and expertise to enter many businesses—jobs were being redefined as managerial or skilled and, therefore, masculine. For instance, as Michael Ignatieff points out, women gaolers were actually excluded by statute as not fitted to the job.[7] Women could manage the family and the household but not the workshop of the factory. Furthermore, a whole series of new financial institutions were being developed in this period which also specifically excluded women—trusts, for example, and forms of partnership. Ivy Pinchbeck has argued that women were gradually being excluded from a sphere which they had previously occupied; it appears that in addition they were never allowed into a whole new economic sphere.

The separation of work from home obviously played an important part in this process of demarcation between men's work and women's work. That separation has often been thought of as the material basis of separate spheres. But once the enormous variety of types of middle-class housing has been established that argument can no longer be maintained. Separating work from home was one way of concretising the division between the sexes, but since it was often not possible it cannot be seen as the crucial factor in establishing domesticity. The many other ways in which the division was established have to be remembered. For doctors there could often be no separation, whereas for ironfounders the separation was almost automatic. In some trades the question of scale was vital—in the Birmingham metal trades some workshops had houses attached but in many cases they were separated. Sometimes there is a house attached and yet the chief employee lived there rather than the family. James Luckcock, for example, a Birmingham jeweller, when he was just starting up in business on his own not only lived next to his workshop but also used the labour of his wife and children. As soon as he

---

[6] G. S. Holyoake, *Sixty Years of an Agitator's Life*, London 1900.
[7] M. Ignatieff, *A Just Measure of Pain: The penitentiary in the industrial revolution 1750–1850*, London 1978.

could afford it he moved out, moved his manager into the house and his wife stopped working in the business.[8] Shopkeepers moving out from their premises and establishing a separate home for their families obviously lost the assistance of wives and daughters in the shop—Mrs Cadbury and her daughters all helped in the shop until the family moved out to Edgbaston.

So far I have tried to suggest that the economic basis for the expansion of the middle class is underpinned by assumptions of male superiority and female dependence. When we turn to the level of the political and social we can see the construction in our period of a whole new public world in which women have no part. That world is built on the basis of those who are defined as individuals—men with property. The Birmingham middle class had developed very little in the way of institutions or organisations by the mid-eighteenth century, but by the end of the century a whole new range had appeared. In the voluntary societies which sprang up in the town the male middle class learnt the skills of local government and established their rights to political leadership. These societies placed women on the periphery, if they placed them at all. Dorothy Thompson has argued in her piece on working-class women in radical politics that as organisations became more formal so women were increasingly marginalised. This process took place earlier for the middle class since their formal organisations were being established from the mid-eighteenth century. As in all other towns and cities Birmingham societies covered an extraordinarily wide range of activities through religion, philanthropy, trade, finance and politics. The personnel of these societies were often the same people who were finding their way onto the boards of local banks, insurance companies and municipal trusts. In Birmingham there were a series of political struggles between the governing classes and the middle class in our period which resulted in the formation of political organisations; to take one example, the Chamber of Commerce first founded in 1785 was the first attempt to bring manufacturers together to protect their interests and had no place for women. The Birmingham Political Union, the Complete Suffrage Union, the dissenting organisations to fight the established church, the organisations which worked for municipal incorporation and the Anti-Corn Law League were all male bodies. It is interesting to note that the BPU made provision for the wives of artisans in the Female Political Union, but

[8] J. Luckcock, *Sequel to Memoirs in Humble Life*, Birmingham 1825.

there was no equivalent provision for middle-class ladies. Women were not defined by the middle class as political—they could play a supportive role, for example fund-raising for the Anti-Corn Law League, but that marked the limit. The only political organisation where they did play an important part was the Anti-Slavery movement where separate ladies' auxiliary committees were set up after considerable argument within the movement, but even here their real contribution was seen as a moral one. Women were appealed to as mothers to save their 'dusky sisters' from having their children torn from them, but the activities which women could engage in to achieve this end were strictly limited. It was often the very weakness of women which was called upon—as God's poorest creatures perhaps their prayers would be heard.

Similarly the relationship of women to new social organisations and institutions was strictly limited. They could not be full members of the libraries and reading rooms, or of the literary and philo-sophical societies, even the concerts and assemblies were organised by male committees. When we look at the huge range of philan-thropic societies again the pattern is that men hold all the positions of power—more specifically the bourgeoisie provide the governors and managing committees while the petit bourgeoisie sit on the com-mittees of the less prestigious institutions and do much of the work of day-to-day maintenance. Women are used by some societies as vis-itors, or tract distributors, or collectors of money, but they are never, formally at least, the decision-makers. Even in an institution like the Protestant Dissenting Charity School which was a girls' school in Birmingham, there was a ladies' committee involved with the daily maintenance of the school, but any decision of any importance had to be taken to the men's managing committee and membership of the ladies' committee was achieved by recommendation from the men. Ladies could be subscribers to the charity but their subscrip-tions did not carry the same rights as it did for the men—for example, ladies could only sponsor girls to be taken into the school by proxy. The ladies' committee had no formal status and relied on informal contact with the men—often taking the form of a wife promising that she would pass some point onto her husband who would then raise it with the men. The constitution of most kinds of society, whether political or cultural, usually either formally excluded women from full membership by detailing the partial forms of membership they could enjoy, or never even thought the question worth dis-cussing. Women never became officers, they never spoke in large meetings, indeed they could not attend most meetings either because they were formally excluded or because the informal exclusion mechanisms were so powerful—for example, having meetings which were centred around a dinner in an hotel, a place where ladies were clearly not expected to be. Nor did women sign the letters and petitions which frequently appeared in the press.

So far I hope that I have succeeded in establishing that at both the economic and political level middle-class women were increasingly being defined as subordinate and marginal; anything to do with the public world was not their sphere. At the same time a whole range of new activities was opening up for men, and men had the freedom to move between the public and the private. It is at the level of the ideological that we find the articulation of separate spheres which informed many of the developments we have looked at. The period 1780–1850 saw a constant stream of pamphlets and books—the best known authors of which are probably Hannah More and Mrs Ellis—telling middle-class women how to behave. But domesticity was a local issue as well as a national one, and the activities of the Birmingham clergy in our period give us plenty of evidence of the way in which congregations were left in no uncertain state as to the relative positions of men and women. John Angell James has already been referred to. He was the minister of the most important Independent church in the town from 1805–57 and was recognised as a great preacher and prolific writer. Carr's Lane had a large membership drawn from both the bourgeoisie and the petit bourgeoisie whilst several hundred working-class children attended the sunday schools. James' books sold extremely well and his series on the family—*Female Piety, The Young Man's Friend and Guide Through Life to Immortality* and *The Family Monitor, or a Help to Domestic Happiness*—were long-term best-sellers.[9] James believed that women were naturally subordinate to men—it was decreed in the Scriptures.

> Every family, when directed as it should be, has a sacred character, inasmuch as the head of it acts the part of both the prophet and the priest of his household, in instructing them in the knowledge, and leading them in the worship, of God; and, at the same time, he discharges the duty of a king, by supporting a system of order, subordination and discipline.

[9] J. A. James, *Female Piety or the Young Woman's Friend and Guide Through Life to Immortality*, 5th edn, London 1856; *The Young Man's Friend and Guide Through Life to Immortality*, London 1851; *The Family Monitor, or a Help to Domestic Happiness*, London 1828.

Furthermore home was the woman's proper sphere:

> In general, it is for the benefit of a family that a married woman should devote her time and attention almost exclusively to the ways of her household: her place is in the centre of domestic cares. What is gained by her in the shop is oftentimes lost in the house, for want of the judicious superintendence of a mother and a mistress. Comforts and order, as well as money, are domestic wealth; and can these be rationally expected in the absence of female management? The children always want a mother's eye and hand, and should always have them. Let the husband, then, have the care of providing for the necessities of the family, and the wife that of personally superintending it: for this is the rule both of reason and of revelation.[10]

James' ideas were not simply spoken from the pulpit; the domination of such ideas was reflected in the organisation of his church and in the way in which church societies were established. Nor were such ideas limited to the Independents. The Quakers and the Unitarians were both important groups in Birmingham—many of the most influential families in the town were in one of these two groups. Both Quakers and Unitarians inherited a fairly radical view of the relations between the sexes but the Quakers in the late eighteenth century were moving towards a more formal subordination of women, introducing, for example, separate seating for men and women. However, the Quakers still offered women the opportunity to preach and thus guaranteed the maintenance of a spiritual significance for women. The Unitarians, though believing in some education for women, maintained strict lines of demarcation as has already been mentioned in connection with the Protestant Dissenting Charity School which was a Unitarian foundation. But it should not be thought that it was left to Nonconformists to lead the way on questions relating to the divisions between the sexes. Birmingham saw a considerable Evangelical revival from the late 1820s, associated with the influence of the Evangelical Bishop Ryder in Coventry and Lichfield. There is substantial evidence of the particular interest which Evangelicals took in the importance of a proper home and family life, and the belief they had in the centrality of the religious household in the struggle to reconstruct a properly Christian community. Christ Church, a large Anglican church in the town centre, was occupied by an enthu-

---

[10] J. A. James, *The Family Monitor* in *The Works of John Angell James*, ed. by T. F. James, Birmingham 1860, pp. 17 and 56.

siastic Evangelical in the 1830s who inaugurated separate benches for men and women; this led to a popular rhyme—

> The churches in general we everywhere find,
> Are places where men to the women are joined;
> But at *Christ Church*, it seems, they are more cruel hearted,
> For men and their wives are brought here to be parted.[11]

The Rev. John Casebow Barrett, the Rector of St Mary's from the late 1830s and a much liked and admired preacher in the town, maintained a similar stance from his pulpit as in his sermon in memory of Adelaide Queen Dowager in 1849 where he extolled her virtues as an ordinary wife and mother:

> As a *wife*, her conduct was unexceptionable; and her devotedness, her untiring watchfulness to her royal consort during his last illness, stands forth as a bright model, which the wives of England will do well to imitate. Here, in her husband's sick chamber, by day and by night, she—then the Queen of this mighty Empire—proved herself the fond and loving wife, the meek and feeling woman, the careful and uncomplaining nurse. *Her* eye watched the royal sufferer: *her* hand administered the medicine and smoothed the pillow: *her* feet hastened to give relief by changing the position: *her* voice was heard in prayer, or in the reading of the words of eternal life. And the character she then exhibited won for her—which we believe in her estimation was more precious than the crown she wore—the deep respect, the high approval, the honest, truthful love of an entire nation, which, whatever its other faults may be, is not insensible to those charities and affections, which give a bright and transcendent charm to the circle of every home.[12]

Domesticity often seems to have an important religious component, but it was not always expressed in religious terms. The local papers often carried poems with a heavily idealised domestic content and the ideology of separate spheres seems to have gained very wide usage. James Luckcock, a Birmingham jeweller who has already been mentioned, was deeply attached to the domestic ideal. He was a political Radical, a great friend of George Edmonds, and was very active in the Birmingham Political Union. There seems to be no evidence that an attachment to domesticity had anything to do with political allegiances—it appears to have cut cleanly across party lines. Luckcock loved the idea of both his home and garden—

[11] W. Bates, *A Pictorial Guide to Birmingham*, Birmingham 1849, p. 46.

[12] Rev. J. C. Barrett, *Sermon in Memory of Adelaide Queen Dowager*, Birmingham 1849, p. 11.

particularly the home which he built for his wife and himself for his retirement in leafy Edgbaston. His relationship with his two sons seems in reality to have been fraught with tension but he continued to celebrate poetically the joys of domestic bliss. At one point when he was seriously ill and thought he might die he composed a poem for his wife about himself; it was entitled *My Husband* and catalogued his thoughtfulness and caring qualities as a husband and father:

> Who first inspir'd my virgin breast,
> With tumults not to be express'd,
> And gave to life unwonted zest?
>   My husband.
> Who told me that his gains were small,
> But that whatever might befal,
> To me he'd gladly yield them all?
>   My husband.
> Who shun'd the giddy town's turmoil,
> To share with me the garden's toil,
> And joy with labour reconcile?
>   My husband.
> Whose arduous struggles long maintain'd
> Adversity's cold hand restrain'd
> And competence at length attain'd?
>   My husband's.[13]

Unfortunately we do not even know the name of James Luckcock's wife, much less her reaction to this poem!

In this brief and introductory paper I have tried to suggest how central gender divisions were to the middle class in the period 1780–1850. Definitions of masculinity and femininity played an important part in marking out the middle class, separating it off from other classes and creating strong links between disparate groups within that class—Nonconformists and Anglicans, Radicals and conservatives, the richer bourgeoisie and the petit bourgeoisie. The separation between the sexes was marked out at every level within the society—in manufacturing, the retail trades and the professions, in public life of all kinds, in the churches, in the press and in the home. The separation of spheres was one of the fundamental organising characteristics of middle-class society in late eighteenth and early nineteenth-century England.

[13] Luckcock, *op. cit.*, p. 49.

Further reading

Behagg, C., 'Custom, class and change: The trade societies of Birmingham', *Social History*, 4, no. 3, Oct. 1979.

Briggs, A., *Victorian Cities*, London 1963.

Foster, J., *Class Struggle and the Industrial Revolution*, London 1974.

Hall, C., 'The early formation of Victorian domestic ideology' in *Fit Work for Women* ed. by S. Burman, London 1979.

Pinchbeck, I., *Women Workers and the Industrial Revolution 1750–1850*, London 1969.

Thompson, D., 'Women and nineteenth-century radical politics: A lost dimension' in *The Rights and Wrongs of Women* ed. by J. Mitchell and A. Oakley, Harmondsworth 1976.

11

Postcolonial perspectives

In this chapter we look at the work and perspectives of historians in the field of postcolonial history. The period since the Second World War has often been described as the age of decolonization. During the past fifty years the European powers have either granted independence to, or been forced out of, colonies acquired over the previous three centuries. The magnitude of European imperial expansion may be measured both by its unprecedented geographic spread, and the millions of human beings whose lives and cultures were irretrievably altered. It is estimated that 'more than three-quarters of the people living in the world today have had their lives shaped by the experience of colonialism'.[1] Imperialism disrupted (or manipulated) traditional patterns of authority within indigenous cultures, created nation-states and integrated colonies into global capitalist production, primarily as sources of raw materials for the imperial power. The great majority of European colonies have acquired political independence, but in economic terms the colonized peoples remain among the most impoverished in the world.

Colonialism sanctioned the spread of Europeans throughout the world on both economic and cultural grounds. The imperial powers justified the migration of settlers into the lands under their control for a variety of reasons: security of strategic trade routes or resources, religious beliefs or overpopulation – the dispersal of unwanted people. The conquest of existing cultures and peoples was also legitimated by the strength of evolutionary thought during the nineteenth and early twentieth centuries. Drawing upon Charles Darwin's *On the Origin of Species* (1859) scholars in a wide variety of disciplines drew analogies between the stages of development evident in the natural world, governed by the 'survival of the fittest', and human society. In the white settler states, a term used to describe America, Argentina, Australia, Canada, Chile, New Zealand, South Africa and Uruguay, settlers pushed aside the indigenous population, frequently asserting that the land they found was empty or unused.[2] The following inscription from a memorial plaque, dedicated to a Cornish farming family on Great Barrier Island, New Zealand, illustrates this popular belief: 'The pioneer Medland family loved this district, where they, finding waste, produced worth.'[3]

Postcolonial historical writing began when the experience of imperialism and colonialism began to be questioned, and this process invariably entailed the revision or rejection of previous historical accounts which narrated European expansion as largely unproblematic. Postcolonial histories include the perspectives of the colonized and often revise the understanding of their experiences. The colonized peoples may be placed at the centre of the historical process. The continuing impact of colonialism is also central to postcolonial accounts of the past. Western narratives which focus upon modernization, the building of the nation-state and economic development in the old colonies have been challenged by alternative perspectives emphasizing the culture and agency of the colonized peoples. The empire is, indeed, writing back.[4]

The term postcolonial is relatively new, and is not without its critics.[5] Is it possible to characterize the historical experiences of so many different peoples under one label? The Australian aboriginal writer, Bobbi Sykes, pin-pointed one difference:

> Postcolonial . . . ? What!
> Did I miss something?
> Have they gone?[6]

In the white settler states the Europeans never went home. This has led the Australian historian Richard Nile to argue that 'these colonies of white settlement are not post-colonial in any sense other than that posited by a strict periodisation between pre-independence and post-independence. In every other respect they are instances of a continuing colonisation, in which the descendants of the original colonists remain dominant over the colonised indigenous peoples.'[7] It is possible to argue that excluding the 'white settler' states implies a static state of affairs in which the changing balance of power between colonized and colonizer does not receive recognition. In Australia, New Zealand and Canada, Aboriginal, Maori and First Nations' peoples are currently engaged in complex negotiations with their respective governments over the return of land and natural resources. Historians in these countries play a key role in reconstructing the historical process of land alienation.

Confining the term postcolonial to those nations from which the Europeans physically departed is also problematic in another respect: the imperial power does not have to be present to continue to exert considerable influence over its old dominions. Indeed, the colonial encounter may live on as either a dynamic or oppressive cultural and economic force long after the physical presence has gone.[8] Many politically independent countries remain economically dependent on, and culturally dominated by, the departed imperial power. While the British may have left India, they left behind intellectual, as well as physical, traces of their occupation; 'mind tracks' as well as train tracks. Among these are the European narratives of modernization, which Dipesh Chakrabarty argues dominate third-world histories.[9]

One of the most powerful critiques of imperialism and colonialism came from the pen of a French doctor, Frantz Fanon. First published in French in 1952, *Black Skin, White Masks* directly confronted both European racism and its corrosive effects upon the colonized peoples. Working in Algeria, then a French colony, Fanon came to empathize deeply with the Algerian independence movement and in 1961 published *The Wretched of the Earth*, 'a revolutionary manifesto of decolonization'.[10] The book is a passionate critique of European religious proselytizing and violent conquest:

> Leave this Europe where they are never done talking of Man, yet murder men everywhere they find them, at the corner of every one of their own streets, and in all the corners of the globe. For centuries they have stifled almost the whole of humanity in the name of a so-called spiritual experience.[11]

Fanon hoped that after liberation, 'nationalist consciousness [would] convert itself into a new social consciousness'. His hopes were not to be fulfilled; in many of the newly independent countries dictatorships or neo-colonial regimes took power. Indeed, there are many postcolonial scholars who have had to go into opposition, culturally and intellectually as well as politically, against their own leadership.[12]

Seventeen years later Edward Said wrote a searing indictment of the way in which French and British writers, in politics, literature and history, had characterized the different peoples conquered by Europeans. In *Orientalism: Western Conceptions of the Orient*, Said examined the production of knowledge about 'the orient' by European scholars. The precise geographical boundaries of the Orient have varied from inclusion of the whole of Asia to a more restricted focus upon those peoples closest to the 'imaginary boundary' between East and West, the Middle East and North Africa.[13] Said describes the Orient as 'not only adjacent to Europe; it is also the place of Europe's greatest and richest and oldest colonies . . . and one of its deepest and most recurring images of the *Other*'.[14] His critical examination of scholarly writing on the Orient has transformed the term orientalism from 'a more or less neutral denotation for "oriental scholarship"' to one with a distinctly 'pejorative connotation'.[15]

Said makes two fundamental arguments. First of all, he suggests that European scholars constructed an essentialist representation of non-Europeans, for whom he uses the term, the 'other'. By the term essentialist, Said means that a set of indispensable characteristics were ascribed to the Orient: politically, as unchanging/despotic or socially, as sensual and cruel. A binary opposition was established between East and West, in which inferior and antagonistic characteristics were enshrined in the concept of the Orient. This is the core of what Clifford has described as 'the key theoretical issue raised by *Orientalism* [which] concerns the status of all forms of thought and representation for dealing with the alien. Can one ultimately escape procedures of dichotomizing, restructuring and textualizing in the making of interpretative statements about foreign cultures and traditions?'[16]

The second major argument made by Said concerns the relationship between the representation of the Orient by Western scholars and imperialism. He argues that the fundamental tenets of orientalism became a 'science of imperialism', which justified the exploitation and domination by European powers. In this sense Said perceives 'orientalism' as a discourse in the terms understood by poststructuralists, in which knowledge was created and actively deployed in the exercise of imperial power. More recently Said has reiterated that 'no more glaring parallel exists between power and knowledge in the modern history of philology than in the case of Orientalism. Much of the information and knowledge about Islam and the Orient that was used by the colonial powers to justify their colonialism derived from Orientalist scholarship'.[17]

There are, of course, criticisms of Said's characterization of 'orientalism', many of which take the position that the European literature about the Orient was much more diverse and oppositional than Said allows.[18] Leaving this aside, Robert Young has also drawn our attention to a contradictory aspect of Said's overall argument. Said defines the discourse of 'orientalism' as a representation with little relationship to any reality, while also arguing that the knowledge generated by scholars of the Orient was actively employed by colonial administrators. In other words, 'at a certain moment Orientalism as representation did have to encounter the "actual" conditions of what was there, and . . . it showed itself effective at a material level as a form of power and control. How then can Said argue that the "Orient" is just a representation, if he also wants to claim that "Orientalism" provided the necessary knowledge for actual colonial conquest?'[19]

Postcolonial historical writing in the past twenty years has developed these two critiques of imperialism and colonialism by deconstructing colonialist discourses, and reconstructing the appalling scale of loss experienced by colonized and indigenous peoples. In many cases the European grand narratives of modernization, which place colonialism within a global trajectory of capitalist development, have been rejected and replaced by a history celebrating 'the virtues of the fragmentary, the local, and the subjugated'.[20] Arif Dirlik has concluded that 'the goal, indeed, is no less than to abolish all distinctions between center and periphery as well as all other "binarisms" that are allegedly a legacy of colonial(ist) ways of thinking and to reveal societies globally in their complex heterogeneity and contingency'.[21]

In this introduction we will look at two examples of postcolonial history, the first from Hawaii and the second, the 'subaltern studies' school of Indian history. These represent the two ends of a spectrum of postcolonial perspectives suggested by Indian historian Gyan Prakash. Looking at Indian history, Prakash locates the first challenge to Western historiography in the anti-imperial nationalist consciousness of the 1920s and 1930s: '[i]t was important for this historiography to claim that everything good in India – spirituality, Aryan origins, political ideas, art – had completely indigenous origins'.[22] The indigenous nationalist perspective on Hawaiian history, written by Lilikalā Kameʻeleihiwa, reflects this aspect of the postcolonial spectrum.

The question animating Kameʻeleihiwa's study is how and why indigenous Hawaiians lost their land and 'slipped to the bottom of society'.[23] She identifies the key event which led to the dispossession of indigenous Hawaiians in the 1848 Māhele, which legally transformed the Hawaiian system of land tenure from communal to private ownership. In an attempt to understand why the chiefly leadership allowed this to happen, Kameʻeleihiwa interprets the sequence of events through three metaphors which, she argues, successfully governed Hawaiian society over the preceding centuries. The three metaphors: 'cherishing the land', that 'everyone has their proper place' (defined specifically in the separation of the sexes and chiefly authority over the people), and 'a metaphor of incest', provide a model through which she seeks to understand the decisions of the paramount chief, the Moi'i, and the four Ali'i Nui (the political council).

There are many difficulties with this type of postcolonial history. In the course of the book, Kame'eleihiwa appears to argue the immutability of cultural inheritance and adopts the very essentialism rejected by Said. She concludes that only through the adoption of these traditional principles can the Hawaiian indigenous people once again live *pono* (in balance). Kame'eleihiwa's invocation of the past as the proper basis for contemporary society may also be perceived as a means to buttress the power of traditional indigenous elites.[24] Finally, Kame'eleihiwa argues that her comprehension of the metaphors implicit within the Hawaiian language enables her to assess more accurately the actions of the paramount chief. But it may be argued that she is still an 'outsider' in terms of time.[25]

Kame'eleihiwa's book also raises the controversial issue concerning who should write indigenous or postcolonial histories. Should the historical experiences of indigenous peoples and the 'subaltern' be reconstructed only by indigenous scholars? Does an emic perspective (that of an cultural insider) have greater merit than an etic perspective (that of an outsider)? In the early 1980s Edward Said warned against this 'kind of possessive exclusivism'.[26] The 'subaltern studies' historians have rejected the concept that postcolonial history can and should only be written by descendants of the colonized, subjugated peoples.[27] However, the indigenous peoples of the United States and the Pacific have been far less comfortable with the expropriation of tribal history by academic outsiders, and frequently seek to retain control over the transmission of fundamental cultural beliefs. The scholarly community in the Pacific has been riven by sharp debates on the issue.[28]

At the other end of the postcolonial spectrum of historical writing are the subaltern studies historians of India who employ contemporary methodology and theory to re-interpret the experience of colonialism. The fundamental perspective of subaltern studies is very simple: 'that hitherto Indian history had been written from a colonialist and elitist point of view, whereas a large part of Indian history has been made by the subaltern classes'. The defining concept of the subaltern classes is derived from the influential twentieth-century Italian Marxist Antonio Gramsci.[29] The subaltern are those of inferior rank, whether of class, caste, age, gender or in any other way. Arguing that Indian history had largely been written from the perspective of the elite, the subaltern studies historians reject the conventional nationalist history of India which 'seeks to replicate in its own history the history of the modern state in Europe'.[30] From 1982 onwards a group of historians, led by Ranajit Guha, published several volumes of essays attempting to answer the question 'why, given numerical advantage, the justice of their cause, the great duration of their struggle, the Indian people were subaltern, why they were suppressed'.[31]

Ranajit Guha has addressed this question in a major study of peasant insurgency in India.[32] His aim is to reconstruct the Indian peasant consciousness from descriptions of 117 uprisings over less than a century of British rule. In this sense, Guha shares many of the same concerns as 'historians from below'. The peasant uprisings, Guha argues, were the major source of unrelenting resistance to British rule, and he concludes that 'Indian nationalism . . . derived much of its striking power from a subaltern tradition'.[33] In this he challenges those interpretations of Indian history from both right and left-wing perspectives that relegate peasant uprisings to the status of spontaneous uprisings, pre-history for either the nationalist or socialist/communist movements.

Both Guha's study of peasant insurgency and Kame'eleihiwa's *Native Land and Foreign Desires* illustrate one of the major problems facing postcolonial historians. Many of the subordinate classes and indigenous peoples have left few written records, and their voice must be reconstituted through the official reports of the colonizer. Kame'eleihiwa utilizes the descriptions of encounters with the Moi'i (paramount chief) and Ali'i Nui (political council) written by European travellers, missionaries and anthropologists relatively uncritically. This is not the case with Ranajit Guha, who utilizes the tools of poststructural analysis (see following chapter) to find the voice of the 'subaltern' in the British reports on peasant insurgency. He comments ironically that the 'fear which haunts all authority based on force, made careful archivists of them'.[34] Within these copious records Guha suggests that the 'mutually contradictory perceptions' of elite and subaltern are so firmly entrenched that 'it should be possible, by reversing their values, to derive the implicit terms of the other. When, therefore, an official document speaks of badmashes as participants in rural disturbances, this does not mean (going by the normal sense of that Urdu word) any ordinary collection of rascals but peasants involved in a militant agrarian struggle.'[35]

It is clear from both these examples that problems of representation have not vanished, and that postcolonial historians face a difficult task in reconstructing the asymmetrical European/indigenous encounter and the continuing consequences of colonialism without recourse to binary or essentialist interpretations of culture. Furthermore, it has been argued that the postcolonial rejection of European grand narratives, particularly that of capitalist expansion, may obscure the strongest single historical narrative relevant to the contemporary plight of indigenous and subaltern peoples.[36] Dipesh Chakrabarty suggests that the way forward for postcolonial historians does not lie in cultural relativism, nativist histories or the rejection of modernity, but in critical engagement with the concepts and ideas that underpin and legitimize the nation-state:

> I ask for a history that deliberately makes visible, within the very structure of its narrative forms, its own repressive strategies and practices, the part it plays in collusion with the narratives of citizenships in assimilating to the projects of the modern state all other possibilities of human solidarity.[37]

This book began with empiricism, a theory of history largely employed in documenting the rise and growth of the nation-state. Some postcolonial historians now suggest that the modernizing narrative of the nation-state has become global and oppressive, denying the legitimacy of alternative and heterogeneous versions of the past. But one of the difficulties faced by postcolonial scholars seeking to re-interpret the experience of colonialism from an indigenous perspective is combining Western epistemology, partly dictated by the nature of written sources, with radically different cosmologies of indigenous oral cultures.[38] This difficulty is evident in a study of Aboriginal murder and dispossession in Western Australia during the 1890s. Howard Pedersen was invited by Banjo Woorunmurra to write a history of the resistance by the Bunaba people, and the leader Jandamarra, to white colonization and the loss of their lands. The account was to draw on both the Bunaba people's oral history and the colonizer's written documents. Pedersen concluded that he was unable to write the book from an Aboriginal perspective:

> I quickly realised that a white historian could not reflect in writing the essence of the Bunaba stories. Jandamarra was magic – a supernatural being who could not be destroyed by police or settler bullets. He could only be

challenged by an Aboriginal man who also possessed these powers. Much of the Bunaba story is about the spiritual significance of land and the law which flows from it. The integration of these stories into a western historical narrative is highly problematic. Much of the information is secret and cannot be written for general public consumption. Also Aboriginal perceptions of the past and explanations about why certain events occurred do not sit easily within western historical chronology and its understandings of cause and effect.[39]

The reading which follows is by Henrietta Whiteman, a professor in the Native American Studies programme at the University of Montana, whose research has examined the 'forced assimilation' of the Cheyenne-Arapaho through the system of education.[40] In this essay, Whiteman describes an alternative history, based upon the cosmology of the Cheyenne and the story of her great-grandmother, White Buffalo Woman. Can you identify the differences between the cosmology of mainstream empirical histories, and that of the Cheyenne? What are the dynamic factors of change in Cheyenne history, and how do these differ from those commonly espoused by empirical historians? Whiteman includes both an emic and etic perspective in her historical interpretation; do you think that she is able to combine them successfully? She concludes that the 'Cheyenne sense of history is one of power, majesty, mystery, and awe'. Does this differ from 'Western' historical narratives, and if so, in what ways? Finally, what is your response to her challenge: is the Cheyenne version of the past 'authentic history'?

Notes

1 Bill Ashcroft, Gareth Griffiths and Helen Tiffin, *The Empire Writes Back: Theory and Practice in Post-Colonial Literatures* (London, 1989), p. 1.

2 See Donald Denoon, *Settler Capitalism: The Dynamics of Dependent Development in the Southern Hemisphere* (Oxford, 1983). For discussion concerning the inclusion of the United States see Amy Kaplan, 'Left Alone with America: The Absence of Empire in the Study of American Culture', in Amy Kaplan and Donald Pease (eds), *Cultures of United States Imperialism* (Durham, 1993), pp. 3–21; Gesa Mackenthun, 'Adding Empire to the Study of American Culture', *Journal of American Studies*, 30 (1996), pp. 263–9.

3 Grace M. Medland, *Great Barrier Calls* (Auckland, 1969), p. 119.

4 Ashcroft, Griffiths and Tiffin, *The Empire Writes Back*. The term postcolonial is certainly present in the historical discourse, but it has a longer history and is better established in critical literary theory. However, the literary definition of postcolonial writing employed by the authors above is very wide, and includes all writing 'affected by imperialism'.

5 For discussion of the conceptual problems, see Anne McClintock, 'The Angel of Progress: Pitfalls of the Term "Postcolonialism"', in Francis Barker *et al.* (eds), *Colonial Discourse/Postcolonial Theory* (Manchester, 1994); Bart Moore-Gilbert, *Postcolonial Theory: Contexts, Practices, Politics* (London, 1997), pp. 5–33.

6 Cited in Linda Tuhiwai Smith, Editorial, *Access: Contemporary Themes in Educational Inquiry*, 11, 2 (1992), p. i. I am grateful to Joan Gibbons for this reference.

7 Richard Nile (ed.), *Australian Civilisation* (Melbourne, 1994), p. 223.

8 McClintock, 'The Angel of Progress', p. 259, argues that the term postcolonial 'actively obscures the continuities and discontinuities of US power around the globe'.

9 Dipesh Chakrabarty, 'Postcoloniality and the Artifice of History: Who Speaks for "Indian" Pasts?', *Representations*, 37 (1992), pp. 4–5. See also Jonathan White (ed.), *Recasting the World: Writing after Colonialism* (Baltimore, 1993), pp. 3–16.

10 Robert Young, *White Mythologies: Writing History and the West* (London, 1990), pp. 119–20.

11 Frantz Fanon, *The Wretched of the Earth* (London, 1961), p. 251.

12 Edward Said, foreword to Ranajit Guha and Gayatri Chakravorty Spivak (eds), *Selected Subaltern Studies* (Delhi, 1988), p. ix.

13 Ulrike Freitag, 'The Critique of Orientalism', in Michael Bentley (ed.), *Companion to Historiography* (London, 1997), p. 621.

14 Edward Said, *Orientalism: Western Conceptions of the Orient* (New York, 1978), p. 1. The Orient is not precisely defined, but appears to include India and the Bible-lands: see p. 4.

15 Freitag, 'The Critique of Orientalism', pp. 620–1.

16 J. Clifford, 'Orientalism', *History and Theory*, 19, 2 (1980), pp. 209–10.

17 Edward Said, 'East Isn't East: The Impending End of the Age of Orientalism', *Times Literary Supplement*, 3 February 1995, p. 4.

18 See Ernest Gellner, 'The Mightier Pen? Edward Said and the Double Standards of Inside-out Colonialism', *Times Literary Supplement*, 19 February 1993, pp. 3–4; C. A. Bayly, 'The Indian Empire and the British Imagination', *Times Literary Supplement*, 12 July 1996, p. 29.

19 Young, *White Mythologies*, p. 129.

20 Partha Chatterjee, *The Nation and its Fragments: Colonial and Postcolonial Histories* (Princeton, 1993), p. xi.

21 Arif Dirlik, 'The Postcolonial Aura: Third World Criticism in the Age of Global Capitalism', *Critical Inquiry*, 20, 2 (Winter 1994), p. 329.

22 Gyan Prakash, 'Writing Post-Orientalist Histories of the Third World: Perspectives from Indian Historiography', *Comparative Studies in Society and History*, 32 (1990), pp. 388–9.

23 Lilikalā Kame'eleihiwa, *Native Land and Foreign Desires/Pehea Lā E Pono Ai?* (Honolulu, 1992), p. 15.

24 See Roger Keesing, 'Creating the Past: Custom and Identity in the Contemporary Pacific', *The Contemporary Pacific*, 1, 1 and 2 (Spring and Fall 1989), pp. 19–42; Epeli Hau'ofa, 'The New South Pacific Society: Integration and Independence', in Antony Hooper *et al.*, *Class and Culture in the South Pacific* (Auckland, 1987), pp. 2–3.

25 See the discussion in Frederic Gleach, *Powhatan's World and Colonial Virginia* (Lincoln, Neb., 1997), pp. 7–8.

26 Edward W. Said, 'Orientalism Reconsidered', in Francis Barker *et al.*, *Literature, Politics and Theory* (London, 1986), p. 229.

27 See Gayatri Chakravorty Spivak, 'Questions of Multi-culturalism', in Sarah Harasym (ed.), *The Post-Colonial Critic: Interviews, Strategies, Dialogues* (New York, 1990), pp. 62–3.

28 See Haunani-Kay Trask, 'Natives and Anthropologists: The Colonial Struggle', *The Contemporary Pacific*, 3 (1991), pp. 159–67; Kara Puketapu and Keri Kaa 'He taonga nui, te tupato', *The New Zealand Listener*, 24 September 1983, p. 98.

29 From the foreword by Said, in Guha and Spivak, *Selected Subaltern Studies*, pp. v–vi.

30 See Chatterjee, *The Nation and its Fragments*, p. 5.

31 *Ibid.*, p. vii.

32 Ranajit Guha, *Elementary Aspects of Peasant Insurgency in Colonial India* (Delhi, 1983).
33 *Ibid.*, p. 335.
34 *Ibid.*, p. 14.
35 *Ibid.*, p. 16.
36 Rosalind O'Hanlon and David Washbrook, 'After Orientalism: Culture, Criticism and Politics in the Third World', *Comparative Studies in Society and History*, 34 (1992), p. 166; see also Dirlik, 'The Postcolonial Aura', pp. 348–56.
37 Chakrabarty, 'Postcoloniality and the Artifice of History', p. 23.
38 See Calvin Martin, 'The Metaphysics of Writing Indian-White History', in Calvin Martin (ed.), *The American Indian and the Problem of History* (New York, 1987), pp. 27–34.
39 Howard Pedersen and Banjo Woorunmurra, *Jandamarra and the Bunaba Resistance* (Broome, 1995), p. xiii.
40 Colin G. Calloway, *New Directions in American Indian History* (Oklahoma, 1988), p. 89.

Additional reading

Chakrabarty, Dipesh, 'Postcoloniality and the Artifice of History: Who Speaks for Indian Pasts?', *Representations*, 37 (1992), pp. 1–26.

Dirlik, Arif, 'The Postcolonial Aura: Third World Criticism in the Age of Global Capitalism', *Critical Inquiry*, 20, 2 (Winter 1994), pp. 328–56.

Fanon, Frantz, *The Wretched of the Earth* (London, [1961] 1965).

Guha, Ranajit, *Elementary Aspects of Peasant Insurgency in Colonial India* (Delhi, 1983).

Guha, Ranajit and Gayatri Chakravorty Spivak (eds), *Selected Subaltern Studies* (Delhi, 1988).

Kame'eleihiwa, Lilikalā *Native Land and Foreign Desires/Pehea Lā E Pono Ai?* (Honolulu, 1992).

Martin, Calvin, 'The Metaphysics of Writing Indian-White History', in Calvin Martin (ed.), *The American Indian and the Problem of History* (New York, 1987).

O'Hanlon, Rosalind and David Washbrook, 'After Orientalism: Culture, Criticism and Politics in the Third World', *Comparative Studies in Society and History*, 34 (1992), pp. 141–67.

Pedersen, Howard and Banjo Woorunmurra, *Jandamarra and the Bunaba Resistance* (Broome, 1995).

Prakash, Gyan, 'Writing Post-Orientalist Histories of the Third World: Perspectives from Indian Historiography', *Comparative Studies in Society and History*, 32 (1990), pp. 383–408.

Richter, Daniel, 'Whose Indian History?', *The William and Mary Quarterly*, 50 (1993), pp. 379–93.

Said, Edward W., *Orientalism: Western Conceptions of the Orient* (New York, 1978).

Said, Edward W., 'Orientalism Reconsidered', in Francis Barker *et al.*, *Literature, Politics and Theory* (London, 1986).

WHITE BUFFALO WOMAN
Henrietta Whiteman

The Grandfather of all grandfathers has existed for all time in all space. He created a universe filled with life and His creation was characterized by beauty, harmony, balance, and interdependence. He considered the Earth Woman to be His most beautiful creation and He intensely loved the human beings. He had made a good world in which His beloved children, the human beings, were to live in a sacred manner.

The Cheyenne Keepers of knowledge, traditions, language, and the spiritual ways maintain a detailed form of this creation story in their oral history. They have taught numerous generations of their children the story of their sacred beginnings. American Indian tribal histories begin with the act of creation. Their unique tribal origins are deeply rooted in the land and in creation, which took place long ago. Unfortunately, the ancient oral histories of these culturally disparate people have been excluded from American history.

To rectify gross historical distortion, White Buffalo Woman and her great-granddaughter will present an oral history and Cheyenne view of history. Their story will cover the important historical events of Cheyennes on their road of life around this island world, which they have walked for thousands of years.

White Buffalo Woman, my great-grandmother, was taught through the oral tradition, just as her mother and grandmothers had been taught. Although White Buffalo Woman began her journey with the people in 1852, she was knowledgeable about their collective tribal experiences beginning with creation. In the way of her people, she, too, understood that the past lives in Cheyenne history. She learned about Sweet Medicine and Erect Horns, the two great compassionate prophets. They had brought the transcendently powerful Sacred Arrows and the Sacred Buffalo Hat and their accompanying ceremonies, the Arrow Renewal and the Sun Dance (Medicine Lodge), as blessings from their Grandfather.

She was taught that the spiritual center of the world was Bear Butte, the lone mountain located near present Sturgis, South Dakota, which is a part of the Black Hills. Cheyennes translate their name for Bear Butte into English as 'the hill that gives,' or 'the giving hill.' They call it that because Sweet Medicine brought their Sacred Arrows and way of life from this holy mountain. Throughout time, many individuals have fasted there or made pilgrimages just to experience its sacredness or to receive the blessings that flow from within it.

Cheyenne sacred history dominates all of life. The act of creation is preserved in their two major ceremonials, the Arrow Renewal and the Sun Dance. The teachings of their prophets are made spiritually manifest in these ceremonies. The Keeper of Sacred Arrows, who represents Sweet Medicine, and who is the highest spiritual leader of the tribe, has said that Cheyennes keep this earth alive through their ceremonies.

Tribal historians divide Cheyenne history into four broad periods and remember each period by an outstanding event rather than by dates. They refer to their earliest experiences as the ancient time when they lived in the far northeast. They believe they lived in Canada in the area between the Great Lakes on the south and Hudson Bay on the north. The historian-elders say they lived there for a long time but were decimated by a terrible epidemic, which left many of them orphans.

The grieving survivors moved south, into their second period of history, which Cheyennes say was the time of the dogs. They tamed the huge part-wolf dogs and, thereafter, walked with them on their road of life. After some time, they entered their third historical period, which the aged wise ones refer to as the time of the buffalo. Compared to earlier times, this was a time of abundance, with the buffalo becoming the people's economic base. The tribe pursued this animal deep into the interior of the Plains.

Finally, on the vast northern Plains the Cheyennes entered into the time of the horse, the last period of history. Long before, Sweet Medicine had described a horse to them. He said they would come to an animal with large flashing eyes and a long tail. It would carry them and their arrows on its back to distant places and they, the people, would become as restless as the animals they rode. Within a brief quarter of a century after acquiring the horse, Cheyennes developed into the classic equestrian hunters of American history. Both the horse and buffalo had a strong impact upon their lives.

Sweet Medicine had predicted that white-skinned strangers would cause even more drastic changes in their way of life. He said they would meet them in the direction from where the sun rises, and he described the unfortunate effects of acculturation, primarily the result of education. He told them that these people would make life easier with many good and wonderful things, such as guns and other items made of steel. Tragically, however, the strangers would attempt to superimpose their values of aggressiveness, materialism, rapacity, and egoism, which would cause cultural disorientation among many Cheyenne youth.

The prophet advised them to be cautious in their association with these people, whom they would call *ve?ho?e*. Thus, white people eventually came to be known by Sweet Medicine's name for them, the same Cheyenne term that means spider. Some elders also say their name is a form of the tribal word that means to be wrapped or confined in something, which is based upon the white strangers' tight-fitting clothing. The connotations are noteworthy from a Cheyenne viewpoint. If white people are wrapped up, they are often narrowly exclusive, insular, and illiberal. If they are not liberal, they are often prejudiced, bigoted, and intolerant. If they are intolerant, they limit other people's freedom. The words and actions of *ve?ho?e* are consistent in that white people have been generally intolerant of everything Cheyenne or everything different, as evidenced by the absence of Indians from American history. White egoism has taken precedence over the presentation of authentic Indian history.

Perhaps because of the trauma and disruption to their lives, only fragments of the initial Cheyenne-white contact have been transmitted in tribal oral history. The Cheyennes were divided into ten bands and came together only for their ceremonials. Consequently, each band must have been contacted at different times under different circumstances. White Buffalo Woman stated that many Cheyennes used to flee from white people and the strange odor they had about them. From a pragmatic point of view, this odor, which had the same effect as a murderer's stench, caused game to avoid the Cheyennes, which threatened their survival as a people. More important, however, from a cultural perspective, they remembered the warning of Sweet Medicine and wished to avoid the misfortune that association with whites assuredly would bring.

White Buffalo Woman's daughter, Crooked Nose Woman, who was born in 1887, did not know the exact details of contact. She stated, however, that when some Cheyenne men saw their first white men, a Cheyenne went up to one of them in a spirit of friendship, shook his hand, and using the male greeting for hello, said, 'Haahe! Englishman.' She also observed that this took place far to the east, on the opposite shore of a big river, which the Cheyennes had to cross in round boats, using sticks as oars. This was probably the Mississippi River, which they refer to as 'The Big River.' White historians agree that initial Cheyenne-white contact occurred in 1680 in the vicinity of present-day Peoria, Illinois, at Fort Crèvecoeur, La Salle's post near the Mississippi River.

Oral history is a living history in that the learners are involved with the historian on a personal level. They hear, listen, remember, and memorize events expressed in the flowing, soft sounds of their own language, describing the collective experiences of the people just as if they happened only the moment before. Their history is more than cold, impersonal words on pieces of paper. Even today, removed by four generations, I know much of what my great-grandmother White Buffalo Woman knew. I, however, have studied white American history, thereby complementing my oral history background.

Tribal history has no memory as to where White Buffalo Woman was born. We know that she was born in 1852, a year after some of the northern Plains tribes, including the Cheyennes, signed the Fort Laramie Treaty. It has been said that she was a beautiful child, with light brown, naturally curly hair, who matured into a phenomenally beautiful lady. Those who knew her have often lamented that none of her many descendants inherited her striking beauty.

The period around the time of White Buffalo Woman's birth was critical. For several years white emigrants had been streaming across Cheyenne hunting grounds on their way west, carrying strange diseases for which the people had developed no natural immunity. In their rush to find gold they spread the 'big cramps' among the Cheyennes, which was so devastating that the band structure was virtually destroyed. It is said that half the tribe died of cholera in 1849.

Disease was only one of the lethal and disorienting results of Cheyenne contact with whites. The ve?ho?e acted as Sweet Medicine had predicted, and White Buffalo Woman witnessed their destructive aggressiveness. White land greed rapidly eroded their once vast land holdings, which became smaller with each successive treaty. The southern bands of Cheyennes and Arapahoes signed the Treaty of Fort Wise on February 28, 1861, in which they agreed to live on a small reservation in southwestern Colorado Territory.

Black Kettle led the band to which White Buffalo Woman belonged, and the band included a large number of mixed-blood Cheyennes and Lakotas. In response to Governor Evans's proclamation, they had declared themselves to be friendly by surrendering at Fort Lyons in Colorado Territory. Black Kettle's Cheyennes and Left

Hand's band of Arapahoes were camped along Sand Creek, assuming they were there under military protection.

Unfortunately, Coloradans operated on other assumptions. They were anticipating statehood, and wanted to extinguish Indian title to Colorado lands by forcing the removal of all the Indians from the territory. They also feared an Indian uprising. Individuals like John Milton Chivington, a former Methodist minister, had political ambitions. He had become a military officer, and on the morning of November 29, 1864, he led his men in a surprise attack upon the sleeping camp of Cheyennes and Arapahoes at Sand Creek. Black Kettle attempted to stop the soldiers by tying an American flag and a white flag to a long lodgepole.

The ruthless slaughter and savage mutilation of the dead continued unabated, however. When it was over, 137 Cheyennes and Arapahoes lay dead. Only twenty-eight of them were men, the rest women and children. White Buffalo Woman somehow managed to escape. Congressional and military investigations were conducted and, although Chivington and other officers were found guilty, no one was ever punished.

Immediately following the massacre at Sand Creek, Black Kettle took his band south. He hoped to avoid further conflict and, thereby, remain at peace. White Buffalo Woman and her family were among the approximately four hundred Cheyennes, representing about eighty lodges, who followed their peaceable chief south.

Treaty-making intensified. The southern Cheyennes and Arapahoes subsequently signed the Treaty of Little Arkansas on October 14, 1865, agreeing to settle on a reservation in Kansas and the Indian Territory (Oklahoma). Three years later, on October 28, 1867, the tribes negotiated the Treaty at Medicine Lodge, the last they signed with the United States Government. They once again agreed to live in peace, made even more land cessions, and consented to live on a reservation in the Indian Territory. Black Kettle signed both treaties.

Believing they were finally at peace, Black Kettle's band was camped along the Washita River in present southwestern Oklahoma. On the morning of November 27, 1868, the nightmare of Sand Creek was repeated. Lieutenant-Colonel George Armstrong Custer and his men attacked the sleeping camp while the military band played 'Garry Owen.' Although Custer estimated 103 dead Cheyennes, later figures place the number between twenty-seven and sixty, most of them woman and children. Black Kettle was among the dead. All he had wanted was to be at peace with the whites—the people who killed him.

Again White Buffalo Woman survived. Within her lifetime she had seen the once large island home of her people become very small. On August 10, 1869, President Ulysses S. Grant created by executive order a new reservation for the southern Cheyennes and Arapahoes. It was on that reservation that White Buffalo Woman and her husband, Big White Man, reared their children. One of them, Spotted Horse Fred Mann, was born in 1890. He later married Lucy White Bear and they had two children, the younger, a son named Holy Bird Henry Mann, born in 1915. Henry's mother died when he was seven or nine months old, and White Buffalo Woman reared him and his sister Mariam. Henry married Day Woman Lenora Wolftongue, another full-blooded Cheyenne. In 1934 I became their first child.

White Buffalo Woman told her grandson Henry that her prayers had been answered in getting to see me, her great-grandchild, and that she could now complete her journey on earth happy in the knowledge that I had come to join the Cheyenne people on their road of life. I have been told that just as she had done for many other infants, my aged great-grandmother lovingly took my tiny body in her hands and, using it as one would a pipe, solemnly pointed me headfirst to each of the six sacred directions of the universe. She thus introduced me to the sacred powers of the world, offered me in prayer as one of the people, and microcosmically traced my life journey on earth with the Cheyennes on their road of life.

Through the ritual my great-grandmother acknowledged my life and charged me with contributing to the good ways of the people. Although we were born in different centuries, our cultural foundation was alike in that we were Cheyenne. Our experiences differed, however. White Buffalo Woman was traditional, and Cheyenne-white history in her time was tragic and sad, but the people were sustained by their strong spirituality. I am bicultural, and tribal history in my time has been generally ignored by white America. Cheyenne history, and for that matter Indian history, has been a story of assimilation, unsuccessfully enforced through 'civilization,' religion, and education.

In 1936 White Buffalo Woman completed her life journey on earth. She taught that understanding was a wonderful thing, and she understood white motivation. She was not cynical but sought only to find the good in people, in the world about her, and in all life.

She and I shared two happy years with the people. Nearly half a century later, I only now understand my great-grandmother's death song: 'Nothing is hard, only death, for love and memories linger on.'

The reservation history of the southern Cheyennes is one of oppression, hunger, broken promises, and rapid environmental degradation. They live solely because of a sheer will to survive. The world in which they once lived in dignity and total self-sufficiency disappeared with the buffalo. Just as Sweet Medicine had predicted, and because of treaty commitments made by their leaders, the Cheyennes as a tribe consented to place their children in the white man's schools in 1876.

From that point on Cheyennes have been subjected to a multiplicity of educational systems. Initially, federally-subsidized schools were operated by the Quakers. The Fort Marion exiles incarcerated in the old Spanish fortress at St. Augustine, Florida, because of their participation in the Red River War of 1874–75, constituted the first Cheyenne adult education class. Lieutenant Richard Henry Pratt was their jailer, and some of them were among his students when he opened the first off-reservation boarding school at Carlisle, Pennsylvania, in 1879. Mennonite mission schools also operated on the reservation, as did federal boarding schools. Their curriculum consisted of industrial training, religion, and academics. Through the Johnson-O'Malley Act of 1934, the Secretary of the Interior was authorized to contract with states for the education of Indian children. With this, Cheyenne children were thrust into the public school system.

Under the provisions of the Indian Allotment Act of 1887, the Cheyenne and Arapaho reservation was allotted in 1891 and was opened to white homesteading in 1892. The Cheyennes' island home was further diminished into 160-acre tracts of individual allotments, checkerboarded throughout seven counties in southwestern Oklahoma. The tribes' traditional forms of governance were supplanted by the adoption of a white form of government in 1937. The Cheyenne-Arapaho Tribes of Oklahoma organized under the provisions of the Oklahoma Indian Welfare Act of 1936, which, like the Indian Reorganization Act of 1934, allowed them to organize for tribal self-government.

In the midst of great environmental, social, political, and educational change, Cheyenne spiritual ways and ceremonies have provided the stability necessary to maintain their uniqueness as a people. Today, just as in earlier times, the Keepers reverently safeguard the Sacred Arrows and the Sacred Buffalo Hat. The Arrow Renewal and Sun Dance are still conducted as they were in the past. Their genesis as a people and the essence of Cheyenneness are preserved in these ceremonies.

This powerful ceremonial life sets the Cheyennes apart as a distinct people with a unique spiritual history. Though their historical genesis extends thousands upon thousands of years back in time, their history is compressed, so that the act of creation is immediate, being preserved in their two major ceremonials. Sweet Medicine and Erect Horns taught them the ceremonies when they brought the transcendently holy tribal symbols to the people as blessings from their Creator. The good teachings of the prophets provide the tribal direction as the people walk their road of life in an historically timeless pilgrimage, following a migration route that extends from the northeastern woodlands of Canada to both the southern and the northern Plains.

In brief, Cheyenne history is a continuum of sacred experiences rooted into the American landscape, with Bear Butte their most sacred and most powerful place. Their continuity as a people requires that they maintain their way of life. Specifically, they must maintain their traditions, beliefs, spiritual life, and, through their ceremonies, maintain their sacred mission to keep the earth alive.

The Cheyenne sense of history is one of power, majesty, mystery, and awe. It is a sacred history, which has been well-preserved in the oral tradition. The people's history and personal history are intertwined in experience. White Buffalo Woman's personal experiences meld into Cheyenne history. Life did not pass her by, nor did history. Her experiences at Sand Creek, the Washita, and at the Little Big Horn all become immediate, personalized history. More important, it is an authentic history, one that reflects her world of personal experiences while simultaneously reflecting the Cheyenne world of sacred experiences.

Cheyenne history is but one tribal perspective. There are many others, all of them constituting authentic American history. Indian history reflects a unique human, spiritual, timeless cosmology. It stands in stark contrast to scientific, secular, dehumanized Anglo-American history. The experiences of Indians and whites reflect two different cosmologies with different missions. As an example, White Buffalo Woman personally suffered the most tragic experiences a people had to tolerate in American history. Yet she maintained her spirituality and did not abandon her sense of history and sacred mission. In the twilight of her life she transmitted this unique sense of history to me as a small child, charging me to keep it alive for the generations of as-yet unborn Cheyennes.

Cheyenne history, and by extension Indian history, in all probability will never be incorporated into American history, because it is holistic, human, personal, and sacred. Though it is equally as valid as Anglo-American history it is destined to remain complementary to white secular American history. In a brief five centuries, Anglo-American experiences have become a secular, scientific history without a soul or direction. The collective stream of American Indian tribal experiences has become a spiritual history with the sacred mission of keeping the Earth Grandmother alive. American Indian history has 25,000- to 40,000-year-old roots in this sacred land. It cannot suddenly be assimilated into American history. Every Indian's personalized experiences today constitute American Indian history of the twenty-first century, just as White Buffalo Woman's history is preserved for all time.

My great-grandmother was a remarkable individual whose life was an historic one and for whom history was life. Our lives together span one hundred thirty years, and being Cheyenne—one of the people—has shaped my distinctive, non-Western view of history. Our history as American Indians is beautiful, rich, valid, and sacred. The challenge lies in understanding and appreciating it as authentic history. The challenge is yours.

12

The challenge of poststructuralism/postmodernism

Currently controversies rage around history and postmodernism, and history and poststructuralism. There seem to be two reasons for this. Firstly, the concepts themselves are relatively new, arising from the 1960s. Historians in the main have been slow to grapple with these ideas, partly because they first developed in a mainly literary milieu. Secondly, while historians have theorized about poststructuralist ideas, there are still few works of historical research that might be labelled poststructuralist. Some reasons for this are examined below.

Before discussing the main ideas of poststructuralism, some definitions are in order. As Caplan pointed out, the terms postmodern, poststructural and deconstruction have been used almost as synonyms by some writers, and conflicting definitions abound. Joyce, following McLennan, for example, describes postmodernism thus:

> it can be characterized as a critique of the 'four sins' of modernist (social) theory: reductionism (seeing a complex whole in terms of its – more basic – parts); functionalism (seeing elements or parts as the expression of a more complex whole); essentialism (assuming that things or structures have one set of characteristics which is basic, or in a cognate sense 'foundational'); and universalism (presuming that theories are unconditional or transhistorical, as opposed to the 'local knowledges' favoured by postmodernism).[1]

When historians first began to discuss the kinds of history suggested by the work of Derrida, Foucault and Lacan, we spoke of poststructuralism. Thirty years on, it is more common to refer to postmodernism. Often, however, the unexplained conflation of these terms leads to confusion. Here, then, following Caplan, we use postmodern as an 'historical description . . . of an age', poststructural as 'a . . . bundle of theories and intellectual practices, that derives from a creative engagement with its "predecessor", structuralism', and deconstruction as 'a method of reading'.[2] In this chapter, therefore, we focus on poststructuralism.[3]

Poststructuralism arose from an engagement with and critique of the tenets of structuralism, a model originating in Saussure's study of language and brought to the social sciences in particular by the anthropologist Lévi-Strauss. Saussure studied language as a system whose properties did not rely on external referents. What was important were the relationships between elements of language or signs. A sign was made up of a signifier or sound pattern and the signified, the concept triggered by the signifier. Signs were distinguished by their difference from others in the set of signs, and signs are arbitrary.[4] While meaning in language derives from the internal system, nevertheless language is a representation of an external reality. Structuralist thinkers extrapolated from structural linguistics to analyse the deep universal mental structures represented by any system of signification; culture and history can also be investigated by this means.

Structuralism posits a closed system (of signification) which can be observed and understood by an external observer. This is similar to the position adopted by the majority of historians with regard to the past. There is a truth back there, which we could discover if only we had all the information, or were examining it from the correct vantage point. Each historian, while not able alone to see the full picture, both due to lack of evidence and an inevitably subjective interpretation, contributes her brick. Eventually the house will be finished, and the person lucky enough to add the paint to the front door knob can stand back and see the completed whole.

A poststructuralist might argue that the house is still only visible from one side; for all the observer can tell, the far wall may be unfinished; as the observer walks to the back door, the front porch may collapse. Maintenance will be necessary and structural alterations are always possible. The system is not closed and never can be. For an historian, this lack of closure implies that there can be no meta-narratives, no overarching explanation of the passage of human history from past to future.

Historians have commonly based their analyses on material artifacts – documents, art and architecture, archaeological remains – and we might label these sources 'texts', collections of signs which conform to some internal system. Through an extension of the idea of language as a system of signification, poststructuralists have enlarged the field known as textual to include other material and non-material texts. For example, Roberta Gilchrist examines the meanings of various arrangements of space in the medieval world: here space is a text. The 'body' is another text commonly used.[5] We can also examine systems of thought as texts: the ideal of feminine slimness, or liberal humanism, for instance. Poststructuralists treat texts of all kinds as systems of signification, whose meanings can be ascertained in part by deconstruction, a method of liberating multiple meanings within the text.

Deconstruction is a method of reading made famous by the French philosopher Derrida in the late 1960s. While for Saussure, the signifier related directly to the signified, this is not so for Derrida. Incorporated in Derrida's sign is always what is absent and what is other. Many words, for example, when deconstructed are found to contain their binary opposite. 'Man' is that which is not 'woman'; when we see 'man' in a text, 'woman' is absent and/or other. However, since 'man' is defined partly by its opposite, even if the sign 'woman' is not mentioned in a text, 'woman' is nevertheless present – at some level we are aware of 'woman', so 'woman' is both present and absent. 'Man' is a necessary word in the text, but at the same time is inadequate to carry its full meaning. Meaning therefore cannot be immediately clear to us.[6]

While the structuralist's system of signification represented an external reality, poststructuralists see a system or text as self-referential, not necessarily and certainly not entirely taking its meaning from the context in which it was produced or from authorial intent. Historians are accustomed to questioning the apparent or stated reasons for a text's production but we frequently do this through a discussion of the circumstances in which it was apparently produced, or by reference to similar texts. Now we are left only with a text, which Derrida tells us is full of opposed and unstable meanings. Furthermore, over time, the text has been read and interpreted differently by various readers, so that our own readings are conditioned by past interpretations as well as our present conditions.[7]

If the meaning of a text is necessarily uncertain, how much more problematic are the historical facts constructed from that text. Facts cannot be independent, and representative of an external reality: they are already historicized, their 'truth' indeterminable.[8] Thus it is not possible to verify another historian's interpretation by reference to the facts; all we can do is re-read an (open) text.

Each text's lack of closure and of an external referent leads us to a multiplicity of histories, and voices from the past, in theory at least as many as there are readers of that text. Poststructuralist historians have tried to represent this multiplicity in various ways. Price, for example, presents a history in four voices, each with its own type-face, so that we hear concurrently the voice of eighteenth-century black slaves (as transmitted by their descendants), the Dutch administrators, the Moravian missionaries, and the historian.[9] Schama has mixed 'fact' and 'fiction' to point out that all historical constructions and interpretations can be regarded as fictions.[10]

For historians researching those marginalized due to their class, race, gender, sexuality, age, the structuralist idea that a sign is distinguished by its difference, by what it is not, by what is 'other', has been helpful. The other, while often implicit, is exposed by the inconsistencies in a set of meanings within a text, so that another meaning is produced by this *différance*, a term referring to absence and difference.[11] For feminist historians, for example, the possibility of reading against the grain of a text to uncover meaning is useful in a world where the majority of historical texts have been produced by men and about men.

Poststructuralists argue that language, as well as representing the world, creates the world. Language, and texts, as collections of signs, are thus reconceived as a social and political force, for which entity the term language is insufficient. 'Language' in its multiple meanings has therefore been replaced in poststructuralist parlance by 'discourse', 'a linguistic unity or group of statements which constitutes and delimits a specific area of concern, governed by its own rules of formation with its own modes of distinguishing truth from falsity'.[12] Analysing the multiplicity of discourses in existence in any one place and time also, of course, produces multiple historical readings.

Various aspects of poststructuralist thought, therefore, result in plural, mutable readings and interpretations, and much of the criticism of poststructuralist incursions into traditional historical practice revolves around this issue. Most basically, poststructuralism supports a relativist position and destroys any claim to historical objectivity. Not only are multiple and sometimes mutually exclusive interpretations possible, they are inevitable, and the truth of an interpretation cannot be verified. All histories are equally representative of reality and therefore equally fictitious. Taken to an extreme, total relativism can result in a nihilism where everything is equally meaningless. How can one be a working, as well as a theoretical, historian under these conditions? Certainly one interpretation cannot be privileged over another, and it can be argued that those interpretations which have been thus privileged in the past owe their position to their conformity to one or another discourse of power. Many theorists believe, however, that this extreme position is unnecessary.

The other issue upon which historians engage poststructuralists and vice versa concerns the use of text and context. If the importance of an historically situated authorial consciousness is denied, critics argue that the text is thus dehistoricized. Since signs (the elements in the text) do not refer to anything material, a text cannot refer to a past reality. Spiegel, who is not dismissive of poststructuralism, points out that 'a historically grounded view of literary and cultural production is extremely difficult to theorize in the wake of the semiotic challenge', but that literary critics have discovered the need for a known history against which to measure their interpretations. She goes on to argue that the controversy around text and context is based on 'incommensurabilities between the objects, tasks and goals facing historians and literary scholars'. While a text is a given, 'the object of historical study must be constituted by the historian' before its meaning can be examined.[13] The historian both constructs (the object of study) and deconstructs (the text) in the present, so that it is hard to reach the past. She also suggests, though more tentatively, that literary critics will be more interested in aesthetics and emotions, whereas an historian focuses on the ideological functions of a text. Spiegel argues that if we view texts as 'situated uses of language' then their full meanings can only be determined by an examination of the social context within which they were produced, even if there is no reference to that context within the text.[14]

Part of the problem for historians struggling to come to grips with poststructuralist practice, we suggest, is that there are few models and examples. Historians have critiqued and theorized poststructuralism for over twenty years, but are only slowly writing from this stance. Perhaps as various solutions to the text/context problem are suggested in writing, some resolution will become possible.

For historians, many poststructuralist topics and methods of investigation are a legacy of the work of Michel Foucault. Foucault studied what he termed the 'history of systems of thought', wanting to discover who we are in the present and how we got to be that way. In Weeks's words, '[t]he central concern of Foucault has been with the rules that govern the emergence and reproduction of such systems, structures of the mind which categorise social life and then present the result to us as truth'.[15] While it is difficult to summarize Foucault's diverse work, we note several issues which have affected historians.

All of Foucault's work examined the workings of power in its various forms.[16] While the operation of power within societies tends to reinforce the dominant discourse of that society, power does not operate from above through a single agency (such as 'the government') but works diffusely, locally; resistance occurs similarly, in a series of local disruptive struggles rather than in a mighty dialectical engagement.[17] Foucault was interested in the control of populations in the present and therefore charted the development of disciplinary practices such as the incarceration of criminals or the insane. *Madness and Civilisation* was not a history of psychiatry but an investigation of the conditions which made the development of the discipline possible.[18]

Much of Foucault's work engaged with the marginalized groups in society (though noticeably not women). He paid attention to the marginalized knowledges of these groups, believing that the work of intellectuals was not to mastermind revolutions, but to uncover such discourses. Significantly, he saw knowledge and power as inextricably connected. In particular, there are no 'truths' but only official or dominant knowledges which impart power to those who know and speak them.

From this we see that history writing can be a form of power: we use our knowledge to control and domesticate the past, although it is only one past. Since all history must be present-centred, we create the way in which people think about the present through our creative fictions (for they can be no other) concerning the past. This is a powerful position. Because the subject of this discourse, the historian, is not external to it, however, she does not in fact create the discourse, nor is it intelligible to her. When one is operating within this exercise of knowledge/power, one cannot understand one's own repression.

Foucault broke from earlier histories in his rejection of meta-narratives, overarching theories of human development through time, and of historical continuity. Instead he discussed a series of discontinuous epistemes (historical periods characterized by the dominance of a particular system of thought). Historical change was therefore not cumulative or progressive, seamless or rational, nor guided by a fixed underlying principle.

Not surprisingly, Foucault's ideas have provoked considerable controversy and even outrage. His rejection of meta-narratives and his refusal to totalize his position by showing connections between the development of diverse phenomena have been disconcerting, especially to those influenced by Marx.[19] Young suggests, however, that conventional historiography has done almost nothing but account for epistemic shifts, and has therefore avoided recognizing 'otherness' in the past. We prefer to seek the similarities and continuities with the present, and thereby dehistoricize the past.[20]

Foucault has also been widely criticized for historical inaccuracies.[21] His arguments are wide-ranging and lateral, but he cites circumstances, events and interpretations for which there is no contemporary source material. In addition, it is difficult to know what to make of an historian who argues that all history is fiction. Most of us believe that our interpretations have some basis in reality, as presumably did Foucault himself, since he supported his arguments with historical evidence. Megill argued, however, that Foucault 'should not be taken seriously as *a historian*', but 'most emphatically *should* be taken seriously *as an indication of where history now stands*'.[22]

A frequent criticism attacks Foucault's apolitical stance. As well as challenging the traditional notion of an intellectual as the 'advance guard of progress and revolution', he jettisons power hierarchies. He does not distinguish between discourses which lead to domination and those that assist liberation, and thus does not address the power effects of his own discourse. Certainly, if we all participate in the discourses of power, it is hard to speak of domination and liberation as diametrically opposed. Nevertheless, it is undeniable that some individuals have less access to power and freedom than others, that some discourses have a monopoly over certain forms of constraint.[23]

What use have historians made of Foucault's legacy? There are two groups which employ poststructuralist notions, although they differ from poststructuralism in significant ways. Roger Chartier, a well-known cultural historian, aims 'to note how, in different times and places, a specific social reality was constructed, how people conceived of it and how they interpreted it to others'. Specific cultural forms create 'imaginative works built out of *social materials*'. Text and context are thus both discursively produced.[24] Bynum, for example, examines women's use of food as symbol to construct and communicate a sense of holiness through asceticism.[25]

While cultural historians study the production of culture, new historicists examine texts as historically specific artifacts. They share Foucault's belief in the 'heterogeneous, contradictory, fragmented, and discontinuous nature of textuality' and, unlike cultural historians, seek 'to disembed the artifact from any process to the present *and* from any present unifying category'.[26] New historicists therefore seek to exhibit the strangeness and thus the historicity of the past, often presenting microhistories.[27] Natalie Zemon Davis recently produced a study comprising three biographies of very different seventeenth-century women, thus showing the discontinuities as well as the similarities in their stories. In her imaginary conversations with her subjects, she 'asked what advantages you had by being on the margins' and enjoyed the adventure of 'following you three to so many different climes'. [28]

Another version of the deconstructionist approach to history is Diane Purkiss's *The Witch in History*.[29] Purkiss examines stories about witchcraft, those told by both early modern and twentieth-century people, by men and women, by misogynists and feminists, by historians, witches and their neighbours. Some of these stories are or were apparently true, others were fantasy or fictionalized. All help to construct the multi-faceted meaning of 'witch' for us. Purkiss uses close reading and psychoanalytic interpretations to show 'how the witch acts as a carrier for the fears, desires and fantasies of women and men both now and in the early modern period'. Both explicitly and implicitly Purkiss also addresses the problems of writing history in a postmodern world:

> early modern assumptions about supernatural signs were less an articulate system than a set of half-formulated working rules. Buried beneath the surface of witch-narratives, they rarely manifest themselves even as an articulate subtext, and the historian's attempt to piece them together is itself a falsification, since it is in the nature of such beliefs that they remain unexamined. It is equally hard for us not to despise people with such beliefs and so to assume that they are all transparent and honest, forthcoming with the truth at all times, incapable of vested interests and theatrical self-fashioning. On the other hand, we may become paralysed by our own scepticism, too cynical to try any longer. Sometimes we are taking stories too seriously, sometimes not seriously enough. Can we ever know about even one story?[30]

While Purkiss, perhaps for polemical purposes, underestimates many historians, the difficulties she outlines are common. To write history, we need to disinter and re-tell histories.

Overall, Foucault's work has pointed to many new historical topics: the histories of marginal people and various institutions, of madness and medicine, of the body (including the body politic), of systems of thought. Studies of these kinds abound. Somewhat ironically, given Foucault's disinterest, feminist poststructuralism is a growing field. For example, *The Classing Gaze* discusses the construction of class and sexuality in nineteenth-century Australia. On a contrasting topic, Donzelot traces the rise of the social and its effect on the family.[31]

From a methodological viewpoint, deconstruction has already shown itself to be an extremely useful historical tool. We have not yet mapped out what a 'poststructuralist history' looks like, nor should we. In Munslow's words, '[p]ostmodern or deconstructionist history converges no longer on the past as such, but on the disjuncture between pastness and presentness'.[32] More fruitful, we suggest, is to speak of a poststructuralist *approach* to history. For Berkhofer, this entails remaking ourselves as readers and reviewers, as well as writers and teachers.[33] Poststructuralist theory, therefore, gives us both the technical and mental tools to develop new histories appropriate to the postmodern age.

City of Dreadful Delight and Judith Walkowitz's earlier book, *Prostitution and Victorian Society* (1980), examine the sexual culture of Victorian England. Walkowitz acknowledges the influence of Foucault, and also that of feminist debates, for example, those concerning pornography. The extract below, from *City of Dreadful Delight*, is characteristic of poststructuralist history. The avoidance of incarceration for insanity by Mrs Weldon, the protagonist of the story, shows the intersection of knowledge and power, and the subversive and contradictory nature of popular discourse.

Foucault argued that power is not purely hierarchical with rules imposed from above: rather it operates diffusely and locally. How is this paradigm of power visible in the story of Mrs Weldon? Do you find it a convincing method of interpretation in this specific case? In what ways can Mrs Weldon herself be seen at the intersection of several discourses about power and powerlessness in Victorian society? Walkowitz argued that '[b]oth sides engaged in a symbolic struggle, in a dialectical battle of words and images, often subverting the same metaphoric language as their opponents'. Find examples of this practice in the extract. Walkowitz also suggests that the 'séance reversed the usual sexual hierarchy of knowledge and power'. In what ways was Mrs Weldon empowered by her experiences?

Do we know the true story of the Weldons' battle? Can we? In what ways does Walkowitz as an historian leave this narrative open, and how does her practice differ from that of some other historians?

Notes

1 Patrick Joyce, 'The Return of History: Postmodernism and the Politics of Academic History in Britain', *Past and Present*, 158 (1998), p. 212, n. 18.

2 Jane Caplan, 'Postmodernism, Poststructuralism, and Deconstruction: Notes for Historians', *Central European History*, 22 (1989), pp. 262–8; for another definition, Thomas C. Patterson, 'Post-structuralism, Post-modernism: Implications for Historians', *Social History*, 14 (1989), pp. 83–8.

3 It should be noted, however, that other writers might define this same set of theories as postmodern.

4 Howard Gardner, *The Quest for Mind: Piaget, Lévi-Strauss and the Structuralist Movement* (New York, 1972), pp. 44–5; F. Saussure, 'Nature of the Linguistic Sign', in David Lodge (ed.), *Modern Criticism and Theory: A Reader* (London, 1988), pp. 10–12.

5 Roberta Gilchrist, 'Medieval Bodies in the Material World: Gender, Stigma and the Body', in Sarah Kay and Miri Rubin (eds), *Framing Medieval Bodies* (Manchester, 1994), pp. 43–61.

6 This discussion is derived from Madan Sarup, *An Introductory Guide to Post-structuralism and Postmodernism* (2nd edn, New York, 1993), p. 33. For more detail, see Chapter 2, 'Derrida and Deconstruction'.

7 Patterson, 'Post-structuralism', p. 84.

8 Keith Jenkins, *The Postmodern History Reader* (London, 1997), p. 19.

9 Richard Price, *Alabi's World* (Baltimore, 1990). See Peter Burke, 'History of Events and the Revival of Narrative', in *New Perspectives on Historical Writing* (Cambridge, 1991), p. 239, for a more extended discussion.

10 Simon Schama, *Dead Certainties (Unwarranted Speculations)* (London, 1991).

11 Caplan, 'Postmodernism', p. 267.

12 Jeffrey Weeks, 'Foucault for Historians', *History Workshop Journal*, 14 (1982), p. 111.

13 The construction of the object of historical enquiry was also mentioned in the discussion of Hayden White in Chapter 8.

14 Gabrielle M. Spiegel, 'History, Historicism, and the Social Logic of the Text in the Middle Ages', *Speculum*, 65 (1990), pp. 73–8. See the debate sparked by this article, in *Past and Present*, nos 131, 133, 135, reprinted in Jenkins, *Postmodern History Reader*.

15 Weeks, 'Foucault', p. 107.

16 For a more detailed but clear discussion, see Alec McHoul and Wendy Grace, *A Foucault Primer: Discourse, Power and the Subject* (Melbourne, 1993), ch. 3. See the bibliography for a list of Foucault's works.

17 Robert Young, *White Mythologies: Writing History and the West* (London, 1990), p. 87.

18 Michel Foucault, *Madness and Civilisation: A History of Insanity in the Age of Reason* (London, [1961] 1967).

19 See, for example, Mark Poster, 'Foucault and History', *Social Research*, 49 (1982), pp. 116–22.

20 Young, *White Mythologies*, p. 75.

21 H. C. Erik Midelfort, 'Madness and Civilization in Early Modern Europe: A Reappraisal of Michel Foucault', in Peter Burke (ed.), *Critical Essays on Michel Foucault* (Aldershot, 1992), pp. 28–41.

22 Allan Megill, 'Foucault, Structuralism, and the Ends of History', *Journal of Modern History*, 51 (1979), p. 502.

23 Poster, 'Foucault and History', pp. 138–40; Weeks, 'Foucault', p. 117.

24 Roger Chartier, *Cultural History: Between Practices and Representations,* trans. Lydia G. Cochrane (Cambridge, 1988), p. 4; Spiegel, 'History', pp. 65–8.
25 Carolyn Walker Bynum, *Holy Feast and Holy Fast: The Religious Significance of Food to Medieval Women* (Berkeley, 1987).
26 David D. Roberts, *Nothing but History: Reconstruction and Extremity after Metaphysics* (Berkeley, 1995), pp. 271–2; Spiegel, 'History', p. 71.
27 See, for example, Carlo Ginzburg, *The Cheese and the Worms: The Cosmos of a Sixteenth-century Miller* (London, [1976] 1992).
28 Natalie Zemon Davis, *Women on the Margins: Three Seventeenth-century Lives* (Cambridge, Mass., 1995), p. 4.
29 Diane Purkiss, *The Witch in History: Early Modern and Twentieth-Century Representations* (London, 1996).
30 *Ibid.,* frontispiece, p. 62.
31 Lynette Finch, *Sexuality, Class and Surveillance* (Sydney, 1993); Jacques Donzelot, *The Policing of Families,* trans. Robert Hurley (New York, 1979).
32 Alun Munslow, *Deconstructing History* (London, 1997), p. 165.
33 Robert F. Berkhofer, Jr., *Beyond the Great Story: History as Text and Discourse* (Cambridge, Mass., 1995), pp. 281–3.

Additional reading

Berkhofer, Robert F., Jr., *Beyond the Great Story: History as Text and Discourse* (Cambridge, Mass., 1995).

Caplan, Jane, 'Postmodernism, Poststructuralism, and Deconstruction: Notes for Historians', *Central European History,* 22 (1989), pp. 262–8.

Carter, Paul, *The Road to Botany Bay: An Exploration of Landscape and History* (Chicago, 1989).

Foucault, Michel, *Discipline and Punish: The Birth of the Prison,* trans. Alan Sheridan (New York, [1975] 1977).

Goldstein, Jan (ed.), *Foucault and the Writing of History* (Oxford, 1994).

Jenkins, Keith (ed.), *The Postmodern History Reader* (London, 1997).

McHoul, Alec and Wendy Grace, *A Foucault Primer: Discourse, Power and the Subject* (Melbourne, 1993).

Munslow, Alun, *Deconstructing History* (London, 1997).

Poster, Mark, *Foucault, Marxism, and History: Mode of Production Versus Mode of Information* (Cambridge, 1984).

Roberts, David D., *Nothing but History: Reconstruction and Extremity after Metaphysics* (Berkeley, 1995).

Sarup, Madan, *An Introductory Guide to Post-structuralism and Postmodernism* (2nd edn, New York, 1993).

Walkowitz, Judith R., *City of Dreadful Delight: Narratives of Sexual Danger in Late-Victorian London* (London, 1992).

Windschuttle, Keith, *The Killing of History: How a Discipline Is Being Murdered by Literary Critics and Social Theorists* (Sydney, 1994).

SCIENCE AND THE SÉANCE: TRANSGRESSIONS OF GENDER AND GENRE
Judith R. Walkowitz

The *Daily Telegraph's* marriage correspondence was only one of many media extravaganzas exposing the plight of wives in the last decades of the nineteenth century. Another cause célèbre was Georgina Weldon's highly advertised campaign against her husband, Henry, and a mad-doctor alienist, L. Forbes Winslow, for conspiring to intern her in an insane asylum because she was a spiritualist. At the height of her fame, when headlines of the half-penny newspapers constantly broadcasted 'Mrs. Weldon again,' the indomitable Georgina Weldon was reputed by one newsclipping service to have commanded as many newspaper columns as a cabinet minister. Mrs. Weldon was a great favorite of W. T. Stead, who admired her pluck, her canny manipulation of publicity, her populist defense of the 'liberty of the subject,' and her struggle against materialist science in the name of female spirituality. On all these counts, she would have provoked a very different response from Stead's contemporary, Karl Pearson, who had little sympathy for a 'woman of the market' such as Mrs. Weldon who used the commercial spaces of the city to parody and campaign against male professionalism.[1]

Mrs. Weldon's 'woman in the city' story celebrates the possibilities of metropolitan life in the 1880s for enterprising middle-class women like herself. Moving comfortably and speedily across the social spaces of London, refashioning different versions of herself, Georgina Weldon was able to publicize her situation and expose the private male plot that failed. Between 1878 and 1885, Mrs. Weldon played out her story in the newspapers and the medical journals, amplified it in street advertisements and processions, extended it to the lecture circuit, the law courts, and ultimately, that premier com-

---

[1] This is a revised version of 'Science and the Séance: Transgressions of Gender and Genre in Late-Victorian London,' *Representations* 22 (Spring 1988): 3–29, © 1988 by the Regents of the University of California. On the marriage debates, see Lucy Bland, 'Marriage Laid Bare: Middle-Class women and Marital Sex, c. 1880–1914,' in Jane Lewis, ed., *Labour and Love: Women's Experience of Home and Family, 1820–1940* (Oxford: Basil Blackwell, 1986), pp. 123–48; Philip Treherne, *A Plaintiff in Person* (London: William Heinemann, 1923), p. 97.

mercial space of the 1880s, the music halls. Combining courage, virtuosity, and slapstick comedy, Mrs. Weldon's campaign of revenge vastly amused the educated reading public, yet it pressed an open nerve about fears of madness and of wrongful confinement, thereby continuing a melodramatic narrative of family-medical conspiracy that Wilkie Collins and Charles Reade had popularized in their sensational novels of the 1860s.[2]

Spiritualism and the mad doctors

Mrs. Weldon was a target of lunacy confinement because her husband tried to use a public controversy between doctors and spiritualists to further his private designs—that is, to rid himself of a nuisance wife. Medical men, alarmed by the growing popularity of spiritualism among the educated classes, had themselves instigated this larger conflict.[3] They caricatured spiritualists as crazy women and feminized men engaged in superstitious, popular, and fraudulent practices. Spiritualists responded by elaborating an iconography of male medical evil, imagining the doctor as a trader in lunacy and as a sexually dangerous man, a divided personality, whose science made him cruel, bloodthirsty, and hypermasculine, because it suppressed his feminine, spiritual part. Both sides engaged in a symbolic struggle, in a dialectical battle of words and images, often inverting the same metaphoric language as their opponents. In so doing, spiritualists and their adversaries took up positions already marked out by feminists and doctors in the campaign against the state regulation of prostitution and echoed contemporaneously in the antivaccination and antivivisection movements.[4]

[2] Peter McCandless, 'Dangerous to Themselves and Others: The Victorian Debate over the Prevention of Wrongful Confinement,' *Journal of British Studies* 23 (Fall 1983): 84–104; idem, 'Liberty and Lunacy: The Victorians and Wrongful Confinement,' *Journal of Social History* 11 (1978): 366–86.

[3] Attendance at séances became a popular craze for the well-heeled in the late 1860s and 1870s, when even Charles Darwin and Francis Galton participated in drawing-room sessions. See Janet Oppenheim, *The Other World: Spiritualism and Psychical Research in England, 1850–1914* (New York: Cambridge University Press, 1985); Ruth Brandon, *The Spiritualists: The Passion for the Occult in the Nineteenth Century* (New York: Knopf, 1983); Alex Owen, 'The Other Voice: Women, Children, and Nineteenth-Century Spiritualism,' in Carolyn Steedman et al., eds., *Language, Gender, and Childhood* (London: Routledge and Kegan Paul, 1985), pp. 31–73; S. E. D. Shortt, 'Physicians and Psychics: The Anglo-American Medical Response to Spiritualism, 1870–90,' *Journal of the History of Medicine and Allied Sciences* 39 (1984): 339–55.

[4] Judith R. Walkowitz, *Prostitution and Victorian Society: Women, Class, and the State* (New York: Cambridge University Press, 1980), chaps. 4, 5; R. D. French, *Antivivisection*

The men who organized the attack on spiritualism were mostly specialists in neurophysiology and psychiatry. They entered the fray after some of their most eminent colleagues, such as Sir William Crookes and Alfred Russel Wallace, had lent their name and reputation to spiritualism.[5] Adversaries of spiritualists believed their own materialist scientific culture was under attack and, as experts in 'morbid' and 'abnormal' states of the brain, they wanted to assert an 'epistemological sovereignty' over the discussion.[6] The brain, insisted William Clifford, the noted physiologist, 'is made of atoms and ether, and there is no room in it for ghosts.'[7]

Throughout the late 1870s, William Carpenter, a professor of zoology, and E. Ray Lankester, a young biologist, waged an unremitting campaign against the 'Epidemic of Delusions.' The extraordinary claims of spiritualists, Carpenter insisted, required extraordinary tests; they must be subjected to the clinical eye of dispassionate observers, not casually verified by their loyal adherents.[8] Lankester intensified the campaign in 1876 by exposing the writing medium, Henry Slade, as a fraud, and, with Horatio Donkin, a Harley Street doctor and later member of the Men and Women's Club, filed suit against Slade under the Vagrancy Acts for being a trickster.[9]

Hostile scientists further repudiated spiritualists as maniacs.[10] Medical critics denounced the trance as a form of hysteria, an 'anomalous state of the brain,' to which women, given their inherently unstable reproductive physiology, were peculiarly liable: wherever

and Medical Science in Victorian Society (Princeton: Princeton University Press, 1975), chap. 9; R. M. McLeod, 'Law, Medicine and Public Opinion: The Resistance to Compulsory Health Legislation 1870–1901,' *Public Law* (1967): 189–211. F. B. Smith, *The People's Health 1830–1910* (New York: Holmes and Meier, 1979), pp. 158–68.

[5] Crookes, for example, extended his patronage to an attractive young test medium (provoking considerable gossip) and published findings that, he claimed, verified the physical phenomena produced by mediums. See Brandon, *The Spiritualists*, pp. 113–26; Oppenheim, *The Other World*, pp. 16–21.

[6] Shortt, 'Physicians and Psychics,' pp. 345, 354.

[7] William Clifford, quoted in Oppenheim, *The Other World*, p. 240; 'Spiritualism and Science,' *Lancet* 2 (1876): 431–33.

[8] Carpenter published a scathing critique of Crookes, 'Some Recent Converts to Spiritualism,' *Quarterly Review* 131 (October 1871): 301; *Lancet* 2 (1876): 832.

[9] He claimed to have snatched a slate away from Slade with a spirit message written on it even before the spirit communication had begun. Mr. Flowers, the police-court magistrate, sentenced Slade to three months' hard labor. The decision was overturned because of a technicality, but Slade fled the country anyway. Oppenheim, *The Other World*, pp. 23, 241; *Lancet* 2 (1876): 474.

[10] 'Mesmeric visions and prophecies, clairvoyances, spirit rappings, tableturnings and liftings,' declared Sir Henry Holland, could best be explained as 'morbid or anomalous states of the brain.' Quoted in Oppenheim, *The Other World*, p. 244.

there were 'strange manifestations,' asserted Dr. George Savage, the director of Bethlehem Hospital, there was 'sure to be found a girl with hysterical symptoms.' Spiritualism, declared Henry Maudsley, ought to have a place among the causes of mental malady. Following the lead of medical scientists, psychiatrists translated spiritualist communications into the esoteric language of materialist science, representing them as local lesions of the brain or unconscious cerebration.[11]

One alienist who enthusiastically joined in the public attack was Dr. L. Forbes Winslow, the operator of two private asylums in Hammersmith. Winslow's own family history was intimately linked to the history of British psychiatry. His father, Forbes Winslow, the great pioneer of psychological medicine, was personally responsible for the legal acceptance of the insanity plea in the 1840s. The son, L. Forbes, was educated at Rugby and Cambridge and groomed to follow in his father's footsteps and take over the family business. Throughout his professional career, the younger Winslow continue to live in his father's shadow: he 'lacked the original powers of his father' and made no 'noteworthy contribution' to his specialty. The medical establishment tended to regard him with some condescension, at best as an undistinguished asylum keeper unconnected to the higher-status specialty of neurology, at worst as a 'trader' in lunacy, soiled by his connection to the market.[12]

Part of Winslow's difficulty lay in the declining status of asylum psychiatry since his father's time, and of private asylum-keeping in particular. Asylum treatment manifested little connection to the new organic theories expounded to professionalize and modernize psychiatry. Alienists still based their diagnosis on behavioral symptoms and other social indicators, which were unconnected to demonstrable lesions of the brain. Somatic theories offered little in the way of cure, and alienists failed to reverse the tendency towards the

---

[11] George Savage, quoted in Jane Marcus, 'Mothering, Madness and Music,' in Elaine K. Ginsberg and Laura Moss Gotlieb, *Virginia Woolf: Centennial Essays* (Troy, N.Y.: Whitston, 1983), p. 33; Alexandra Owen, *The Darkened Room: Women, Power, and Spiritualism in Late-Victorian England* (London: Virago, 1989), pp. 144–46.

[12] L. Forbes Winslow, *Recollections of Forty Years* (London: John Ouseley, 1910); Obituary, *Lancet* 1 (1913): 1704; Obituary, *BMJ* 1 (1913): 1302; Dr. A. L. Wyman, 'Why Winslow? The Winslows of Sussex House,' *Charing Cross Hospital Gazette* 64 (1966–67): 143–46. The *Lancet*'s obituary coldly described him as one 'who was well known in lay circles as an alienist,' while the *British Medical Journal* peremptorily dismissed him as a publicity hound: 'His opinion in any case that happened to interest the public was apparently highly valued by some newspapers, but with his own profession it carried less weight.' Quoted in Wyman, 'Why Winslow?'

'silting up' of institutions with chronic patients in the late nineteenth century. As long as alienists were connected with asylums, they were tainted by association with low-status patients, enjoyed very limited access to research and hospital appointments, and were essentially trapped in a dead-end specialty.[13]

An enterprising man nonetheless, L. Forbes Winslow seems to have compensated for unimpressive professional credentials by pursuing a career as expert witness and medical publicist. By his own account, he testified at 'practically every major murder trial of criminal insanity'; and he further enhanced his reputation in lay circles by producing a number of popular texts on forensic psychiatry.[14]

Following the lead of E. Ray Lankester, Winslow became an enthusiastic 'ghost grabber,' who exposed a public medium as a fraud in 1877 by squirting red ink at his 'spirit face.'[15] In *Spiritualist Madness* (1877) he identified spiritualism as the principal cause of the increase of insanity in England, particularly among 'weak-minded hysterical women' (psychiatrists like Maudsley had merely listed it among significant causes), and he claimed that upwards of forty thousand spiritualists were interned in American asylums.[16] Winslow's pamphlet generated a wave of anxiety among spiritualists;[17] it also

[13] L. S. Jacyna, 'Somatic Theories of Mind and the Interests of Medicine in Britain, 1850–1879,' *Medical History* 26 (1982): 233–58; Michael Clark, 'The Rejection of Psychological Approaches to Mental Disorder in Late Nineteenth-Century British Psychiatry,' in Andrew Scull, ed., *Madhouses, Mad-Doctors, and Madmen: The Social History of Psychiatry in the Victorian Era* (Philadelphia: University of Pennsylvania Press, 1981), pp. 271–312; Shortt, 'Physicians and Psychics,' p. 353; W. F. Bynum, 'Themes in British Psychiatry: J. C. Prichard (1786–1918) to Henry Maudsley (1835–1918),' in Michael Ruse, ed., *Nature Animated* (Dordrecht: Reidel, 1983), pp. 225–42.

[14] Winslow's record was to testify at three murder trials in a week (*Recollections*, p. 139). L. Forbes Winslow, *Fasting and Feeding Psychologically Considered* (London: Balliere, Tindall and Cox, 1881); idem, *Insanity of Passion and Crime, with 43 Photographic Reproductions of Celebrated Cases* (London: John Ouseley, 1912), p. 205. His writings claimed a somatic basis for disease yet identified the signs of criminal insanity in terms of behavioral symptoms: 'external signs of speech behavior and acts,' a failure of the rational will, that displayed a want of 'prudence and foresight.' Winslow also presented himself as an expert on 'the borderlands,' that newly identified twilight region where personal eccentricities shaded off into mental disorder. Winslow had a penchant for alarmist prediction of a 'Mad Humanity': 'Insanity is advancing by progressive leaps,' he wrote in 1912, as 'is shown by the official annual reports during the last fifty years.' *Insanity of Passion*, p. 205.

[15] Winslow, *Recollections*, p. 60.

[16] L. Forbes Winslow, *Spiritualistic Madness* (London: n.p., 1877), p. 32. He coupled this 'sensationalism' with a scientific explanation of spiritualist madness as a 'physiological' condition of the 'nervous system,' once again following the lead of more prestigious scientists like Lankester and Maudsley.

[17] In response, spiritualists organized defense funds and stepped up their own campaign against the lunacy laws. Owen, 'Subversive Spirit, chaps. 5, 6; S. E. Gay, *Spiritual-*

brought him to the attention of Henry Weldon, who asked him to interview his wife and then find an asylum for her. Winslow clearly regarded Weldon's request as routine.[18] As lunacy certification required the signature of two doctors (independent of the asylum operator) who had conducted separate examinations of the prospective patient, Winslow concocted a scheme to interview Mrs. Weldon: he and his medical colleagues would visit her, under the guise of interested philanthropists inquiring about her orphanage. After these interviews were completed, he suggested a companion for Mrs. Weldon; when told by Mr. Weldon that would not be 'practical,' he readily accepted her as a patient for an annual fee of £400.[19] Unfortunately, both Weldon and Winslow had underestimated the ingenuity, determination, and performing skill of their adversary, Georgina Weldon.

The talented and beautiful daughter of a Welsh landed gentleman, Georgina Treherne had married the impecunious Henry Weldon against the wishes of her family in 1860.[20] Their 1860 marriage was a 'love match,' but also a way for Georgina to escape the control of her authoritarian father and gratify her desire for a theatrical career. Since Harry had only a small private income, she insisted that, as a condition of their marriage, he agree that she be permitted to 'go on the stage and make a fortune.'[21]

Georgina soon learned that a marriage contract—even with an inadequate breadwinner—was no ticket to the stage. Once married, Henry reneged on his promise and Georgina had to settle for amateur theatrics and charity musical-benefits. She kept the household afloat by observing the 'strictest economy' and by 'singing for her supper' at Society events.[22] However, by the late 1860s, Georgina's popularity began to wane, and she herself found the role of performing amateur increasingly distasteful. Disillusioned with her childless marriage and fed up with 'singing for her supper,' she returned to

istic Sanity: A Reply to Dr. Forbes Winslow's 'Spiritualistic Madness' (London: Falmouth, 1879); 'A Vigilance Committee,' The Spiritualist (London) (10 Dec. 1880): 287.

[18] Over 400 patients had been placed in his asylums through lunacy certification. The Times (London), 11 July 1884.

[19] Winslow, quoted in The Times, 28 Nov. 1884.

[20] Treherne, Plaintiff; Edward Grierson, Storm Bird: The Strange Life of Georgina Weldon (London: Chatto and Windus, 1959); 'Mrs. Weldon's Orphanage,' Spiritualist (21 Sept. 1877).

[21] Mrs. Weldon, quoted in Grierson, Storm Bird, pp. 26, 27.

[22] She was a well-known figure in society circles, a frequent visitor to Little Holland House and friend of the pre-Raphaelites. Ibid., p. 43.

teaching as a new avenue for fulfillment. In the ninth year of her marriage, she developed the idea of a National Training School to teach music to poor children in a 'naturalistic' mode.[23] She persisted in this plan, over the objections of her husband, who disliked her proposal to recruit 'dirty, diseased orphans' from the streets and place them 'beneath his roof to be fed, clothed and educated.'[24] As a result, Harry Weldon (who in the meantime had come into a comfortable inheritance) separated from his wife in 1875, giving over to her the lease to Tavistock House, their Bloomsbury townhouse, and a thousand pounds a year.

Mrs. Weldon's philanthropic scheme, coupled with her marital troubles, estranged her from genteel society and her own family.[25] Society was further shocked by the unconventional regime at Tavistock House. Mrs. Weldon's progressive methods thoroughly violated social and class decorum.[26] The children 'were taught to sing and recite from the earliest age, they were sent to the opera'; they were brought up as vegetarians; they were not allowed to cry; they were permitted to go barefoot and yell for a quarter of an hour; they were not subjected to rigid rules nor were they trained up in a manner that would fit them for a menial station in life.[27]

Equally unconventional and indecorous were her advertising techniques on behalf of the orphanage. The children were carted around from one event to another in an advertising van, a retired horse van with 'Mrs. Weldon's Sociable Evenings' emblazoned on it in enormous letters—an object so 'outlandish' that her brother begged her to 'keep it from his door.' The sociable evenings themselves were only slightly less outlandish; frequently Mrs. Weldon combined musical

[23] 'Mrs. Weldon's Orphanage.'

[24] Ibid.

[25] Mrs. Weldon was not an isolated pioneer in this kind of undertaking. During the 1860s and 1870s a number of women opened small, private, rescue homes for prostitutes; their 'personal style of philanthropy,' to quote Josephine Butler, was a self-conscious challenge to the impersonal and repressive regimes of evangelical penitentiaries that had been founded and administered by men in the early Victorian period. By and large, these female philanthropists were middle-class Quakers and nonconformists, not members of fashionable society. If they engaged in personal charity at all, society ladies of the 1870s generally restricted themselves to home-visiting of the poor, not importing 'street arabs' into their own residences. See Josephine Butler, *An Autobiographical Memoir*, ed. by G. W. Johnson and L. A. Johnson (Bristol: Arrowsmith, 1928), pp. 81–83.

[26] Middle-class Victorian conventions called for the rigid segregation of children from adults and their training in self-restraint rather than self-expression. Middle-class observers expected poor children to be even more regimented.

[27] Georgina Weldon, *The History of My Orphanage, or the Outpourings of an Alleged Lunatic* (London: Mrs. Weldon, 1878); Grierson, *Storm Bird*, pp. 147, 148.

entertainment with a reading of the history of her orphanage, and the entire evening culminated with a dramatic recitation of the 'Spider of the Period,' performed by Sapho-Katie, aged three.[28]

Meanwhile, Mrs. Weldon plunged deeper and deeper into heterodox activities. She became an enthusiast for rational dress: 'I had simple tastes. . . . I did not take to crinolines when they were in fashion. . . . I wore my hair short. . . .' She embraced a number of other 'eccentric' causes associated with radical politics and popular health: vegetarianism, mesmerism, the occult.[29]

Spiritualism was a natural extension of her countercultural interests. Her progressive views on child-rearing were compatible with the innovative pedagogies of the spiritualist Progressive Lyceums, that featured, according to one historian, 'variety, learning-by-doing and dancing, no harshness.'[30] Mrs. Weldon also participated in the larger community of spiritualists: she won the praise of the spiritualist press as a 'keen and true friend' for her defense of the notorious Mr. Slade and for her gratuitous singing at spiritualist meetings.[31] She even experimented in 'social levelling' within her own household by enlisting her maid and her orphans in spirit communication.[32] Given her own marital difficulties, Mrs. Weldon may have also sympathized with the spiritualist critique of patriarchal sexual power within marriage and its insistence that women be the 'monarch of the marriage bed.'[33] Humble female mediums with marital problems frequently looked to the spiritualist lecture and séance circuit as a source of employment and refuge from unhappy homes. Before very long, Mrs. Weldon would herself appeal to spiritualists for collective protection and support against patriarchal plotting.

As a spiritual practice, spiritualism had particular appeal to women, who significantly outnumbered men as adherents and mediums. The private, homelike atmosphere of the séance, rein-

[28] Grierson, Storm Bird, p. 148.

[29] Georgina Weldon, How I Escaped the Mad Doctors (London: Mrs. Weldon, 1882), p. 6; Grierson, Storm Bird, p. 233.

[30] Logie Barrow, 'Socialism in Eternity: Plebian Spiritualists 1853–1913,' History Workshop 9 (Spring 1980): 56.

[31] 'Printed Allegations against Mrs. Weldon,' Spiritualist, 19 April 1878; 'Notes and Comments,' The Medium and Daybreak (London), 17 Oct. 1879.

[32] 'Topics of the Day be the Heroes of the Hour,' Pall Mall Budget (London), 21 March 1884. On social leveling and spiritualism, see Morell Theobald, Spirit Workers in the Home Circle: An Autobiographic Narrative of Psychic Phenomena in Family Daily Life Extending over a Period of Twenty Years (London: F. Fisher Unwin, 1887); Owen, 'The Other Voice,' pp. 55–57; Light (London), 26 March 1887.

[33] Medium and Daybreak, 24 Aug. 1888, 7 Sept. 1888.

forced by the familiar content of spirit communication with dead relatives, was a comfortable setting for women. The séance reversed the usual sexual hierarchy of knowledge and power: it shifted attention away from men and focused it on the female medium, the center of spiritual knowledge and insight. As the scene of popular 'hands on' female healing, the séance also constituted a female consumer challenge to orthodox allopathic medicine.[34]

Equally important was the fact that spiritualism provided spectacular entertainment directed at all the senses. Most private séances featured trance or inspirational speaking, but a wide assortment of 'physical phenomena' was included in the repertoire of professional or 'test' mediums: table-tilting, floating furniture, musical instruments playing by themselves, the wafting of mysterious incense in the air.[35] Even more dramatic sexual displays and inversions were accomplished at materializations: a medium, usually an attractive young girl, would be placed in a cabinet, bound and gagged, while a fanciful spirit would issue forth, sometimes a red Indian, sometimes a swearing buccaneer, sometimes a lovely young female spirit in a diaphanous white gown who sat on the laps of her favorite gentlemen.[36]

As other historians have noted, trance conditions legitimized a wide range of 'bad behavior' on the part of women by allowing them to engage in a subtle subversion—but not repudiation—of the 'separate sphere' construction of 'true womanhood.' Spiritualists deemed women particularly apt for mediumship because they were weak in the masculine attributes of will and intelligence, yet strong in the feminine qualities of passivity, chastity, and impressionability.[37] Female mediums were receptive vessels for other spirits—usually male spirits—who acted as the medium's control or 'guide' in the

[34] Miss March, a healing and trance medium, observed a lady in pain at her séance in 1887, 'brought her into the center of the room and placing her hand on her back and chest, indicated the whereabouts of her pains' to the woman's evident surprise. On other female healers, see also *Medium and Daybreak*, 7 Oct. 1887, 13 July 1888; Owen, *Darkened Room*, chap. 5.

[35] Mrs. Henry Sidgwick, 'Results of a Personal Investigation into the Physical Phenomena of Spiritualism,' *Proceedings of the Society for Psychical Research* 4 (1886–87): 45.

[36] Owen, 'The Other Voice,' pp. 45, 47; Florence Marryat, *There Is No Death* (London: Kegan Paul, Trench, Trubner & Co., 1891), pp. 202–4; George Sitwell, to the editor of *The Times*, reprinted in *Spiritualist*, 16 Jan. 1880; R. Laurence Moore, 'The Spiritualist Medium: A Study of Female Professionalism in Victorian America,' *American Quarterly* 27 (1975): 207, 214.

[37] Moore, 'Spiritualist Medium,' p. 202.

spirit world.[38] This form of male impersonation reflected the contradictory dynamic operating around gender in spiritualist circles: women could authoritatively 'speak spirit' if they were controlled by others, notably men; their access to male authority was accomplished through the fragmentation of their own personality.[39] There was a further irony and danger: these special female powers also rendered female mediums vulnerable to special forms of female punishment, in particular, to medical labeling as hysterics and to lunacy confinement.

Mrs. Weldon undoubtedly found spiritualism's penchant for theatricality very appealing.[40] What most attracted her were the opportunities it offered women for vocal performance. As we have seen, ever since she was a young woman, Mrs. Weldon had tried to devise ways to perform in public, from amateur theatrics to charity benefits, to her sociable evenings. Not surprisingly, she was attracted to the séance, a home-based entertainment that featured women *speaking* rather than *being*.[41]

Mrs. Weldon first attended séances in France, but soon found that she was temperamentally unsuited for mediumship. Although she continued to experiment with other forms of spirit communication, her taste tended to run to the mystical (hence, her attraction to French spiritualism and to a heterodox Catholicism) and she herself had little interest in the physical phenomena of spiritualism. During her first séance in France, for example, when she 'desired ardently' to communicate with dead friends, 'scarcely any phenomena occurred.' When at the advice of the medium, 'she remained perfectly passive, marked manifestations of the table began.' But clearly Georgina Weldon was not the type to remain 'perfectly passive' for

[38] According to a spirit census conducted by psychical researchers in the 1880s, 58 percent of the mediums were women, while 63 percent of the spirit controls were male. Spiritualists explained the tendency of female mediums to be possessed by a 'masculine spirit force' on the grounds that men were most likely to experience a violent death, and these earthbound spirits were most likely to communicate at séances. Ostensibly a defense of individuality, since it insisted that spirits preserved their own identity even after death, spiritualism also demonstrated the fragility of the holistic, undivided self and of gendered subjectivity in particular. Vieda Skultans, 'Mediums, Controls and Eminent Men,' in Pat Holden, ed., *Women's Religious Experience* (London: Croom Helm, 1983), p. 17.

[39] Owen, 'The Other Voice,' pp. 37, 38, 67, 68.

[40] Mrs. Weldon first attended séances in France, at a fashionable drawing room, where she tried to communicate with dead friends and received some 'test messages' spelled out through rappings on the table. *Spiritualist*, 23 June 1876.

[41] Owen, 'The Other Voice,' p. 35.

long, or to allow herself to become a transparent vessel for other spirits. She was insufficiently passive and impressionable. Her energy and determination would serve her well in her impending struggles against the 'plot that failed.'[42]

The plot that failed

In 1878, Mrs. Weldon and her orphans were visiting a convent in France, when she had a premonition that she must return home. Perhaps she had heard rumors that her husband, grown dissatisfied with the terms of their separation, wanted to retrench and sell the lease of their Bloomsbury townhouse, Tavistock House. Leaving her orphans in the care of the convent nuns, she immediately crossed the Channel and returned to London. She soon became embroiled in a criminal charge against a servant who, she claimed, stole possessions from the house. During her cross-examination, the defense counsel tried to cast doubt on her testimony by claiming that she was suffering from delusions. Within a few days of this public accusation, Mrs. Weldon found herself visited by a series of mysterious strangers.[43]

As she recounted her story—and what follows is a summary of her own account—Mrs. Weldon was dusting the music books in her library on 14 April 1878, when a servant announced that two visitors, Mr. Shell and Mr. Stewart, were in the hall. Thinking they were her music publishers, she had them admitted. Instead, they turned out to be two strangers, an older gentleman who sat 'on the middle of his spine' with his hands clasped on his stomach, and a younger one resembling a 'Christy minstrel,' 'all blinks, winks, and grins.' They introduced themselves as fellow spiritualists interested in her work on musical reform and children. She told them she was a 'firm believer in spiritualism.' After a half-hour conversation, they went away.[44]

[42] *Spiritualist*, 23 June 1876. Mrs. Weldon's spiritual taste reflected her class position. According to Logie Barrow, there were notable class differences in religious practice among spiritualists: plebian spiritualists tended to be vehemently anti-Christian, less mystical, more empiricist and materialist than their middle-class counterparts. Treherne, *Plaintiff*, p. 208; Logie Barrow, *Independent Spirits: Spiritualism and English Plebeians, 1850–1910* (London: Routledge and Kegan Paul, 1986), chap. 5.

[43] Weldon, *How I Escaped*; 'Printed Allegations.'

[44] Mrs. Weldon repeated her version of the 'plot that failed' (Treherne, *Plaintiff*, p. 58) in a wide array of articles, pamphlets, newspaper interviews, and courtroom testimonies. See for example, Mrs. Weldon, quoted in 'Some Medical Men at their Work,' *Spiritualist*, 17 May 1878; *The Times*, 15 March 1884.

At eight o'clock her servant announced that the visitors had returned. They rushed into the room, and to her surprise, they were another set of complete strangers, this time, a 'Tubby One' and a 'Taciturn One' with the aspect of a 'seedy dentist's assistant.' They too asked her about her spiritual communications; whether any of her children were mediums and whether she believed her animals possessed souls.[45]

During these initial encounters, Mrs. Weldon answered their questions positively and directly. 'I did not think it strange; I suspected that it was all about some rich and mysterious orphans.' After they left, she gradually came to realize that the mystery pertained ominously to herself. Mrs. Weldon began to feel 'dreadful' and sensed 'some horrible trap.' She remembered there were rumors afoot about her suffering from delusions and began to suspect that this masquerade might be part of an attempt to confine her for lunacy. She told the servant to 'lock and bolt up the house.' Within twenty minutes a carriage arrived and the bell rang. 'Who's there?' 'A gentleman and two ladies to see Mrs. Weldon!' Bell, the caretaker spoke to them outside. Finally he shut the door in their faces. 'They knocked and they rang three times, but we turned out the gas; they got tired of waiting, and at last we heard the carriage drive off.'[46]

'*For the first time in my life* I felt nervous.' '[S]omething I call my guardian angels, had given me a sign warning me I was in very immediate and grave danger.'[47] '[P]ale and trembling,' Mrs. Weldon posted letters to several friends to warn them of her predicament.[48] She sent one letter to W. H. Harrison, editor of the *Spiritualist*, who had published a series of letters from Mrs. Louisa Lowe. In her letters, Mrs. Lowe, a former inmate of a private asylum, had warned spiritualists of the dangers of wrongful confinement in lunatic asylums. Nothing in England, wrote Mrs. Lowe, 'was easier than to get a sane person into a lunatic asylum.'[49] None were more likely to be 'put away' without due cause than 'women in general' and 'wives in

---

[45] Mrs. Weldon, quoted in 'Some Medical Men.' The visitors took copious notes on her description of visions, including one featuring a shower of stars and Christ on the cross.

[46] Ibid.

[47] *How I Escaped*, p. 13.

[48] Mrs. Weldon, quoted in 'Some Medical Men.' Sir Charles Dilke and William Gladstone were among her correspondents.

[49] Louisa Lowe, quoted in Treherne, *Plaintiff*, p. 61. For other discussions of Mrs. Lowe's activities on behalf of lunacy law reform, see Peter McCandless, 'Build, Build: The Controversy over the Care of the Chronically Insane in England, 1855–70,' *Bulletin of the History of Medicine* (1979): 87; Owen, *Darkened Room*, chap. 7.

particular.'[50] 'All the morning I was thinking,' wrote Mrs. Weldon, '"Oh that I dared to go out to Mrs. Lowe."'[51]

At 2 P.M. the following day, the 'bell rang again.' 'A note from Mrs. Harrison introducing who—but Mrs. Lowe!!! The very woman I was longing and praying for.' Mrs. Weldon had begun to tell her story when the bell rang again. The caretaker appeared much agitated: 'Those three have come have pushed their way in and say they will wait till they come to see you.'[52]

Mrs. Lowe took command of the situation and went off to fetch the police; when she arrived with 'two stalwart policemen,' a newly emboldened Mrs. Weldon confronted the 'trio' at door. The two women 'darted upon me and seized me.' Mrs. Weldon felt inclined to fetch a poker and break their heads, but Mrs. Lowe advised a more discreet course. 'Give them in charge for assaulting you,' said Mrs. Lowe. 'Policeman,' said I, 'take them in charge, they are assaulting me.' 'I might have spoken Hebrew or Chinese; they never moved, and I feel convinced they would have let me be carried off bodily.' On the advice of Mrs. Lowe, she barricaded herself in her room.[53]

At last, a friendly policeman (who had been warned the evening before) arrived and forced the trio to produce the lunacy order, signed by her husband and a family friend, General de Bathe, who had briefly visited Mrs. Weldon the previous afternoon. 'They then left, I telegraphed to my husband to come and save me.' Mrs. Weldon insisted her husband's signature must be a forgery, but the cynical Mrs. Lowe responded, '[You] don't know how bad husbands [are].' Both her servant and the kindly policeman supported Mrs. Lowe's advice to 'go' rather than to trust to her husband's benevolent intervention. '[S]o in greatest haste, I threw my cloak over my shoulders, my bonnet, without waiting to put on my boots, in a pair of wonderful old slippers ran down the square, the policeman stopped a cab ('I am not looking at the number!' he said) jumped into it, Mrs. Lowe took me to her house and I was . . . SAVED!!!!' When the 'madhouse-keeper' Winslow returned that night, he was furious to learn that his quarry had escaped. 'Mrs. Weldon is a dangerous lunatic! Where has she gone? A thousand pounds for any one who can find her.'[54]

---

[50] Louisa Lowe, The Bastilles of England: or the Lunacy Laws at Work (London: Crookenden, 1883).
[51] Mrs. Weldon, quoted in 'Some Medical Men.'
[52] Ibid.
[53] Ibid.
[54] Weldon, How I Escaped, pp. 17, 19; The Times, 28 Nov. 1884; Winslow, quoted in Treherne, Plaintiff, p. 63.

Mrs. Weldon first accompanied Mrs. Lowe to her home and then went underground for the seven days that the lunacy order remained in effect. When she surfaced, she was determined to avenge herself on the parties responsible for the assault. Acting on her own behalf, she appeared before Mr. Flowers of the Bow Street Police Court. Mr. Flowers sympathized with her ordeal and condemned the action of Dr. Winslow as 'an unjustifiable design upon her liberty'; but he could offer no legal redress against the assault. Legal authorities were powerless to take up her case, he explained, unless she had been confined in a lunatic asylum; nor could she, a married woman, institute a civil suit against them.[55]

Georgina had nonetheless won a moral victory. Mr. Flowers's statement of sympathy legitimated her case and quickly established her sanity, even to the medical press, who acknowledged her to be a 'lady abundantly capable of enjoying her liberty without harm to herself or others.'[56] Even though she had been debarred from pursuing her case in court, Mrs. Weldon proceeded to assail her enemies on all other fronts. Following the advice of Charles Reade, the novelist, she adopted an 'American' style of publicity.[57] She published her story in the spiritualist press, offered interviews to the daily newspapers, tried to provoke libel suits from the participants, stood on public platforms and embraced the cause of lunacy reform, hired sandwichmen to parade in front of Winslow's home with signs denouncing him as a 'bodysnatcher,'[58] and launched a public concert career, as well as continuing her social events at home, where between musical performances she read her lecture 'How I Escaped the Mad Doctors.'[59]

Mrs. Weldon's narration: a story retold

Mrs. Weldon survived her husband's conspiracy and proved herself a forceful antagonist to psychiatric medicine. She was able to elicit support and sympathy, even from unusual quarters like *The Times* and the medical press, for a number of reasons. Mrs. Weldon was a female rebel who retained the 'aura' of 'true womanhood.' Although

[55] Mr. Flowers, quoted in 'Mrs. Weldon and the Lunacy Laws,' *Spiritualist*, 18 Oct. 1878.

[56] *BMJ* 1 (1879): 39. *Truth* demanded a 'searching inquiry' (quoted in *Spiritualist*, 18 Oct. 1878). The *British Medical Journal* further castigated Winslow for improperly trying to confine Mrs. Weldon in the hope of deriving pecuniary profits.

[57] Treherne, *Plaintiff*, p. 119.

[58] Weldon, quoted in 'Some Topics of the Day.'

[59] Grierson, *Storm Bird*, p. 176. In the early 1880s, Mrs. Weldon temporarily reconstituted her orphanage. By 1884, however, the orphanage was defunct and the children dispersed. Grierson, *Storm Bird*, p. 245.

the turmoil and drama of her life were the direct result of her determined resistance to the conventions of gender, she presented herself
as a sweet, gracious lady with a feminine voice who led a 'quiet,
domestic life.' In stretching but not repudiating the boundaries of
'separate spheres,' she adopted a strategy similar to other female
spiritualists.

But in other ways, she manipulated her femininity very differently than did spiritualist performers. As Regenia Gagnier notes, she
tended to parody those same female domestic virtues—from maternal feelings to musical soirées—that she claimed to uphold.[60] Moreover, the same 'unfeminine' qualities that made her temperamentally
unsuited for mediumship—her strong personality and her active,
restless temperament—enabled her to fight back in public, to break
out of the controlling dynamics that rendered other female spiritualists, particularly mediums, more vulnerable to medical supervision.
Even her spirit communications were of an intensely practical sort,
counseling self-protection and decisive action.

Class and age also set Mrs. Weldon apart from the nubile, young
women of artisanal and lower-middle-class background who performed materializations and became 'test mediums' under the
patronage of some wealthy gentleman.[61] With more resources at her
disposal, Mrs. Weldon could choose a more independent means of
public presentation. To be sure, there was some affinity between Mrs.
Weldon and materializing mediums; in her search for employment,
she would eventually turn her hand to commercial performances,
and she too had a penchant for a certain linguistic cross-dressing.
Instead of hypermasculine lower-class sailors or soldiers, her impersonations extended to authoritative, elite men of the law. Having
experienced considerable difficulty with musical impresarios, Mrs.
Weldon would dispense with male patronage altogether when she
went public as a 'lunatic lawyer in petticoats.'

Differences of class, age, and temperament could not protect her
from lunacy certification—they only enabled her to escape incarceration once threatened. When Mrs. Weldon finally read her lunacy
order, she learned 'for the first time' that 'because I was a spiritualist they wished to examine the state of my brain.' More precisely,
because she was a spiritualist *and* the estranged wife of a man who
wanted to 'retrench,' her liberty was endangered. But her social posi-

---

[60] See Reginia Gagnier, 'Mediums and the Media,' *Representations* 22 (Spring 1988).
[61] Brandon, *Spiritualists*, pp. 113–26; Oppenheim, *The Other World*, pp. 16–21; Owen, *The Darkened Room*, chap. 3.

tion was also her defense: well-connected and self-possessed, she was able to turn the tables on her enemies, the psychiatric 'body-snatchers,' and to seriously undermine their public credibility.[62]

Mrs. Weldon was also a very good storyteller. As a campaigner and 'lunacy lawyer' she triumphed over her enemies because she was able to explain her plight in ways comprehensible to a reading public. As soon as she sensed her 'danger,' she recognized the outlines of a familiar plot. She immediately thought of Mrs. Lowe's letters in the spiritualist press, themselves derivative of Reade and Collins's sensational narratives of family intrigue and betrayal.[63] Like other sensational novelists of the 1860s, Collins and Reade had revised the representation of sexual danger enacted in traditional stage melodrama, to focus on middle-class marriage. For them, female powerlessness and vulnerability began at home; women were less endangered by illicit sexual encounters outside the family than by male sexual abuse within its circle. Marriage no longer resolved the female dilemma; it compounded it. The insane asylum simply amplified the danger of the domestic asylum; it was a supplementary patriarchal structure, a place of madness and sexuality where doctors substituted for tyrannical husbands as the keepers and tormenters of women.[64]

In her public pamphlets, Mrs. Lowe had characterized her experience of the asylum in much the same way: as a place to stash away unwanted wives (or relatives) and as a place of sexual danger. She accused her husband of arranging for her incarceration after her spirit writing had exposed his adulterous activities. She described the lunatic asylums where she was confined as places of institutionalized irrationality, where the doctors were crazier than their patients and the whole atmosphere was suffused with an unrestrained sexuality and indiscipline designed to drive any rational person mad.[65]

By drawing on the tradition of the sensational novel filtered through Mrs. Lowe's own 'history,' Mrs. Weldon retold an older

---

[62] Mrs. Weldon, quoted in Treherne, *Plaintiff,* p. 98; Lowe, *Bastilles of England.*

[63] Wilkie Collins, *The Woman in White* (London, 1859–60; rpt., Harmondsworth, Middlesex: Penguin, 1974); Charles Reade, *Hard Cash: A Matter-of-Fact Romance* (London: Chatto and Windus, 1895; rpt., Collier, New York, 1970).

[64] Winifred Hughes, *Maniac in the Cellar* (Princeton: Princeton University Press, 1980).

[65] Lowe, *Bastilles of England; My Outlawry; A Lecture Delivered in the Cavendish Room* (London, 1874); *My Story: Exemplifying the Injurious Working of the Lunacy Laws and the Undue Influence Possessed by Lunacy Experts* (London, 1878); Dr. Maudsley, testimony before the Select Committee on the Lunacy Laws, *Parliamentary Papers,* 1877 (373), 13, Q. 7328; Dr. Fox, Q.7642.

narrative of entrapment. In this story of male villainy and female vic-
timization, Mrs. Weldon cast herself as an endangered heroine, who
was assisted in the nick of time by Mrs. Lowe, another sister 'lunacy
lawyer in petticoats.'[66] Together they were able to foil a patriarchal
plot to deprive her of her liberty. Her first installment of this story,
summarized above, included a full repertoire of melodramatic motifs
and tropes: rapid action, the profusion of secrets, stereotyped, inter-
changeable villains who possessed no psychological depth, extreme
states of being and danger, multiple disguises and impersonations,
the operation of sinister forces directed by some unknown mastermind.[67] As in stage melodrama, servants and policemen embodied
comic relief—they were sympathetic but impotent figures, powerless
to repel the advances of menacing invaders. Only the courage and
determination of Mrs. Weldon and Mrs. Lowe saved the day and
turned the 'bloodhounds from the door.'[68] To escape incarceration,
Mrs. Weldon had to flee her own domestic asylum, the safe and
comfortable scene of daily life, and go disguised as an anonymous
denizen of the city. Later she would resurface as a 'public' woman
bent on vindicating her honor and sanity.

'Truth is stranger than fiction,' declared the *Medium and Daybreak*,
commenting on the Weldon case. '[S]omething is radically wrong
when a virtuous and highly-talented woman can with impunity be
torn from her home and doomed to worse than penal servitude.'[69]
But who was the ominous force behind these machinations?[70] Mr.
Weldon's involvement remained obscure until the climax of the first
scene, when the lunacy bill was finally read and his signature dis-
closed.[71] Only then were the actions of the mad doctors unveiled as
part of a 'little family conspiracy' and only then did Mrs. Weldon
come to realize, in Mrs. Lowe's words, 'how bad husbands [are].'[72]

Mrs. Weldon's melodramatic story of her 'escape' remained the
same throughout its many recitations, with one important elabora-

---

[66] *Spiritualist*, 26 April 1878.

[67] For a discussion of melodramatic themes, see Hughes, *Maniac*, passim; Peter
Brooks, *The Melodramatic Imagination: Balzac, Henry James, Melodrama, and the Mode of
Excess* (New Haven: Yale University Press, 1976); Michael R. Booth, *English Melodrama*
(London: Herbert Jenkins, 1965).

[68] 'Mrs. Georgina Weldon,' *Medium and Daybreak*, 17 Oct. 1879.

[69] *Medium and Daybreak*, 22 Aug. 1879.

[70] Mystery was structured into Mrs. Weldon's narrative order. In her first account,
she introduced her story *in media res*, making the invasion of the mad housekeeper and
his assistants initially appear as a mysterious act of violence. See 'Some Medical Men.'

[71] In stage dramas this climax would be visually fixed into a dramatic tableau.

[72] 'Mrs. Georgina Weldon.'

tion: the progressive sexualization of her story as her husband's involvement became clarified. Shortly after her escape, in an interview in the *London Figaro*, Mrs. Weldon accused her husband of conspiring with General de Bathe to get rid of her in order to marry de Bathe's young daughter; she further claimed that de Bathe had nurtured a long-standing grievance against her for having spurned his sexual advances when she was a girl.[73] Mrs. Weldon interpreted the male conspiracy of doctor-family friend-husband as a 'traffic in women,'[74] in which doctors colluded in the private sexual designs of men by defining female resistance as madness.[75] Contemporary observers, commenting on her story, further amplified and extended the theme of sexual danger. The spiritualists likened the actions of the 'mad doctors' to the sadistic pleasures of the hunt; while even the *British Medical Journal*, not commonly given to Gothic allusions, invoked the example of Rochester and Jane Eyre to illustrate how men might use lunacy confinement to further their sexual self-interest.[76]

[73] *Spiritualist*, 4 July 1879. As a result of this interview, Mr. Weldon, who insisted the idea of marrying de Bathe's daughter never entered his head, successfully sued the *Figaro*'s publisher, Mr. Mortimer, for libel. For our purposes, the veracity of her accusation is less important than her loyal adhesion to a conspiratorial representation of sexual danger.
[74] Gayle Rubin, 'The Traffic in Women: Notes on the "Political Economy" of Sex,' in Rayna Reiter, ed., *Toward an Anthropology of Women* (New York: Monthly Review Press, 1975), pp. 157–210.
[75] This triangular relationship echoed Freud's famous Dora case. See Charles Bernheimer and Claire Kahane, eds. *In Dora's Case: Freud-Hysteria-Feminism* (New York: Columbia University Press, 1985).
[76] The '"mad doctors" method of hurting their prey is exciting and truly sportsmanlike,' *Medium and Daybreak* observed sarcastically ('Mrs. Georgina Weldon'). For the response of the medical press, see 'Lunacy Law Reform: The Power of the Keys,' *BMJ* 1 (1879): 245. Notice that the spiritualists focus on the sexual perversions of the doctors, while the medical press concentrated on the husband.

Index

Note: 'n.' after a page reference indicates a note on that page.